# Jewish Identity in American Art

*Judaic Traditions in Literature, Music, and Art*
Ken Frieden, *Series Editor*

The preparation and publication of this volume was made possible
by a grant from the Memorial Foundation for Jewish Culture
as well as by the generous support of:

The Mr. and Mrs. Raymond J. Horowitz Foundation for the Arts

Jean and Dr. Jerry Friedman

An anonymous donor

# Jewish Identity in American Art

## *A Golden Age since the 1970s*

**Matthew Baigell**

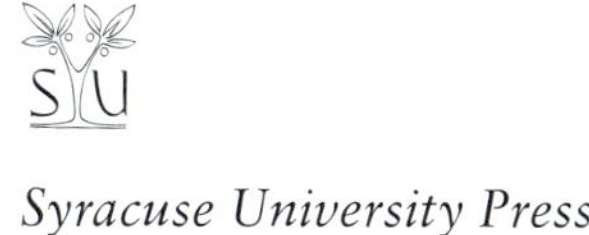

*Syracuse University Press*

First Edition 2020

20 21 22 23 24 25 6 5 4 3 2 1

∞ The paper used in this publication meets the minimum requirements of the American National Standard for Information Sciences—Permanence of Paper for Printed Library Materials, ANSI Z39.48-1992.

For a listing of books published and distributed by Syracuse University Press, visit https://press.syr.edu.

ISBN: 978-0-8156-3675-5 (hardcover)
978-0-8156-3685-4 (paperback)

**Library of Congress Cataloging-in-Publication Data**

Names: Baigell, Matthew, author.

Title: Jewish identity in American art : a golden age since the 1970s / Matthew Baigell.

Description: First edition. | Syracuse, New York : Syracuse University Press, 2020. | Series: Judaic traditions in literature, music, and art | Includes bibliographical references and index. | Summary: ""Jewish Identity in American Art" is about the first Jewish American generation of artists who are both comfortable as assimilated Americans and who also respect and revere their religious heritage"—Provided by publisher.

Identifiers: LCCN 2020003655 | ISBN 9780815636755 (hardcover) | ISBN 9780815636854 (paperback)

Subjects: LCSH: Jewish art—United States—20th century. | Jewish art—United States—21st century. | Jewish artists—United States. | Art, American—20th century—Themes, motives. | Art, American—21st century—Themes, motives.

Classification: LCC N6538.J4 B354 2020 | DDC 704.03/9240730904—dc23

LC record available at https://lccn.loc.gov/2020003655

*Manufactured in Canada*

*For my grandson Soyer*

*and*

*my great-granddaughter Ivy*

# Contents

## Illustrations

# Preface

I initially wanted to title this book *We Are Living in a Golden Age of Religiously Themed Jewish American Art and We Really Don't Know It*, but that title contained too many words to put on the book's cover. Nonetheless, I believe that we are living in such a golden age and that most people really don't know it. I hope the reader will in the end agree that those artists born from the 1930s to the 1960s who explore religiously themed art have created such an age. I base my opinion on almost thirty years of interviewing dozens of artists, asking about their reasons for finding inspiration in the Hebrew Bible, the Talmud, kabbalah, the midrashim (legends), and commentaries as well as in the holiday and daily prayer books. The text here is based on notes, email messages, telephone conversations, as well as interviews recorded in the privacy of studios or in noisy coffee shops (in one instance on a park bench almost blown away by strong winds clearly heard on the tape), and reconfigured passages from earlier relevant publications listed in the works cited section.

The book includes an introduction, an overview chapter that suggests the range of attitudes about Judaism over the decades, a brief review of Jewish feminist art, eleven chapters on individual artists, and a conclusion. Some quotations and information (such as birth and life dates) are repeated when it seemed necessary because not every reader will start on page one and read consecutively to the last page.

My idea was to present the artists as part of a general survey showing the wide range of and approaches to their subject matter. As a result, I rarely mention specific artistic influences on particular artists, believing that such concerns belong in more specialized, scholarly articles. The same holds true for discussing the iconographical motifs found in the ancient texts. Some motifs are very complex and depend on the kind of Talmudic knowledge that neither I nor most readers have. On occasion, I clarify in some detail meanings and representations but prefer to explain only enough about a particular work to make the content comprehensible rather than to exhaust the possibilities of interpretation. Anybody who has looked into the Talmud and the various *responsa* knows that there are endless interpretations of the interpretations, the counterinterpretations, and the reinterpretations.

An indispensable set of volumes is Louis Ginzberg's *The Legends of the Jews* ([1909–38] 1917–87). The set I used is boxed, each book having matching covers, but the volumes were originally published over a period of years. I thought it would be confusing to include the particular date of publication for each volume when cited in the text, so I give the range of publication dates when citing Ginzberg. Also, because over the years certain source materials, such as newspaper clippings and exhibition brochures, have been deleted from artists' websites, in the works cited list I have indicated that copies of such sources are in a certain artist's files.

I should also note that artists were often kind enough to give me copies of biographical records as well as personal documents, typed statements concerning their art, and copies of magazine articles. So when in the text I mention such statements, it is to be understood, unless otherwise indicated, that they are copies of these statements now in my own files. This general reference here eliminates distracting phrases such as "from my files" or "in my possession" from the text.

And during the course of my research, the Talmud and several books of midrashim (legends, tales) were digitized and placed on the Sefaria website. When possible, I included references in the text. Otherwise, book references are included in the works cited list.

I want to acknowledge foremost all of the artists, who often answered patiently my queries about their ideas, feelings, and sources as well as about their works. Because some responses date back to the 1990s, their views might have changed, but I have included remarks as expressed at the time they were given. Some artists are quoted more often than others only because they spoke more volubly or wrote letters and emails more revealingly. But all were very cooperative, and I am ever thankful to them for sharing their knowledge, insights, and wisdom gained from their years of studying and creating works based on the ancient texts. I especially want to thank those whom I repeatedly pestered for graciously providing me with references to both ancient and modern texts that inspired their works. Otherwise, on several occasions I would have lost my way chasing down sources on the Internet and in libraries.

It is important to acknowledge Ruth Weisberg, founder and president of the Los Angeles–based Jewish Artists Initiative, and Yona Verwer, founder and director of the New York–based Jewish Art Salon, for their extraordinary service to artists and their growing public as a result of their promotion of Jewish-themed art in this country and abroad through exhibitions and related events.

I thank Renee Baigell, Ephraim Edelstein, and Shloma Edelstein for patiently answering my questions over many decades about religious matters far beyond my own limited knowledge. I also thank Laura Kruger, curator at the Hebrew Union College–Jewish Institute of Religion Museum, New York, the most knowledgeable curator of Jewish-themed art in America, for her many astute observations over the years. Thanks to my rabbi, Zach Fredman, for alerting me to the Prophet Joel's predictions. Mark Podwal was very generous to allow me to see page proofs of his latest book, *Kaddish for Dąbrowa Białostocka* (2018), which focuses on the community in Poland in which his mother was born.

I owe a profound debt of gratitude to Deborah Manion, Kelly Balenske, and the staff at Syracuse University Press, whose patience, support, encouragement, and good cheer are to be cherished by any author lucky enough to work with them. And a special thanks to Annie Barva, whose inspired and meticulous copy editing reduced the number of inadvertent errors and who in clarifying several passages made the text more readable.

And finally but by no means last, I want to give more than a thanks, a shout-out, to those donors who so generously and graciously provided funds for the large number of color illustrations. The preparation and publication of this volume were made possible by grants from the Memorial Foundation for Jewish Culture, the Mr. and Mrs. Raymond J. Horowitz

Foundation for the Arts; Jean and Jerry Friedman, Beverly Hills, CA; and one anonymous donor.

The cover image, *Girl Blessing the Torah* (1997) by Brian Shapiro, captures the overall attitude of this generation of artists. The subject is both traditional and radical. It is traditional in the way the young woman grasps the Torah, evoking its centrality to Judaism as well as honoring the respect and love the artists hold for their cultural and religious heritage. But it is a young woman who holds the Torah, not a man, an image unthinkable until recent decades. So the painting also updates tradition, symbolizing the artists' desires to assert the religion's contemporary relevance and ability to change with the times.

# Jewish Identity in American Art

# Introduction — *A Unique Generation*

This is a story that needs to be told. It is not about American artists who happen to be Jewish but who ignore or denigrate Jewish subject matter or about artists involved in political issues or about those who might provide interesting but traditional visual transpositions of the ancient texts or common scenes such as Grandma lighting the Sabbath candles. Rather, it is about one of the most interesting and arresting developments in the history of Jewish American art—the great number of artists born from the 1930s to the 1960s who since the 1970s have explored Jewish religious as well as secular themes in ways never before seen in the history of Jewish American art.

One might think that these artists who have little or no direct experience with the great East European immigration around the turn of the twentieth century, let alone memories of life in eastern Europe, and who were too young to remember the hardships of the Depression of the 1930s or to comprehend fully the meaning of the Holocaust as it was happening in the early 1940s—some were born well after that event—would be largely absorbed into the American artistic mainstream. After all, they matured at a time of relatively little overt anti-Semitism in America. They instead grew up as part of a unique generation, the first generation of largely American-born and American-educated artists who feel quite comfortable as assimilated Americans but—and this distinguishes the artists with whom I am concerned—have also exhibited an overwhelming desire to explore their cultural and religious heritage. These artists—the ones who search out, challenge, and build on subject matter that they find in the ancient texts, including the Hebrew Bible, the Talmud, kabbalah, midrashim (legends and commentaries), as well as the holiday and daily prayer books—are for me the most vital and interesting artists within the history of contemporary Jewish American art, the ones most willing to take risks with their material, the ones who have opened up new ways to think about and create art with Jewish religious and secular content. (For more on third-generation Jews in America, see Herberg [1955] 1960, 187–90; Glanz 1977, 123; Sarna [1986] 1997, xiii–xv.)

Let me describe them in an analogous way. The literary historian Julian Levinson makes an important point in his book *Exiles on Main Street: Jewish American Writers and American Literary Culture* (2008) when he notes that writers such as Gertrude Stein, Lillian Hellman, Arthur Miller, and Norman Mailer did not "evince any particular inclination to return to Jewishness" or to have much to say about "the ways in which Judaism and Jewishness have been reimagined and reconfigured" (4). Levinson contrasts these authors with Emma Lazarus, Ludwig Lewisohn, Alfred Kazin, and Irving Howe, among others, whose works do embody such qualities. In other words, the fact that an author is Jewish does not mean that he or she has contributed to the development of a Jewish American culture.

The artists considered here have contributed! It also needs to be emphasized that all the artists I have contacted over the past thirty years assert that they are Americans who happen to be Jewish, not Jews who happen to be American. They also say that they prefer to be known as artists who are Jewish rather than to be tagged as Jewish artists. Further, in all our years of conversations and correspondences, they have mentioned the names only of those artists in mainstream Western art history. Or, to be precise, they have little or no contact, let alone special connections, with artists from other countries who are Jewish. Their subject matter is framed by feminist and gender issues, spiritualism, a desire not to allow their heritage disappear through assimilation, as well as their great curiosity about the ancient religious texts central to Judaism. Their searches in and responses to what they have found inform their present-day attitudes, and as a result they have created what I believe is a golden age of religiously themed Jewish American art of which we have been largely unaware.

By turning to the original sources, they have leap-frogged back over the centuries, past the experiences of their recent and more distant elders, to find inspiration and subject matter directly in the ancient texts as well as in their readings of current events. As a result, there is no sustained line of descent to them from earlier figures either in approach to subject matter or in attitudes toward Judaism, as indicated in chapter 1. I do not mean to imply that the contemporary figures I discuss are ignorant of their predecessors or are not thankful and do not appreciate their predecessors' achievements, but they do not consider artists such as Jennings Tofel (1891–1959), Ben-Zion (1897–1987), Ben Shahn (1898–1968), Jack Levine (1915–2010), and Leonard Baskin (1929–90) as role models. The Jewish insularity of these and other earlier figures as well as the separation from the Jewish community of abstract expressionists such as Barnett Newman (1905–70) and Mark Rothko (1903–70) play little part in the more contemporary artists' desire to continue to work out their own ways to connect to the Jewish past and contribute to the Jewish present.

In their religious themed works, their return home is to the original home as presented in the ancient texts, a return they make with a critical but nevertheless loyal eye. They do not, for example, read the Hebrew Bible to figure out God's intentions, as the Orthodox might. Rather, they create modern midrashim that give the old stories contemporary relevance. They present their sense of Judaism in an up-to-date manner so that it is for them a living religion, its stories applicable to contemporary experiences. In an email dated January 22, 2009, Archie Rand (b. 1949) summed up nicely the pleasant situation in which these artists find themselves:

> We are Jews in diaspora—permanently—and we live in this world, now. In America, at least at this moment, this allows us movement and provides a certain obligation towards self-realization, identification, fulfillment, and then, if necessary, moving on. But we are not entombing anyone. And certainly not in shame, expedience, or disassociation.

Rand also stated, most importantly, that he would not indulge in "static religious symbolism" but rather devote his efforts to create a Jewish-themed art appropriate to the present.

Rand's observations are quite profound and mark this generation as special. Yes, depending on one's point of view, Jews outside of Israel live in the Diaspora, but the artists, by their thoughts and in their art, reject opinions based on earlier conditions that existed and still exist

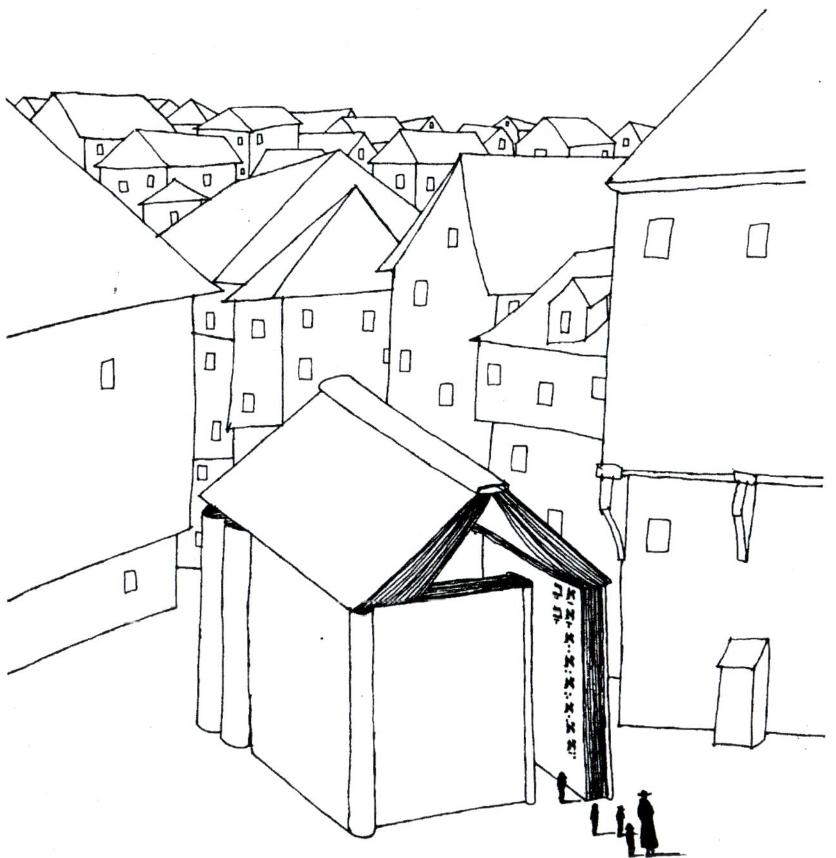

1. Mark Podwal, *Heder (School for Jewish Children)*, 1977. Ink on paper, 14 × 11 in. © Mark Podwal.

primarily in Europe and Asia. For example, literary critic George Steiner famously said that the Bible is the Jews' homeland, that its study is "the central motion of personal and national homecoming" (1996, 304–5). Mark Podwal (b. 1945) captured the tone of Steiner's comment in his early drawing *Heder (School for Jewish Children)* (1977) (fig. 1), which shows children entering a school in the form of a book, but Podwal must have known that by this date, 1977, this notion was already an anachronism. True, the artists I focus on study the Bible and other ancient texts, but they are not diasporic artists in the sense of considering themselves to be in exile and finding the Bible to be their surrogate homeland. For them, the words said at the end of the Passover meal, "Next year in Jerusalem," marks the end of the meal, not a fervent wish.

Svetlana Boym quotes a phrase from *The Theory of the Novel* (in German 1916, trans. 1971) by Georg Lukacs, the Marxist literary critic, that also does not describe this generation of artists: "transcendental homelessness," meaning that there is the desire to be at home in the world, the desire to find in religion a "totality of existence hopelessly fragmented in the modern age" (Boym 2001, 24). In this sense, the homeland exists as a state of mind rather than as a place. For the artists, America is their place, plain and simple. What might have applied to earlier generations, especially those who lived in Europe or were born in Europe, lacks validity here. Whereas, for example, one might refer to a "German Jew" but never a "Jewish German," it is very easy to say "Jewish American." America is not a host culture. It is home. The artists are Jewish and American. They do not have to choose which adjective modifies which noun.

As Uzi Rebhun, a demographer at Hebrew University in Jerusalem, has stated, "You have Jews in the West who live very comfortably under pluralistic governments that give them unprecedented social and economic opportunities and let them live Jewish lives" (quoted in Kraft 2008; see also Aviv and Shneer 2005). And in 1985 in America, at the same time that significant works had already been created by the artists considered here, prospects for Jews in America looked very good. Stephen J. Whitfield considered this positive outlook in a review of then recent books by Charles E. Silberman (1985), Chaim Waxman (1983), and Steven Cohen (1983). He concluded that the Jewish community in America was no longer a community of fate and that "for the first time in the history of the Diaspora, the sense of exile has evaporated" (1985, 49). Individuals no longer had to convert to gain social or financial success but were free to remain Jewish or, if they so desired, to "disappear into the general population" (49).

Whitfield mentioned but did not discuss the fraught issue of how to transmit and transform that heritage to the next generation, but the artists discussed here have accepted that challenge and as of this writing are still creating works that they consider appropriate to their time and that will appeal to a public interested in searching for ways to connect their American selves to their Jewish heritage. But it is also necessary to mention that despite their optimistic outlook the artists are not unaware of an ever-lurking feeling of disaster that has sometimes cropped up in our conversations. Perhaps this feeling is a Jewish reflex learned in childhood from adults and from the artists' own knowledge of history. My point in mentioning this feeling is to say that the artists have not and are not escaping into myths, legends, kabbalah, Talmudic discourse, and the ultimate source, the Bible. They are grounded in reality, as their works based on secular events indicate, but they are profoundly motivated to bring the ancient texts into contemporary discourse, to take timeless stories and give them an historical resonance for the present moment. In any event, Archie Rand gave expression to this feeling when he said to me when he had heard some unpleasant news, "In fear, I hold tight to what has nourished me in exile. I announce my Jewishness knowing that there is a potentially hostile if not lethal Other out there."

This book, then, is about the artists' efforts rather than a survey of their careers. And I choose to emphasize this approach because when I mentioned my plans to some acquaintances, they wanted to know if the book would include jokes, inquiries into Orthodox thinking, or information about Israel. That is, their knowledge of contemporary Jewishness was limited largely to stand-up comedy via Jerry Seinfeld, Sara Silverman, and others, to the more visible Orthodox movement, and to their sense that it has something to do with another country. Their grasp of Jewish history as well as the religion and its rituals was limited, and they were mostly unaware that artists might attend Orthodox, Modern Orthodox, Conservative, Reconstructionist, or Reform services or that they might be interested in biblical history and want to explore Jewish spirituality. Other acquaintances wanted to know what took so long for somebody to write a book such as the one I envisioned and why art historians, art critics, and mainstream art journal editors have largely avoided this material.

This is not the place to speculate about such matters except to say that I hope this book prompts further research and even book-length monographs on what is to my mind an extraordinary generation of artists. The artists, of course, feel that the seriousness of their intentions has not been acknowledged and appreciated, let alone rewarded financially, that their differing approaches to their subject matter has been ignored, and that their significant contributions to a modern Jewish art and culture have been little noticed—in contrast to the attention given to Jewish novelists and Hollywood figures. But they persist.

It has often been said, most recently and most bluntly in a review by art critic Jason Farago about books on Jasper Johns and exhibitions of his work, that contemporary artists "have had no choice but to get smart about the economics of art. The result has been that any remaining formalist commitment to the autonomy of painting or sculpture is now well and truly dead" (2018). No denying that, but the artists considered here have chosen to find their motivation elsewhere than in the art market. They have found it, most broadly speaking, in their religious and cultural heritage.

As is obvious, these artists matured during the post–Second World War decades and no doubt responded to many events and shared many experiences with others of their generation. Rather than outline broadly those events and experiences extensively discussed in recent books on Jewish social and religious history, including those by Jonathan D. Sarna (2004), Sylvia Barack Fishman (2000), and Jack Wertheimer (2018), I think it appropriate and more to the point of this book to draw material specifically from what the artists have said and written about their memories, feelings, interactions, and intentions—that is to say, their lives—during these years.

The most relevant observation is that they do not form a distinct body operating within certain parameters of style or approach to subject matter because they come from too many different religious, cultural, and social backgrounds. Most did not know and were not aware of other like-minded artists in the 1970s and 1980s. All of them interpret their subject matter in highly personal ways sustained by their particular set of beliefs and notions of self-identity. As Arnold Eisen, the chancellor of the Jewish Theological Seminary, has observed, one's Jewish identification is now quite personal. "It is primarily in private space that American Jews define the selves they are and want to be" (2008, 127, 128; see also Cohen and Eisen 2000). In effect, Eisen indicates that each person, autonomous and sovereign, decides which rituals and practices to observe (see also Wertheimer 2018, 8–10, 254–60). By extension, each artist is the arbiter of what might or might not be included in a work and from which point of view that subject matter might be examined.

And that is exactly the point of this book—to look at a sampling of works by those contemporary artists who do not desire on the one hand to join the mainstream art world or on the other hand to maintain old traditions by illustrating Jewish texts in a traditional narrative manner but who rather choose to explore and reveal their own feelings and points of view largely through Jewish subject matter derived from secular and biblical or religious history. They personalize their subject matter and reveal intimate feelings in their statements, both of which mark a departure from the more guarded and religiously determined images and comments of artists of previous generations (considered in chapter 1). Their works often seem to be extensions of their conversations, their pointed comments and observations, rather than visual transcriptions of passages from religious texts.

Beginning in the 1970s, while responding to contemporary artistic, cultural, and social developments, these artists also began to seek ways to meld together their daily American experiences with their religious and cultural backgrounds. Like other artists of the time, they asserted their prerogatives as creative artists by exploring various attitudes, modes, means, and materials—their thematic interests leading them to enlarge the parameters of Jewish-themed art in ways unimaginable in earlier decades.

The feminist historian Savina J. Teubal reminds us that the biblical authors were creating religion, not writing history (1997, xiii). They wrote statements of faith, not fact. Current scholars search for facts but can also have strong opinions that influence their presentations of their arguments. To the mix of scholarship, religious precept, liturgy, and attitude filtered through their imaginations, artists have also contributed to our envisioning of the past and its applications to the present. As a result, they have developed new Jewish iconographical motifs and new ways to interpret well-known biblical stories. The artists certainly revere the ancient texts, but they do not hold them sacrosanct or infallible. Instead, they take nothing for granted and have no inhibitions about challenging their sources or using them as points of departure for their own imaginative flights.

There are at least three facts with which the artists might agree. First, it is safe to say that the paintings made by Archie Rand in 1974 to fill the interior of the B'nai Yosef Synagogue in Brooklyn, New York, are the most important early works of this period (fig. 76). Second, it is also safe to say that one of this generation's defining features is the extensive use of biblical narratives, a form of presentation common to Christian art for centuries but extremely rare in Jewish American art until the 1980s. And third, as a result of the feminist movement, both male and female artists portray the biblical matriarchs as well as other women mentioned in the Bible in greater numbers than did artists of previous generations. Beyond these facts, no overall consistent chronological and stylistic characteristics distinguish one decade of works by these artists from another decade of works except perhaps for those within an individual artist's oeuvre. A happy anarchy reigns.

With works so personally varied, it needs to be kept in mind that knowledge not just of the biblical sources but also of ancient midrashic writings and the artists' own midrashic observations is essential. The texts augment meanings the viewer can find in the paintings, and the paintings enhance textual interpretations that might occur to the viewer. The easiest way to understand the new attitude is to realize that even though the Bible is still a sacred text and various religious and liturgical traditions are still honored, the artists' interpretations are what really matter—what they choose to emphasize, confront, or reject, quite often with little or no inhibition.

This is not to say that they see themselves as revolutionaries but that they decide the emotional and intellectual tone of a work and that their imagery is not necessarily subservient to traditional interpretations of the subject at hand. Whatever their personal reasons, they also look on the ancient texts as both familiar and unfamiliar terrain open to intellectual adventure and exploration, as a means to formulate value judgments, and they look on their own works as a way to give the texts a contemporaneity and relevance we might not ordinarily find in them.

Whatever social and artistic factors as well as world events are in play, each artist has his or her own reasons for turning to religious subject matter. Nonetheless, the following generalizations can be made on the basis of what I have heard and noted over the years. First, Israel's success in the Six-Day War of 1967 gave Jewish Americans a new sense of pride in their religion and culture as well as the psychological incentive to explore Jewish themes. Second, the near defeat of Israel in the Yom Kippur War of 1973 revealed to many, perhaps for the first time, their profound connection to Judaism and to Israel. Third, the civil rights movements of the 1960s, although associated mainly with African Americans, gays and lesbians, and feminists, also inspired Jews to assert themselves—to come out, as it were, as Jews within mainstream culture. Fourth, the feminist movement especially encouraged women artists to explore their Jewish heritage and to question traditional patriarchal versions of biblical history. A fifth related factor revolves around the complete freedom of American artists to create whatever they wish. Without central rabbinic or religious authorities who might inhibit open-ended explorations and examinations of biblical materials and without guiding traditions of any type, but rather with the example of the current various liberation movements that encouraged reevaluation of traditional modes of thinking, artists began to restudy the sacred texts. A sixth important factor might very well be the negative responses to the strong assimilative tendencies after the Second World War and to the often demeaning and unpleasant ways deracinated Jews were portrayed in American popular culture by figures such as Philip Roth and Woody Allen (B. Rubin 1995, chap. 4). A seventh factor centers on the both subliminal and obvious responses to the rise of the multifaceted Jewish Renewal movement in the 1980s, with its concerns for spiritual regeneration and renewed Jewish identity, in part a reaction experienced by some artists to the overly cerebral, desiccated religious services they attended as youngsters (Baigell 2006b, 135; see also Aryeh Kaplan 1985, 1990; Lerner 1994; Schachter-Shalomi 2001, 104).

Even if we narrow the focus to individual artists within this larger framework, there is no simple or single explanation or overarching theory for the turn to religious subject matter. In fact, several explanations I received from them are quite varied, vague, even antithetical. For some of these artists, subjects emerge randomly in their imaginations. They just seem to happen. For others, growing up in a comforting Jewish environment created by parents and grandparents was crucial. In contrast, some were raised in completely secular households and turned to Jewish subject matter based on their personal desire for spiritual elevation and to feel they were part of something larger than themselves. What might that something be? Rabbi Neil Gillman thinks it has to do with belonging: "[belonging,] that intuitive sense of kinship that bonds a Jew to every other Jew in history and in the contemporary world. Whatever Jews believe, and however they behave as Jews, serves [*sic*] to shape and concretize that underlying sense of being bound to a people with a shared history and identity" (1990, xvii).

We might also say that some artists ally themselves with Judaism but not necessarily with Jewishness, with religion but not ethnicity, with their own concerns but not those of the Jewish polity. Although some might have their arguments with the concept of God, they are not scholars who question who wrote the Bible or follow the latest archaeological excavations that might determine the accuracy of the ancient texts. Nor, for that matter, are they focused on the issue that God might change the rules, as in, say, the story of the daughters of Zelophehad, who inherited their father's land because there were no sons (Numbers 27:1–8). For some, the sense of Yiddishkeit and the eastern European culture and language of their grandparents and great-grandparents are not a significant part of their experience. Nor, for that matter, do they desire, as mentioned earlier, to disappear as Jews or to be absorbed into the American artistic mainstream. Their interest in Jewish themes might suggest at some remove a desire to re-create that sense of togetherness and concern for the Jewish community that characterized life in the European shtetl and the early days of immigrant life in America. Virtually all of the artists with whom I have communicated have described the desire to belong to or have contact with a Jewish community, however loosely defined; their sense of an internalized Jewish identity that they feel but cannot easily describe; their connection to Jewish history; and, for some, their discovery of newly found spiritual needs that can be fulfilled only within a Jewish context.

Whatever sense of group identity they might have, compared to that of earlier generations, is based more on their readings of the ancient texts than on common generational experiences. But it should be noted that with respect to Judaism as a performative religion, some honor certain traditions and laws concerning prayer, food consumption, and religious ritual that do connect them to Jewish traditions, if not to a specific community (Orthodox, Reform, and so on).

It is worthwhile noting in this context that by insisting on exploring their religious and cultural heritage, these artists reject the kind of universalism that had been the goal of many Jewish artists since the emancipation in Europe in the nineteenth century. With the rise of anti-Semitism in the nineteenth and twentieth centuries, culminating in the Holocaust, always an ever-present, gnawing memory, does this rejection mean that the artists have lost faith in the progression of liberal values and are creating their own separate artistic future apart from the mainstream? Or might it mean that recent past history is no longer relevant because of the decline of overt anti-Semitism in their lifetimes and that therefore the artists feel freer than in the past to express their heritage? I honestly do not know. Whichever way this binary can be argued, the fact is that they no longer feel it is necessary to abandon or hide their Jewish identity in order to fit into the mainstream culture of the place where they live. They identify as both mainstream and minority at the same time, a privilege largely unknown to previous generations, which had to choose between 100 percent Americanism or 100 percent something else, an issue still a matter of concern as late as the immediate post–Second World War years (Baigell 2015b, 191–92; Rosenberg 1950).

Three works created by Archie Rand, Richard McBee (b. 1947), and Carol Hamoy (b. 1934) in the 1980s and 1990s give some inkling of the material to follow. (See their individual chapters.)

Concerning Rand, I want to compare one of his images of rabbis with *Jew with Torah* (1949) by the European-born artist Ben-Zion (fig. 2). In the years after the Second World War, Ben-Zion painted a few versions of men cradling Torah scrolls. By their appearance, all no doubt had earned the rabbinical ordinations awarded to graduates of rabbinical institutions. The men are usually advanced in years, and each embodies the spirit of tradition and continuity of Judaism and therefore of the Jewish people, especially important in the years just after the Holocaust. They are repositories of biblical history, maintainers of religious liturgy, and teachers of the next generation. Ben-Zion would have known, of course, that such men are respected, even venerated beyond all others, and considered to be *ben torah*s, sons of Torah (the first five books of the Hebrew Bible). In *Jew with Torah*, by showing the man holding the Torah scroll close to his face, his eyes closed as if in a trance, the artist clearly indicated the man's "love of Torah" (a common phrase still used today), his love of learning, his spirituality, and his exemplary presence and centrality to the Jewish community.

By contrast, in a set of paintings titled *The Rabbis 1* in 1985 (fig. 3) Rand created a series of figures who neither look nor act like Ben-Zion's figures. They do not look as wise as Ben-Zion's rabbis, nor do they hold lovingly detailed religious objects. Barely outlined and casually arranged decanters, candlesticks, and other objects used in religious ceremonies are instead placed in the background. Rand's rabbis, in the company of not very intelligent-looking friends or followers, seem to be passing by on a street. Rand has admitted that a "cultural raucousness" (his words) invaded these paintings in the way objects are casually strewn around in the background as well as in the way the figures are dressed and positioned.

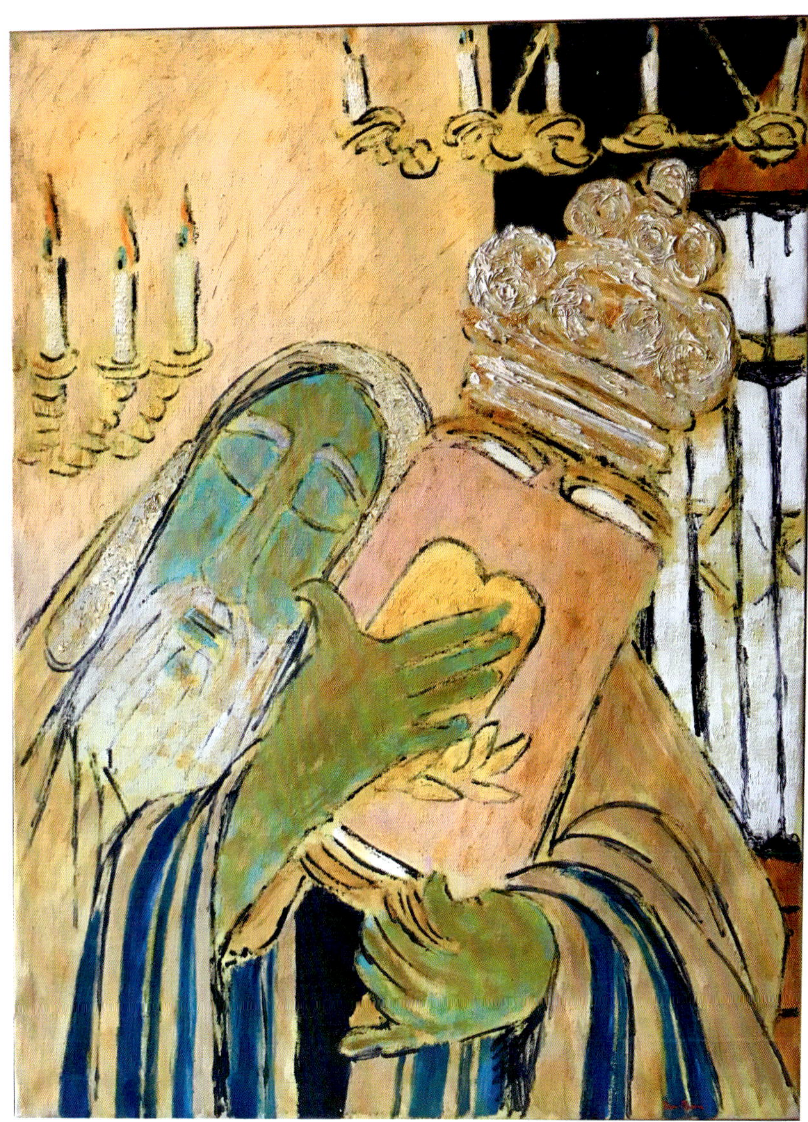

2. Ben-Zion, *Jew with Torah*, 1949. Oil on canvas, 40 × 30 in. Courtesy of the Ben-Zion Estate.

He said, "I like my rabbis. They're funny, vulgar, wise, and righteous. They are a humanizing element in my work. It's humbling to see them content as they are with the knowledge of the inherent 'averageness' in the most noble strivings. It's all very Jewish" (qtd. in *Jewish Themes* 1986, 2:34).

There is a decided element of independent thinking in Rand's paintings. What he means by "Jewish" relates more to everyday life than to the exultation of religious figures. His rabbis are not the awesome arbiters of religious doctrine, nor are they the community leaders conjured up by Ben-Zion in the 1940s. They are ordinary people one might pass on the street, their religious and ceremonial functions obliquely and casually indicated by the objects in the painting's background. One senses that not every rabbi would receive Rand's respect, let alone veneration, if it were unearned. Perhaps Rand would not even stand up briefly when a rabbi entered the room, a traditional form of respect. By dethroning rabbis from their highly venerated positions, he announces himself as the arbiter of the overall tone and effect of his paintings, obedient to nothing but his own imagination and intentions, albeit within a Jewish framework.

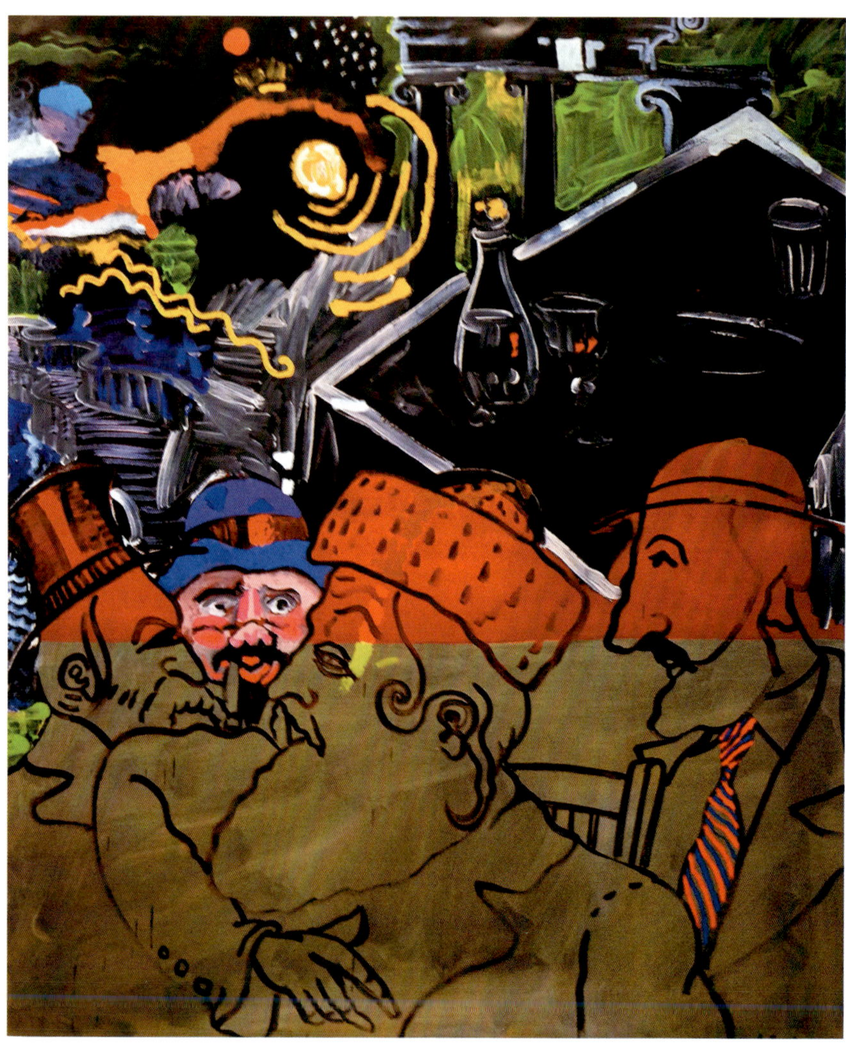

3. Archie Rand, *The Rabbis 1*, 1985. Acrylic on canvas, 58 × 48 in. Collection of Sylvia and Carl Freyer, Israel. Courtesy of the artist.

Works with an obvious feminist slant as well as those based on kabbalist sources were not common before the 1970s (Baigell 2007a, chap. 9). The second work to think about is *Sabbath Bride* (1985) by Carol Hamoy (fig. 4), a sculpture that could not have been made before the 1970s because it combines a feminist approach with kabbalist overtones. *Sabbath Bride*, a seminal work in Hamoy's career as well as in the history of Jewish feminist art, is based on sources that combined her then newly developing religious concerns with both her feminist interests and her secular background. A daughter and granddaughter of workers in the needle trades, Hamoy played with fabric remnants, beads, and threads as a youngster and still uses them as primary materials for her assemblages and constructions, thus honoring, as she says, her foremothers. A mixed-media construction about thirty inches tall, *Sabbath Bride* is a motherly-wifely figure composed of fabric, beads, candles, feathers, and a bird's nest. The feathers incorporated into her gown evidently were plucked from the chicken that had been prepared during the afternoon for the Sabbath meal.

But the bride's gown is not meant to be a Jewish joke about mothers and housewives. Rather, the iconography of *Sabbath Bride* grows more complex the more it is studied. Hamoy intended the title to suggest the figure described in the song "Lechah Dodi," written

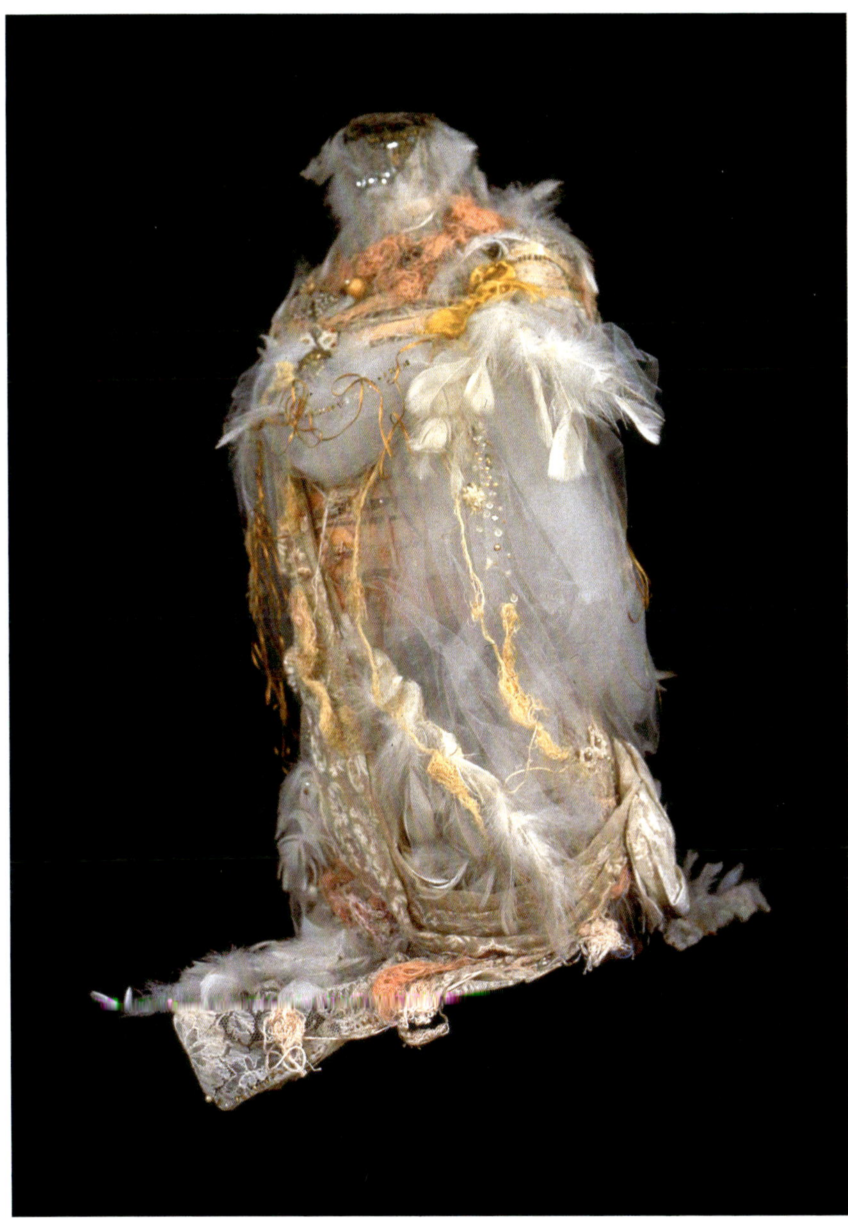

4. Carol Hamoy, *Sabbath Bride*, 1985. Mixed media, 38½ × 18 × 32 in. Collection Hebrew Union College–Institute of Religion Museum, New York. Courtesy of the artist.

by the sixteenth-century kabbalist Shlomo Ha Levi Alkabetz, which ushers in the Sabbath at Friday-evening services in synagogues around the world. In that song, the Sabbath Bride is welcomed by Israel, the groom. Other interpretations of the meaning of the Sabbath Bride indicate that she is the spiritual mother of Israel, that she is Israel the bride of God, that Israel is the spouse of the Sabbath, and that the Torah is the bride of Israel (Ginzberg [1909–38] 1917–87, 3:77, 92, 94, 455; A. Heschel [1951] 2005, 51–62, 109–13; Patai [1967] 1990, 265–73).

*Sabbath Bride* might also symbolize Jerusalem. One of the lines in "Lechah Dodi" is "Shake off the dust—arise! Don your splendid cloths," which refers to the passage in Isaiah 52:2 in which the prophet urges Jerusalem to rise up and dress in her finery. Hamoy's *Sabbath Bride*, then, is wife, mother, bride, queen, and symbol of Jerusalem who also welcomes her viewers to the Sabbath celebrations. For

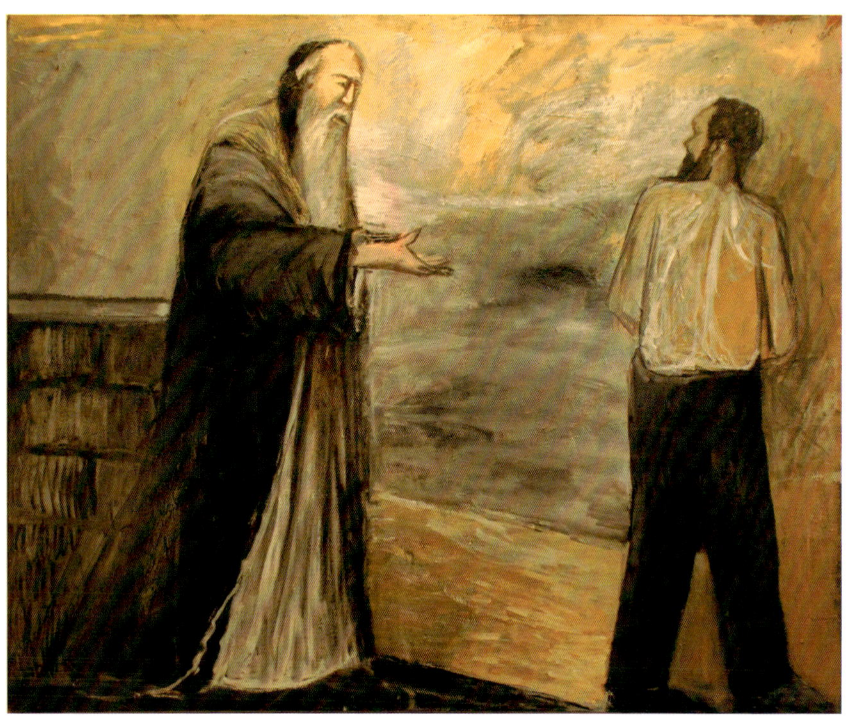

5. Richard McBee, *After*, 1994. Oil on canvas, 68 × 84 in. Courtesy of the artist.

sixteenth-century kabbalists, as the scholar Raphael Patai has observed,

> she [the Shekinah, the female aspect of the Deity] played the role of spouse as well as mother to her people. She also assumed the form of a divine queen and bride who joined them every Friday at dusk to bring them joy and happiness on the sacred Sabbath. To this day, in every Jewish temple or synagogue, she is welcomed in the Friday evening prayers with the words "Come, O bride." ([1967] 1990, 33)

Hamoy's visualization of the Sabbath Bride thus represents one of the most complex, multilayered concepts in all of modern Jewish art.

Various passages in the Bible and other texts might also raise questions to which artists might seek or invent answers. They might imagine "what ifs," or they might assert, "I need more information here" or "There is an issue that needs resolution," or they might ask, "Because the Bible is blank on this matter, what if I embellish the text here?" For example, after Abraham binds Isaac but does not sacrifice him as God initially commanded and instead substitutes a sacrificial ram, we are left catching our collective breaths. The Bible says only that "Abraham then returned to his servants, and they departed together for Beer-sheba" (Genesis 22:19). But what about Isaac?

This example leads to the third work I want to consider here, *After* (1994) (fig. 5) by Richard McBee, who has made more than one hundred paintings on the Binding of Isaac as well as on the lives of Sarah and Hagar. *After* raises the issue of the subsequent relationship between the father and the son. Will they be able to communicate with each other as before or be permanently estranged? In this psychologically illusive painting, McBee perhaps suggests that the latter is the more likely answer. Abraham, in ancient garb, reaches out to Isaac, dressed in modern clothing. Abraham's facial expression seems to show remorse as well as a desire to apologize and to explain his actions. But Isaac pulls away. Even in his profile we see fear and incomprehension still expressed. The space between the two also suggests both unbridgeable generational differences between father and son as well as the more obvious lack of trust Isaac must feel for his father (see Baigell 2009b, 116). My point here is that Abraham and Isaac no longer live only in the Bible. McBee takes the passage and provides it with a human dimension, updates it, and makes it relevant to contemporary life. It is no longer about mythic people who lived who knows when and whose actions have no bearing on our lives. The Bible can tell us stories about ourselves and our relationships.

McBee's painting, part of his ongoing series of works on the story of Abraham and Isaac, marks one of the defining characteristics of the art of this generation: the creation of narrative series, whether focused on a single event or person or on a general theme or subject. These series have been created over periods of time or in single campaigns and are based on material found in the Bible, kabbalah, and the Psalms. Although the creation of such series is not unique—earlier series abound, ranging from Ben Shahn's twenty-three paintings completed in 1931–32 on the trial and execution of the two Italian anarchists, Nicola Sacco and Bartolomeo Vanzetti, accused of murder to the comic strips and graphic novels created by a host of Jewish artists—series are not found in such abundance until the end of the twentieth century.

When asked why they needed or desired to create so many series, the artists have said that there are stories they want to tell, that the series mode marks a way to record what they have learned, to understand the ancient texts' figures as individuals, and to explore motives or experiences similar to those of today. I think what they are really saying is that they want the texts, especially the Bible, to be a living experience, not just books about a bunch of people who are so remote from their lives as to be expendable or who are portrayed in movies wearing robes and sandals and speaking in fake English accents.

I should mention how I selected Rand, Hamoy, and McBee as well as the other artists for this book. Having discussed issues with so many artists over the past three decades, I might have ended up writing what would have become a biographical dictionary of sorts. I preferred instead for the sake of coherence to discuss the art of eleven artists who I think have produced a reasonably consistent body of work that is based on religious sources and that has enlarged the parameters of Jewish-themed art through the artists' explorations of subject matter and modes of presentation.

So as not to ignore the efforts and contributions by other deserving artists, I have included some of their statements throughout the following chapters. Their comments help define the moods, intentions, and aspirations of their generation. It should be understood that their remarks are a representative rather than an exhaustive account of the thoughts of a very socially and religiously responsive and articulate generation of artists. It is my hope as well that my choices will be challenged and that those who do the challenging will write their own books and articles on artists of this generation. As far as I am concerned, the more public knowledge of these artists' efforts the better.

After I selected the eleven artists I wanted to focus on for extensive commentary, organizing the order of chapters became problematic. I had unintentionally divided male and female artists into separate groups, which I decided to leave intact. Feminist concerns are much more apparent in the women's art, and, perhaps primarily for that reason, their works in general are more concerned with social values and more interested in finding similarities between ancient and modern patterns of behavior. This is not to say that the works by the men are devoid of social values—I know the male artists are very concerned about these things—but the women more often use stories from the Bible to critique current events as well as misogynist behavior over time.

The works of the male artists by contrast, range widely, hewing closer to story lines, inventing backstories, and riffing imaginatively on the stories. Their styles and approaches to subject matter are distinct (as are the women artists' works) and do not easily connect in a single group or in-groups.

Mark Podwal's work is considered in the first of the individual artists' chapters because his sensibility and subject matter invoke most nearly the Jewish experiences and memories of the European past. Four chapters on women artists—Ruth Weisberg (b. 1942), Janet Shafner (1931–2011), Carol Hamoy, and Siona Benjamin (b. 1960)—follow. The next two chapters, on Robert Kirschbaum (b. 1949) and Tobi Kahn (b. 1952), are linked because of the idealism and spirituality implicit in their works. The chapters on Richard McBee and David Wander (b. 1954) are paired because both have created many narrative series. The last two chapters on individual artists are linked because both Archie Rand and Joel Silverstein (b. 1957) introduce many interesting objects, forms, and figures into their works that can enhance, destabilize, or de-familiarize one's readings of their works. (With the exception of Benjamin, born in Mumbai of Bene Israel inheritance, all of the artists are of Ashkenazic, or eastern European, descent.)

Taken altogether, the artists of the 1930s–1960s generation study, interpret, and even exult in their heritage and want to see it perpetuated. Their aim is Jewish continuity, not Jewish rupture—a continuity appropriate to a decentered twenty-first-century Judaism in America. Their general attitude is perhaps best summed up in Egon Mayer's observation that the "cultural open-endedness of late-twentieth century America" has allowed blending of "the universalistic components of American identity with a multitude of particularisms" (2008, 269–70).

In an email message to me dated October 27, 2012, Archie Rand gave a shorthand assessment of what was going on in the minds of many artists as they were starting their artistic careers. "It was the '60s. We recoiled when asked to invest in the traditional. Alternate deposits which could provide a stem of trust as strong as that provided by religion, government, nationality had to be located."

Common denominators, such as they are, include the desire to communicate personal feelings, to express spiritual and religious concerns, and to project a sense of personal authenticity. In this regard, the artists have repudiated irony, dissembling, and values associated with twentieth-century postmodernism even if they use some of its devices. They might instead be considered post-postmodernist in that they find through their explorations of Jewish secular and religious themes ways to express what is meaningful and relevant in their lives and to communicate those qualities to their viewers.

Some artists study religious texts with rabbis, are active in synagogue activities, or are members of *havuras*, independent study and worship groups, feeling that secular culture alone offers little ethical guidance. All would like their art to contribute to improving world conditions as much as and even more than responding to art-market values. Ruth Weisberg, for example, stated in a letter dated October 22, 2003:

> Jewish observance and ritual provide . . . sustenance and at their best have many rewards: providing a moral compass, a true sense of community, and an opportunity for collective repair of the world. I have also found that the study of Torah can integrate all aspects of ourselves, be they moral, intellectual, or spiritual. I love Judaism's embrace of all my capacities. I do not have to disengage my mind. As in art,

it provides moments in which all you know is in tune. Intuition and knowledge provide new insights and a renewed integration of body, soul, and experience.

In an undated letter to me, she returned to the notion of repairing the world:

> What I do feel very strongly is that my desire to make art, to create meaning and to be generative is a conscious commitment I make to be affirmative in the face of the knowledge of great systematic cruelty and inhumanity. To remember and to affirm have for me a specifically Jewish sense of renewal. It is the part I can play in the repair of the world—Tikkun Olam [*sic*].

The phrase "repair of the world" stands out in her letter, acknowledging that by the early 1980s the Hebrew term *tikkun olam*, initially a complex religious concept, had entered common usage as a catch-all secular phrase for Jews and non-Jews to describe activities that contribute to the betterment of humankind—or repair of the world. It connotes notions of mending and restoration and has both secular and religious aspects, such as performing good deeds, giving to charity, and engaging in religious activities and practices, perhaps as a form of personal redemption (Scholem [1941] 1961, 246–75, 1971c, 13; Soltes 2008, 251–54, 294–300). Of course, creating a single work of art, whether a painting, construction, or performance piece, will not change the world—artists know this—but the idea of contributing to societal betterment, however minimally, provides a way to connect to society at large beyond the confines of the studio and gives their art purpose.

But why is the idea of *tikkun olam* so popular today among so many people? A few possible answers. First, because people feel increasingly powerless in today's globalized world, small acts of kindness contribute both to a sense of personal redemption as well as to the larger societal good in either a religious or a secular sense.

Second, those inclined to spiritualism might feel that deeds that promote uplift will raise humankind to their own level of aspiration as well as help transform the world by bringing people closer to a sense of universal harmony.

Third, for Jews, as communal obligations for each generation become less and less binding and significant, acts of *tikkun olam* serve as a reasonable substitute for their once shared common religious heritage and communal responsibility. Today, for many, only a vague sense of kinship has replaced earlier attachments to collective activities, whether religious, secular, or political (D. Myers 2009, 37; Schwartz 1984, 68). But if polled, many artists would probably agree with the basic Jewish attitude succinctly stated by the popular twentieth-century theologian Abraham Joshua Heschel: "Who is a Jew? A person whose integrity decays when unmoved by the knowledge of wrong done to other people." Judaism "leads us to regard injustice as a metaphysical calamity" (1996, 32, 7).

Fourth, the literary historian David Roskies has pointed out that in Yiddish and Hebrew fiction around 1900, as traditional roots grew more distant, writers were drawn back to the shtetl as the idealized home, a paradise lost (1984, 93, 109–11). Thus, one hundred or so years later, acculturated Jewish Americans might look on *tikkun olam* as an ideal type of Jewish behavior, a secular Garden of Eden for the soul.

Fifth, performing acts of *tikkun olam* indicates a refusal to lose hope for humanity after the Holocaust and any number of other genocidal calamities and horrific events (Berger 1985, 5; Levenson 2000, 283).

Sixth, *tikkun olam* connotes for Jewish feminists "[the] creat[ion of] a just society to which a just Judaism can contribute and flourish"

(Plaskow 1990, 225). Or to state more bluntly what needs repair and mending in this regard: "When the Bible speaks of the beginnings of the people of God, it refers to the 'Fathers'" (Fischer 2005, 1).

Seventh, as a summing up, it can be said that at a time when religious belief can be so private and so antiauthoritarian, individuals invoke the term *tikkun olam* as part of their sense of self-identity. Arnold Eisen concludes that each person, autonomous and sovereign, decides which rituals and practices to observe (2008, 127–28). By extension, each artist is the arbiter of what might or might not be included in a work.

For the artists considered here, the issue of religion or the practice of religion does not revolve around belief or nonbelief but rather around commitment to, as Eisen has suggested, a "live relation with aspects of our inheritance that speak with 'inner power'" (1997, 28). Probably all would agree with the following general and open-ended observation: "One is Jewish if one identifies with Jewish history as one's own. This involves positioning oneself in relation to Jewish history, however central or tangential" (Krausz 1993, 272). The artists discussed here have positioned themselves more centrally than tangentially.

# 1 Comparing Generational Responses

Although there were Jewish artists in America in the nineteenth century, it was not until the beginning of the Great Migration in the 1880s that a serious presence can be discerned. Since that time, we can identify roughly six major generations of artists: the Yiddish-language magazine cartoonists, the early-twentieth-century modernists, the political artists of the 1930s, the abstract expressionists of the 1940s, the post–Second World War generation, and the current generation. Insofar as some born around the turn of the twentieth century lived into the 1960s and 1970s and participated in activities as well as employed painting styles associated with succeeding generations, there are considerable overlaps. Max Weber (1881–1961), for example, was a major early modernist and studied with Henri Matisse in Paris. Yet he was also very active politically in the left-wing, antimodernist art world of the 1930s. And Barnett Newman (1905–70), who published material hostile to the figurative American Scene movement of the 1930s, is one of the figures central to the rise of abstract expressionism in the 1940s (see Baigell 2007a).

It follows that statements about an artist's relationship to Judaism might vary over the years depending on his or her political, social, and artistic concerns at different moments, on how Jews were perceived in those moments, and on his or her closeness to or distance from his or her eastern European heritage and immigrant experiences. I argue as a generalization that artists born before the 1930s–1960s generation never became fully assimilated Americans because they were well aware of and influenced to greater or lesser extent by overt anti-Semitism in the United States and Europe, which became much less obvious after the end of the Second World War, and by the ever-present even if decreasing importance of their eastern European heritage. The artists considered here, the children and grandchildren of immigrants, appear to be able to objectify to a greater extent their attitudes about Judaism. Unlike the older artists, they do not feel as if society has imposed a religious label on them because of their ancestry and therefore that they have to accept or respond in some way to that label. They do not think of themselves automatically as an intimate part of the larger Jewish community but rather as people who chose to be or remain Jewish through personal negotiation.

Very little has come down to us concerning Jewish artists in America in the nineteenth century. We know that photographer and painter Solomon Nunes Carvalho (1815–97) involved himself in local Jewish affairs wherever he traveled (Carvalho [1853–54] 1953–54; Gutmann 1963, 26–27). And sculptor Moses Jacob Ezekiel (1844–1917) preferred to be known as an artist who was Jewish rather than as a Jewish artist, but not much is known about his connections to Judaism (Gutmann and Chyet

1975, 21, 42–46). According to Ezekiel's own account,

> I must acknowledge that the tendency of the Israelites to stamp everything they undertake with such emphasis is not sympathetic to my taste. *Artists* belong to no country and to no sect—their individual religious opinions are matters of conscience and belong to their households and not to the public. In reference to myself, this is my stand point [*sic*]. (Ezekiel 1975, qtd. in Philipson 1922, 9, emphasis in original; see also Baskind 2007, 102)

Many of the relatively few Jewish inhabitants of the United States at that time were immigrants from Germany and belonged to Reform congregations, if to any congregation at all. They desired to fit seamlessly into American society, and therefore Ezekiel's position seemed a logical one. But those who arrived during the Great Migration from eastern Europe that began in the 1880s and ended in 1924 with the establishment of US national quotas were largely Orthodox in religious orientation and background and part of a widely based Yiddish culture in whichever country they came from. Unfortunately, available archival records of art instruction in American settlement houses reveal very little, and a search of articles on art in old Yiddish- and English-language magazines and newspapers indicates that authors rarely, if ever, quoted artists directly about their heritage, probably because few artists and authors thought to question it. They grew up within Jewish communities in eastern Europe and in America and often spoke Yiddish or other eastern European languages at home, and if material in the Archives of American Art at the Smithsonian Institution is any indication, they often wrote articles in Yiddish and letters to each other in a variety of languages. Raised in their traditional cultures, they found Jewish identity less an issue—they certainly knew who they were and where they came from both literally and metaphorically—than the impact of American culture and concerns about assimilation. Furthermore, whatever their political or religious convictions, they thought of themselves and were thought of by the mainstream press as part of the larger Jewish community even as they sought to come to terms with their ambivalent status as Jews in America. This definition of them is of some consequence because several artists of this generation, whether European or American born, lived on into the 1960s and beyond and therefore for more than half a century helped set the tone of what it meant to be a Jewish artist in America.

Two factors in this history stand out. First, art critics and observers tended to think about Jews as a melancholic people, and, second, Jewish art critics and observers often asked artists to represent their community rather than join the mainstream. For example, in *The Spirit of the Ghetto* ([1902] 1965), a series of essays about Jewish life on New York's Lower East Side first published in 1902, Hutchins Hapgood described Jacob Epstein (1880–1959), the American-born illustrator, in the following way: "The artist has a melancholy, wistful face. . . . Epstein is filled with a melancholy love of his race, and his constant desire is to paint his people just as they are—to show them in their suffering picturesqueness" (249).

A non-Jewish critic characterized portraits painted by Abbo Ostrowsky (1889–1975), who arrived in the United States from Russia in 1908 and ran the important art school of the Educational Alliance on the Lower East Side of New York from 1917 to 1954, as revealing "the melancholy temperament of the Jewish People" (Chamberlain 1914, 193).

In articles written by Jews, *melancholy* as a descriptive term sometimes devolved into words such as *pathos* and *sadness*. Artist and critic Saul Raskin (1878–1966) questioned the loss of pathos in art in an article about the

Dutch Jewish artist Josef Israels (1824–1911). Humanity, Raskin held, yearns for pathos. He then asked:

> Who will be the one to return pathos to us? Why not us Jews? We can resurrect it. After all, Jews are the most pathos-like people among all of the past and present nations. Jews have experienced the worst sorrows and horrors and have suffered through the ages in their wanderings over the earth. They have suffered for their God and for their people. So they are the ones who can and will bring back pathos to the world. (1911, cols. 21–22)

In the same article, Raskin also insisted that Israel's "glance is filled with pity, not on a generalized person but on the unique individual" (col. 22).

Artist and writer Benjamin Kopman (1887–1965), who helped establish the Jewish Art Center in New York in 1925 to promote and maintain a secular Yiddish culture in America, wrote in 1928 that the portraits by Max Weber "express real suffering and sorrow. The Jew cannot shed his past." According to Kopman, Weber's Jewish soul illuminated his works (1928, 355). Weber evidently agreed. Of his painting *The Rabbi* (1934), he wrote that his subject was a "symbol of spiritual leaders whose dignity, faith, and moral conviction surmounted pain and bitterness throughout history."[1] And in 1938, the anti-Semitic policies instituted by Hitler in 1933 when he became chancellor of Germany certainly validated such observations. The Communist author Moishe Olgin (1878–1939) noted that a painting of Job by Ben-Zion (1898–1987) is "steeped in the anguish of the Jewish people" (Olgin 1938, cited in Kainen 1938).

In the face of many defections to the mainstream art world early in the twentieth century, Jewish artists were constantly reminded to maintain community contacts, especially by Abbo Ostrowsky and Dr. John Weichsel (1870–1946), who founded the People's Art Guild in 1915, the most important Jewish art organization of its time (it lasted until 1918). Ostrowsky, insistent and emphatic about encouraging and fostering the development of an art that reflected community culture, mentioned in a letter in 1914 that he wanted "to help Jewish art students develop a spirit for Jewish art." He rejected modernist art because he felt it was detrimental to sustaining Jewish heritage and therefore irrelevant to the Jewish community. It reflected only an artist's individual nature.[2] Weichsel, equally insistent, encouraged artists to remain attached to their community both for the sake of their own artistic development and for raising the cultural level of the community.[3]

Through the 1920s, the notion persisted that Jewish artists should remain tied to their community. In a review of an exhibition of Educational Alliance Art School students, artist Louis Lozowick (1892–1973) noted that artists should draw inspiration and spiritual sustenance from the community, identify with it, and embody its cultural heritage in their art. If they did so, the school would become "a great refining and elevating force in the life of

1. From an undated (c. 1934) clipping from unidentified newspaper, clipping file, Max Weber Papers, New York Public Library.

2. Abbo Ostrowsky to Dr. Alex Wolf. July 29, 1914, roll 1394, frame 364; "Autobiography," n.d., roll 1394, frame 656; and "The Armory Show," n.d., roll 1394, frame 677, Abbo Ostrowsky Papers, Archives of American Art (AAA) Microfilm Center, New York, Smithsonian Institution.

3. Dr. John Weichsel, "A Prospectus," 1916, roll N60-1, frame 464, Dr. John Weichsel Papers, AAA; "Catalogue of Exhibition at Forward Building," n.d., roll N60-1, frame 601, Weichsel Papers, AAA; "Prospectus for a Jewish Museum," n.d., roll N60-1, frame 686, Weichsel Papers, AAA.

the New York Jewish community" (Lozowick 1924, 465–66).

To be sure, Lozowick's preference for artists conveying the life of their community probably grew from his leftist political beliefs, but he might also have wanted art to play a role in keeping the community from fracturing and losing its Jewish identity through assimilation. The latter condition was certainly part of the motivation for Jennings Tofel (1891–1959), Benjamin Kopman, Abraham Walkowitz (1878–1965), and the literary figure David Ignatoff (1885–1954), editor of the magazine *Shriftn*, to found the short-lived Jewish Art Center in 1925 (it closed in 1927). Quite simply, Tofel and the others wanted "to encourage the creation of a distinct Jewish culture within a pluralistic society" and planned to do so through exhibitions, lectures, and musical presentations (Tofel 1927, 53; see also Kampf 1990, 57; Werner 1976, 10). Another motivating factor was that "despite all openness, they [Tofel and the others] always felt like outsiders in the largely gentile art establishment" (Werner 1976, 10).

Tofel worried that "an older generation of Jewish artists in America rejected Jewishness as something disturbing and detrimental" (1927, 54). He did not mention names but probably meant those artists who sought to exhibit in "uptown" galleries or gravitated toward the Stieglitz circle (Alfred Stieglitz [1864–1946] was the major proselytizer for and popularizer of modernist art). Tofel preferred to think of a time when, like that imagined by Ostrowsky, Weichsel, and Lozowick, the Jewish community and its artists would grow closer together. "[Each] artist will [then] sense the clarity of his source and that will enable him to traverse the whole world of appearance and be his own, an authentic human being" (Tofel 1927, 55), meaning that in his opinion an artist's Jewish identification alone could be the source of artistic inspiration.

More than that, however, Tofel felt that a "new dignity was bestowed on the concept of nationality" (1927, 55). Therefore, a Jewish artist did not need to identify as an American in America but could remain part of an imagined Jewish polity. In effect, Tofel thought in terms of a Jewish nationality, and loyalty to that concept was of uppermost importance. The last sentences of his article about the Jewish Art Center in 1927 were: "And who discovered the Jew in me? Who finds it essential that I should remain a Jew? Nobody except Me [*sic*]" (56). Tofel also held that Jewish artists like him should remain Jewish, create Jewish art based on biblical sources, immerse themselves in their heritage, and align themselves with what he called "the Jewish character," a term too imprecise to define today. In a hand-written note probably dating from the 1930s, Tofel continued in this vein. "Judaism is a nation and a religion. They [Jews] lost their land and were scattered among the people of the world. Still they persisted as a nation."[4]

If I read Tofel correctly, he sought a place in which one could reside but remain relatively impervious to local customs and traditions if they conflicted with one's "national" heritage. Or perhaps he took to heart notions of cultural pluralism put forth by figures such as Horace Kallen (1882–1974) and Randolph Bourne (1886–1918), according to which America could be composed of a mosaic of nations, each contributing its share to the national entity (Bourne 1916a, 1916b; Kallen 1915).

Clearly, Jewish identity was central to Tofel's self-definition as a person and as an artist. Other artists of his generation had similar feelings. Ben-Zion stated: "As a Jew, being adopted by America, and adopting it, my contribution to its art expression can only be within

4. Jennings Tofel, handwritten note, n.d. [c. 1930s], roll 65–38, frame 15, Jennings Tofel Papers, AAA.

the realm of my experience."[5] A few years later he elaborated on this thought, indicating that he was tied less than Tofel to a profoundly parochial and distinct Jewish point of view:

> Although identification of an artist must be first and foremost with humanity as a whole, nevertheless the really genuine one never dissociates himself from his creed. On the contrary, he thrives on the sources of his origin, and through projecting his background reaches humanity which no matter how multiple and different its creeds and upbringing may be—at the roots is the same humanity. (Ben-Zion 1963)[6]

Sculptor Aaron Goodleman (1890–1978), whose politics were well left of center and therefore more universal than parochial, nevertheless acknowledged the influence of his Jewish heritage when he wrote: "The more profound the artist's understanding of the rudiments of nature, of his surroundings, of the origins, the social aspirations, *the culture and the tradition of his people*, the larger the personality of the artist, the more significant his achievements in art, and the greater his contribution to society" (qtd. in "Aaron Goodleman" 1947, 66, emphasis added).

Such thoughts, no doubt, are common to those who were born in one culture and have lived in another. In an interview in late 2018, Alfonso Cuarón, a Mexican now resident in Italy, the writer and director of the motion picture *Roma* (2018), and knowledgeable of international developments in film history, observed: "For almost a decade, I lived in that chimera of cosmopolitanism. And I do believe that we are all citizens of the world, but if you're not centered and deeply rooted in a cultural identity, then that cosmopolitanism turns infertile" (qtd. in Valdes 2018).

Such statements by Tofel, Ben-Zion, Goodleman, *and* Cuarón basically assert that the universal can be attained through the local, that whatever their heritage all people aspire to the same goals. In this regard, it is interesting to note that one of the best-known social realist artists, Ben Shahn (1898–1967), made perhaps the most overtly religious statement by an artist of his generation when explaining his religious mindset as a youth:

> At that time [as a youth in Lithuania], I went to school for nine hours a day. And all nine hours were devoted to learning the true history of things, which was the Bible. Time was to me, then, in some curious way, Timeless. All the events of the Bible were, relatively, part of the present. Abraham, Isaac, and Jacob were "our" parents—certainly my mother's and my father's, my grandmother's and my grandfather's, but mine as well. I had no sense of imminent time and time's passing. (1963, 5)

To this day, Hasidic and ultra-Orthodox individuals still refer to "Father Abraham" and "Mother Sarah."

In such statements, one can see how religious, cultural, and communitarian values and memories merge. So it is not beyond reason to assume that despite or perhaps because of the strong presence of a secular, socially concerned art in the 1930s and the devastating emotional and psychological effects of the Holocaust in the 1940s, Tofel and others affirmed their continued commitment to Judaism, symbolized by the creation or re-creation of the Jewish Art Center in 1948, which was sponsored by the World Jewish Congress for Jewish Culture, evidently an organization in some way still connected to whatever remained of the

5. "Ben-Zion Autobiographical Sketch," 1959, typescript, n.p., Collection Ben-Zion House, New York.

6. "An Artist's View of a Jewish Museum," Sept. 13, 1963, roll N69-122, frame 153, Ben-Zion Papers, AAA; see also Baigell 2006a, 47–48.

organizational radical Left. The leaders of the Jewish Art Center, primarily European-born artists well into their middle years—the Arts Committee included Chaim Gross (1904–91), Ostrowsky, Raskin, Tofel, and Walkowitz—still thought of themselves as sharing a similar Jewish heritage and culture as well as Jewish values and experiences.[7] But for us today, the new Jewish Art Center symbolizes the last gasp of the Lower East Side ethos of this era. Looking more to the pre-Holocaust past than to the future and clearly motivated by the desire to maintain time-tested socialist attitudes held since the late nineteenth century, the center planned to "support Jewish plastic and pictorial arts, to bring the culture of art into all Jewish homes . . . , the fulfillment of which we, together with the artists, look for encouragement and sympathy from the wide Jewish folk masses." To do so, the Arts Committee called for "building and consolidating existing Jewish cultural forces [and] stimulating Jewish creativeness." It hoped that exhibitions here and abroad would "knot more closely together all the Jewish artists of the world."[8]

Discussing these intentions in his article "Art Comes to the Jewish Community," included in the document describing the Jewish Art Center's aims and aspirations in 1948, David Ignatoff visualized a future built on the past, a continuation of where they had been in the 1920s rather than where the Depression of the 1930s and the six million murdered in the 1940s had left them.[9] Ignatoff reeled off names of biblical prophets, devoted considerable space to the importance of Alfred Stieglitz, Dr. John Weichsel, and members of Die Yunge, a radical group of writers that flourished early in the century, and then outlined plans for exhibitions, lectures, and art classes, as if continuing the activities of the Educational Alliance and the People's Art Guild.

In another essay appended to the aims-and-aspirations document titled "Artists and Scholars View Yiddish Art," Nochum B. Minkoff reiterated various opinions about the nature of Jewish art offered by assorted artists and writers, whose definitions of its character essentially limited it to an art created by eastern European Jewish men born around the turn of the century, such as Marc Chagall (1887–1985).[10]

Around the same time that Tofel and others were trying to resurrect their old organization, another group of artists had largely separated from the Jewish community in favor of international mainstream concerns. They were the abstract expressionists and included sculptor Seymour Lipton (1903–86) and painters Adolph Gottlieb (1903–74), Mark Rothko (1903–70), and Barnett Newman. Although they made very few comments specifically about their religion, we can extrapolate Jewish inferences in their works. (For these works, see the indexes in Baigell 2001, 2006a, 2007a, 2015b.)

In an interview, Lipton said: "I don't practice the formal credo of Judaism although I am deeply aware of my position as a Jew, both nostalgically, as to my parents, and politically, as one of a minority group" (in Grossman 1967, 96). In the same year, Gottlieb stated: "The idea of being a so-called Jewish artist is like being a professional Jew. I think art is international and should transcend any racial, ethnic,

7. *Jewish Art Center: Aims and Aspirations* (1948), reel N60-2, frames 122–44, Weichsel Papers, AAA.

8. *Jewish Art Center: Aims and Aspirations.*

9. David Ignatoff, "Art Comes to the Jewish Community," 1948, in *Jewish Art Center: Aims and Aspirations*, roll N60-2, frames 125–27, Weichsel Papers, AAA.

10. Norman B. Minkoff, "Artists and Scholars View Yiddish Art," 1948, in *Jewish Art Center: Aims and Aspirations*, reel N60-2, frames 9–15, Weichsel Papers, AAA. See also Baigell 2005b, 77, 2007a, xviii–xix.

religious, or national boundaries" (in Grossman 1967, 47).

Perhaps in private conversations Rothko and Newman spoke as openly as Lipton and Gottlieb, but nothing similar from them seems to be recorded in print. Rather, their references to brutality and terror in the modern world strongly suggest that they had in mind the callous destruction of eastern European Jewry (of the many references, see *Mark Rothko* 1987, 80; Newman 1990, 100; Sandler 1970, 64).

Artists born in America between, say, 1915 and the late 1920s were less reticent but perhaps more conflicted about their Jewish background. Most were born and educated in America, but their ties to the immigrant generations were still apparent. And they were undoubtedly aware of the open and even virulent anti-Semitism that climaxed in the 1940s (Baigell 2007a, 129–45; Dinnerstein 1994, 78–149). Therefore, between friction at home with tradition-minded parents, hostility on the street, and uncertainty regarding their place in American society, artists such as Jack Levine (1915–2010) and Leonard Baskin (1922–2000), two artists who spoke most openly about their religion, projected a sense of disquietude, perhaps even embarrassment, about it, as recorded in their relevant statements. (In his later years, Levine became more accepting of his heritage and created several Jewish-themed works, but Baskin less so, even though he made a great number of such works [Baigell 2006a, 118–40]).

Of his series of paintings of biblical figures begun in the early 1940s, Levine said:

> My father's death in 1939 started me on the path of those Jewish sages. It was his religion, not mine. . . . It wasn't Judaism bursting out of me, but a kind of museumology. . . . I haven't gone into Judaica out of some sort of religious piety. There are craft reasons—textures to deal with and atmospheric passages to paint. . . . In a way, my involvement with Jews is political, and in a way history-mongering. It brings me closer to some kind of artistic precedent I have my eyes on. But as for people who say I shouldn't be involved with gold-leaf backgrounds and Hebrew letters, and then with beards and turbans making hieratic gestures, the hell with those people. (qtd. in Brown and Frankel 1989, 37–38)

By distancing himself from his father's religion and by discussing craft issues, Levine diffused the significance of his Jewishness, as if he had to explain and apologize for his choice of subject matter. Even as late as 1957, he was recorded as saying, "I'm a Jew of the American seaboard [he was born in Boston], looking east. I've never managed to feel fully indigenous. I've been part of a tolerated minority. That has affected the subject matter as well as the style of my painting" (in Rodman [1957] 1961, 202).

Levine's relationship to the Jewish community always remained ambivalent in that he wanted it both ways—to identify as Jewish but not too Jewish, to acknowledge tradition but not be bound by it. In 1962, he offered the following assessment of his position:

> I think I have tried to express in my work some sort of ethic which may stem from some of our traditions, but it is not necessarily turned back within the Jewish community. I try to paint for everybody . . . and consequently it hasn't been an introverted expression, let's say, in the ethnic sense. But there is no question in my mind that after some fashion, I'm true to my tradition and to my teaching. (Levine 1962, 35)

This statement is a near perfect example of Charles Liebman's thesis about ambivalent American Jews: "What is striking . . . is the constant search for a universalistic ethic which would cut through the differences that an older tradition had impressed, but which would permit the Jew to retain at least nominal identification as a Jew" (1973, 157). One might say of Levine and certainly of Baskin that they were not European but not fully American either. Baskin, born in New Brunswick, New Jersey, the son of an Orthodox rabbi, recalled in 1961:

> I went to Yeshiva . . . and loved God with all my heart and all my soul. Until the age of sixteen I was steeped in traditional Judaism. Slowly my mind found its way elsewhere. The lustrous other world with its ranks of possibility became apparent. I stretched into it and was incapable of ever returning, but my brain is serried with the infinity of memory-traces that recall the sound and smell of *shul* [synagogue], of home, of Yeshiva, or the nearly all-Jewish street. (Baskin 1961, 295)

Baskin also noted that "Yiddish is the inner language of aliens. Anyone can learn Hebrew," meaning that Yiddish was more than a language but rather a stand-in for self- and group identity distinct from American identity (1961, 294). At the same time, he was able to state that "as a Jew, I have never had a bad experience, but I identify as a Jew, I feel very Jewish, very Yiddish particularly" (qtd. in Jaffe 1980, 127).

Of all of the artists born in the 1920s, George Segal (1924–2000) seems to have been least bothered by being Jewish in America—or, for that matter, in the world—despite the fact that he was the child of immigrants, had heard stories of pogroms from his parents and accounts of Holocaust atrocities from neighbors, and spoke Yiddish and Hebrew as a child. "There was pressure [at home] to learn English. I stopped speaking Yiddish and Hebrew by the time I was five because it was shameful," he said when I taped an interview with him in 1992. "I feel myself very strongly American . . . and the product of the American university system." At the same time, however, his past is present in his creative work. The author of several sculptures based on biblical figures, he stated that whether a particular work is secular or Jewish themed, "my Jewish background contributes some kind of heavy weight myth and spirituality," a neither-here-nor-there kind of statement. He simply meshed, as he said, his Jewish heritage with many aspects of American democracy—suburban living, movies, and so on. "I'm after some kind of synthesis," he said. He was also very supportive of Israel. He mentioned that after the Second World War "the only response for Jews was to work incessantly for the establishment of the State of Israel. I think it is essential that Israel survive as a homeland for Jews." By the early 1980s, he had traveled there four or five times. (Some of these observations are also based on my conversations with Segal at the home of mutual friends during the many years we lived a few miles from each other in New Jersey.)

By contrast, the comments by the artists born in the 1930s and after, unencumbered by the experiences Levine and Baskin had, are much more affirmative, assertive, and positive. With a greater sense of integration into American society and because anti-Semitism, although always present, was less overt as they were growing up, they have communicated their religious interests from a position of comparative psychological and emotional strength. They are not embarrassed by or feel they need to gloss over the fact that they are Jewish. This is not to say that they deny the continued existence of prejudice, but rather that they feel, perhaps for the first time in American history, comfortable in being open about their religious heritage. For them, the hidden meaning of what Baskin called "the language of aliens" is just another and not very important part of their being and self-definition. They do not speak and, I would bet, do not understand Yiddish. Their associations are by far more American than eastern European.

Nor are they defensive or confrontational about choosing Jewish subject matter. They do not share Levine's adversarial stance vis-à-vis Christians because certain thoughts no longer need articulating. Even as late as the 1980s, Levine believed "that it was my purpose . . . to be a propagandist for the Old Testament, for my own group" (qtd. in Brown and Frankel 1989, 134). He is also reported to have said that he "painted Old Testament scenes partly in answer to the Christians who constantly painted them, thus reclaiming them for Judaism" (qtd. in Amishai-Maisels 1993, 483 n. 92).

The artists of the 1930s–1960s generation would also reject out of hand art critic Hilton Kramer's hostile observation when reviewing an exhibition of paintings of Jewish subjects by Hyman Bloom (1913–2009). In an issue of *Commentary* in 1955, Kramer admitted that "for the observer who had associations with this imagery from childhood onwards, Bloom's paintings stimulate the same surprise and dismay one feels at finding *gefilte* fish at a fashionable cocktail party" (1955, 586; see also Baigell 2002a, 34). When Kramer was confronted with obvious Jewish subject matter, his embarrassment and culturally induced Jewish self-hatred were palpable, as if to say it is all right to have schnapps and herring at home but only Scotch and canapes in public.

Beginning in the 1970s and continuing to this day, Kramer's disdain for Jewish subject matter was and is no longer acceptable. A tremendous explosion of interest and pride in subjects based on the ancient sacred texts has invigorated the works of Jewish artists in recent decades. Over the past forty–fifty years, such artists have also expressed their intentions and interests quite publicly. Janet Shafner (1931–2011), who made many feminist works that challenge biblical patriarchy, noted in an email dated April 25, 2007, "In the eighties, when I began my paintings inspired by *Tanach* [the first five books of the Bible or the Torah, the Prophets, and the Writings], I felt like I was alone. Now, I read about Jews everywhere exploring what it means to be Jewish and to do art that circles their tradition."

In an interview on January 12, 2012, Boston-based painter Fay Grajower (d. 2017) used words that artists of the abstract expressionist generation might have had difficulty saying out loud: "Being a Jew is who I am."

New York–based artist Archie Rand (b. 1949), who had already achieved an initial mainstream success as a modernist, switched almost exclusively to Jewish-themed art in the mid-1970s. Perhaps he best sums up the change in attitude in his statement that "I am by no stretch of the imagination [a religiously] observant person, but I demand the right to proclaim my Jewishness. . . . I just came in and invaded it" (qtd. in Rosen 2001, 57; see also Cembalest 1994).

New York–based artist Mark Podwal (b. 1946) said:

> Neither from a religious family nor observant, I nonetheless derive continued inspiration from my heritage. Fascinated by Jewish history, moved by its teachings, enchanted by its legends and folklore, and delighted by Yiddish proverbs, I have attempted through my work to enliven its traditions, wisdom, beauty, and wit in a visual way.

He continued: "I am very proud to be Jewish. . . . I look at Judaism as something that can offer me creativity" (in Cipolla 2006).

Chicago-based painter and printmaker Ellen Holtzblatt[11] said in an email on April 21, 2007, that she had once avoided Jewish content because of the art world's rejection of it, but

11. I have been unable to find the birth dates of Holtzblatt and a few other artists mentioned in this chapter, and they won't tell me.

that rejection no longer concerns her. "At this point in my life, Jewish text is intimately relevant, and that is all that matters. Art making cannot be compartmentalized from my intrinsic nature." And Los Angeles–based artist Ruth Weisberg (b. 1942) proclaimed in a letter on October 22, 2003: "I love Judaism's embrace of all my capabilities. I do not have to disengage my mind. As in art, it provides moments in which all you know is in tune. Intuition and knowledge marry and produce new insights and a renewed integration of body, soul, and experience."

Los Angeles–based photographer Bill Aron (b. 1941) explained his turn to Jewish subject matter in a statement published by that city's Jewish Artists Initiative in 2007 (see the discussion of art organizations later in this chapter): "I began photographing at a time in my life when I was trying to figure out what connected my past to my present and what my future might be. My father believed in the unity of the Jewish people, yet he also believed in the American Dream. He wanted me to be an American but to respect where I came from" ("Artist Statement, Bill Aron" 2007). In an email dated May 20, 2009, he wrote that "work has always been about the Jewish content in my head. I never thought about pursuing any other subject matter."

In the Jewish Artists Initiative publication *A Gathering of Sparks* in 2011, other artists expressed similar feelings. Eileen Levinson stated: "I'm in JAI to join the generation of artists that are shaping Jewish creative life in Los Angeles." Benny Ferdman found that "my connection to JAI puts me in dialogue with other artists who share a common idea—that it is possible to create authentic Jewish art within the culturally scattered reality of Los Angeles." Carol Es holds that "being part of JAI transforms my severed connections to the Jewish community and grants me acceptance of who I really am—a part of a tribe of kin, which in many ways brings me closer to God." And Ruth Weisberg said that she values JAI "because it creates a real sense of community and encourages us to explore the immense source of inspiration which is Judaism" (*A Gathering of Sparks* 2011, 43, 25, 24, 56).

Some artists have described a more problematic but not dissonant or antagonistic relationship with Judaism. For example, photographer Jason Francisco (b. 1967), who has searched out and photographed inhabitants of Jewish neighborhoods in several countries, revealed another aspect of contemporary views of Jewishness in an interview on November 4, 2004. Raised in a minimally religious family, he wants to aid "in the definition, or redefinition, of Jewishness in my own time. This is very important. . . . I'm finding out what it means to have already been Jewish." He sees himself as a "Diaspora Jew who lives in America. America is where I live, where I was born. I am an acculturated American . . . , but not an involuntary American."

Others grew up under totally different circumstances. New York–based fiber artist Laurie Wohl (b. 1942) said in an interview on December 27, 2005: "My maternal grandfather was an Orthodox rabbi, and I was very, very close to him. Some of my earliest memories of Shabbat [the Sabbath] were [of] going to shul [synagogue] with him and sitting with him. And that sort of seeped in."

In contrast, Los Angeles–based artist Sam Erenberg (b. 1943) spoke to the loss of community or, rather, of never quite being part of a community in a letter dated May 1992, where he described his feelings at that time.

> Since I am not an "observant Jew," nor do I attend temple, I do not have a communal "Jewish identity." But I might define "identity" as one who possesses "Jewish roots," and if one believes that "blood" and "soul" are not just biological and religious terms

> but metaphysical ideas, then, of course, I do have Jewish identity. I also believe that the notion of "memory" might work in a similar fashion, although more acculturation is involved here. . . . Yet my memory comes from a deeper part of my being. It is like a "longing," the pathos often described and alluded to in Jewish literature. This longing (or guilt?) is the deep feeling for mankind that my father tried to instill in me.

Another Los Angeles–based painter, Pat Berger (b. 1929), unlike artists of earlier generations who chose to leave members of the Jewish community to reinvent themselves as Americans or who exhibited what can only be called embarrassment at admitting they were Jewish, wrote in a letter dated May 5, 1992, that as she became older and "became aware of discrimination and anti-Semitism, there was a kind of yearning inside me to identify more with Jewishness."

Others have expressed feelings of outrage in thought and deed, unimaginable before the 1960s, at art teachers and mainstream art critics and gallerists who have ignored and belittled Jewish-themed art. For example, New York–area painter Joel Silverstein (b. 1957) described his feelings in an email dated January 22, 2012:

> I frankly think that a lot of Jewish artists, including myself, got such an anti-art feeling in the traditional Jewish community and anti-Jewish feeling in the art world, including specifically from secularized Jews in key art positions[.] I think every self-proclaimed Jewish artist has war stories replete with unpleasant comments—and repetitions of these [comments] are often not even bound by the qualities of specific works, but merely [by] unfair and obnoxious attitudes. At Pratt Institute [which he attended in the 1970s], the rhetoric was decidedly secular and unspiritual. Certainly, Jewish identity as an aspect of the work of art was never applauded or welcomed by any faculty member, some of them Jewish, and by gallerists, curators, and others in the art world.

Feminists equally committed to their religion have raised different issues—obviously regarding Jewish patriarchy, as discussed in chapter 2—that could not have been articulated before the late 1960s and the rise of Jewish feminism then. New York–based artist Helène Aylon (b. 1931) summed up many Jewish female artists' thoughts when she said: "I still love the culture, but feel it needs a real airing out. I love the word Torah, but when I look at it, I feel betrayed. I'd still take the good parts, but those aren't enough. . . . I want to be Jewish. I love being Jewish. . . . At the same time, I can't swallow this" (qtd. in Paulson 2001).

And Carol Hamoy (b. 1934), also based in New York, has devoted her art to setting the record straight. In an email dated November 27, 2011, she wrote: "It occurred to me that the Torah is really his/story—a collection of experiences told by men about men. I decided it would be my job to fill out the population of those five books by telling her/stories of the women who were in those pages at the very same time. . . . I felt it would be a real bonus to review aspects of this religion from another point of view—a twenty-first-century feminist perspective."

Some artists have expressed the importance of spirituality as an element of motivation. For example, in an interview on August 22, 2006, Jill Nathanson, a nonfigurative, nonrepresentational painter in New York who created a series of four abstract paintings in 2004 based on Moses's second ascent of Mt. Sinai to receive a new set of tablets, explained the feeling she sought to capture of this most seminal event in all of Jewish history. "Within Judaism, there is an inner visualization of prayer or the divine that is internal and abstract. I try to get a hold of this inner meditative, abstract visualizing in my work" (see also Baigell 2008; for other like-minded artists, see Baigell 1999, 2006b). And Santa Monica–based artist Bruria Finkel (b. 1932) noted in an email in July or August 2003 that "in prayer, religion sometimes enables one to reach states close to a spiritual space. The major aspect of the spiritual experience is to reach a state of bliss when one follows certain processes [e.g., meditation] that bring you to that state."

Other artists believe that because God created the universe, whatever we do or make should honor God. Los Angeles artist Laurel Paley has stated this position very plainly: "The role I see for the artist is similar to the role I see as a Jew. What a Jew does is to 'sacralize' and elevate the everyday and make it holy. . . . An artist can take mundane materials, like goo and newspaper and trash and ink, and make it something spiritual and extraordinary that can create meaning in people's lives" (qtd. in Kushner 1998, 4). The theologian Abraham Joshua Heschel summed up this point of view well, explaining that one of the goals of the Jewish way of living is "to experience commonplace deeds as spiritual adventures, to feel the hidden love and wisdom in all things." And "the highest peak of spiritual living is not necessarily reached in rare moments of ecstasy; the highest peak lies wherever we are and may be ascended in a common deed" (1955, 49, 384).

Still others invoke the concept of *tikkun olam*. New York–based abstract painter and sculptor Tobi Kahn (b. 1952) has often said in many conversations over the years that he wants his art to bring about a better world, acknowledging that "in the rabbinic tradition we are mandated to continue God's work, partners in renewing the world (*tikkun olam*)" (Kahn c. 1985), and "we praise and protect the natural world while acting to repair the brokenness—in ourselves and in the global community" (Kahn 2009, 12).

Notions of *tikkun olam* can reach beyond the artist's studio, the scholar's study, or the synagogue, especially among those artists who incorporate elements of the landscape into their art. For instance, Atlanta-based artist Maxine Hess creates works inspired by the Torah that she feels "command personal responsibility, respect for others, and caring for G-d's sacred creation" (in *Song of the Land* 2012, 14). In effect, one is a steward rather than a despoiler of the land, a modern gloss on the Talmudic dictum *hiddur mitzvah* (Shabbat 133b), based on Exodus 15:2, "This is my God and I will enshrine (extoll) Him." In the context here, *hiddur mitzvah* means, as Hess intends, to honor God's creation. She bears public witness to her religious concerns.

In an odd way, such artists are not unlike the social concern artists of the 1930s who applied the sense of responsibility inherent in their religious heritage to secular political concerns (Baigell 2015b, 1–9). But the difference between the two generations lies in the fact that the younger artists are more concerned with their desire to find meaning, often of a personal nature, in the ancient texts than in encouraging social action. They find in their inventions of midrashim a way to explore and comment upon those texts, a way to emend and tease out nuanced interpretations of various passages they choose to visualize in their work. No less than poets, scholars, and theologians, these artists, especially the feminist artists (see chapter 2), have found ways to recast and rewrite, as it were, stories and characters "drawn in outline in the biblical narrative" (Steinmetz 1988, 35).

Just as the desire to fill in the blanks in that outline inspired the creation of the Talmud long ago, so artists as well as scholars, especially but not exclusively feminist scholars, have interpreted biblical narratives or have written commentaries based on current concerns and interests. Artists also find ancient midrash to be a valuable source of information and a trigger for their own interpretations, as Siona Benjamin (b. 1960), Archie Rand, and Ruth Weisberg, whose works are considered in detail later, have attested. In a written statement dated November 17, 2000, Benjamin said,

> I like to make parallels to stories and circumstances today. . . . It's all about bridging and understanding that almost nothing has changed from the myths of old to today. Midrash is not just a Jewish point of view, it is a very humanistic point of view. . . . I explore the women of the Bible and bring them forward to combat the wars and violence of today in a midrash of intricate paintings.

In Archie Rand's view,

> we need [*midrashim*] as an intercessor to certify the *kashrut* [meaning, in this context, authenticity or appropriateness] of what we know to be a discussion between our Jewish faith, our God, our universe, and ourselves. . . . I propose that God replies to our questions through *midrash*. . . . It is in the story, the *midrash*, that one is assured of a community, a share in the continuance, beyond one's own arbitrary time and place. The story, the *midrash*, is the tether to meaning which fastens human beings to this earth and connects us to the past and future. (1999b, 3–4)

This passage makes at least two notable points. First, studying midrashim becomes another avenue to approach the events and personalities in the ancient texts; second, such study reflects an artist's own relations to eternity and community, whether these relations are personal or congregational and traditional. On another occasion, in an email dated August 31, 2010, Rand emphasized the connection to the community: "I refer to [midrash] as a bonding link to the arc of the culture. . . . To engage midrash is to rejoin and support and [to] ask [for] acceptance and announce an understanding and love and respect for the values of the community."

According to Ruth Weisberg,

> *Midrash* has many roles; sometimes it fills in missing parts of the story; and at other times it answers an implicit question. *Midrashic* commentary often adds a human dimension or a psychological insight to the narrative. More than anything, it tends to enliven the archetypal stories for successive generations. Visual art can also function in these ways, in its use of specific images, its sensory appeal, and its direct emotive power. (2004a, 138)

In one such instance, the outline of the story of the Noachian Flood was insufficient for Ellen Holtzblatt, who in a personal midrash in 2006 embellished it with fourteen woodcuts titled *Hamabul* (The Deluge). In a series of emails in 2012, she wrote that the story was obviously riveting, but she found the biblical text to be "spare and emotionless" and in need of considerable elaboration. "The story clearly depicts the scope of the devastation, but [has] blanks on details that my imagination has since filled in." Holtzblatt has stated elsewhere that she decided to look "beneath the outer coats of the stories into a deeper and more mystical realm" and found there "layers of personal, emotional, and spiritual meaning," implied but not spelled out in the text. She continued that she viewed her art as "visual midrash. The images are my means for exploring and developing personal insights and connections to the text. They become a vehicle for learning about myself and the world" (qtd. in Baigell 2013b, 9).

Evidently, Holtzblatt's thoughts are an echo of ideas sounded through the centuries. As Richard McBee (b. 1947) has noted, "The extremely terse nature of the biblical narrative cries out for the kind of textural deconstruction that the rabbis in the *midrashic* literature pursued" (2013–14, 49). Such personal and autonomous engagement in place of acceptance of traditional interpretations has been described as an important element in the search for "privatized spirituality" among many Jewish Americans. According to Rabbi Dana Kaplan, "American Jews are increasingly asking themselves how Judaism can help them explore their spirituality. They yearn for a Judaism that can address their deepest emotional needs and help them to expand their notion of God and how religion can enrich their lives" (2009, 55). For artists, midrashim, whether ancient or of one's own invention, certainly help in that endeavor.

I have included here just some of the responses I have culled from various publications or directly from artists over the years. The takeaway is that the artists admit or assert—some without qualification, others with questions—that Judaism is one of the elements central to their lives. The degree of centrality, however, is now entirely personal. As historian Noam Pianko has noted, "Interest in religion has shifted from an emphasis on or sense of group consciousness to individual searching, a renewed interest in spiritual and religious practice without any necessary collective allegiance or identification" (2015, 121–22). Pianko has also asserted that "feminism challenges the very idea that there could be one static essence that defines the Jewish people" (112). As pointed out in the introduction, Arnold Eisen, chancellor of the Jewish Theological Seminary in New York, has stated similarly and succinctly, "It is primarily in private space and time that American Jews define the selves they are and want to be." He has also noted that each person, autonomous and sovereign, decides which rituals and practices to observe, if any (2008, 127, 128; see also Cohen and Eisen 2000). Saying essentially the same thing but in a more religious context, Rabbi Neil Gillman has asserted: "When a Jew says that he observes the Sabbath in a way that is 'meaningful' to him . . . , he is echoing, however unconsciously, existentialist individualism . . . , a very strikingly new and modern departure from the more authoritative and communal style of traditional Jewish thinking" (1990, 183). By extension, each artist becomes the arbiter of what might or might not be included in a work and from what point of view.

But Eisen does remind us that the individual who decides how to observe his or her religion is not a rank egotist who inevitably will substitute individual autonomy for inherited wisdom or always remain in search of self-identity at the expense of ignoring what might be considered the sacred. Rather, Eisen holds that one can desire to "seek an abiding significance . . . that goes beyond daily activities and the limits of [one's] own reason or mortality" (2008, 129). Whatever their degree of religiosity, spirituality, and desire for independence, most artists discussed here would agree with Stephen Whitfield's formulations: "There is simply no longer a serious way of being Jewish—and living within Jewish culture—without Judaism," and "only religion can form the inspirational core of a viable and meaningful Jewish culture" (1999, 237, 224). What I am implying here is that the future of Jewish-themed art in America cannot be defined only by associations with basically superficial aspects of Jewish culture (e.g., eating bagels and lox on Sundays, laughing at Jewish-themed jokes by Jewish comedians, or adding a Star of David to a painting for no apparent reason) but must be linked integrally to Jewish history, memory, and religious practice.

For assimilated Americans, then, the connections to Judaism and to the Jewish community will always remain problematic, something that can no longer be taken for granted and understood with a nod of one's head. In an email exchange on February 1, 2016, about this matter and as if in response to Leonard Baskin's observation that Yiddish is "the language of aliens," meaning that Jews are still bonded together as an alien community, Rand wrote: "Our private language is being erased by freedom. You have to be nuts to desire those components that created that language—exclusion and pogroms."

To offset potential atomization but also in no way compromising individual autonomy or suggesting stylistic or thematic guidelines, two major art organizations were formed early in this century, the Jewish Artists Initiative in Los Angeles in 2004 and the Jewish Art Salon in New York in 2008. Each advocates dialogue and exchange of ideas about Jewish-themed art, exhibitions of such art, and consideration of issues of Jewish identity in the twenty-first century. Together, their memberships number in the hundreds.

There is also a larger issue here, one that combines assimilation with the desire to perpetuate Jewish-themed art and therefore some kind of contemporary Jewish cultural identity. As Archie Rand wrote in his flip but often profound way in an undated letter in the spring of 2016, "A culture's art is a normalizing accessory, a banner of self-recognition that allows that culture to sit at the table and ante up." The artists I profile here want to sit at the table and ante up as both Americans and Jews.

# 2 Jewish Feminist Art: *A Short Review*

There is no question that Jewish feminist artists since the 1970s have been leading figures in exploring religious subject matter. Not all women artists, however, have found constant inspiration in the ancient texts. Figures such as Eleanor Antin, Judy Chicago, Mierle Laderman Ukeles, Elaine Reichek, and Martha Rosler have made important contributions to the history of Jewish American art, but for the most part they have explored secular themes concerned with gender issues, assimilation, the eastern European past, and the Holocaust rather than subjects based on the ancient texts. Their Jewish identity is more cultural than religious (Bloom 2006, 2). Those who do find subject matter in religious texts are serious students of these texts and fearless in presenting images they consider important and relevant to their own lives and the lives of other women. Their overall contribution to the development of Jewish art in America is both generous in scope and progressive in that their wide-ranging interpretations ignore traditional patriarchal readings of these texts. They are the first generation of women artists to do so perhaps in the entire history of world Jewish art. Ultimately, they might be considered among the most important artists in our time to have fostered this approach to biblical subject matter. In fact, one can imagine several books and articles yet to be written about the many new and different ways women in the Bible have been portrayed in art since the 1980s.

A statement written about thirty years before that decade is applicable to Jewish feminist art today: "Social action is not politics or sociology or economics, though it involved all of them. It is the essence of religion, certainly the Jewish religion" (Vorspan and Lipman 1956, 23–24). The cogency of this statement is borne out by similar assertions I have received over the past twenty-odd years by feminist artists who have written or told me about the reciprocal relationship between their feminism and their Jewish heritage. The concern for a strong, gendered self-identity manifested through feminism provoked their interest in a more vital Jewish identity, and the social and political values inherited from their Jewish cultural and religious backgrounds played a key role in their interest in equality for women. For them, feminism and Judaism are inextricably intertwined, so that it is impossible to separate the one from the other. It should also be said that within the Bible, for example, they can find narratives larger than their own experiences, and their individual concerns are reciprocally enhanced through their interpretations of biblical characters and events.

Perhaps these are key reasons for the large representation of Jewish women artists in the Jewish feminist movement. The study of the Bible and other ancient texts helped establish a common culture, shared experiences, and shared aims based on shared subject matter. For the artists, it became a way of belonging to something—a community however tightly or loosely knit—and a way to share similar values with others rather than to be stranded alone within one's individual beliefs or to be a solitary fragment in a fragmented, incohesive American Judaism or, for that matter, in the mainstream art world.

In this regard, the Bible contains ready-made stories of both patriarchy and of event-making women able to change systems of governance and tradition. Such stories can provoke both rage and affirmation, pointing out, on the one hand, male overt or covert hostility to women and, on the other, the fact that the ancient Israelites to the extent possible had already provided examples of the power of women to change the course of history—reasons enough to find the ancient texts outrageous or gratifying as well as historical and contemporaneous. As Janet Shafner, whose works are considered later, has pointed out,

> I found that the dramatic lives of our biblical ancestors were strikingly contemporary, and I was fascinated by the connections. Everything that touches us deeply today has a parallel occurrence in the Bible—family jealousy, sexual obsession, enduring love and sacrifice, murder, rape, incest, man's inhumanity to his fellows, even ethnic cleansing—it was all there. (2003, 3)

As Shafner indicates, because the Bible is open to individual interpretation, its stories are both dated and timeless and can easily be conflated with contemporary concerns about morality and ethics and, in addition, can fulfill the desire to learn about one's own heritage and historical past.

Jewish feminist concerns emerged as part of the larger feminist movement in the late 1960s and soon gained momentum when some scholars began to emphasize specifically Jewish issues as they experienced anti-Semitism at feminist conferences. But, more to the point, these scholars emphasized the necessity for religious reform and the dismantling of patriarchic traditions or the persistence of patriarchal ideology in articles and books. As the historian Noam Pianko observes, "Feminism challenges the very idea that there could be one static essence that defines the Jewish people" (2015, 112).

Of course, the Bible cannot be rewritten. Tradition has to be confronted or ignored. In the 1970s, Jewish feminists' principle tasks, then, were to call for inclusion, participation, empowerment, and renewal within modern Judaism (Fuchs 2000, 16, 20; Munich [1985] 2005) and, as a corollary for both male and female artists, to be aware of the possibilities of gendered Jewish-themed art. As Susannah Heschel observed several years ago, "When a woman looks to Judaism, she should not see only a reflection of the experiences of Jewish men" (1983b, xxxii). And when looking at an artwork with Jewish content, one should not see only a male point of view.

A case in point: Pat Berger's painting of Tamar after she is raped by her half-brother Amnon (Second Samuel 13:11–14). Tamar sits on a stool in a field, distraught and already mourning for herself (fig. 6). Berger's sympathies obviously lie with the young woman. Because Amnon is infatuated by Tamar, it is jarring to note, as Rachel Adler has pointed out, that "when sexuality becomes an expression of caring and sharing, rather than just *having*, that rape becomes an atrocity" (1998, 130, emphasis in original). Among those male artists who have been attracted to the attack on Tamar as a subject to paint, the conclusion of the episode has been the most popular. They ignore Tamar entirely and portray instead Absalom, Tamar's full brother, killing Amnon in revenge, thus engaging in violent action

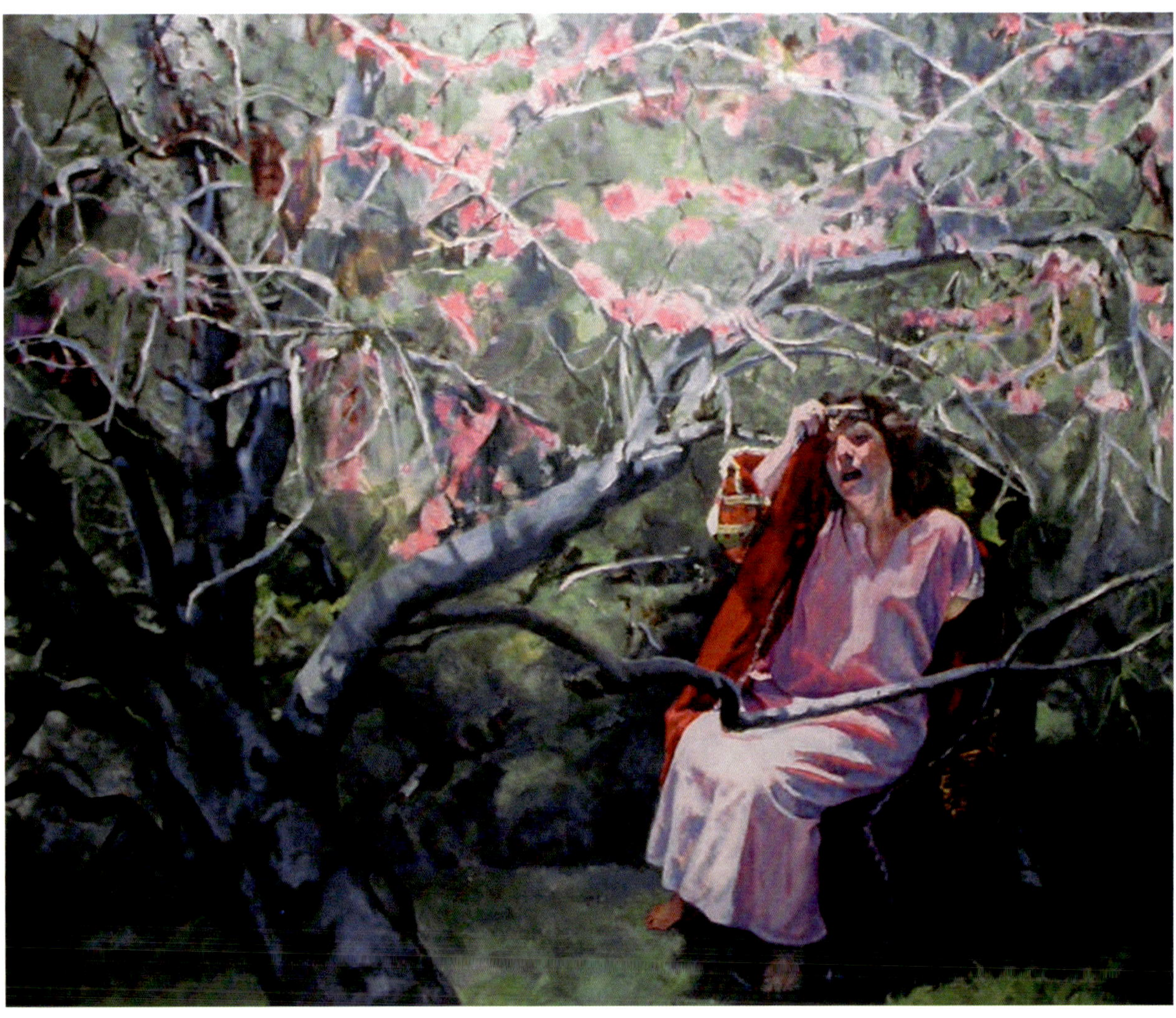

6. Pat Berger, *The Rape of Tamar*, 1991. Acrylic on canvas, 60 × 72 in. Courtesy of the artist.

against the perpetrator rather than showing compassion for the victim. This is not to say that male artists favor the wrong approach but that they might view the event from a different perspective. Within a general Jewish point of view, it is worthwhile pointing out Rachel Adler's observation: "There is not and never was a Judaism unaffected by the gendered perspectives of its transmitters and augmenters" (1998, xiv).

By 1971, women began to organize prayer and study groups, and in 1973 the North American Jewish Students' Network organized the first national Jewish women's conference. Around the same time, women joined Conservative and Reform minyans (quorums of ten required for a religious service, heretofore entirely male). In 1972, a woman was ordained a rabbi within the Reform movement, followed by women ordained in the Reconstructionist and Conservative movements in 1974 and 1985, respectively. Within Orthodox Judaism, the Jewish Orthodox Feminist Alliance was founded in 1997 to enhance lives within the parameters of halacha, or Jewish law. (In the vast literature on Jewish feminism, see Fishman 1993; S. Heschel 1983a; Plaskow 2005; Umansky 1988.)

With these changes in perspective promoted by the feminist movement, male experiences, heretofore considered normative, were challenged in word as well as in deed. In 1976, a feminist or at least a nonsexist daily prayer book, or siddur, entitled *Siddur Nashim: A Sabbath Prayer Book for Women*, compiled by Naomi Janowitz and Maggie Wenig, was published. Through the 1970s and the early 1980s, several authors called for a modern Jewish theology that acknowledged women's experiences. For example, Judith Plaskow asserted, "I cannot . . . write a theology that abstracts from my experience and ignores part of myself, or that abstracts from the community of which I am a part." For Plaskow, Jewish life had to be transformed. "Feminism demands a new understanding of Torah, God, and Israel" (2005, 23, 63). To that end, the development of new rituals "asserts women's presence in the present" (Plaskow 1989, 48). And Susannah Heschel held that "a feminist theology of Judaism must resonate with women's experience, must ground women's lives in a Jewish dimension. The outcome may be new or revised traditions, observances, and prayers," so that women "will become receivers and transmitters of Judaism, not onlookers" (1983b, xxii).

The Bible directly absorbed its fair share of criticism with the feminist movement. For example, poet Alicia Ostriker has stated, "If the Bible is a flaming sword forbidding our entrance to the garden, it is also a burning bush urging us toward freedom. It is what we wrestle with all night and from which we may, if we demand it, wrest a blessing" (1993, 86; see also Fuchs 2000). Naomi Graetz notes that biblical authority raised complex questions with no easy answers. The Bible represented morality in the broad sense, but it was open to critique insofar as virtually all women were controlled, bought and sold, and achieved status only through marriage and sexual purity. In effect, they were not considered fully human or equal to men (2005, 6, 24; for a counterargument, see Haas 1992). And Rabbi Rachel Bearman has noted,

> The rabbis of the Talmud were not the "journalists" of their time. Journalism is the work of discovery and distributing truthfully factual information. The Talmud is a collection of opinions, knowledge, and insights that come from various schools of thought. It is a reflection of the men (and here, it is only the men) who lead and shaped our religions for generations. (2018)

One way to get beyond what in the literature (and in conversations) of the 1970s and 1980s appeared to be nonstop critiquing of the Bible and the patriarchy was, as noted earlier, to employ midrashim to make the Bible relevant to contemporary life. For example, Naomi Graetz states, "We must start imaginatively to re-engage with our sacred texts by writing *midrash.* Only in that way can all voices, not only a few, be part of the partnership" (2005, 51). Her argument is that midrash will also help develop one's sense of moral inquiry and self-understanding. Another scholar, Naomi Mara Hyman, states forthrightly: "*Midrash* has, in many respects, been the way in which Jews have attempted to put themselves and the issues of the times into the ancient story. . . . The process of *midrash* not only offers contemporary Jews an authentic way of making the text our own, but also provides a precedent for such activity" (1998, xviii).

To enhance the educational, imaginative, and interpretive possibilities for individuals who want to translate midrashim into visual images, Tobi Kahn and Dr. Leon Morris formed in 2001 an instructional unit they called Beit Midrash in Temple Emanuel, New York, to guide student artists who want to create visual commentaries derived from ancient texts. And Dr. Jo Milgrom, based in Israel, developed in November 2009 the website Visual Midrash, which provides samples of Jewish-themed art created over the centuries.

Several other statements are also cited by feminists who do not accept the manner in which women are treated in the Bible stories or the way these women are considered today by religious traditionalists. Undoubtedly, all feminists would completely reject the spirited but no longer tenable account offered by the great Talmudic scholar Rabbi Joseph B. Soloveitchik, who stated that marriage creates an existential community—not just a partnership between husband and wife—that allows the covenantal relationship with God to be passed on from parents to children down through the generations. Even though both parents are intimately involved with educating their children, Rabbi Soloveitchik repeatedly pointed out that women are more concerned with motherhood than fathers are with fatherhood. "The woman is bound up," he wrote, "with the child and she experiences her motherhood role in all her thought and feeling." Her "self-sacrifice and superhuman devotion [are the ways] in which a woman finds self-fulfillment" (2000, 106, 52).

On Rabbi Soloveitchik's behalf, it must be said that he did acknowledge that the destiny of humankind and the perpetuation of the covenantal community were shaped by the activities of the Founding Mothers, Sarah, Rebecca, Leah, and Rachel. And he did consider, if all too briefly, the nonmotherly, nondomestic activities of figures such as Miriam and Deborah, but he never allowed the reader to forget that, for him, biology is destiny. That belief is reinforced weekly when traditional-minded, observant men recite before the sanctification of the Sabbath on Friday evenings verses 10 through 31 of Proverb 31, popularly known as "Eishet Chayil" (Woman of Valor) in praise of their wives' efforts within the household and as breadwinners.

But as one feminist scholar has asked, "[Is] the detailed delineation of *the perfect wife* in Proverb 31 . . . a reflection of a real woman or merely a man's dreamy construction?" (Bach 1999, xiv). Another scholar has stated that women have complained that the verses "describe a woman who is a wife, mother, hard worker, teacher of children, and provider for her family," but the verses do not ask, "Is she [also] somebody in her own right[?]" (P. Adelman 2005, 8). Many men would answer, "Yes, of course." "She is like a merchant fleet" (verse 14) bringing food to the family and tending to business among her many responsibilities. Feminists would say that this depiction merely perpetuates women's servanthood. And the very fact that women are singled out for praise suggests that they are objects of study, exploration, and observation by men, that men experience life but in contrast women are objects to be experienced (Aschkenasy 1986, 8). From this patriarchal view, women exist only in relation to men, have no inner life worth exploring, are solely mothers and nurturers, and are granted little or no autonomous selfhood.

Those women who are not Orthodox would agree with this critique of Proverb 31. But those who remain within that community offer a counterargument. In my limited conversations with Orthodox women, they say that they find empowering the words that are sung (or said) to them in the "Eishet Chayil" and are quite pleased by the recognition that their activities engender within the family. Mothers, after all, are responsible for the education of their children and therefore for the continuity of the religion and thus, in effect, for the religious and moral health of the next generation. For those willing to take on such responsibilities and obligations, the tasks are demanding, but the rewards especially fulfilling—within the context of the community's values, which are accepted without question. Orthodox mothers have said to me after a son's successful completion of the bar mitzvah ceremony how gratifying it is to have raised such a religious son who made no mistakes in reading unhaltingly and knowingly from the Torah.

So here we have a flashpoint: those willing and eager to accept what they consider to be awesome responsibilities and those who find themselves diminished and in a kind of imprisonment. When we translate this situation into artistic settings, then it becomes easy to understand why Jewish feminist artists think of the biblical stories as palimpsests to explore their own feelings about their religion, the kinds of commitments they make to it, and how they might relate to the entirety of biblical history and the place of women in it.

I want to consider now two works and the different ways the artists have responded to biblical patriarchy. Neither artist is the subject of an individual chapter, but the works in question, I feel, are important markers in the history of the 1930s–1960s generation. The first is by Arizona-based artist Beth Ames Swartz (b. 1934) and the second by Helène Aylon (b. 1931).

Swartz, a decidedly spiritual artist, has studied the Bible, kabbalah, and a variety of eastern religious systems. Her work *Israel Revisited* (1981), created in Israel, honors ten women, for whom she invented ten ritual performance pieces and created ten individual collage constructions based on biblical and kabbalist sources—creations unthinkable without the feminist movement.

Before discussing this work, I need to explain Swartz's interpretation of the Shekinah. Artist-critic Saul Raskin wrote the following in his book of illustrations for the Pirkei Avot (Wisdom of the Fathers): "When ten people sit together and occupy themselves with the Torah, the Shekhina [*sic*] abides among them" ([1940] 1969, 39). Raskin invoked the presence of the Shekinah in its Talmudic sense. What this means, according to the great scholar of kabbalah Gershom Scholem, is that "in Talmudic literature and non-kabbalistic rabbinical Judaism, the Shekhinah [*sic*]—literally in-dwelling, namely of God in the world—is taken to mean simply God himself in His omnipresence and activity in the world and especially in Israel." But to kabbalists, the Shekinah is also "an aspect of God, a quasi-independent feminine element with Him" (1965, 104–5).

Scholem also contrasts Talmudic and kabbalistic attitudes toward God by pointing out that in the Talmud the concept of the Shekinah's exile means that the Shekinah was with the people of Israel in the Diaspora, their exile from Israel. But in kabbalistic thought, exile does not mean traveling with the Israelites but rather that "a part of God Himself is exiled from God. . . . The exile of the Shekhinah [is] in other words the separation of the masculine and feminine principles in God" (Scholem 1965, 107, 108; see also Gross 1979, 167–73; Patai [1967] 1990, 96–111; Scholem 1991, 140–96). In the Talmud, then, God is one; in kabbalistic thought, God is also one but has multiple emanations or aspects (*spherot*), including a feminine aspect.

The kabbalist rather than Talmudic interpretation of the nature of the Shekinah became popular in the 1970s because of the rise of feminism as well as the growing interest in kabbalah at that time. Feminists began their search for a nonpatriarchal God or, at least, nonpatriarchal aspects of God. Kabbalists also held that Creation and the desired reunification of the masculine and feminine principles of the Deity would be completed through the concept of *tikkun olam*, or repair of the world (Scholem [1941] 1961, 268–76).

The combination of the feminist and kabbalist lines of thought are manifested in Swartz's work *Israel Revisited*. This work is, to my knowledge, among the first, if not the first, contemporary, large-scale feminist project in which the Jewish subject matter is derived from the Bible and kabbalah, and, as such, it is among the most historically significant Jewish American

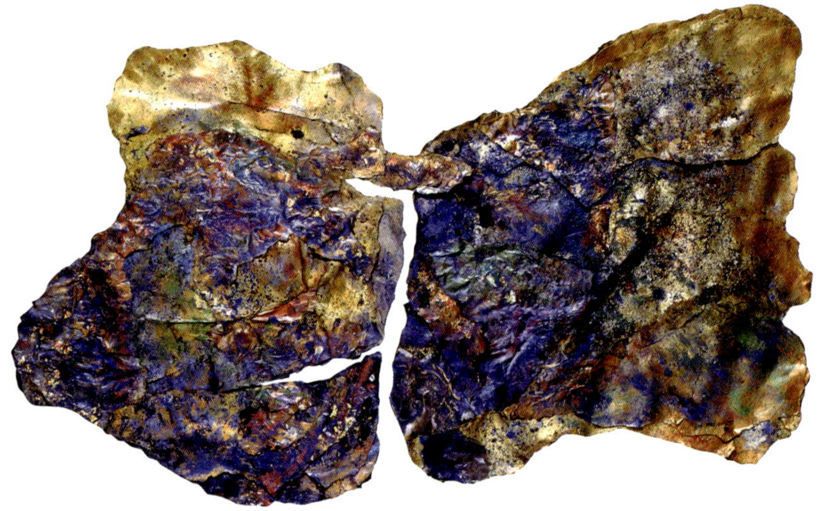

7. Beth Ames Swartz, *The Cave of Machpelah #1*, 1980, ID#: 010. Fire, earth, acrylic, variegated gold leaf, and mixed media on layered paper, 31½ × 54½ in. 

feminist artworks of the 1980s. Swartz chose ten sites in Israel in 1980, the same number as the ten *spherot*, emanations or aspects of God described in the *Zohar*, a major kabbalistic text written in Spain in the late thirteenth century (Applehof 1981). At each of the ten selected sites, Swartz, dressed in white, created a ritual and a performance piece to honor not only the Shekinah but also the queen of Sheba; the biblical matriarchs, including Rebecca, Rachel, Deborah, Miriam, Beruriah, and Huldah; Doña Gracia (a sixteenth-century Portuguese woman); and the Unknown Woman. In a conversation Swartz and I had in 1998, she said she was especially interested in honoring the Shekinah and mentioned that she prays to the Shekinah, the nonmasculine aspect of God. "I began to feel that the Shekinah exemplified the concerns of this project, that God has many names and can speak through women as well as men and that feminine energy is part of everybody's heritage." (See also Weissler 2005, 61–65.)

To create the individual pieces, Swartz placed long sheets of paper on the ground at each site, cut and punctured them, rubbed each with glue, poured acrylic gel on them, set them on fire, and covered them with soil. After returning to her home with the remnants, she rearranged each one, then colored and, as she said, "froze" them.

Swartz associated each of the women she had selected with a specific spherotic emanation of the Deity. Rebecca was paired with the emanation Binah, or understanding, and the color indigo because of her self-determination and self-knowledge. The completed work dedicated to her memory, entitled *The Cave of Machpelah #1* (1980, fig. 7), marks the place where Rebecca, Sarah, and Leah are buried. Swartz also noted that Rebecca "exercised her freedom of choice and was willing to leave the security of her native land to start a new life." She represented those women who "ventured into the world to find personal fulfillment" (*Beth Ames Swartz: Israel Revisited* 1981, 20; Genesis 24:57–61). Swartz paired Deborah, the prophet, with the emanation called Gevurah, or power and judgment, and with the color red. She paired Miriam with Hod, or intelligence, and the color orange because of her willingness to speak her mind concerning the marriage of Zipporah, a Cushite, to her brother, Moses, as well as because of her role as a prophet (*Beth Ames Swartz: Israel Revisited* 1981, 29; Numbers 12). And Huldah, paired with Malkuth, the emanation of God closest to our own world, and the color russet, is represented by

Jerusalem. Huldah, a prophet who lived in Jerusalem, predicted the destruction of that city after the death of King Josiah (Second Kings 22:17–20). Swartz chose colors for their associations with the different *spherot*, and a different color dominates each work in *Israel Revisited*. Given the vagaries of Swartz's process of firing and reconstruction, the semblance of a Hebrew letter might seem to appear in the interstices of a piece, but no specific message is intended.

For our purposes here, performance art in which rituals concerned with women's lives, women's space, and women's relation to the earth as well as with ways the Goddess is invoked is of particular relevance. In the 1970s and 1980s, several artists besides Swartz performed rituals, created sacred spaces in both public and private settings, acted as shamans in healing rituals, and celebrated time cycles such as those of the various solstices in order to express women's revelations of the soul and spiritual quests heretofore not openly articulated. By 1976, Swartz was using fire in her ritualistic performances, as had artists such as Judy Chicago, Mary Beth Edelson, and Geny Dignac. In addition, the Israeli artist Miriam Sharon performed desert rituals to exorcise patriarchal models "that constricted alienating cityscapes of concrete over ancient earth shrines and sacred sites" (Orenstein 1988, 75). Sharon also developed meditation rituals and used the desert as a temple for meditation. And in 1977, a group of ten women sat and chanted within a ring of fire in a mourning ritual ceremony in La Jolla, California, to create a holy space for women.

According to one observer, Swartz's connection to these performance and ritualistic events also had a specifically Jewish dimension. These events provided "an emotional identification with her heritage, and [she] began to realize that from the Burning Bush, through which God spoke to Moses, to the 20th century Holocaust, fire was inextricably bound with Jewish history" (Reed 1981, 43; for additional material on kabbalah in American art and on Swartz and rituals, see Baigell 1999; 2001, 229–42; 2006a, 35–39, 81–85, 109–11, 116–17, 151–52; 2006b; and 2007a, 174–75, 189–211; as well as *Beth Ames Swartz: Inquiry into Fire* 1978; Christ 1979, 273–87, and 1980, 125–29; Nelson 1984; Orenstein 1988, 1994; D. Rubin 2002, 15; Wortz 1982).

With this short description of Swartz's artistic processes and religious and spiritual proclivities as well as of the feminist context in which she worked, I mean to suggest that *Israel Revisited* is a prime example of how secular, traditional religious, and kabbalist feminist concerns can complement each other and why this work is part of both "American American" and Jewish American art history.

Helène Aylon's history and artistic efforts are quite different. She was raised in an Orthodox community and abandoned it as an adult. Among the most confrontational and fearless feminist artists, she has found since the 1990s subject matter in the ancient texts by challenging patriarchic and misogynist passages in the Bible. Where others have found comfort and solace, she has found insults. Where others have interpreted and commented upon the events in the lives of women in the Bible, Aylon wants to know who hijacked the Bible from God and added all those terrible passages about women and who simply ignored women's presence in history (Aylon 2012; Baigell 2006a, chap. 10; Orenstein 2007).

Perhaps Aylon's most famous work is *Liberation of G-D* (1990–96) (fig. 8), a large, mixed-media installation composed of fifty-four books comprising the fifty-four chapters of the Torah (the first five books of the Bible) and five stands on which Bibles are placed. In each of the books, she has underlined with a pink marker on transparent parchment covering each page the "empty spaces" where a woman's name or presence has been omitted

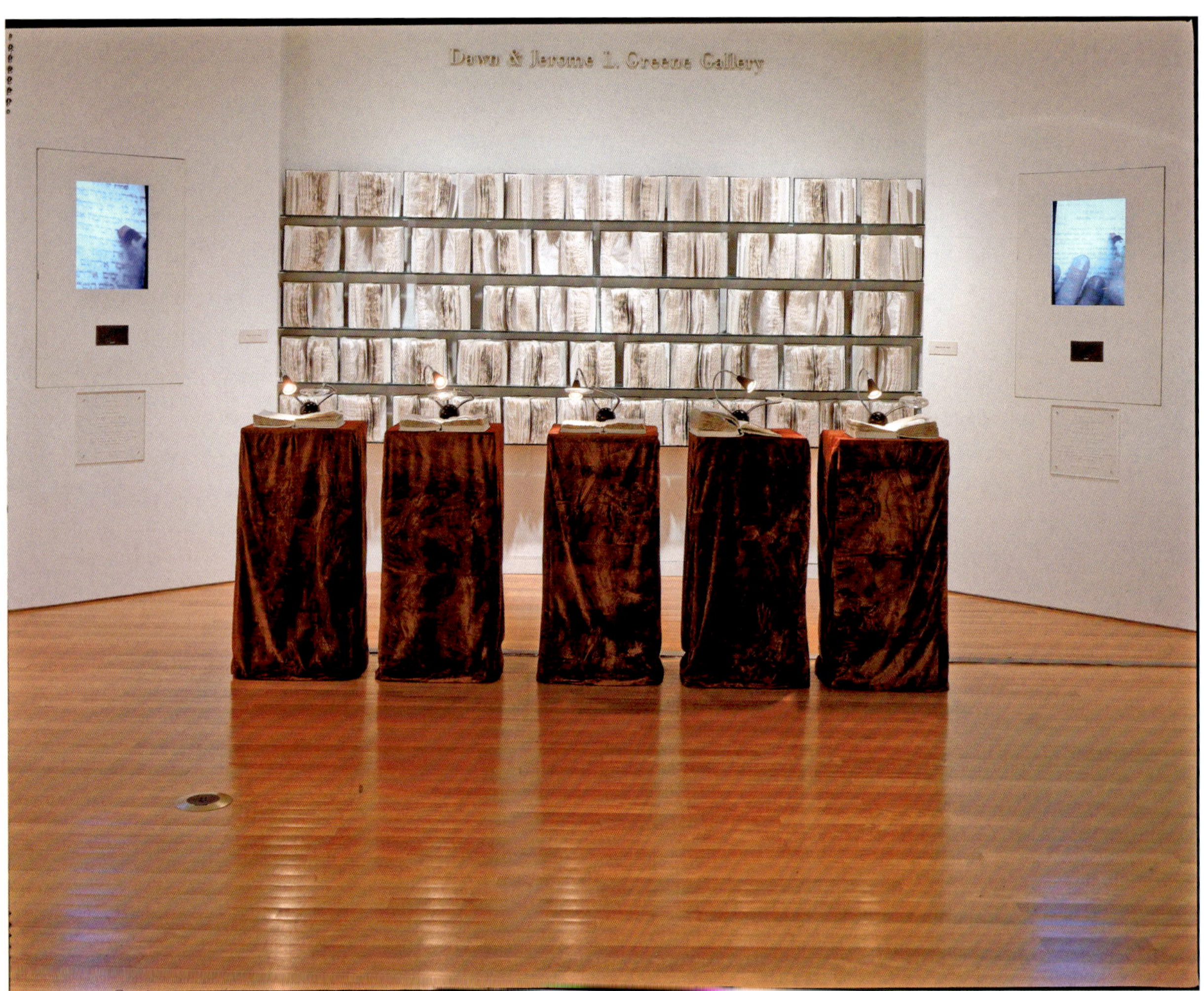


8. Helène Aylon, *The Liberation of G-D*, 1990–96. Multimedia installation, dimensions variable. Purchase: Dobkin Family Foundation and Fine Arts Acquisitions Committee Funds, Estate of Phyllis Frey, and Mr. and Mrs. George Jaffin Fund, 2000-17a-aaaa. The Jewish Museum, New York. Photograph courtesy of the Jewish Museum, New York, and Art Resource, New York. © 2018 Helène Aylon. Licensed by VAGA at Artists Rights Society (ARS), New York.

and where words of vengeance, deception, cruelty, and misogyny appear instead (Aylon 2012, 230–31; Baigell 2006a, 176–79; Berlind 1999; D. Cohen 1997; Gefen 1999; Kleeblatt 1996a, 32–33; Stanger 1996, 40).

In the "Proclamation" that accompanied *The Liberation of G-D*, Aylon wrote: "I began *The Liberation of G-D* searching in the five books of Moses for sections where G-d has been spoken for. I look into passages where patriarchal attributes have been projected on to G-d as though man has the right to have dominion even over G-d" (qtd. in Gass 2000, 13). For Aylon, the Bible was somehow hijacked from God, meaning that "*The Five Books of Moses* are the five books of Moses" (qtd. in Gass 2000, 16). In effect, as one observer notes, "God needs to be liberated, she [Aylon] tells us. The Divine Being could not have written this misogynous text" (Gefen 1999, 72).

Although Aylon knows that the Bible cannot be rewritten, her project in this work and in similar works is to question why the male perspective has been accepted—at least until the 1960s—as the normative perspective in virtually all aspects of the religion. It is important to note here that Aylon does not ridicule the religion or target stereotypical representations of people or institutions within contemporary Jewish culture, as others have done (in Kleeblatt 1996a, see, for example, 13, 16, 23, 30, 31, 32, and in the edited volume Kleeblatt 1996b, 138, 141, 148, 149), but rather she displays an appropriate anger similar to that of many others, ranging from novelist Cynthia Ozick to religious historian Judith Plaskow, who have sought to identify and create contributive roles for women in religious practices and contemporary Jewish culture (see, for example, Ozick 1983 and Plaskow 1990). In her exasperation, Aylon has chosen to critique rather than to engage in a dynamic interaction with the Bible. She wants the women of the Bible to be recognized by name and for their achievements, not marginalized or ignored. (Carol Hamoy has created a long list of women mentioned in the Bible, some named but mostly anonymous.) As Cynthia Ozick so pithily put it in the early 1980s, "When my rabbi says 'A Jew is called to the Torah,' he never means me or any other living Jewish woman" (1983, 125). (In Conservative, Reform, and Reconstructionist congregations, women are now called to give blessings over and to read from the Torah.)

◆ ◆ ◆

Some of the statements quoted in this chapter find their visual parallels in works by Siona Benjamin, Carol Hamoy, Janet Shafner, and Ruth Weisberg. But I did not want to place the individual chapters on them and their artistic production immediately adjacent to this chapter, as if to suggest that their art should be considered solely in a feminist context rather than as part of the remarkable development of new approaches to Jewish-themed subject matter common to the generation of artists I profile here.

# 3 Mark Podwal

Mark Podwal was born in New York in 1945. A physician, he has jokingly considered medicine his avocation and art a vocation to which he turned increasing attention while in medical school. At that time, the late 1960s, he began to make drawings about the American conflict in Vietnam as well as the Six-Day War in Israel. In the following years, he drew mostly secular images for the *New York Times* op-ed page until he decided that he preferred to create Jewish-themed works instead.

Podwal has mentioned that the ultimate source of his interest in this subject matter grew from his experiences in a Jewish summer camp when he was twelve years old. Until that time, he had some knowledge about Judaism, but exposure to its art and culture at camp prompted him to learn the prayers well enough to lead Sabbath services by the end of the summer and to help with the ornamentations for a newly built synagogue. Today, Podwal calls himself a "nonobservant Orthodox Jew" who enjoys Orthodox traditions more as an observer than as a participant. (Additional information about his background can be gleaned from video interviews with him on the Internet, located using his name for the search.)

Podwal did not begin to draw Jewish subjects until he was twenty-four years old. By that time, he said in an interview on February 2, 2012, he felt very comfortable exploring Jewish subject matter in his art and enjoyed reading as much as possible the biblical and midrashic literature. His early commitment to such subject matter is not to be taken lightly. Like Joel Silverstein's experiences in art school noted in the introduction and the negative critical responses to Robert Kirschbaum's and Archie Rand's interest in mining the ancient texts (see chapters 8 and 12), Podwal's attraction to Jewish subject matter was also questioned. Specifically, when purchasing Podwal's art, William Lieberman (1923–2005), former curator of modern and contemporary art at the Metropolitan Museum of Art, advised him to get out of "the Jewish rut."

Clearly, he did not, and today he is among the most knowledgeable artists of Jewish secular and religious history. Podwal is also among the most productive and has an extraordinarily quick and fertile imagination. For example, when asked to contribute to an exhibition of small book-size works at the Museum of Biblical Art in New York in 2013, he immediately suggested a series of twelve drawings built around three themes from the Book of Ezekiel—Call of the Prophet, the Doom of Jerusalem, and Israel Restored—and delivered them within days (Baigell 2013a, 18–19). Prague has almost become a second home for him since the leaders of the Altneuschul asked him to create designs to be embroidered on the tapestries and the textile coverings of the synagogue's religious objects.

He now worships there regularly during his many trips to that city. (He also created embroidery designs for the Brno Synagogue in the Czech Republic.)

Because Podwal was born at the end of the Second World War, his sensibility is profoundly marked by his Jewish heritage and is attuned to events in ancient Israel, the history of Jews in eastern Europe, including traditional life in shtetls, or small towns and villages, as well as experiences during the Holocaust. Of all the artists considered here, he seems to have internalized most profoundly the events, both major and minor, in Jewish secular and religious history. But he remains, as he has said, grounded in American culture and history and with a deep-seated sense of relief feels that the Wandering Jew, the figure of anti-Semitic myth, is now at home in America.

As much a reader as a listener, he obviously has no personal memory of the Second World War or the immediate postwar years, except for fragments overheard in conversations by his elders. But these fragments seem to have affected him deeply. He has mentioned, for example, that even though his mother immigrated to New York in 1929, long before the outbreak of the war, he heard family stories of difficulty and hardship in Europe. "Perhaps my family history is why I often dwell on Jewish suffering," he writes. "My heart is with the Jewish experience" (Podwal 2018, 40). An uncle who was not admitted to America in 1929 and who remained in the ancestral shtetl died of typhus in the Treblinka death camp during the Second World War. "I've been told that my uncle David drew very well. I'd like to believe that my talent in art is a gift to his memory," the artist has stated (Podwal 2018, 1, 40).

In several works, we can observe his desire to commemorate and honor the inhabitants of destroyed Jewish communities as well as the lives of those who either died in or survived the round-ups, the ghettos, and the murder and concentration camps. However, his images are not filled exclusively with doom, gloom, and destruction but are balanced with the saving grace of Jewish belief in redemption and hope for a better future. *A History* (1988) (fig. 9), for example, is a remarkable example of how he tempers one of the worst episodes in all of Jewish history, symbolized by the train tracks and entrance to the Auschwitz murder camp, by balancing it against an image of Jerusalem—that is, utter violence countered by the single place in the Jewish world that signifies redemption, the Temple Mount. (Of the many books with devastating Holocaust imagery, see Amishai-Maisels 1993.) An open Torah scroll appears in the foreground. Immediately above the scroll, a fire blazes over the Temple in Jerusalem. The path to the right, train tracks to Auschwitz in the form of an upside-down menorah, signifies distress, like an upside-down American flag. Behind the death camp's entrance is the black smoke of the crematorium. To the left, we see the upright menorah signifying survival and resurrection in the land of Israel and perhaps the hope for the arrival of the Messiah.

*A History* also reflects Podwal's overall approach to such subject matter and the manner in which he presents these kinds of images. He will show burning buildings but not violent activities or brutal actions against individuals. Even in his series of paintings of the golem, the legendary figure created from clay by Rabbi Judah Ben Loew (between 1512 and 1526–1609) to protect Prague's Jews, Podwal does not show the figure engaged in destructive activities (Podwal 1995, 2016, 106–8). Well aware of the attacks on Jewish communities through the centuries, he does not paint pogroms in progress but rather imagines shtetls and ghettos surrounded by huge Torah scrolls and houses covered by prayer shawls, as if the scrolls were fences and the shawls protective coverings, suggesting simultaneously holiness,

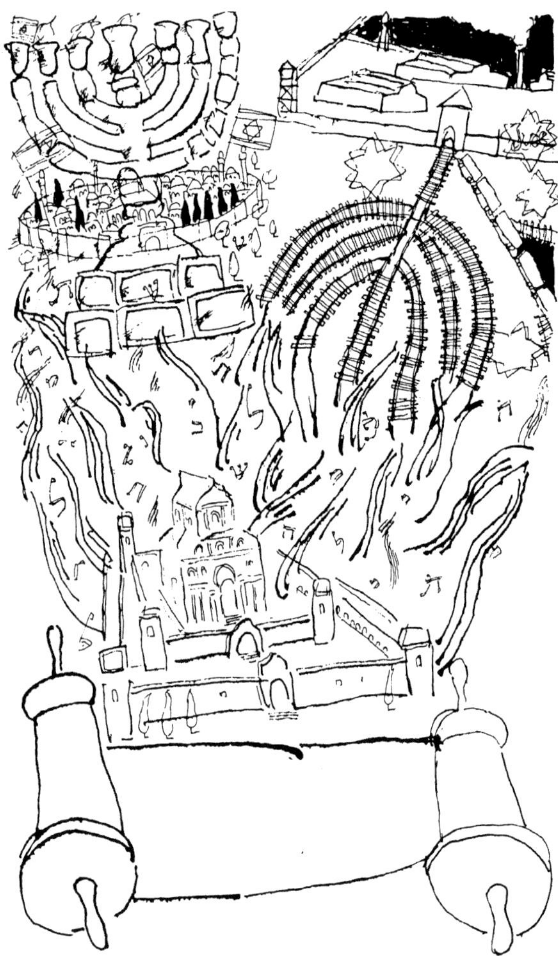

9. Mark Podwal, *A History*, 1988. Ink on paper, 11 × 14 in. © Mark Podwal.

comfort, security, and the embracing solace of life lived within religious boundaries.

Devastation pure and simple, however, is the theme of *Destruction of the Temple* (1999) (fig. 10). It alludes to the destruction of Jerusalem and King Solomon's Temple in 586 BCE as well as to other disasters in ancient and modern Jewish history, including the dismantling of the Second Temple in 70 CE. These events are annually commemorated on Tisha B'av, one of the saddest days in the Jewish calendar, by fasting and reading Lamentations. In the painting, a giant menorah representing the city and the Temple—set against a lurid red sky, its candles aflame—reaches from the bottom to the top of the painting. It is as if the entire Jewish world is on fire. Sitting on top of a blue field suggestive of the top of the Temple Mount, a mosque appears, possibly heralding future denial of access for Jewish prayer. At the base of the blue field, a base suggestive of the Western Wall, Podwal has placed helmets of soldiers from the distant and near past who have murdered Jews, implicating others who denied access to the Temple Mount for prayer.

Podwal's source was probably these passages from Lamentations: "From above He sent a fire down into my bones" (1:13); "She [Jerusalem] has seen her Sanctuary invaded by nations which You have denied admission into Your community" (1:10); and "The Lord has rejected his altar, disdained his Sanctuary. He has handed over to the foe the walls of his citadels" (2:7).

The fate of Jews past and present is never very far from Podwal's thoughts, especially when family is involved. The illustrated book he published in 2018, *Kaddish for Dąbrowa Białostocka*, is about the shtetl in which his mother was born. The word *kaddish* in the title refers to the prayer for the dead. In 1904, according to Podwal, there were 1,800 inhabitants in Dabrowa, and Jews composed 78.2 percent of the population. It was the highest percentage of Jews in a town in the entire Grodno region and one of the highest, if not the highest, percentage of Jews in the Russian Empire. In 1941, the Germans burned the town to the ground. No Jews live there today. Podwal includes eighteen illustrations, a number that honors the memory of his mother's hometown. Each letter of the Jewish alphabet is traditionally assigned a number. The letters that spell the Yiddish word for "life," *chai*, add up to eighteen. So in remembering the death of his mother's community, Podwal, evoking Jewish numerology, raises a glass, as it were, to life. The town lives at least in one's memory. Podwal appropriately depicts the pleasant world of his mother's youth rather than the

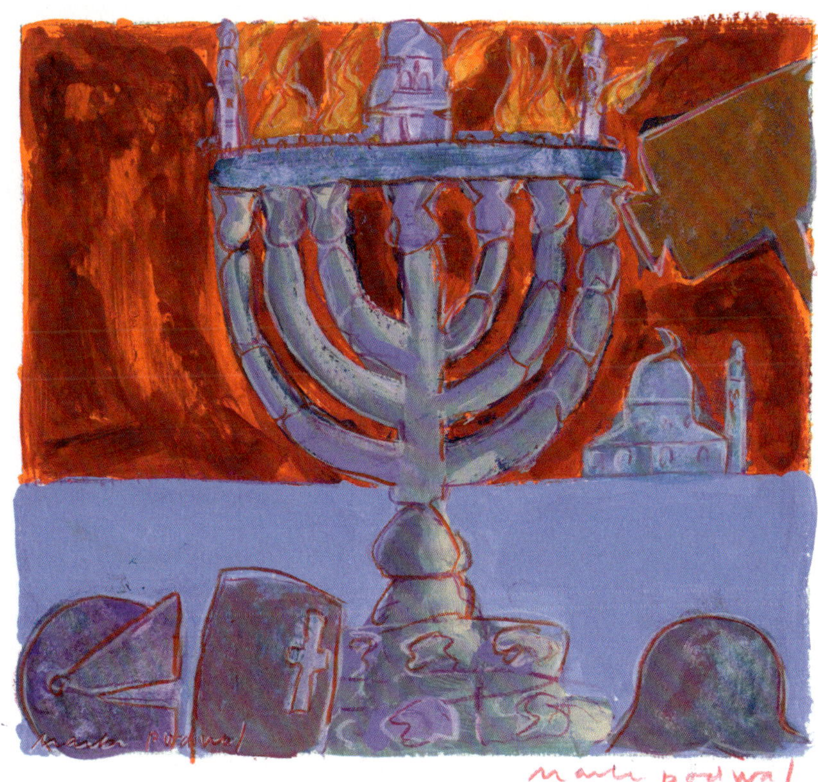

10. Mark Podwal, *Destruction of the Temple*, 1999. Acrylic, gouache, and colored pencil on paper, 10 × 12 in. © Mark Podwal.

horrific scenes of murder and mayhem during the Holocaust.

A few years earlier, in 2014, he exhibited a group of forty-two paintings and drawings titled *All This Has Come upon Us* at the Terezín Ghetto Museum in the Czech Republic (which was established in 1991 to commemorate the lives and deaths of Jews shipped to the ghetto/concentration camp located there). In contrast to the paintings commemorating his mother's hometown, these forty-two paintings and drawings illustrate moments of distress in Jewish history dating back to the years of captivity in Egypt. Podwal's title for the exhibition is taken from Psalm 44:18 and is appropriate because Jews often recite psalms in times of despair. (These illustrations can be viewed at the Mark Podwal website, http://markpodwal.com/projects.html, "Terezin Portfolio.")

One of the paintings in the exhibition, *Expulsion 1492* (2013) (fig. 11), is a sad–happy painting that acknowledges the expulsion of

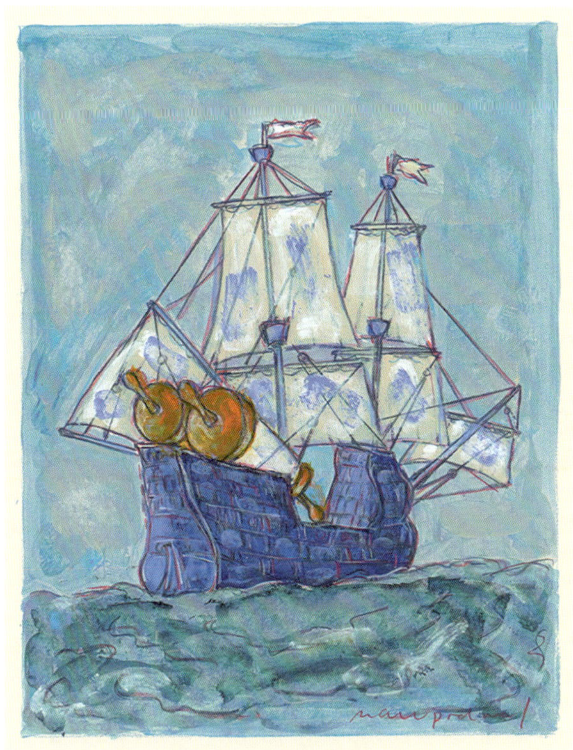

11. Mark Podwal, *Expulsion 1492*, 2013. Acrylic, gouache, and colored pencil on paper, 22 × 30 in. © Mark Podwal.

Jews from Spain in 1492 by King Ferdinand and Queen Isabella. Podwal has appended to this painting a passage from Psalm 119:54: "Your laws are songs to me wherever I may live." And so he illustrates that thought by showing the exiled Jews carrying their religion with them in the form of Torah scrolls. However far the ship might sail, on whatever shores the ship might dock, and whatever hardships the passengers will encounter, the scrolls and therefore the religion will survive.

Of the forty-two works in the Terezín Ghetto Museum exhibition, I selected this one for reproduction because certain subjects, such as the expulsion from Spain, are depicted by other artists as well, notably Ruth Weisberg (see chapter 4). Whether one artist influenced another is not relevant here; what is relevant is that certain events in Jewish history as well as particular stories in the Bible can be visualized more easily or are simply more powerful and more exciting to think about than others. The important point is that each artist interprets an event or story according to his or her concerns and interests.

It should be noted, then, that Podwal has painted works on subjects similar to those explored by virtually all the other artists featured here. For example, both he and Ruth Weisberg have created works honoring those murdered in the Holocaust and, as just indicated, those expelled from Spain. Weisberg created a series of three paintings juxtaposing the expulsion from Spain with Jews fleeing German-controlled countries by ship in the early 1940s and with the liminal state of immigrants who have left their homes but who have not yet arrived in a safe haven. And like David Wander (chapter 11), Podwal has portrayed the destruction of Jerusalem. He shares with Siona Benjamin (chapter 6) an interest in the figure of Lilith, who in legend was the first wife of Adam. He has, like Janet Shafner (chapter 5), explored kabbalist interpretations of the creation of the universe. Like Robert Kirschbaum (chapter 8), he has evoked the symbolism of the Temple Mount in Jerusalem, and along with Archie Rand (chapter 12) he has portrayed the elevation of Elijah to heaven. Not least, he and two other artists, Weisberg and Wander, have illustrated Haggadahs, the book read at Passover seders: Podwal providing images for three different Haggadahs (Podwal 1972 or *Let My People Go* 1972; Podwal 1993 or *A Passover Haggadah* 1993; and Podwal 2012 or *Sharing the Journey* 2012), Weisberg for one (Weisberg 2002 or *The Open Door* 2002), and Wander for one (Wander 1985 or *Wolloch Haggadah* 1985).

Like other artists, Podwal finds a vast trove of material in the ancient texts, including subjects in the many legends that have accrued over the centuries. Unlike Siona Benjamin's valorization of Lilith's feminist aspects, his version of the Lilith legend concentrates on the number of children she presumably killed. In Podwal's *Lilith* (2006) (fig. 12), we see a headless woman with babies tumbling about. According to legends, she, like Adam, was created from dust and was his equal (Ginzberg [1909–38] 1917–87, 1:65; 2:233; 3:280; 4:5; 5:87, 148). But she abandoned him and was told that if she did not return, she would lose one hundred demon children daily. Not intimidated, she did not return, and among her many vengeful misdeeds she injured baby boys soon after their birth and killed children often by strangulation. The large owl present in the painting is not mentioned in the legends but in early European, African, and Native North and South American mythology, owls are harbingers of death, night monsters, evil omens, and bearers of supernatural danger, which is how Lilith is depicted as well.

But all is not forbidding and grim in the Jewish past or in Podwal's universe. In fact, the bright colors and quick brush strokes of the artist's work *Adam Kadmon* (2000)

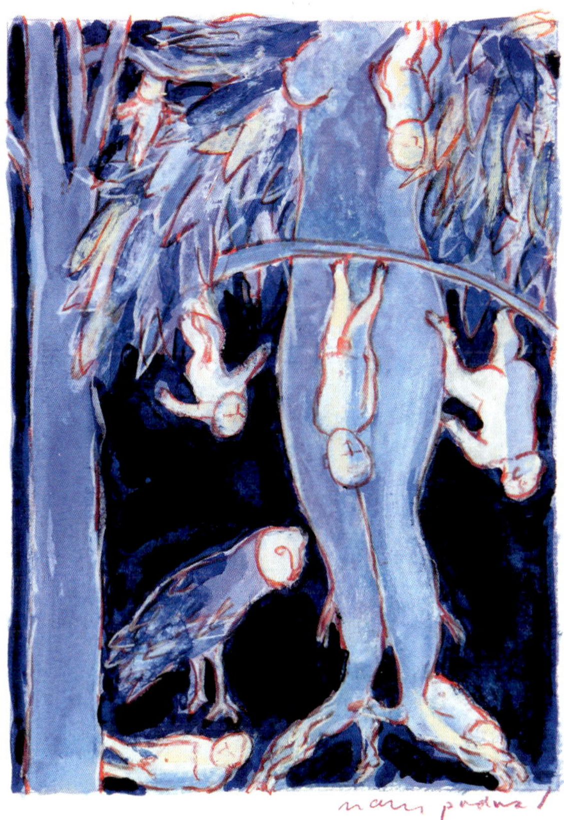

12. Mark Podwal, *Lilith*, 2006. Acrylic, gouache, and colored pencil on paper, 12 × 10 in. © Mark Podwal.

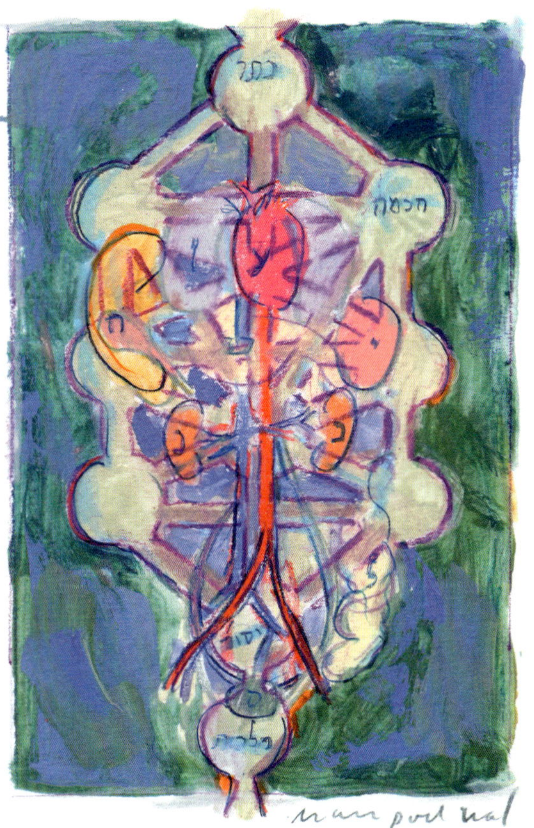


13. Mark Podwal, *Adam Kadmon*, 2000. Acrylic, gouache, and colored pencil on paper, 12 × 10 in. © Mark Podwal.

(fig. 13) mark it as a near delirious painting announcing the birth of our universe. It also reveals Podwal's familiarity with kabbalah. The easiest way to explain this painting is to refer briefly to the creation of the universe as propounded by Rabbi Isaac Luria (1534–72), who lived in what is Safed in current-day Israel (Scholem [1941] 1961, 213–15). God withdrew from encompassing all space to provide space for the creation of the world. The first shaft of light that appeared in that primordial-primeval space was Adam Kadmon (not the Adam of the Garden of Eden), representing the first configuration of the divine light, the essence of things, and all that is potential in the universe emanating from God. Even though kabbalists believe that God was so remote that such a force could be known only to God, they nevertheless identify ten emanations, or *spherot*, of God that came to be arranged on what has been called the Tree of Life. Podwal indicates these emanations by the ten symmetrically placed circles in the painting. The red circle in the center, one of the *spherot* superimposed on the Tree of Life, is attached to a stick figure, most probably symbolizing Adam of the Garden of Eden, the physical manifestation of Adam Kadmon. The Hebrew word in the topmost circle, *keter*, represents the unknowable God. On the upper-right circle, Podwal wrote *hokhmah*, "wisdom." Toward the bottom, he wrote *yesod*, the foundation of all the active forces of God, and at the bottom, the lowest of the *spherot*, he wrote *malkhuth*, which refers to our world and the Shekinah, the feminine aspect of God.

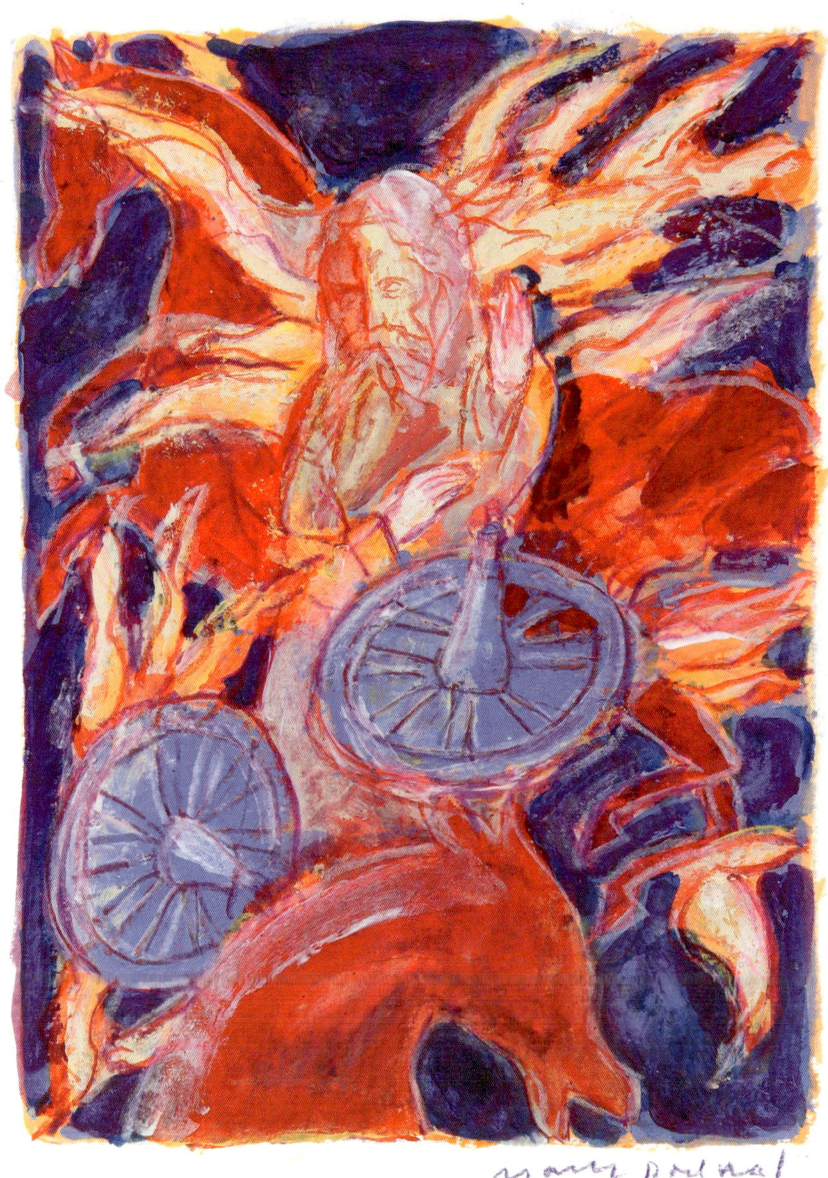

14. Mark Podwal, *Elijah's Metamorphosis*, 2006. Acrylic, gouache, and colored pencil on paper, 12 × 10 in. © Mark Podwal.

So the painting is composed of three elements. First, its title indicates that it marks the beginning of the world, and the red line down the center represents the first appearance of the divine light or force known as Adam Kadmon. The second element is the kabbalists' Tree of Life, indicating the ten manifestations of God. And third, the red stick figure also represents the presence of the first human as recorded in the Bible—together, the birth of the world, God's relation to the world, and the first human presence in the world, all done in bright, cheerful colors. In comparison to Janet Shafner's depressing and Robert Kirschbaum's abstract conceptions of Creation (see chapters 5 and 8), Podwal's image in *Adam Kadmon* offers a glimmer of hope for humankind despite the travails the artist has recorded in other works.

Equally colorful but in a different register, *Elijah's Metamorphosis* (2006) (fig. 14) depicts Elijah's journey to heaven. As described in the Bible, Elijah and Elisha are in conversation when Elijah, who knows he is to be taken, asks Elisha what he can do for him (Second Kings

2:9–11). Elisha asks for a double portion of Elijah's spirit. "As they kept on walking and talking, a fiery chariot with fiery horses suddenly appeared and separated one from the other, and Elijah went up to heaven in a whirlwind." Less a view of a scene than a projection of Elijah's intense state of mind, the painting portrays Elijah looking down at Elisha as if projecting his spirit onto his disciple. He is surrounded by two red horses, two chariot wheels, and tongues of fire set against an azure sky, certainly as dramatic an entry into heaven as one can imagine.

As in America, recognition of this generation's achievements through exhibitions in Europe, let alone purchases, has been minimal. Podwal is the exception. He has exhibited abroad and has created works for Prague's Altneuschul. His connection to that synagogue began before his personal association with it, when he made drawings of the building beginning in 1978 for Elie Wiesel's book *The Golem* (1983). The drawings for that book were published by the Prague Jewish Community beginning in 1985, and Podwal's work was subsequently exhibited in that city in 1997. Between 2004 and 2006, Podwal visited Prague several times as the executive producer and writer of a Public Broadcasting System documentary on the Old Jewish Cemetery there. By 2011, the chief rabbi of Prague, familiar with his art, asked Podwal to design textile coverings for religious objects, noted at the beginning of this chapter.

Perhaps prompted by knowledge of the synagogue's history and religious rituals, Podwal painted a scene surprisingly quite rare among artists of his generation. Several American artists do attend both daily and weekly services, but they do not create works recording scenes during a service. Podwal's painting *Yom Kippur in the Altneuschul* (2008) (fig. 15) shows a moment in an actual service. Men wrapped in their prayer shawls are standing or walking presumably toward the bema, where the Torah will be read, while three seated men read from their high-holiday prayer books. (Torah scrolls are taken from the Ark at least three times a week for Torah readings.)

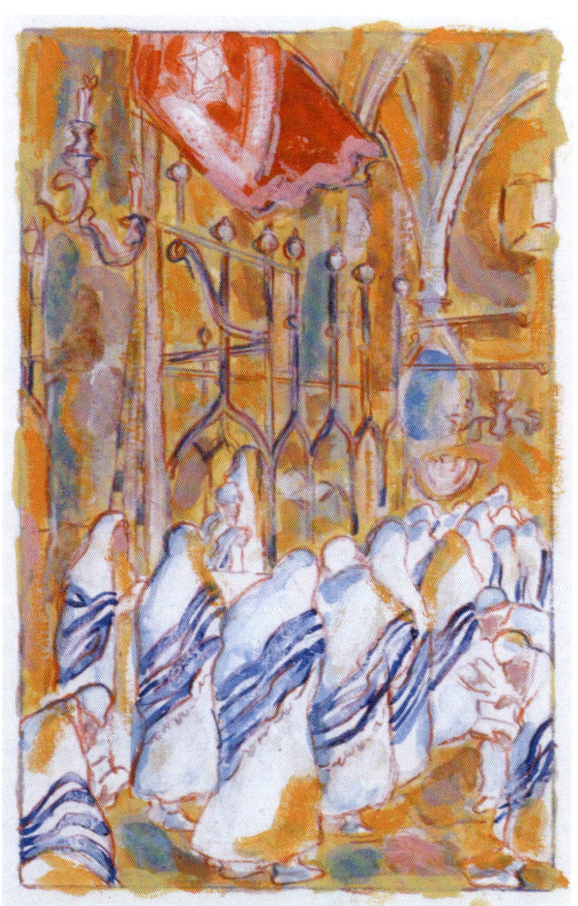

15. Mark Podwal, *Yom Kippur in the Altneuschul*, 2008. Acrylic, gouache, and colored pencil on paper, 16 × 12 in. © Mark Podwal.

Because we do not see the men's faces, Podwal might be suggesting that the men are lost in thought or that their anonymity marks a scene repeated by generations of participants. Given the events of the mid–twentieth century in central and eastern Europe, this painting is also about survival, redemption, the tenacity of belief, and the insistence on perpetuating a religious culture despite whatever difficulties might have overtaken these congregants in the street, in their homes, and in their place of worship.

*Yom Kippur in the Altneuschul* well summarizes Podwal's art in that it is saturated with Jewish history. Through the literal performance of religious ritual in that synagogue, it evokes and acknowledges both directly and indirectly the sorrows, determination, and continuity of the larger community in Europe and America as well as around the world and makes an argument for the centrality of ritual in the survival of the religion. In this regard, the painting gains an outsize importance along with a several other works—such as Carol Hamoy's *Sabbath Bride* (1985) (fig. 4), Ruth Weisberg's *The Scroll* (1986) (figs. 17–20), Archie Rand's *Chapter Paintings* (1989) (fig. 77), David Wander's five scrolls, and Richard McBee's continuing series on the Binding of Isaac—that illustrate the range and depth of interest exhibited by artists of this generation, who have determined to read the history of Judaism from their own perspective and to depict those aspects that have touched them most profoundly.

# 4 Ruth Weisberg

Ruth Weisberg (b. 1942) was there at the beginning. She moved to Southern California in 1969 and shortly thereafter became a powerful presence in the feminist art movement. At that time, it was the most important and best-organized feminist art group in the country. Judy Chicago (b. 1939) and Miriam Schapiro (1923–2015), key figures in this development, started the Feminist Art Program at the California Institute in Valencia, which lasted from 1971 to 1973, and opened Womanhouse in 1971 in Los Angeles, almost immediately attracting several like-minded figures to the area. Weisberg, already a recognized presence in the Los Angeles art world, participated in the first exhibition around 1973, a two-person show with Chicago.

But as close as Weisberg was to these artists at the time, she was not one of them in one crucial way. Although several were Jewish, they identified themselves almost entirely by gender rather than by religion. In the very rare instances when they dealt with Jewish themes, they did so in an almost completely secular way (Baskind and Silver 2011, 198; Bloom 2006). Not so Weisberg, for whom religion was important. As she said in 1990, "I am nourished by the history of the Jews, the history of art, and by the unwritten history of women" (qtd. in McCloud 1990, 21; see also Weisberg 1999, 4). And as she later reiterated in an email on July 16, 2003, "Just as I am always female, I am always Jewish. So, no matter what I am working on, I bring to bear certain fundamental beliefs, values, and habits of mind." But she did share with Chicago, Schapiro, and the other artists at least one significant attitude toward subject matter. As critic Arlene Raven so succinctly states, "Most of all, personal narrative entered women's visual vocabulary as expression and public disclosure" (1988, 8; see also Raven 1973, 1994). Weisberg explained that "it seems pointless to me to make art that doesn't have a kind of passionate attachment to what you are saying. I want to share with people, and I want them to be able to project themselves into my images" (in Barrett 1990, 15).

All narrative is of course personal. But in the context of feminist art, Raven meant that many women artists began to create works influenced by personal experiences or by events experienced only by women. For instance, in 1981, as part of *The Birth Project*, Chicago created embroideries of women giving birth, which she titled *Creation of the World* and *Birth Tear Embroidery*. Chicago and Schapiro asked, "What does it feel like to be a woman? To be formed around a central core and have a secret place which can be entered and which is also a passage way from which life emerges?" (Chicago and Schapiro 1973, 11; see also Broude and Garrard 1994; Raven 1988, 104–5).

Weisberg, writing retrospectively in 2004, felt much the same way, stating that women's stories had not yet been told. In a series of works dating from 1972, for example, she was among the earliest to allude to the birthing experience (although in a much less obvious way than Chicago) by creating works of women floating underwater, intimating, as Weisberg said, memories of a *mikvah* (a pool of running water that brides use just before marriage and in which married women "purify" themselves after menstruation) as well as notions about creation, pregnancy, and the idea of giving birth to one's own self (Byrne 2001, 17; Weisberg 2004b). In other works down to the present, including *The Scroll* (1986), Weisberg has created images that inscribe attitudes and describe experiences not usually found in works by male artists.

By 1972, it had become clear that Weisberg's path had diverged from that of her sister Jewish feminist artists. Whatever their similar family backgrounds (eastern European origins, political concerns, and activism), Weisberg embraced rather than distanced herself from her Jewish heritage. As a result, she became a pioneer and a leading figure in the exploration of Jewish subject matter from both feminist and nongendered points of view. As she explained at the end of that decade, "[I am] nourished by the history of the Jews, the history of art, and by the unwritten history of women" (qtd. in Ball 1979, 1, cited in J. Myers 2007, not paginated).

Weisberg is among those artists who grew up in an environment that encouraged Jewish identification, but in a more secular and cultural than religious manner. Her family was intensely secular, pro-Zionist, and pro-feminist. During several conversations, she indicated that issues of social justice and ethical values were emphasized rather than synagogue attendance or observance of religious rituals. Her maternal grandfather, who had emigrated from Austria, visited the Soviet Union in the late 1920s to work on engineering designs for the Moscow subway system and in the early 1930s to help establish Birobidzhan as a Jewish Republic. Earlier, in 1911, he had also helped establish a Zionist utopian colony in Utah that taught its members community values, self-sufficiency, and self-reliance (G. Hirsch 1985–86, 41; Jackson 1988, 12).

In 1960, Weisberg interrupted her studies at the University of Michigan to attend the Academia di Bella Arti in Perugia, where she received her Laurea degree in 1962. While living in a country and community predominantly Catholic, she began to feel her difference as a Jew, not by experiencing significant anti-Semitism but rather as a means of self-identification. On returning to Michigan, where she received a master's degree in art in 1966, she decided to learn as much as possible about her heritage. She initially was attracted to Jewish mysticism, in particular Gershom Scholem's ([1941] 1961, 1965) accounts of kabbalah.

When she moved to Los Angeles, she connected with Rabbi Laura Geller, director of Hillel at the University of Southern California, who was instrumental in encouraging Weisberg to explore Jewish themes in art. At first, Weisberg found historical rather than religious subject matter more amenable to her artistic interests. Nevertheless, over the course of her career she has created works based on both historical and religious Jewish as well as non-Jewish sources. Nor has she limited herself to making art alone. She was president of the College Art Association, the professional association of artists and art historians, from 1990 to 1992; dean of the University of Southern California Roski School of Art and Design from 1995 to 2010; and founder of the Jewish Artists Initiative of Southern California in 2004.

Her first important work with Jewish content was the series of nine intaglio engravings that make up the artist's book *The Shtetl: A*

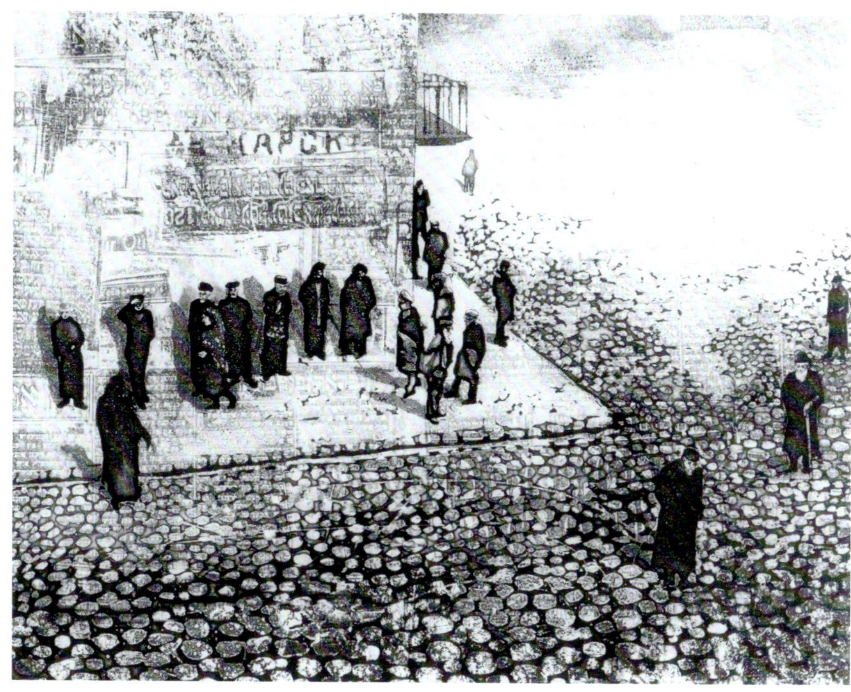

16. Ruth Weisberg, *Waiting*, from *The Shtetl: A Journey and a Memorial*, 1971. Intaglio on paper, 11⅞ × 15⅝ in. Courtesy of the artist.

*Journey and Memorial* (fig. 16), published in 1971, one of the earliest works by an artist in her generation to memorialize the Holocaust. Its immediate source was *yiskor* books—accounts of shtetls, or Jewish communities, destroyed during the Holocaust, especially the account of her grandmother's shtetl. Rather than illustrate scenes of violence, in *The Shtetl* Weisberg emphasized the shtetl inhabitants' reactions by showing a very vulnerable community anticipating the unimaginable.

The cold fear and psychological immobilization already apparent in that community's inhabitants is still palpable to the viewer today, as if the shtetl's destruction occurred yesterday. As Weisberg said, "I have the need to hold onto history. . . . I need to preserve things from destruction or death. In wanting to carry on a tradition, a continuity, I preserve a love of humanness" (qtd. in G. Hirsch 1985–86, 44). And like many Jewish Americans who understand in ways too profound for mere words to express that they are lucky to be alive because their parents or grandparents immigrated to America, she sensed that such a project would redeem the memory of those murdered and give her art a purpose. She has said: "I might have been among them, but I was born in Chicago in 1942. I am a branch, a resting place for their souls. This book [*The Shtetl*] is my life's journey in place of theirs" (qtd. in McCloud 1990, 23).

As one observer has noted, "The idea of 'witness' as well as a growing sense for the redemptive value of art in extracting meaning from pain, chaos, and loss increasingly became a motivation in [Weisberg's] work" (Jackson 1988, 12). But aside from the fact that *The Shtetl* was very specific in meaning, it was also important as an example at that early time of how Jewish artists could express themselves more openly, not just by illustrating a biblical story but by addressing a disastrous event in Jewish history in a profoundly personal way, thus enlarging the possibilities and increasing the availability of subject matter for a Jewish-themed art.

The idea of creating a narrative, whether as a linear story or as a series of related episodes, must have intrigued Weisberg. Some years later, in 1984–85, while traveling and working in Italy, visiting churches, and renewing her acquaintance with the many religious mural cycles she had first seen in 1960, she, like many Jewish people who have marveled at these works, realized that there was no parallel pictorial Jewish narrative tradition that provided human form to biblical stories. What, for example, would Jewish interpretations of the story of Abraham and Isaac look like or the story of Queen Esther, not in single, isolated pictures, but as interconnected works in a narrative series or as a sequence of paintings built around a common theme?

After returning to Los Angeles, Weisberg commenced an eleven-painting cycle entitled *A Circle of Life* (1984–85), which would include a mix of Jewish history, autobiography, and the Jewish world to come. The thoughts motivating this cycle encompassed how to visualize continuity with the past, nourishment of the present by the past, and conflation of the past with the present, the latter a particularly Jewish trait—as in conflating disasters such as the destruction of the Temple in Jerusalem in 586 BCE, the murder of Jews during the Crusades in the twelfth century, and the Holocaust in the twentieth century (Funkenstein 1993, 250, 253; Hertzberg and Hirt-Manheimer 1998, 11; Roskies 1984, 13, 16, 17, 259; Yerushalmi 1982, 22, 36, 96). The first painting in *A Circle of Life*, titled *The Great Synagogue of Danzig*, presents a double file of nine children standing in front of a wooden gate that walls off the Danzig synagogue. All of the forms, human and inanimate, are to greater or lesser degree transparent, suggesting both a time-bound moment in the 1940s and a timeless moment of destruction and survival in Jewish history. Another painting, *Survival*, depicts a woman in a fetal position underwater, an image to which Weisberg has returned, and evokes for her the passage in Genesis 1:6—in which the waters of the earth are separated from those above, which fall as rain, and those below, which include oceans, lakes, and rivers—as well as, most important for this painting cycle, purification in a *mikveh*, birth, and sustenance. That is, Weisberg is expressing simultaneously ritual and creation on both personal and cosmic levels. In the final painting of *A Circle of Life*, titled *The World to Come*, a ladder rises almost from the bottom to near the top of the painting. The ladder is surrounded by faintly painted, barely visible people, who represent humanity. We do not know what is in the world to come, but if we assume that the circle is closed, then it leads back to the Danzig synagogue and another round of destruction and survival until the Messiah comes and breaks the circle in the timeless world that will follow (Holo 1986).

Weisberg later noted in an email on September 26, 2010, that around the time she completed *A Circle of Life*, "I had become very aware [years ago] that although Jewish texts had tremendously rich narrative and imagistic elements, Jewish artists had not yet taken advantage of these elements." By chance, she met Dr. Lawrence Hoffman of New York's Hebrew Union College, who offered her the possibility of creating a continuous narrative on a subject of her choice with no strings attached. The offer could not have been better timed in the evolution of Weisberg's career because it provided her with the opportunity to bring together her established interest in Jewish and feminist subject matter with her developing regard for continuous narrative painting. She then began to plan the creation of *The Scroll*, which she completed in 1986.

To the best of my knowledge, *The Scroll* was the first extended narrative painting in the history of Jewish American art concerned with the sacred texts, historical events, and the artist's personal life. For this reason alone, *The Scroll* is of historical importance. But it is important for another reason. It is the first extended narrative that addresses subject matter from a Jewish feminist point of view (Baigell 2007b, 14–25; Gouma-Peterson 1988; *Ruth Weisberg: The Scroll* 1987). Weisberg did not create a survey of "great men in Jewish history" or "highlights in Jewish history" (e.g., victorious battles, miraculous occurrences) but rather a contemporary exploration of the ways Jewish history can be made relevant to contemporary Jewish life and thought and of the ways one's own experiences can be linked to events in the recent and distant past. *The Scroll* is about Weisberg's Jewish memory—selective, personal, nontraditional, pathbreaking. In it, Weisberg combined narrative elements from the Bible, legends and commentaries, lifecycle events, festivals, personal history, and contemporary events, which she structured and programmed with an inner logic that one can discern as one moves from image to image. It is her story of the Jewish people, interspersed with events in her own life, a work unthinkable in the past, with explicitly feminist sections unimaginable before 1970. As she has said of her work, "I'm making visual things that have been written about a lot, but no one has ever drawn" (qtd. in B. Brown 1991, 20).

*The Scroll*, ninety-six feet long, was created as a huge, open circle as if it were an open Torah scroll that allows the viewer to enter and be surrounded by the images. Recurring images of the tallith, or prayer shawl, and a Torah wimple undergird the entire work. A wimple, made from the fabric wrapped around an infant boy at his circumcision, is considered to be a physical link between the covenantal relationship of the circumcision and the Torah. The ritual probably dates from the seventeenth century. After the circumcision ceremony, the cloth is cut into thin strips, which are then sewn together and often embroidered with an inscription bearing the child's name, birth date, and a blessing. It is often used years later to wrap the Torah from which the child reads during his bar mitzvah and might be buried with him at death (Wertlowsky and Wigdor 1999, 698). The wimple depicted in *The Scroll* has embroidered on it the words "a life of Torah, wedding, and righteous deeds," combining a personal event (wedding) with two of the three foundational premises of the Jewish world, the study of Torah and charity, the third being worship.

All of these images are encompassed within the symbolic protection offered by the open Torah-like arrangement of *The Scroll*. In like manner, artists as varied as the American Seymour Lipton (1903–86) and the Russian Yefim Ladyzhensky (1911–82) portrayed men wrapped in a tallith as a symbol of strength and protection (Baigell 2002b, 27; 2003, 144, 176; 2004b, 37). The author Cynthia Ozick describes in her short story "The Shawl" ([1980] 1990) how a protective, magical shawl provides life-giving sustenance to three women during the Holocaust on their incarceration in a concentration camp. The shawl has been interpreted as "a literary symbol of the *tallit*. . . . Wrapping oneself in a prayer shawl is tantamount to being surrounded by the holiness and protection of the commandments, as well as conforming to the will of God. The wearer of the *tallit* is a member of the covenant community" (Berger 1985, 53). So the scroll in Weisberg's work envelopes those within its open circle.

Read from right to left as in Hebrew script, *The Scroll* is divided into three main sections—"Creation," "Revelation," and "Redemption," each linked with one of the festival holidays: Passover, physical freedom; Shavuot, receiving the Torah at Mt. Sinai; and Sukkot, the harvest festival. The first image in "Creation" is of a group of people surging forward, which suggests a group of immigrants beginning their lives in a new country. Immediately adjacent to them, thus juxtaposing contemporary history with an ancient legend about new life, an angel touches a baby in utero.

According to the midrash, the baby does not want to be born, but the angel touches "the babe on the nose, extinguishes the light at his head, and brings him forth into the world against his will. Immediately the child forgets all his soul has seen and learnt[,] usually interpreted as complete knowledge of the Torah, and he comes into the world crying, for he loses a place of shelter and security and rest" (Ginzberg [1909–38] 1917–87, 1:58). The baby then emerges from the birth canal. All in all, "Creation" offers a unique and daring Jewish version of birth imagery compared to the imagery created by other feminist artists (see chapter 2). In the distance, one sees the mountains and deserts of the Sinai as well as the Red Sea, which are not only indicative of future difficulties and a confirmation of the loss of that shelter and security before birth but also symbolic of the creation of the Jewish people. The Covenant with God is confirmed in the next image, the circumcision ritual that ends this particular unit.

The next image in "Creation" focuses on the progression from childhood to adulthood. Three circles of children are seen dancing: the first group smiling in the Indiana sand dunes of Weisberg's childhood; then a group of Polish Jewish children, haunted by the Holocaust; and, finally, several youths dancing arm in arm in a displaced-persons camp just after the end of the war, delighted by the prospect of settling in Jewish Palestine. These images flank the bat mitzvah of Weisberg's daughter, marking her symbolic entrance into Jewish adulthood. Rabbi Laura Geller indicates the passage in the Torah to be read as Weisberg and her sister, Naomi, look on (fig. 17). The emphasis placed on the newly developed rituals for this important event and the women surrounding the youngster were also highlighted in the Jewish feminist literature of the time, especially by Judith Plaskow (1979; see also Geller 1995, 246, and Gottlieb 1995). Here, Weisberg gives visual emphasis to Plaskow's assertion that "ritual asserts women's presence in the present" (2005,

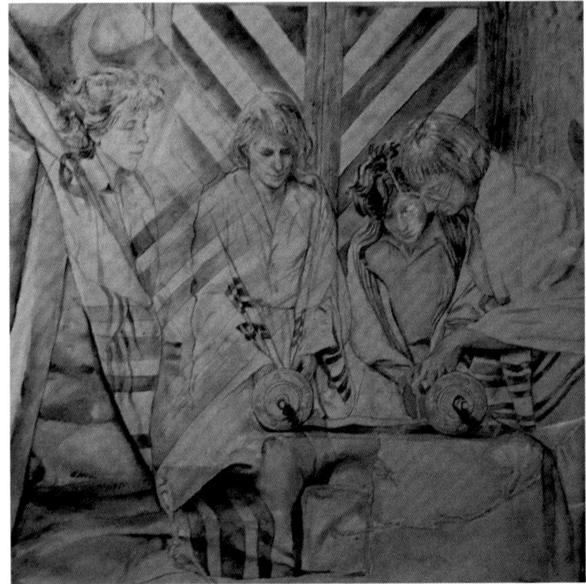

17. Ruth Weisberg, *Bat Mitzvah*, detail from *The Scroll*, 1986. Mixed-media drawing on paper, 4½ × 94 ft. SCC 41.377, Skirball Museum, Skirball Cultural Center, Los Angeles. Gift of Sandy and Adrea Bettelman.

63). Portraying the bat mitzvah also asserts a covenantal gesture for women, just as the circumcision does for men. In fact, by portraying her daughter's bat mitzvah, Weisberg added a new and important image to Jewish American visual iconography.

The second section, "Revelation," describes a wedding ceremony, the bride and groom, as is the custom, held aloft on chairs for a few moments by mixed groups of men and women. The women dancing around the couple allude to Miriam and the women who danced after the Jews passed successfully through the Red Sea (Exodus 15:20) as well as to the commandment to entertain the bridal couple after the wedding ceremony. Placed between the dancing scenes, a couple ascends a flight of steps to the chuppah, or marriage canopy, supported by a giant tree and under which they are to be married (fig. 18). A male rabbi officiates. The groom wears a *kittle*, a symbol of purity as well as the garment that subsequently might be his

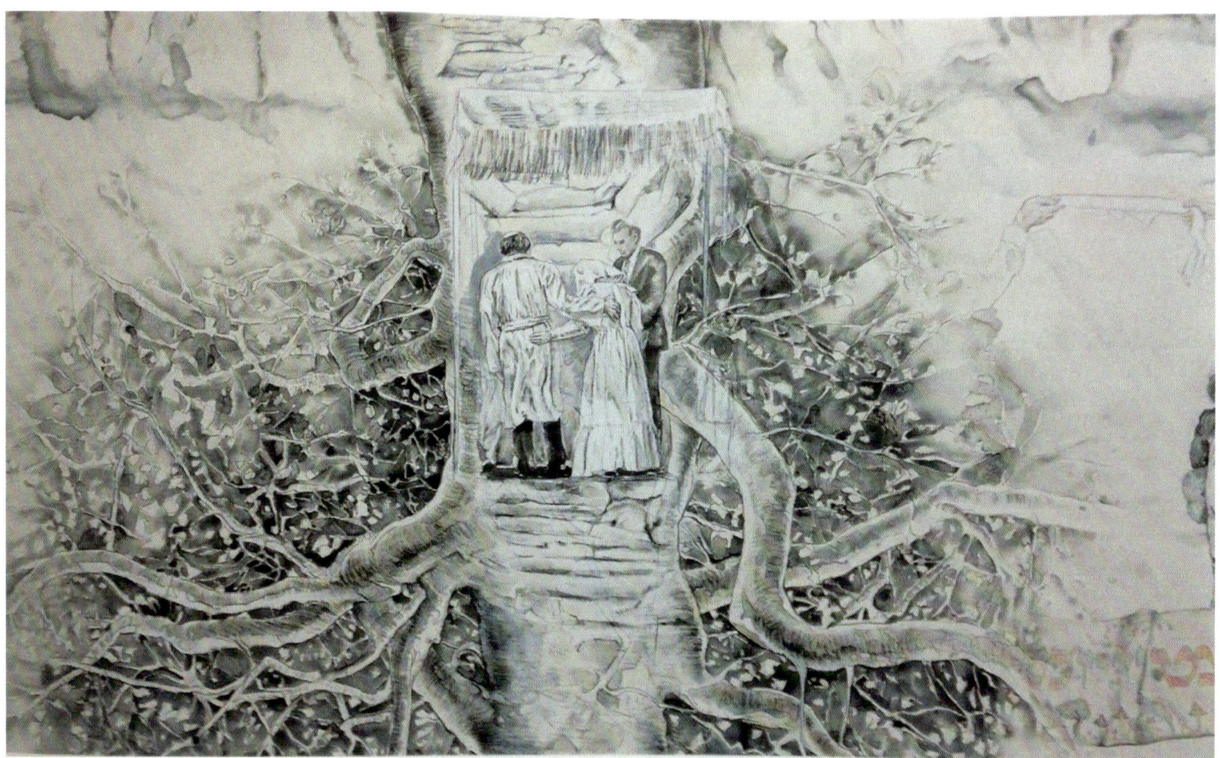

18. Ruth Weisberg, *Wedding*, detail from *The Scroll*, 1986. Mixed-media drawing on paper, 4½ × 94 ft. SCC 41.377, Skirball Museum, Skirball Cultural Center, Los Angeles. Gift of Sandy and Adrea Bettelman.

burial shroud. Usually, only Orthodox grooms wear a *kittle*, but this couple touch each other in public under the chuppah, an impossible act if this were an actual Orthodox ceremony. I assume, then, that Weisberg portrayed the figures in this way to make the point that the ceremony encompasses both traditional and modern points of view, a celebration for all those committed to having a Jewish wedding ceremony.

The joining of two people as one and with God also marks a spiritual occasion, symbolized by the tree that encompasses the couple. Its roots are inverted—that is, located at the top—meaning that it is the Tree of Life, the mystical tree of kabbalah that represents the Divine and its emanations, or *spherot*. In kabbalistic renderings of the tree, the Ein Sof, the Infinite or the Divine, the Unknowable that is known only to itself, is figured at the top. The Shekinah, that emanation closest to humans, is at the bottom. According to Gershom Scholem, the great explicator of Jewish mysticism, "The cosmic tree grows downward from its root, the first *Sefirot* [sic], and spreads out through those *Sefirot* which constitutes its trunk and through which make up its branches and crown. This image is first found in the *Sefer ha-Bahir*" ([1974] 1978, 106, 42). (The *Sefer ha-Bahir* is the earliest work in kabbalistic literature in which this notion appears. It was written in Provence between 1150 and 1200 but was based on earlier sources [Scholem (1974) 1978, 42, 106, 214].)

In "Revelation," the steps rise to a prismatic curtain, a direct reference to the description of the Sanctuary in the Temple in Jerusalem by Josephus (b. 37 CE), the historian who wrote *The Jewish War*. In his book, Josephus describes the twelve steps that led to the Sanctuary and the curtain in front of its entrance, "a Babylonian tapestry embroidered with blue, white linen thread, scarlet, and purple. The mixture of materials had a clear mystic meaning. . . . Worked in the tapestry was the whole vista of the heavens except for the signs of the Zodiac" (1984, 303). Weisberg seems to suggest here in "Revelation" that just as humans cannot truly fathom the Ein Sof, so they cannot gain entrance to the Holy of Holies or visualize the Divine, which lies behind the curtain. But by placing the newlyweds and therefore the newly formed couple near the Sanctuary, Weisberg enjoins them and the viewer to lead a good life, to elevate their spiritual level, to emulate the Divine, but with the knowledge that they can never be in its presence. Nevertheless, in the joining of the bride with the groom one glimpses or has a revelation of eternity. As the foundational tenets of Judaism indicate, each individual is required to study Torah, to worship, and to enact righteous deeds. By locating an event that many have experienced (marriage) in proximity with the ancient Temple and all that it symbolizes, Weisberg undoubtedly meant to provoke serious personal reflection on the history of Judaism, on one's own life, and on one's personal and religious obligations. Taken altogether, this section of *The Scroll* is one of the most profound and richly allusive in the entire history of Jewish American art. I have described it in detail here to make the point that Jewish religious iconography is extraordinarily rich and largely unknown.

The next group of images includes an unfolded Torah scroll (fig. 19). On the viewer's side, there are several women wearing prayer shawls and children. The scene describes a ritual Rabbi Geller has enacted in which people are literally surrounded by the Torah. On the other side, behind the unfolded scroll, older men and women dressed in Orthodox fashion sit as if watching the parade, or the future, go by. Quite possibly, the younger people, who can view and therefore read the text, are meant to symbolize the acquisition of knowledge through study of the Torah as they pass in front of those who remain stationary and cling to the past.

In Talmudic fashion, however, a counterinterpretation is also possible. In the prophecy of Joel 3:1, it is stated: "I will pour out My spirit on all flesh; Your sons and daughters shall prophesy; Your old men shall dream dreams, And your young men shall see visions." This verse is interpreted in an accompanying column suggesting a glorious future for the faithful, however young or old. "Prophecy, dreams and visions were the three recognized ways in which human beings received communications from God" (*Jewish Study Bible* [1985] 2004, 1172 n.). This interpretation is especially appropriate insofar as the open Torah scroll that envelops the youngsters and is also seen by the older generation indicates to the faithful that they are in the presence of the Word of God.

In the third section, "Redemption," a distant vision of Jerusalem floats above the Israelite tents in the desert where the people are camped on their journey to the Promised Land during their exodus from Egypt or during their diasporic travels over the centuries (fig. 20). Immediately adjacent to this image, concentration-camp uniforms hang on clotheslines, reminding the viewer of those murdered both long ago and in our own time before they could reach the Promised Land and live freely and peacefully. The juxtaposition of these two images evokes two different but equally heartbreaking passages from well-known liturgical sources. First, the last lines of the Haggadah recited at the end of the Passover meal, "Next year in Jerusalem! Next year, may all be free!," might have been on the minds of many camp inmates, but such a happy fate would not come to pass. And, second, because it is common to recite certain psalms in moments of crisis, many in the camps might have had in mind, especially in their misery, the lines of Psalm 137 that are said before Tisha B'av, the day set aside

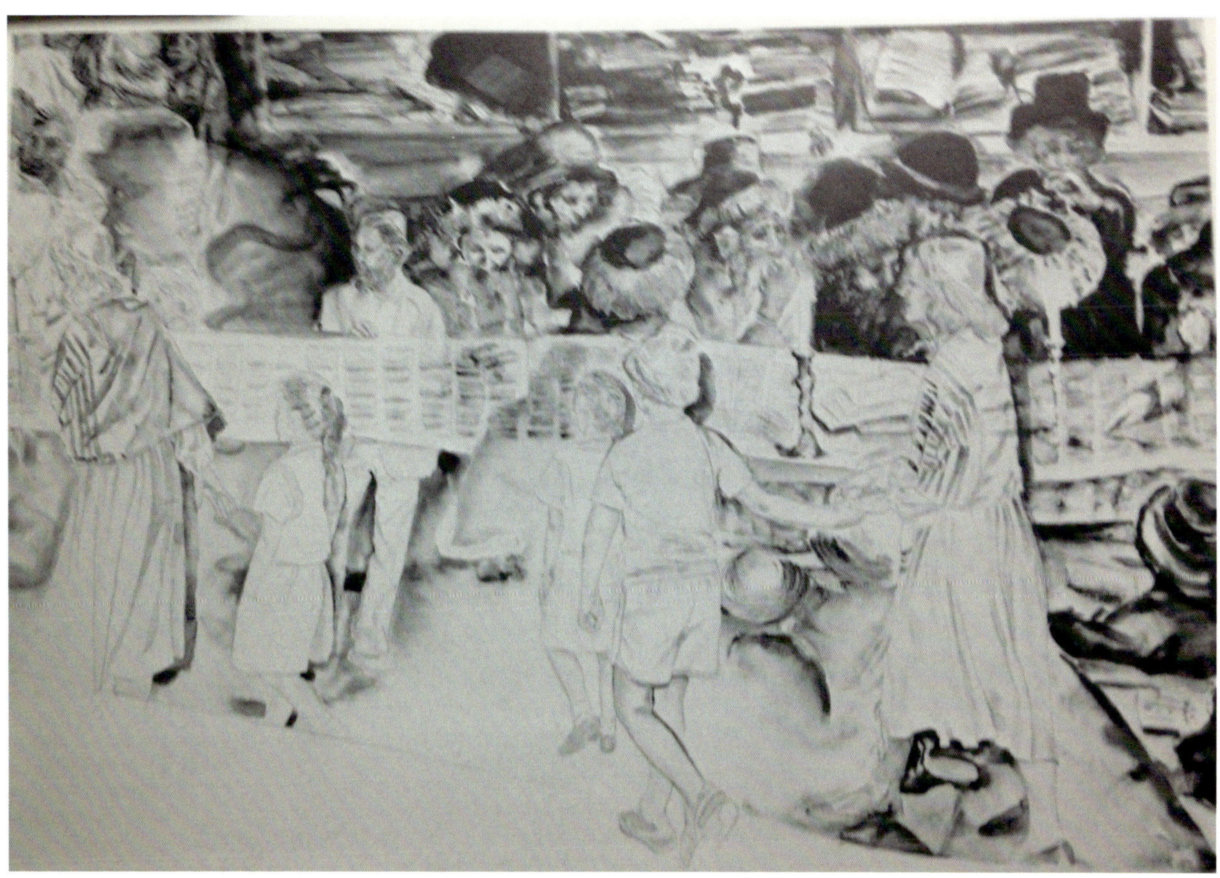

(*Above*) 19. Ruth Weisberg, *Open Scroll*, detail from *The Scroll*, 1986. Mixed-media drawing on paper, 4½ × 94 ft. SCC 41.377, Skirball Museum, Skirball Cultural Center, Los Angeles. Gift of Sandy and Adrea Bettelman.

(*Below*) 20. Ruth Weisberg, *Camps and Jerusalem*, detail from *The Scroll*, 1986. Mixed-media drawing on paper, 4½ × 94 ft. SCC 41.377, Skirball Museum, Skirball Cultural Center, Los Angeles. Gift of Sandy and Adrea Bettelman.

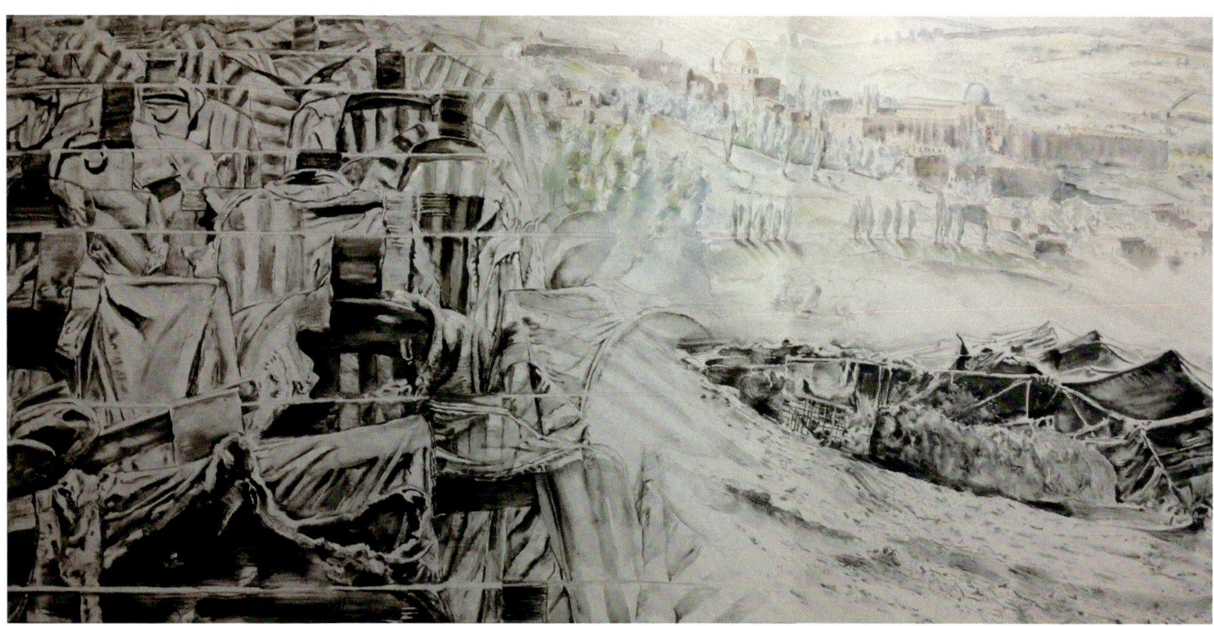

to commemorate the destruction of the Temple: "By the rivers of Babylon, there we sat, sat and wept, as we thought of Zion. . . . If I forget you, O Jerusalem, let my right hand wither; let my tongue stick to my palate if I cease to think of you, if I do not keep Jerusalem in memory even at my happiest hour" (lines 1, 5–6).

Adjacent to these images, large wings and hands are meant to suggest comfort and protection and, not least, the airborne evacuation of Ethiopian Jews to Israel. *The Scroll* ends as it begins, with the portrayal of a stream of people—ancestors, figures from past generations—perhaps inhabiting the hoped-for messianic and redeemed world, a world noted in prayers and by the prophets.

In some sections, *The Scroll* is obviously transgressive to Orthodox and patriarchal beliefs and modes of thought. Notions of a "woman's place" is made irrelevant by the presence of so many women involved in Jewish activities. Where once women were portrayed, say, lighting the Sabbath candles, a role reserved for them, Weisberg has moved them into rituals once assigned to men. Like other artists considered here, she has also given emphasis to autobiography and modern religious practices while also acknowledging traditional and "official" texts. This emphasis means that she has made herself arbiter of what she deems important and personally acceptable in religious tradition. Her sense of self-definition therefore is as important as her biblical knowledge and religious commitment in choosing images to portray. For her, fulfillment lies less in adhering to unquestioning religious belief than in filtering that belief through her own values. Furthermore, she is much more concerned with the activities of individuals, with relating easily to them, than in presenting abstract ideas or standard historical highpoints. (See comments by Eisen and others at end of chapter 2.)

*The Scroll* is in every sense of the word "her/story," not "his/story," and is based on what Weisberg deems important historically, culturally, and religiously. Think about it! The making of *The Scroll* was an immense challenge—taking on thousands of years of Jewish history and memory and then combining in narrative sequence individual life experiences and celebrations; past and present public events; a cycle of birth, life, and death; historical triumph and tragedy; legend and fact. And it all was done without precedent.

Two comments should be pondered in thinking about the significance of *The Scroll* as a statement of both contemporary Jewish art and contemporary Jewish thought. Gershom Scholem says that there are two types among those who study kabbalah: those who think it a great achievement merely in memorizing everything and those who acknowledge tradition but also challenge it.

> So far as the consciousness of future generations is concerned, only the men [and women] of this [latter] type are the true carriers of tradition, for tradition is living creativity in the context of revelation. Precisely because tradition perceives, receives, and unfolds . . . , it is the force within which contradictions and tensions are not destructive but rather stimulating and creative. (1971b, 297)

Social observer Hilary Putnam holds that Judaism can be spiritually enriching when it substitutes reinterpretation for "slavish adherence[,] . . . for all genuine appropriation of tradition involves continued reinterpretation, and tradition that is not constantly reappropriated and reinterpreted becomes fossilized" (1993, 115). *The Scroll*, then, is one of the most important visual statements in the entire history of Jewish American art as well as a statement of contemporary Jewish thought.

In the years following the completion of *The Scroll*, Weisberg created at least three works with narrative intentions, one based on a spiritual interpretation of biblical events, another based on historical events, and the third raising questions about moral and family values in a biblical story. The first, *Passing Over* (1991), is a drawing and mixed-media installation twenty-four by thirty-five feet that depicts an actual stone-lined passageway placed vertically to a mural. The passageway opens onto a band of raked sand and a real ladder that arcs in exaggerated foreshortening several feet over the gallery or museum floor until it touches an area above the mural. The scenes depicted in the mural include views of the stunning, distant mountains of the southern Sinai, with Mt. Sinai at the very center. The varied panoramic landscape alludes to the period between the exodus from Egypt and Shavuot forty-nine days later, when the Israelites received the Torah at Mt. Sinai, symbolizing the passage from physical freedom to spiritual enlightenment. The period between the two events is considered a time for self-reflection and self-improvement. Of *Passing Over*, Weisberg said: "I'm basically trying to recreate [*sic*] the landscape of Passover and the Revelation [at Sinai] to give the viewer the experience of moving through the metaphorical landscape from darkness to light" (qtd. in Nilson 1991).

The second work, the historical triptych *1492–1942* (1991), is on the one hand about Columbus sailing for the New World and the expulsion of Jews from Spain in 1492 and on the other about the inability of Jews to find a safe haven in the early 1940s because of virulent anti-Semitism in German-controlled countries and restrictive immigration policies in potentially safe-haven countries. The three panels are titled *Expulsion*, *Refused Permission to Land*, and *Bound for Nowhere*. Each includes Columbus's ships in the lower half and modern ships from which Jews were unable to disembark in the upper half. In her research, Weisberg came to believe that some of the funds Columbus received to outfit his ships were confiscated from Jews in 1492 and that his ships actually sailed past ships filled with refugees forced to leave Spain. The most famous of the modern ships seen in the upper parts of the three paintings is the *St. Louis*. Unable to allow the great majority of its passengers to disembark in Cuba or the United States in 1942, it returned to Europe with its cargo of about 930 Jews, of whom 254 were ultimately murdered in the Holocaust (see "Voyage of the *St. Louis*" n.d.).

Weisberg created the third set of narrative paintings, *Sisters and Brothers* (1994) (figs. 21–22) expressly to connect the moral and ethical issues in the actions of Rachel and Leah and of Jacob and Esau to contemporary life, issues that provoke serious discussion about proper and improper modes of behavior between siblings as well as between parents and children and about how these biblical figures' actions call attention to matters of truth and falseness as well as to the mundane and the spiritual. As Weisberg said,

> I deliberately chose the story of Jacob, Esau, Leah and Rachel, as I felt it had the psychological complexity and spiritual depth to sustain a monumental project. Over a period of several years, I worked on drawings and paintings that culminated in a two-tiered steel structure, 14 feet by 18 feet, containing fourteen paintings on canvas narrating the story of two brothers and two sisters with their mirrored stories of betrayal, estrangement, struggle, and reconciliation. (1999, 2)

This story is, in fact, a modern nondenominational one. Weisberg wanted to show the Bible as a book relevant to modern life rather than as one filled with mythic characters engaged in mythic activities.

In brief, the biblical story begins with the birth of Esau and Jacob to Isaac and Rebecca (Genesis 25–33). Various events set the boys against each other, especially when Jacob buys Esau's birthright and tricks their father into blessing him in place of his older brother. Subsequently, Jacob is tricked by his uncle, Laban, the father of Leah and Rachel, into marrying Leah instead of Rachel, Jacob's true love. And at the consummation of Jacob and Leah's marriage, the sisters and their father, Laban, maneuver Jacob into thinking he has married Rachel. Ultimately, the brothers and sisters reconcile with each other to greater or lesser degree. Over the centuries, a great number of midrashim have been written about the compelling nature of their stories—especially about the births of the brothers, their various deceptions, their marriages, and their complex relationships with each other (Ginzberg [1909–38] 1917–87, 1:313–69, 4:310, 5:278–99; Lifshitz 1994, 224; *Midrash Rabbah: Exodus* 1983, 2; *Midrash Rabbah: Genesis II* 1983, 559–650; Stern 2004, 1869–71; Tuchman and Rapoport 2004, 212–17).

Weisberg faced at least two questions before beginning her *Sisters and Brothers* cycle: which episodes to choose and how to place them in appropriate sequences. She readily admitted that Marilyn Lavin's book on Italian Renaissance narratives, *The Place of Narrative* (1990), provided some answers. Lavin asserts that narratives have always played a didactic role in Western church decoration and that "they remained a major medium of public communication for over a thousand years" (1). This declaration resonated with Weisberg's interest in Jewish themes, and so, realizing that there were no equivalents in Jewish American art, she searched for an appropriate subject to explore, one in which the story line would be filled with psychological and emotional complexity. Lavin also posits the notion that, depending on the story being presented, narrative panels can be and have been organized for maximal effect regardless of the chronology of the particular story or event. Different organizational schemes were "developed," Lavin holds, "to broadcast messages of greater than narrational value . . . [and to offer] new relationships and juxtapositions of scenes, knowing they would constitute new meanings" (1990, 6).

Weisberg decided on a two-tiered sequence of panels facing inward in a tentlike arrangement. As with her other works, her studies of Renaissance art influenced her choice of style. Individual panels on the four siblings, placed on the lower level, symbolically support the narrative panels on the upper level. Weisberg then placed similar or related episodes opposite each other, such as Isaac blessing Jacob across from Leah's deception of Jacob on their wedding night, as if to key viewers to the subtext of duplicity in both instances. *The Blessing* (fig. 21) shows Jacob, who takes the place of his brother, approaching their father as Esau looks on from behind a door. This is a key moment in the brothers' relationship with each other, the moment of supreme deception. Jacob says, "I am Esau, your first-born." And when asked by Isaac, still not certain if he is Esau, Jacob repeats, "I am" (Genesis 27:19, 24). Both ancient writers of midrashim and modern scholars have had a field day with Jacob's answer, explaining why Jacob says that Esau is the first born, what Jacob "really" says, and what he might have or was supposed to have said (see especially Ginzberg [1909–38] 1917–87, 1:336, and Stern 2004, 180–71). In Weisberg's panel, Isaac seems troubled and looks away, his poor eyesight preventing him from seeing his son, perhaps knowing somewhere in the back of his mind that he has been tricked by his wife, Rebecca, and Jacob.

In the panel opposite *The Blessing*, *The Uncovering* (fig. 22), Weisberg shows Jacob and Leah consummating their marriage as Rachel stands hidden behind the door. The text in Genesis 29:23 is very simple and clear. Laban, Leah and Rachel's father, tricks Jacob into marrying Leah. "When evening came, he took

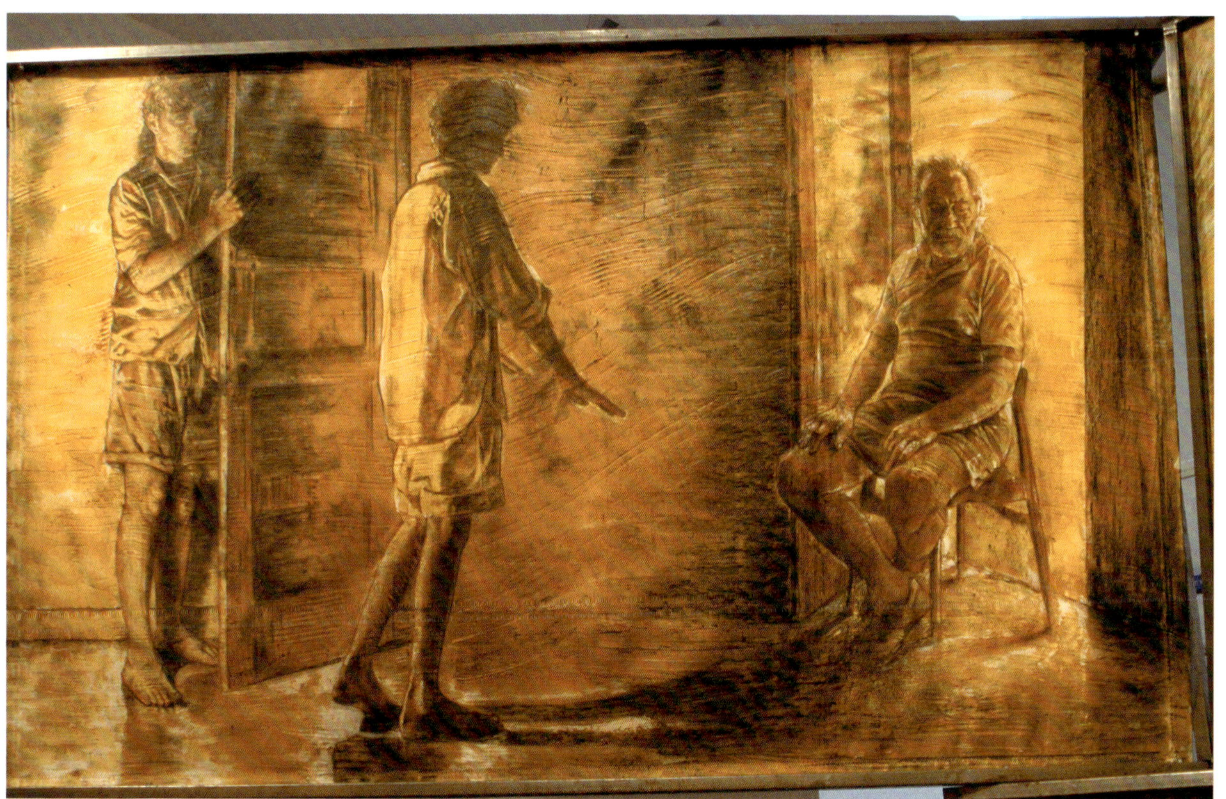

21. Ruth Weisberg, *The Blessing*, from *Sisters and Brothers*, 1994. Steel, canvas construction, charcoal, wax, graphite, powdered pigment, 6 × 10 ft. Entire construction 13 × 18 ft. diameter. Courtesy of the artist and Jack Rutberg Fine Arts, Los Angeles.

his daughter Leah and brought her to him; and he cohabited with her." In the legends, Leah and Rachel know which sister would marry Jacob. They have worked out a series of signals to fool Jacob into thinking that Leah is Rachel. In one version, Rachel hides under the bed and answers when Jacob calls her name—which makes us wonder if Jacob has depth-perception hearing issues (Ginzberg [1909–38] 1917–87, 1:357, 4:310, 5:294). The following morning, Jacob discovers the deception and angrily questions Leah. She replies that she has learned about deception from Jacob's example (Ginzberg [1909–38] 1917–87, 1:357). In addition, then, to Laban and his daughters' deceptions, the exchange between the newlyweds, at least in legend, suggests that their marriage will be a rocky one, certainly an ongoing and unpleasant experience faced by many contemporary viewers.

In other panels, Weisberg added her own midrashic embellishments to the siblings' interactions. In *Struggle*, as Jacob and Esau wrestle with each other, Esau stares at Jacob. The latter, perhaps acknowledging his deception, is unable to return Esau's gaze. In contrast to fraternal belligerence, Weisberg portrays the sisters in *Wellspring* if not exactly cooperating with each other, then at least helping to sustain their community by measuring the disbursement of water, a task identified with women in the Bible.

In all of these scenes, Weisberg did not want merely to illustrate passages in the Bible but instead to help the viewer to realize that a particular biblical passage and its visualization can also have relevance to contemporary experiences many have shared: deceitful activity between siblings, parents, and married couples. As she has said, "It seems pointless to me to

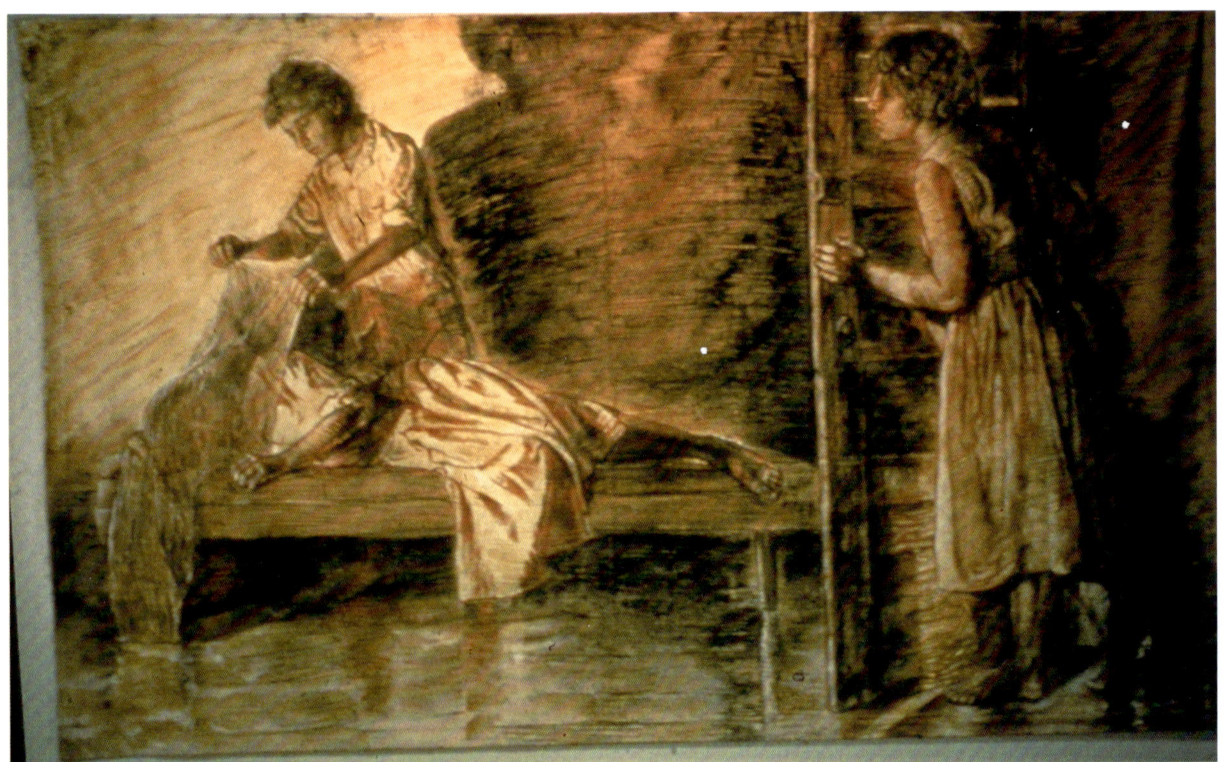

22. Ruth Weisberg, *The Uncovering*, from *Sisters and Brothers*, 1994. Steel, canvas construction, charcoal, wax, graphite, powdered pigment, 6 × 10 ft. Entire construction, 13 × 18 ft. diameter. Courtesy of the artist and Jack Rutberg Fine Arts, Los Angeles.

make art that doesn't have a kind of passionate attachment to what you are saying. I want to share with people, and I want them to be able to project themselves into my images" (in Barrett 1990, 15). To make that point even stronger, the figures are dressed in timeless clothing not tied to any particular period, thus encouraging viewers to relate to them as real rather than distant, mythic figures. In this way, it is perhaps easier to reinterpret both the past in terms of present experiences and the present in terms of past experiences. One can identify with the biblical figures as human beings involved in very human and sometimes less-than-savory activities. Weisberg's intention was to make invisible the interface between events in the Bible and contemporary life, to draw comparisons between the ancient past and the present, and to find in the old stories hints about ways to deal with one's own predicaments. That is, she hoped to personalize the Bible for her viewers. Or as she has succinctly stated, "We excavate image, text, and our own experience in order to create meaning for ourselves and others" (Weisberg 1999, 4).

The idea of passage is never far from Weisberg's thoughts—physical, moral, spiritual, psychological passage, as in escaping from something old to something new, looking forward to a better life by abandoning impossible conditions, finding safety through avoiding danger. *Floating World* (2003) (fig. 23) zeros in on those on shipboard who had to leave their homes in order to gain safety—from Spain in 1492, from Europe in the early 1940s, or from African, Asian, and Latin American countries in our own time.

This painting, suggestive of starting a new life in another country with a different language

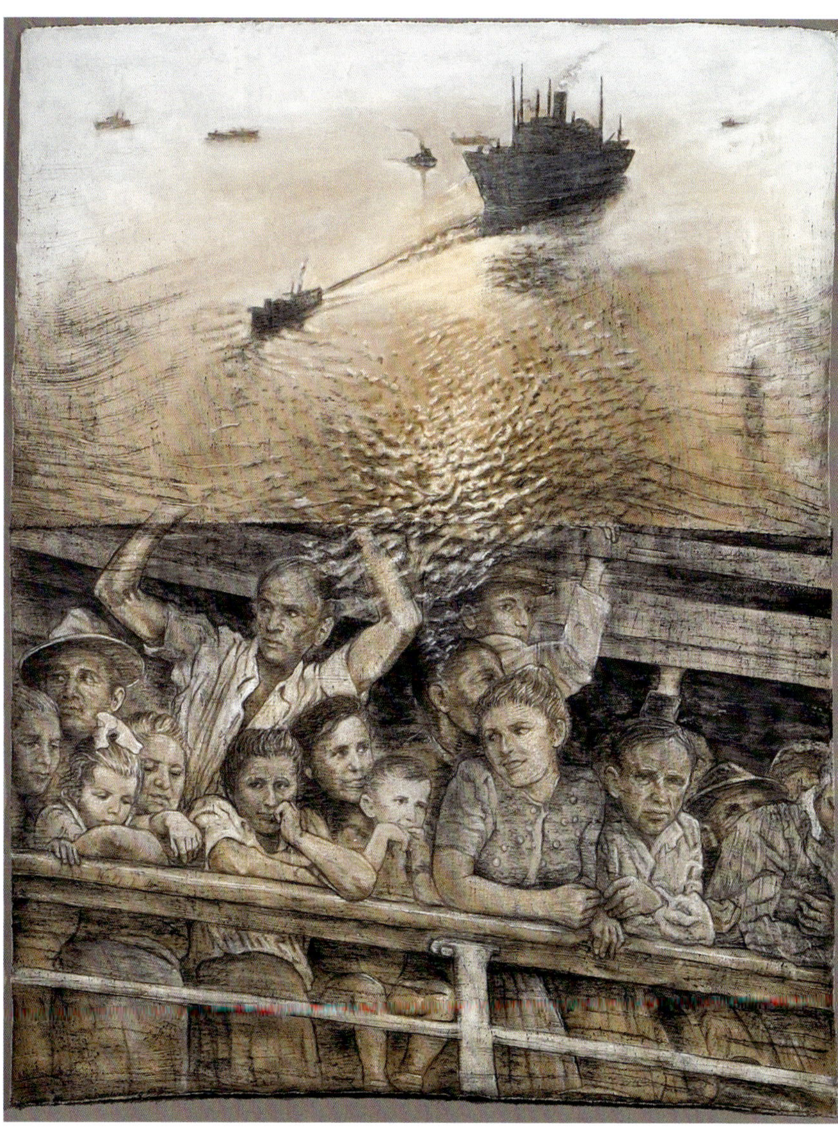

23. Ruth Weisberg, *Floating World*, 2003. Mixed-media paint on unstretched canvas, 78 × 61 in. Courtesy of the artist.

and customs, puts the viewer in the proper frame of mind to realize the enormous task Weisberg faced when organizing the episodic narrative that makes up the twenty-nine-foot-long mural titled *New Beginnings: One Hundred Years of Jewish Immigration* (fig. 24), created for the Jewish Federation headquarters in New York and completed in 2006.

The challenge Weisberg faced was to capture in a single work the history of Jewish immigration to America and Israel from European pogroms early in the twentieth century, from Nazi-controlled countries in the midcentury period, and from the Soviet Union and Ethiopia toward the end of the century—undoubtedly the most complicated work about passage that she has attempted so far. Her organizational scheme presents a succession of episodic images in three parallel registers, all looking as if seen in a hazy dream, which in effect was the dream of all of those millions of immigrants over the generations who sought to arrive at a better place for themselves and their families. In an email of February 6, 2006, Weisberg provided the following outline (edited here):

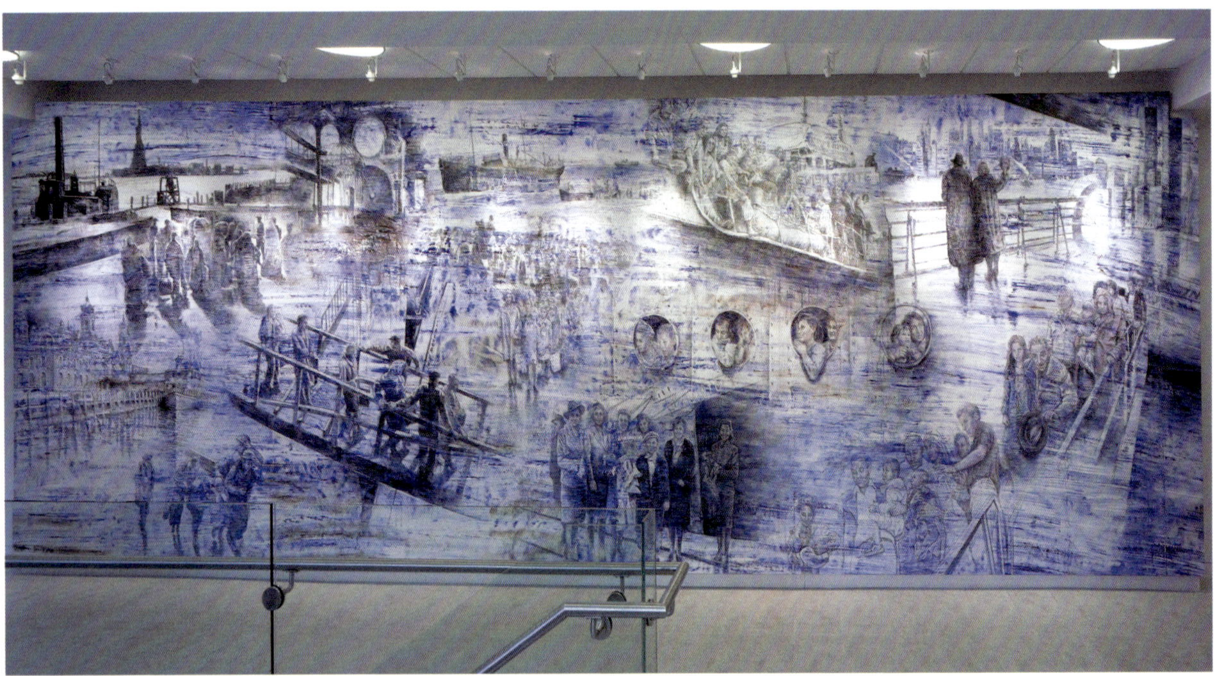

24. Ruth Weisberg, *New Beginnings: One Hundred Years of Jewish Immigration*, 2006. Mixed-media drawing, 114 in. × 29 ft. Collection of United Jewish Appeal of New York. Courtesy of the artist.

1. Starting in the upper left, a group of immigrants, ca. 1905, move toward a ferry landing. The Statue of Liberty appears in the distance.
2. To the right is the Essenweinstrasse Synagogue, Nuremberg, that was partially destroyed on Kristallnacht, November 8, 1938, the night when throughout Germany Jewish institutional buildings and private property were destroyed or vandalized and individuals attacked.
3. The images in the upper right are of a Jewish ship that evaded the British blockade of Jewish Palestine just after the Second World War. It is discharging passengers while a sympathetic crowd watches from the shore. A nearby ship has been renamed the *Jewish Star*.
4. The final image is a couple looking out at the New York skyline with the Twin Towers of the World Trade Center in the distance, a purposeful inclusion because the mural depicted Jewish immigration from 1900 to 2000, and what better way to indicate the year 2000 than still-intact Twin Towers!
5. In the second register, Ellis Island appears at the extreme left adjacent to a seemingly floating gang plank with people walking across. For Weisberg, this image is key to the entire mural because it suggests the liminal state of immigrants, having departed but not having arrived.
6. A series of four adjacent portholes framing children invokes the unfortunate history of the *St. Louis* in 1939, when, unable to discharge its passengers in free countries, it docked in Antwerp. A year later Germany invaded Belgium.
7. On the right, Soviet Jews on a jetway arrive in Israel.

8. On the lowest band at the far left, a group of immigrants head toward the Ellis Island ferry.
9. In the center, a group of immigrants disembark from the *Serpa Pinto*, the first ship to arrive in New York with legal immigrants after the Holocaust. It is another key image because it is the only group, together with the Ethiopians, seen just below, who are no longer between departure and arrival. The passengers have made a safe passage.
10. The image in the lower right refers to Operation Moses in 1985 that brought Ethiopian Jews to Israel.

Probably her single most joyous depiction of traveling to a better place, which also shows the conflating of past with present, is her drawing titled *The Parting of the Red Sea* (2002), among her illustrations for the Passover Haggadah *The Open Door* (Weisberg 2002 or *The Open Door* 2002, 60–61). It shows the moment when the Red Sea parted for the Israelites to escape the Egyptians. Jews are enjoined to relate the story of the Exodus every year, and participants at the seder in which the Haggadah is read are to imagine themselves, like the Israelites, fleeing from oppression and therefore to understand at a profound level the true meaning of freedom. Thus, in the drawing, the young and the old, their bodies transparent—as if we see them in a vision, as they were imagined by millions over the centuries—but dressed in contemporary clothing, pass both solemnly and thankfully into their future through the dramatically colored but nonthreatening parting waters.

Other illustrations in *The Open Door* show women and young girls participating in the preparations of the seder meal and the accompanying rituals. As in the text of this Haggadah, Weisberg favors the experiential and the personal as well as the desire to connect past and present history that emphasizes the ritual's eternal contemporaneity. By comparison, the Haggadahs illustrated by Ben Shahn and Leonard Baskin depict biblical scenes in an impersonal manner and stress patriarchal presences (Shahn 1965 or *The Haggadah for Passover* 1965; Baskin 1974 or *A Passover Haggadah* 1974). The three Haggadahs tell the same story, but the generational and gendered differences (a worthwhile comparative study in itself) between the illustrations by Shahn and Baskin and the illustrations by Weisberg are obvious and important to note in defining and assessing the overall mindset of the artists born in the years just before and after Weisberg.

# 5 Janet Shafner

In an email dated November 29, 2005, Janet Shafner (1931–2011) wrote that she was a "New York City kid" who lived in East Harlem until she was twenty years old. Her parents were leftist, Yiddish-speaking, nonreligious Russian immigrants, and she realized only later in life that "there was a long and profound intellectual history in Jewish life and culture." After becoming an observant Jew, she began to concentrate on painting biblical subject matter in the late 1980s as her way of "learning in the traditional sense of exploring the text to uncover esoteric and profound connections" (see also her autobiographical statement, Shafner 2003, 3). Her interest coincided with the nationwide stirrings of the growing Jewish art movement. As she noted in an email of April 25, 2007, "In the eighties when I began my paintings, inspired by *Tanach* [the first five books of the Bible, the works of the prophets, and the Writings], I felt like I was a lone voice. Now, I read about Jews everywhere exploring what it means to be Jewish and to do art that circles their tradition."

In her readings, she, like other artists, found many parallels between present-day activities and those recorded in the ancient texts. Or if she could not find an exact parallel, she could use an ancient story to comment on a current situation. As a result, Shafner invited her viewers to ponder the relevance of the Bible to contemporary life, to find in it not just religious messages or an ancient history that did not seem to relate to modern living but rather how the ancients handled similar kinds of ethical, moral, and social issues. Like other students of biblical history, she found in the private and public lives of biblical and contemporary individuals similarities often despicable and cruel in their application. In effect, human nature had hardly changed or evolved beyond the unscrupulous, the unethical, and the immoral (Shafner 2003, 3). It is evident that despite her own very positive view of life, to which everybody who knew her will attest, she did not hold out much hope for humanity.

Whereas Ruth Weisberg presented issues for thought and discussion in *Sisters and Brothers* (figs. 21 and 22), Shafner offered her own conclusions in her paintings. This assessment is borne out by several of her works based on the Bible. To be sure, there were triumphs by event-making women such as Queen Esther and Ruth, but there were also a significant number of setbacks and victims, such as Tamar, the daughter of King David, and the Concubine of Gibeah, not to mention Adam and Eve, who were banished from the Garden of Eden.

Shafner might very well have agreed with Rabbi Neil Gillman's assessment that "Judaism is pervaded by a basic confidence in our human ability to do the right thing . . . , [that] in no way is the evil outcome predetermined by the fact of our humanness, by our intrinsic

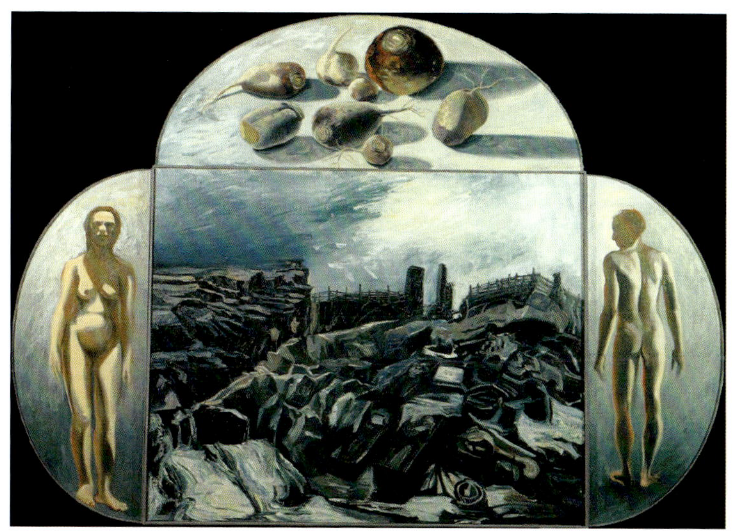

25. Janet Shafner, *Adam and Eve: Entropy*, 1990. Oil on canvas and wood, 60 × 84 in. From the website janetshafner.com.

character" (1990, 46), but perhaps as a result of reading about so much mayhem and murder in the Bible and having lived through so many extraordinarily senseless acts of murder, violence, and destruction, especially in Europe, during her lifetime, she might have wondered if humanity could ever redeem itself, a thought that found expression in her art.

In her more positive works, Shafner did add a redeeming feature that attests to her desire to know as much as possible about the subject she was then working on. As she wrote in her autobiographical statement about her turn to Jewish subject matter, "I began to read commentaries and associated texts such as *midrash*, which explores the inner meaning of the Hebrew writings" (2003, 3). She amended this statement in an email of November 17, 2005: "By linking contemporary social and political issues with related narratives in the traditional Jewish writings, or by juxtaposing multiple images from the biblical and *midrashic* events, the layers of meaning of these paintings are visually and intellectually deepened."

One wonders, then, what might have prompted Shafner to create two paintings about Adam and Eve: *Adam and Eve: Entropy* (1990) (fig. 25) and *Adam and Eve: The Sparks* (1999) (fig. 26), with the latter being one of a group of three paintings about the first biblical family. In the earlier painting, composed of somber mustard yellows, browns, blues, and blacks, Adam is seen walking away from the viewer and Eve walking toward the viewer. They are not connecting with each other. They are also unclothed, indicating that they have not yet eaten the forbidden fruit. They flank a scene of entropy in which once-inhabited spaces have fallen into a state of ruin that approaches complete inertia, a permanent condition.

The arched lunette at the top of *Adam and Eve: Entropy*, a unit Shafner often added to her paintings to suggest further meaning or a possible softening of the apparent message of the central panel or a note of possible redemption, is composed of turnips. Shafner added this particular vegetable because Holocaust survivors found only turnips to eat when they returned to their hometowns. It symbolized for her "our eternal hope for the continuation of life on earth after the destruction—both man-made and God-made—which began with Adam and Eve" (Shafner 2003, 82). This is a heavy weight and responsibility for turnips to bear, and one doubts if they portend an optimistic outcome in the face of so many millennia of destruction, disillusion, and disappointment dating back to the first biblical family.

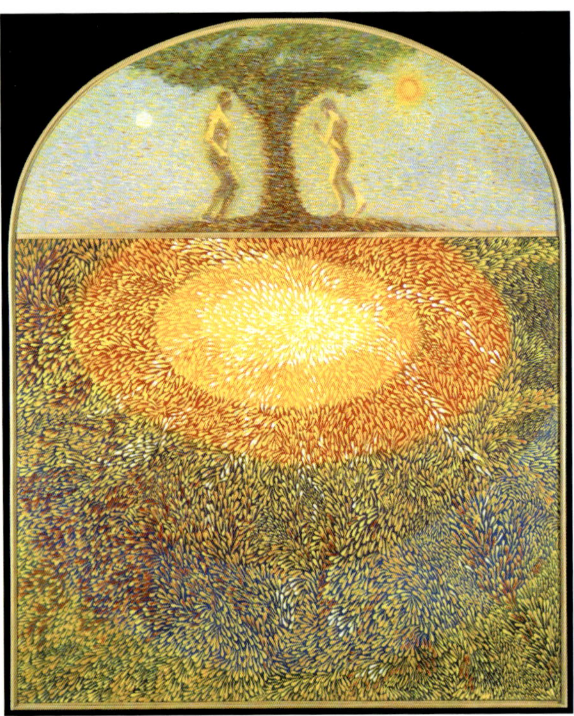

26. Janet Shafner, *Adam and Eve: The Sparks*, 1999. Oil on canvas, 58 × 50 in. From the website janetshafner.com.

In *Adam and Eve: The Sparks*, Shafner combines brilliantly in a single painting the first inkling of trouble in the Garden of Eden with the initial rupture and fracture of Creation. The couple appears in the lunette flanked by the sun and the moon. Between them stands, presumably, the Tree of Knowledge of Good and Evil. They are forbidden to eat its fruit, but the figure on the right—possibly bearded, so it must be Adam—holds the fruit that he will eat.

There is trouble ahead. This is suggested in the large area below Adam and Eve, which is composed of hundreds of brightly colored brushstrokes. These brushstrokes represent both the creation of the world and the introduction of evil into it, illustrating Rabbi Isaac Luria's (1534–72) belief that during the Creation the Divine Light was so intense that it broke the vessels that held it (Scholem [1941] 1961, 244–86). The shattered vessels allowed sparks of light to descend into the human world, creating the existence of evil—the moment we see in the painting—which, according to Rabbi Luria, prevents the coming of the Messiah until all of the sparks are scooped up and returned to the vessels by good deeds and acts of human kindness.

None of this bodes well for Adam and Eve. Who ultimately is to blame? According to Gershom Scholem, it is poor Adam. "If Adam had not sinned [by taking the apple], the world would have entered the Messianic state on the first Sabbath after creation with no historical process whatever. Adam's sin returned the universe . . . to its former broken state. What happened at the breaking of the vessels happened again" (1971a, 46). As Shafner described this process, "Man, created in the image of God, has been given the mission of the spiritual repair of the world by gathering these sparks and elevating them to their source by acts of goodness" (2003, 10). (This is the meaning of *tikkun olam*, mentioned in the introduction.)

By combining the biblical story of the eating the apple with a kabbalist interpretation of the Creation, the shattering of the vessels, Shafner locates Adam and Eve as actors in a cosmic scheme of creation, acquisition of knowledge, introduction of evil, and the remote possibility of redemption—all in a single painting.

The questions remain: Will it be possible to return into the vessels all of those sparks Shafner painted? Can humans do enough good deeds to control the desire to commit evil and therefore to contemplate the ultimate arrival of the Messiah and the granting of eternal life (*The Torah: A Modern Commentary* 1981, 38–40)? Probably not. Shafner's message, then, is a grim one despite the painting's bright, sparkling colors. This line of thought is continued in her series of four paintings titled *The Divine Ecology* (2003–4). The paintings are shown on her website (janetshafner.com), each with a description: *The Tree of Knowledge*, focusing on the tree that brought free will and suffering to humankind; *The Tree of Life*, focusing on the tree that would provide eternal life but is surrounded by the Tree of Knowledge; *The Four Rivers*, illustrating a topic described in Genesis 2:10–14; and *The End of Paradise*, showing the sealing of Adam and Eve's and, by extension, our own fate. This latter painting, a bright eggshell-like form surrounded by spiky red lines extending out over a blue field and thus suggesting streams of fire, provides a last look at the receding Garden of Eden. Shafner includes the following midrash as a challenge:

> When God created the First Human Beings, God led them around the Garden of Eden and said, "Look at my works! See how beautiful they are. How excellent for your sake I created them all. See to it that you do not spoil and destroy my world. For if you do, there will be no one else to repair it." (*Midrash Ecclesiastes Rabbah* 7:13)

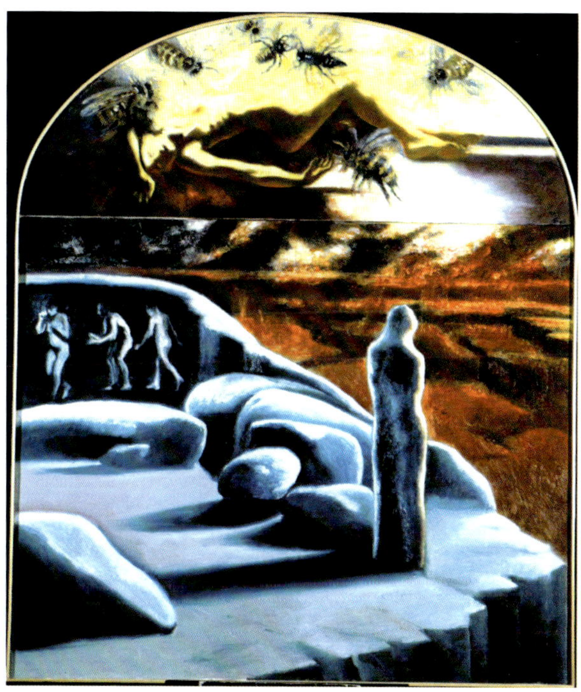

27. Janet Shafner, *Lot's Wife*, 1996. Oil on canvas, 58 × 50 in. From the website janetshafner.com.

In the years before Shafner completed this painting, she created at least four that commented negatively on the choices that humans might make: *Lot's Wife* (1996) (fig. 27) and three paintings titled *The Concubine of Gibeah* (1998–99) (fig. 28 is the second one). Lot's wife self-destructs, and the concubine is murdered.

The story of Lot and his wife is told in Genesis 19. The wife is nameless in the biblical account but is also known as Idit in legend (Ginzberg [1909–38] 1917–87, 5:241 n. 180; Hammer 2001, 253). Lot invites two angels or messengers into his home in Sodom. They tell Lot to leave because the city will be destroyed. He departs with his wife and their two unmarried daughters. They are instructed not to look back or stop (Genesis 19:17), but Lot's wife nevertheless looks back (19:26) and is turned into a pillar of salt. No explanation is given, but at least one legend has filled in the story: "Her motherlove made her look behind to see if her married daughters were following. She beheld the Shekinah [God's earthly manifestation] and she became a pillar of salt" (Ginzberg [1909–38] 1917–87, 1:255), the moment Shafner portrays in her painting.

In the background, the naked Lot is in a cave with his two unmarried daughters, where they will seduce their father (Genesis 19:33–38). The lunette, showing a young woman stung to death by bees, recounts an event that occurs in the town of Admah inhabited by individuals as vicious as those who live in Sodom (Ginzberg [1909–38] 1917–87, 1:250; Shafner cites the *Babylonian Talmud, Tractate Sanhedrin 109b:7* as her source [Shafner 2003, 30]). A young woman is condemned to death for giving a stranger water and bread. Smeared with honey by townspeople, she is attacked by bees and stung to death. It is this event that prompts God to destroy Sodom.

The murder of the concubine of Gibeah, one of the most sordid episodes in the Bible, is just as grisly. She is raped and dismembered (Judges 19), as illustrated in *The Concubine of Gibeah 2* (fig. 28), a night-time vision scene.

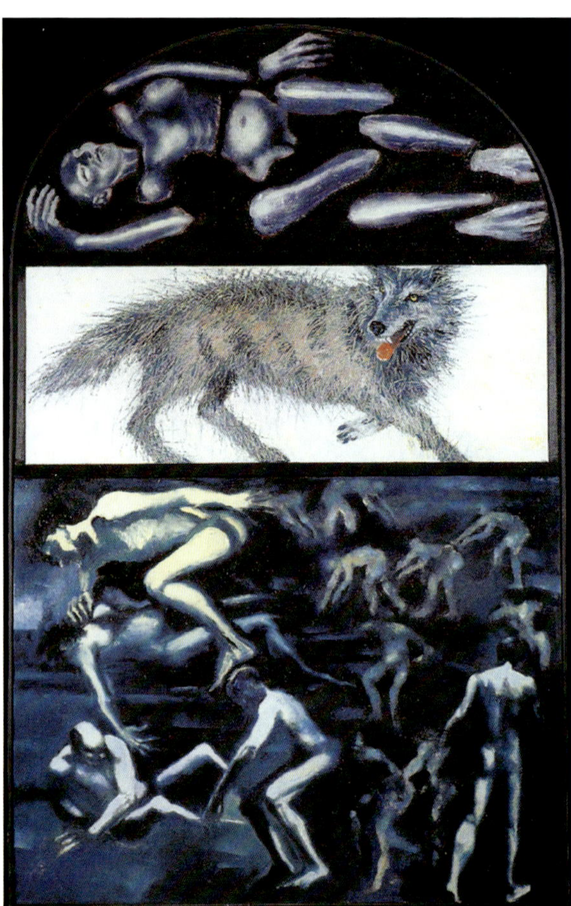

28. Janet Shafner, *The Concubine of Gibeah 2*, 1998–99. Oil on wood and canvas, 63 × 40 in. From the website janetshafner.com.

The concubine/wife of a Levite from the hill country of Ephraim abandons her husband and returns to her father's house in Bethlehem in Judah. After her husband reclaims her, they pass the night in Gibeah, which is in territory controlled by the Benjaminites. During the evening, the wife is gang raped and dies. The following morning the husband returns to his home with his deceased wife. He then cuts up her body into twelve pieces and sends one piece to each of the tribes of Israel. Seeking revenge, the tribes make war on the Benjaminites. Thousands of lives are lost, and the patriarchal tagline for the entire sordid episode is basically a shrug of the shoulders: "In those days there was no king in Israel, everyone did as he pleased" (Judges 21:25). Richard McBee describes this state of affairs more elegantly: "Irresponsible passions lead to unspeakable crime and retributions escalate into anarchy" (2003). Shafner remarked in a conversation that she painted this work after reading about the great numbers of women who were raped during the Serbian–Bosnian war between 1992 and 1995.

In the lower part of the painting, Shafner envisions the rape scene. The cut-up body lies in pieces in the lunette. In the intermediate zone, a wolf prowls across the picture's surface, referencing Jacob's prophetic vision at the time of his death concerning the warlike temperament of his son Benjamin and his descendants: "Benjamin is a ravenous wolf. In the morning he consumes the foe, and in the evening he divides the spoil" (Genesis 49:27).

Women fare much better in other works by Shafner. They include Esther, Ruth, and the daughters of Zelophehad. The Scroll (or Book) of Esther tells the story of Haman's plan to destroy the Jewish population of Persia. Mordechai alerts Queen Esther, his relative, who then intervenes with King Ahasuerus. Haman's plot is discovered, he is killed, and the Jews survive. For *Esther and Mordechai* (2002) (fig. 29), Shafner's immediate point of departure is the opening words of chapter 4, verse 1, of the Scroll of Esther, when Mordechai notifies Esther of Haman's intentions: "Do not imagine that you, of all the Jews, will escape with your life by being in the king's palace" (4:13). She says that she will try to see the king, although, if he does not agree to an audience, the visitor (even if it is Esther) might be killed. And at this moment, she becomes an event maker in Jewish history because of her response to Mordechai. "If I am to perish, I shall perish!" (4:16). She does not perish, and in the subsequent chain of events she has initiated, she saves the Jews from annihilation.

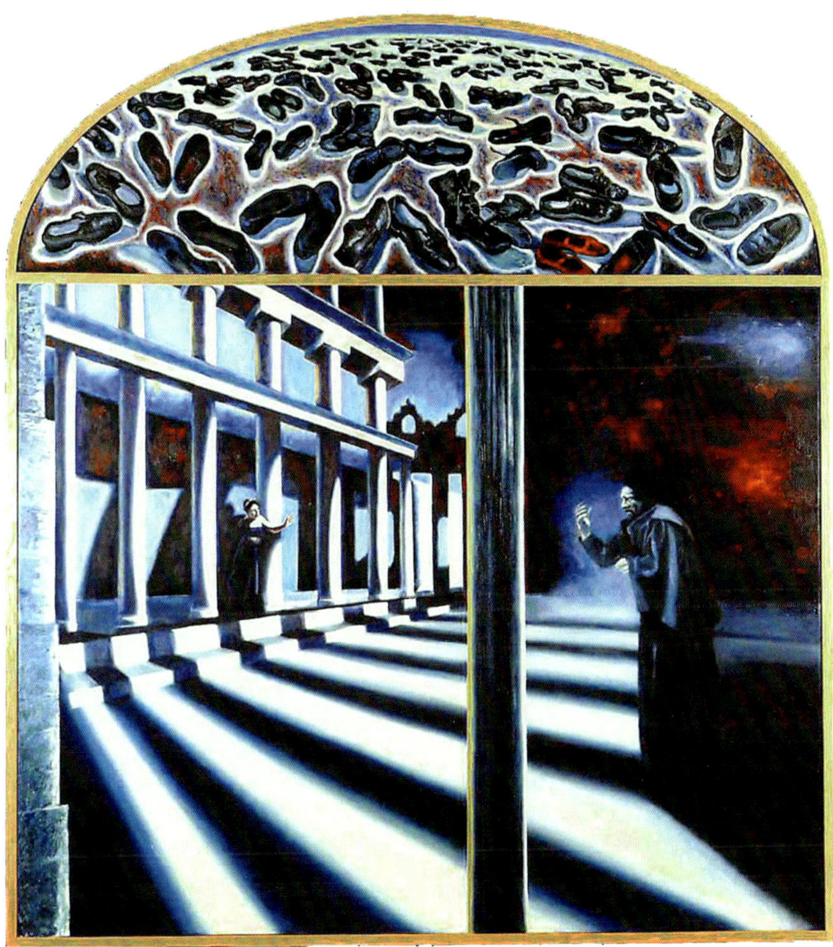

29. Janet Shafner, *Esther and Mordechai*, 2002. Oil on canvas, 66 × 59 in. Collection of the Bernard Heller Museum at Hebrew Union College–Jewish Institute of Religion, New York. From the website janetshafner.com.

Shafner took a few liberties with the text. She placed a column between Esther and Mordechai to indicate their different positions in society. She also eliminated the intermediary mentioned in the biblical text who carries messages back and forth. In an email of June 14, 2006, Shafner wrote that she placed Mordechai in a dark space surrounded by sparks of red, green, and blue to suggest a sacred moment. She also set the scene at night, perhaps aware of the observation made by one commentator, who, basing her remarks on a midrash and a passage in the Talmud (Yoma 29a:3), connected Esther's name to the darkest hour of night, the hour before dawn (Ronson 1999, 337). The name "Esther" means "hidden one," and Esther remains hidden, as it were, until the light is needed. In this instance, she changes the course of events and saves the Jewish people from the planned genocide.

In the email of June 14 and in another one dated July 23, 2006, Shafner explained the seemingly infinite landscape of shoes in the lunette. Abandoned shoes meant to her stasis, that people cannot move, escape, or control events. This suggests that such events have overtaken the shoes' former wearers. Abandoned shoes also suggest "the abrupt ending of the journey of life," an obvious reference to the piles of shoes exhibited at Auschwitz and at the United States Holocaust Museum in Washington, DC, taken from the Jews systematically murdered in the concentration and death camps during the Second World War. In

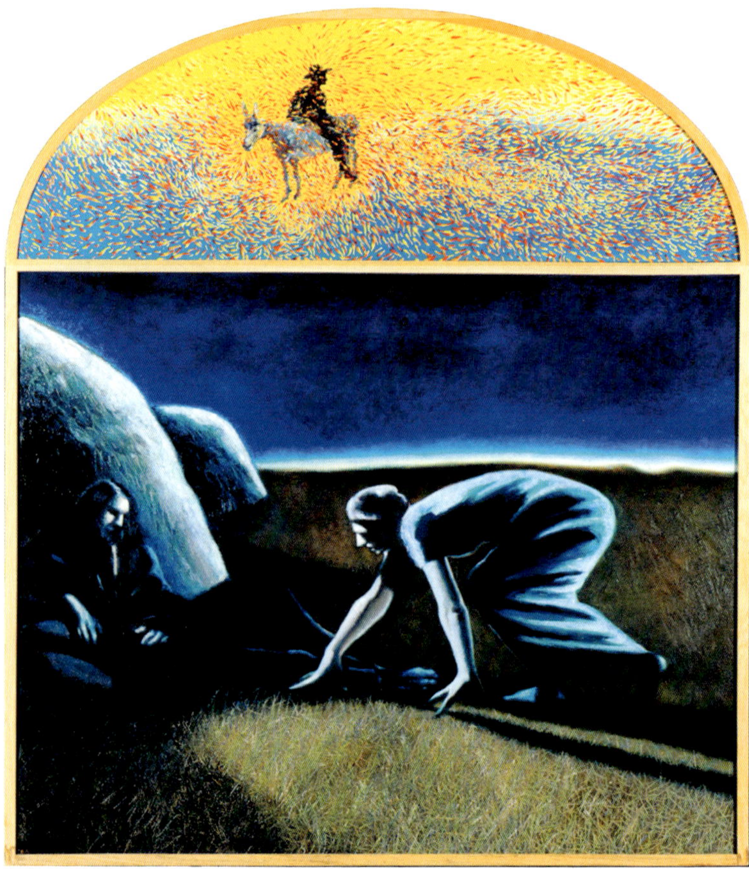

30. Janet Shafner, *Ruth and Boaz*, 1999. Oil on canvas and wood, 50 × 50 in. Collection of the Bernard Heller Museum at Hebrew Union College–Jewish Institute of Religion, New York. From the website janetshafner.com.

effect, in *Esther and Mordechai* Shafner intimates that there were not enough Esthers in the 1940s to save the Jews.

There are at least two different lessons to be learned from studying the biblical account of Esther's actions, both of them applicable to contemporary life. First, do not remain passive in the face of danger or evil, or, in the anti-Semitic context here, use whatever means are available to counter it. And, second, with Esther's actions in mind, through careful personal diplomacy remain loyal to one's heritage and manage to lead a fulfilling life by understanding one's own vulnerabilities as well as the limits and possibilities of living in exile (Laniak 1998, 6, 90).

Esther saves a people. Ruth, through divine intentions, perpetuates a dynasty of kings that includes David and Solomon and the future Messiah. For her painting *Ruth and Boaz* (1999) (fig. 30), Shafner selected the pivotal moment in the Book of Ruth, the moment when Ruth, taking the initiative, also becomes an event-making woman:

> She went down to the threshing floor and did just as her mother-in-law [Naomi] had instructed her. . . . She went over stealthily and uncovered his [Boaz's] feet and lay down. In the middle of the night, the man gave a start and pulled back—there was a woman lying at his feet. "Who are you?" he asked. And she replied, "I am your handmaid Ruth. Spread your robe over your handmaid, for you are a redeeming kinsman." (3:6–9)

For both those concerned with the destiny of the Israelites and those attentive to feminist interests, *Ruth and Boaz* is a major painting. Naomi lives in Moab with her two widowed daughters-in-law, Orpah and Ruth. When Naomi returns to Bethlehem, Ruth accompanies her. Normally, one of the dead husband's brothers would marry his widowed sister-in-law, but in this instance there are no such brothers. Boaz, a kinsman but not an in-law, is not obligated to marry a widowed relative. Ruth, however, reminds Boaz that he is a kinsman, and Boaz, being a kind man, ultimately marries Ruth. They have a child, Obed, who fathers Jesse, the father of David, the paternal line that will ultimately lead to the Messiah. Naomi takes Obed as her own child, and Ruth disappears from the Bible, having fulfilled her procreative role by providing a son.

According to legend, Boaz is an octogenarian and Ruth forty years old at the time of their wedding (Ginzberg [1909–38] 1917–87, 4:34). One scholar notes that Ruth, a smart and clever person, has become acquainted with the Israelites' religious laws and social customs even though she is not one, learns about the tradition of responsibility by kinsmen, and thus finds in Boaz her mate (Aschkenasy 1998, 151–56). In the lunette of Shafner's painting, the Messiah appears as described in Zechariah 9:9: "Rejoice greatly, Fair Zion; Raise a shout, Fair Jerusalem! Lo, your king is coming to you. He is victorious, triumphant, yet humble, riding on an ass." Shafner surrounds the figure with the divine light of Creation (Shafner 2003, 48).

By seeking out Boaz, Ruth enlarges the meaning of kinsmen's responsibilities and as a result alters a tradition. So, too, do the daughters of Zelophehad, who successfully challenge the custom according to which only male children inherit a father's estate (Numbers 27:1–8). According to one scholar, the daughters' actions can be considered the most relevant story in the Bible about gender equality (Hammer 2001, 272; see also Ronson 1999, 233–37). In *Daughters of Zelophehad* (2006) (fig. 31), Shafner honors all five daughters: Mahlah, Noah, Hoglah, Milcah, and Tirzah (Numbers 26:33). Having no brothers who would normally inherit their father's estate, they petition Moses, who does not know what to do, so he asks God, who says that he "should give them an hereditary holding among their father's kinsmen; transfer their father's share to them" (27:7). But they "may marry anyone they wish, provided they marry into a clan of their father's tribe" in order to keep the ancestral portion for the tribe. They marry cousins (36:6–8, 10). According to legend, God says: "The daughters of Zelophehad have the law on their side, for what they desire is in accordance with the law that was written in heaven by Me" (Ginzberg [1909–38] 1917–87, 3:394).

In an email of June 25, 2006, Shafner noted that even though the Israelites were still in the desert and the land had not yet been divided, the daughters' desire to share in it signaled their faith in Israel's eventual possession of its promised land. But her inclusion of the wall in the upper left of the painting, which encloses parts of modern Israel, raises the politically sensitive question of just where boundaries might ultimately be drawn for that nation.

Whatever the medium, artists have also painted self-portraits either as stand-alones or as part of a particular work that might be secular or religious in nature. Late in life, Shafner included a self-portrait in a work based on both the Bible and the legends: *The Assumption of Serach bat Asher* (2010) (fig. 32). It is one of Shafner's most heartfelt paintings. The seated figure is a self-portrait. Serach (also Serah) is mentioned only once in the Bible and then only in passing as a child of Asher (Chronicles 7:30). But in the legends she plays a central role in telling Jacob that his son Joseph is alive (Ginzberg [1909–38] 1917–87, 2:115–16). Jacob's sons are afraid to tell their father the good news. They ask Serach to play the harp while singing to Jacob that Joseph is alive. Jacob is so elated that he prophesies: "My daughter, may death

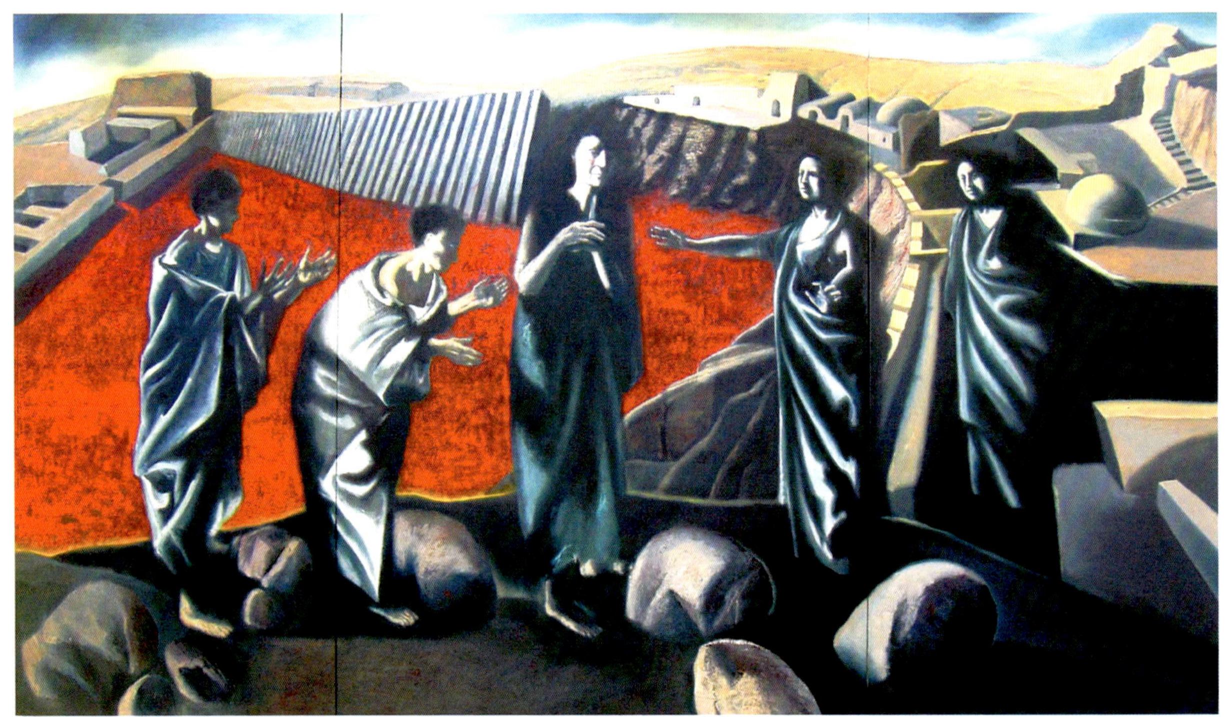

31. Janet Shafner, *Daughters of Zelophehad*, 2006. Oil on canvas, 48 × 84 in., three panels. From the website janetshafner.com.

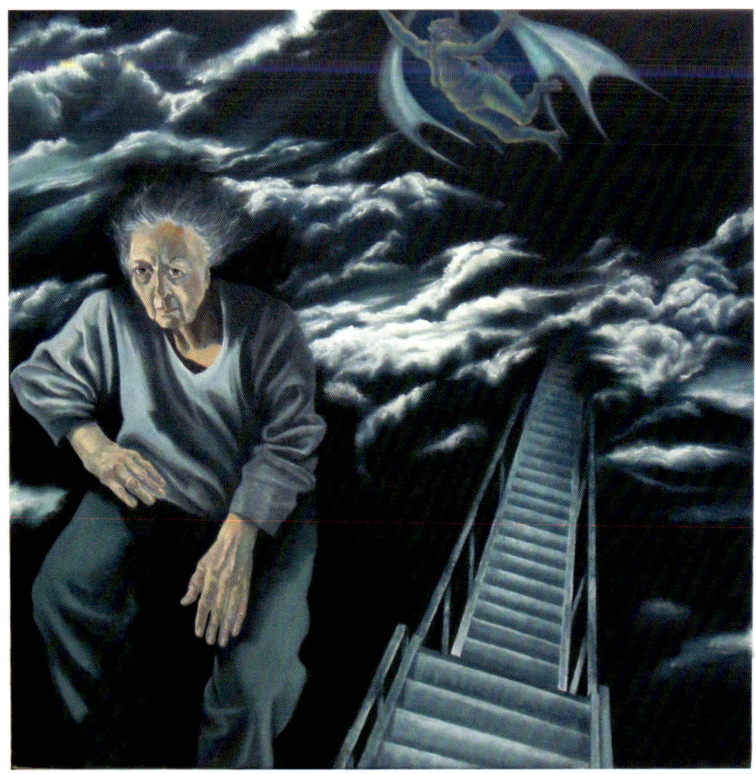

32. Janet Shafner, *The Assumption of Serach bat Asher*, 2010. Oil on canvas, 50 × 50 in. From the website janetshafner.com.

never have power over thee, for thou didst revive my spirit." His prophesy comes true, for she does not die but enters paradise alive. (See also Ginsberg [1909–38] 1917–87, 5:96, 165, 369.) And when the Israelites decamp from Egypt, only Serach knows where Joseph, who wanted to be interred in the Holy Land, is buried. His coffin is carried through the forty years of wandering in the desert.

In the painting, Shafner shows herself contemplating Serach's assumption to paradise. The strong physical presence of the ladder that binds Shafner to this world is no match for the wings that carry Serach to paradise. In the self-portrait, one of the great self-portraits of our time, Shafner stares with an inquisitiveness and intensity that reveals no fear of what can only be the abyss.

Paintings such as this one can seemingly sum up an entire career. The subject is biblical/secular and seen through a feminist lens. This self-portrait is not a matter of painting what is seen in a mirror but of linking the artist to an ancient and still vital community. Shafner knew that in the annual prayer that would commemorate the day she passes, she would be remembered in the traditional ceremony, and perhaps her spirit, like Serach, would enter paradise—thoughts that provide comfort and solace. Such thoughts lead to the notion that all of the artists mentioned here create works as much for the present moment as for memorializing and linking themselves to generations past. As suggested in the introduction, these artists stress continuity, not rupture. But more than that, Shafner must have identified herself with Serach because her paintings invoke Jewish memory and hopes just as Serach carries in her memory the Israelite sojourn in Egypt, the arrival in the Promised Land, and, ultimately, entry into paradise.

# 6 Siona Benjamin

Siona Benjamin (b. 1960) is an anomaly. She was not born in America or in eastern Europe but in Mumbai and therefore has a different relationship to the United States than artists of earlier generations as well as those of her own generation. Unlike the older artists, she was not part of a massive immigration in which individuals, despite the dislocations of arriving in a strange country, could find comfort and familiarity among those with whom they shared a common religious and social culture. Coming to America alone as a college-age student who grew up within Indian culture, Benjamin still finds America, even decades later, after raising a family, to be a foreign country—considerably less foreign than when she first arrived but still measurably strange to her in various ways. She often says that she occupies a not uncomfortable liminal space that is no longer Indian but not yet American. She chooses to identify herself as an artist, a Jewish woman of color, and a feminist—and also in her own way as an American.

Her story is an interesting one, but the fact that she is very open about her identities speaks to an important moment in Jewish American art history. Within the broad context of the relationship of Jewish artists to the America of the late twentieth century, she has been able to articulate her sense of difference in ways unknown and impossible for artists of earlier generations. It is worthwhile noting that, first, unlike those who decades ago preferred to remain within the parameters of their religion and cultural heritage and, second, unlike those who chose to ignore their religion and heritage in order to reinvent themselves as Americans and, third, unlike those who exhibited levels of anxiety about acknowledging their religious background, she has stated in a very open, thoughtful, nonadversarial, and nondefensive manner where she comes from, the importance of her Indian and Jewish heritages, and how she has combined past experiences with present encounters. As a result, she has set herself apart without any sense of apprehension or embarrassment from both the American mainstream and Jewish artists whose backgrounds are eastern European. There is no compunction to avoid or totally embrace or feel hesitant about explaining who she is and how she represents herself through her art.

Such an attitude could not have been assumed so blithely and easily and, most important, so honestly before the last decades of the twentieth century. For example, in the years during and after the First World War, one was either 100 percent American or 100 percent something else (Hegman 1999, 52–57; Higham 1984, 165, 175; Ribuffo 1983, 9). And in the years after the Second World War, Jews were reminded to keep a low profile about their Jewishness. The philosopher Sidney Hook thought the best advice for Jews was to lead dignified, respectable lives and contribute to a democratic, secular, albeit diverse American culture rather than to flaunt their religion or heritage (1949, 468, 480). The art critic Harold Rosenberg was aware of the issue of choice, of the necessity to be "a single thing" rather than a "hyphenated thing." "Isn't it the . . . modern impulse," he noted, "to be one who is one-hundred percent something that makes Jews so uncomfortable when they debate whether one can be both an American and a Jew? In comparison with apparently single identification of others, being twice identified seems embarrassingly ambiguous." Rosenberg was further puzzled not by "any actual, greater singleness among non-Jewish Americans than among Jews, but the prevalent *ideology* of total choice with its exclusion of the *possibility* of being anything else" (1950, 510, emphasis in original).

Among Benjamin's various typed statements and taped interviews, here is one from 2004 in which she provided an answer to a hypothetical question about her relation to mainstream artists:

> I feel both a connection and a disconnection. It's like sitting on top of a fence. Sometimes it feels safe to fit into a compartment and fall either way from the fence, but then I am reminded that although precarious, this position gives me a wider perspective on being able to see both sides. I feel there is a strong transcultural movement now more than ever and this will only get stronger. America is a country of immigrants and I feel that this diversity is our strength. Sometimes I share my art world with the rising group of South Asian–American artists and sometimes with diasporic Jewish artists, both groups feeding the core of my being. I am also solidly an American artist. As to the environment in which I have lived since 1984, it inspires me.

Born into an observant Bene Israel family in Mumbai (her given name, "Siona," translates as "Zion"), she attended Zoroastrian and Catholic schools and grew up with Hindu and Muslim friends. Anti-Semitism was never a problem, and familiarity with other religions, their rituals and myths, was quite common among the Indian Jews where she lived. She came to America to attend graduate school, eventually receiving a master of fine arts degree from Southern Illinois University in 1989 and another from the University of Illinois in 1993, where she majored in theater set design.

She initially worked in abstract modes, and when she turned to representational forms, she realized that her figures, especially their faces, were dark and indistinct. Told by her instructors that she should emulate nonethnic Western rather than Indian art and that she should paint large-scale figures, she needed time to think through the kind of imagery that made sense to her—the hidden faces evidently symbolizing her confusion about her identity as an Indian, a woman, and an artist living in a foreign country. Who wouldn't be confused? To an Indian, Westerners seemed ethnic others. And where is it written that one should paint large-scale figures, swinging a brush from the elbow or shoulder, as it were, rather than bending a wrist or fingers? She decided to work on a small scale and to find inspiration within her Indian and Jewish heritages.

By the mid-1990s, she had combined into a recognizably personal style features of Indian and Persian miniatures and obvious references to comic books, Bollywood, memories of ornate synagogues of her youth, and the illustrations of the Polish Jewish American illustrator Arthur Szyk (1894–1951). Elements of pop art began to appear in her work around 2005. In terms of subject matter, she combines even obvious contemporary American references with mythic and religious images of Indian deities. She usually paints figures blue, a color with which she identifies for a variety of reasons. For Benjamin, "being blue is a symbol of being other" (qtd. in Anand 2018). She also thinks of blue as a universal color insofar as the oceans and the sky are blue. The god Krishna is usually painted blue. This color, then, suggests universality, tolerance, diversity, worldly and unworldly presences, and, perhaps most importantly, transcultural beingness ("Elizbeth Greenberg" 2016, 39). This meaning is of some consequence: adding various forms and figures (biblical, Hindu, mythic, personal) to a work gives a transnational presence to an anecdotal account of a specific scene.

Her first important series, *Finding Home*, dating from the late 1990s, is at the root of her subsequent work, focusing on the constant search for and reflection on where one's home is and how it can be found and defined. The series initially contained primarily American and Indian references. A representative work, *Finding Home #9* (1998), shows the Statue of Liberty standing on a flattened lotus leaf carrying in her six arms a suitcase, a guitar, a small private house, a menorah, a twirling toy, and a tablet inscribed with the Hebrew letters that spell "life." (Most of the paintings in the *Finding Home* series are shown at the website Art of Siona Benjamin, at https://artsiona.com/paintings/finding-home-2/. See also J. Goldman 2003; Orenstein 2000; Soltes 2016, 9.)

Benjamin began to read Jewish and feminist literature around 2000 after moving to Montclair, New Jersey, home to many Jewish people, and began a program of study with a local rabbi, ultimately seeking further study at the Jewish Theological Seminary in New York. She discovered that she was especially attracted to midrashic stories, legendary tales about individuals and events found in the Bible that evoked memories of the many mythic Hindu and Muslim tales she had heard in India. Although, as she has said, she is Jewish to the core, she also treats these stories with the same valence and provides them with universal meaning as they bear on her thoughts about contemporary events. She considers the stories as mythological tales that can be brought up to date and applied to present-day situations. In that sense, she views herself as a contemporary artist who finds in past tales contemporary application.

In the early 2000s, she began to identify with outsider women such as Lilith, Adam's first wife in legend; Asnat, Joseph's Egyptian wife; and Hagar, mother of Ishmael, the progenitor of the Arab peoples. By 2004, these and other figures began to appear in her paintings in a series titled *Finding Home (Fereshteh)* (*fereshteh* means "angels" in Urdu). In a typed statement dated 2004 about the *Fereshteh* series, Benjamin explained her intentions. She wanted to explore "women of the Bible and bring them forward to combat wars and the violence of today" in what she termed "a *midrash* of intricate paintings." Her intention was to create a dialogue in the viewer's mind between ancient and modern events and experiences in order to confront unresolved issues. The figures in each painting "become characters that act out their parts, recording, balancing, rectifying, restoring, and absorbing." She felt that through these works she "[could] dip into [her] personal specifics and universalize, thus playing the role of artist/activist." Certainly an amalgamation of her various cultural heritages, these works also have the concept of *tikkun olam* at their heart—they contribute to the repair of the world, in her mind as good a justification for creating paintings as there is. By projecting positive acceptance and integration of her exotic background in her paintings, she hoped that their viewers would "transcend this apparent exoticness and absorb the core message—tolerance of diversity."

One should not expect in Benjamin's works, therefore, literal translations of biblical texts into traditional images but rather should view the texts as departures for her thought-provoking observations of contemporary events

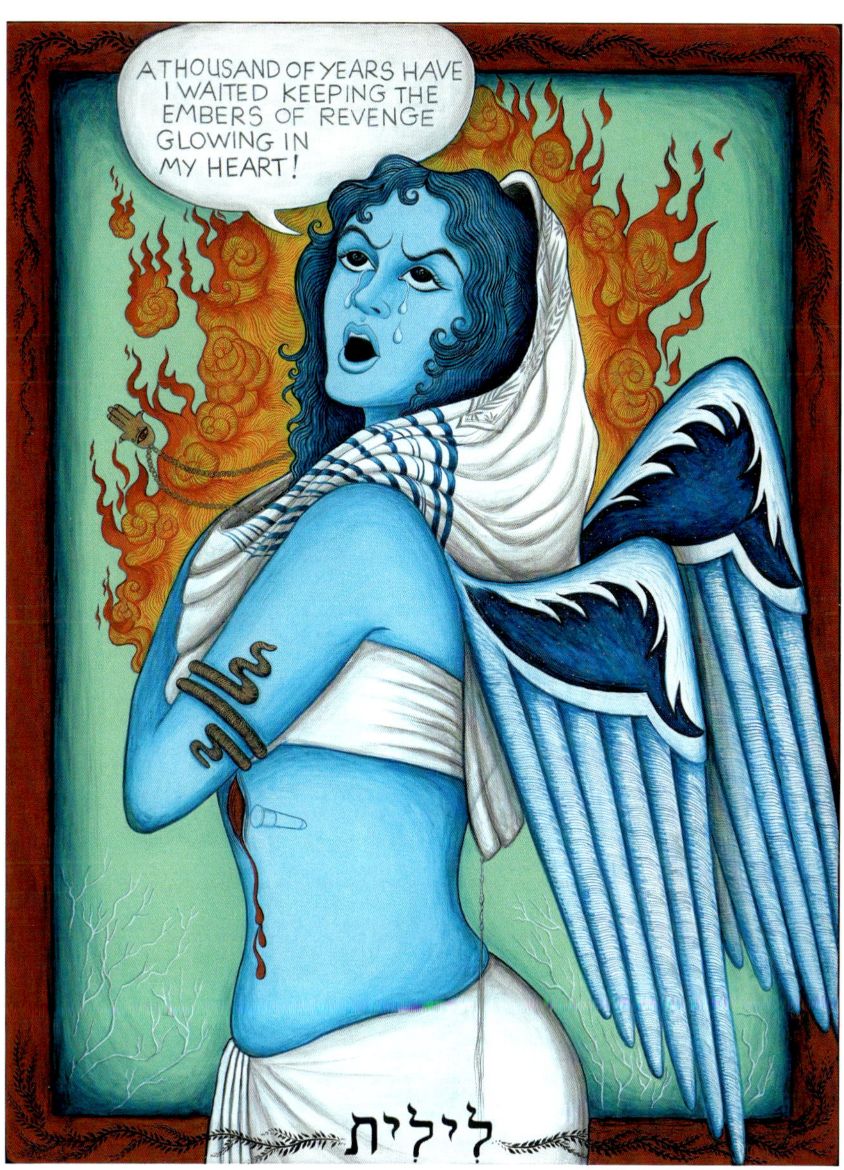


33. Siona Benjamin, *Finding Home #74 (Fereshteh) "Lilith,"* 2006. Gouache on wood panel, 30 × 24 in. Private collection. Courtesy of the artist and ACA Galleries, New York, www.artsiona.com.

and the strengths, weaknesses, and successes of women. Benjamin also comments on men's patriarchic attitudes. For example, in Indian mythology the concept of Ardhanarishvara is one in which a character can be half-man and half-woman, whose strength is then projected through female figures.

The most powerful figure in Jewish legend is a woman, Lilith, who appears *only* in legend and is especially popular among feminists. But knowing Indian legends, Benjamin also views Lilith in androgynous terms. She has created a subset of paintings about Lilith within the *Fereshteh* series, dating from 2005 to 2010. One of the most memorable is *Finding Home #74 (Fereshteh) "Lilith"* (2006) (fig. 33).

Lilith, with a capital L, is not mentioned in Isaiah 34:14, but rather "lilith," with a lowercase *l*, is included as a kind of demon. In our own day, feminists consider her a model and have named a journal after her. In the many stories associated with her, she is Adam's first wife, created like him from dust rather than from his body and therefore his equal (Ginzberg [1909–38] 1917–87, 1:65–66, 2:233, 3:87, 5:148; Hammer 2001, 448–50; Patai

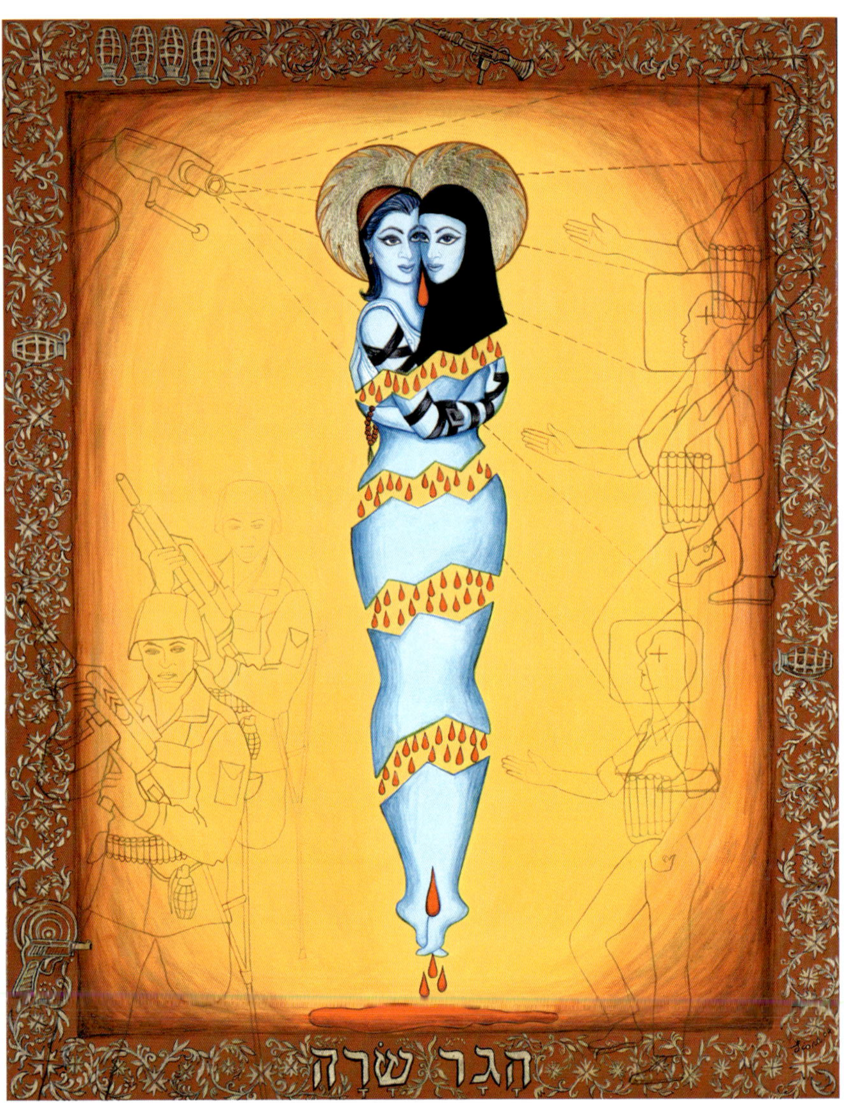


34. Siona Benjamin, *Finding Home #61 (Fereshteh) "Beloved,"* 2003. Gouache and gold on paper, 20 × 16 in. 2012.1.34, Donald Rothfeld Collection of Contemporary Israeli Art, American University Museum. Courtesy of the artist and ACA Galleries, New York, www.artsiona.com.

[1967] 1990, 246–69). She will not accept a secondary role, and because she angers God by calling him by name, she is banished from Eden. In addition, she becomes a mother who loses hundreds of her own children and is considered a menace to other children. She is also supposed to seduce and kill single men and to be potentially harmful to mothers.

Benjamin presents Lilith in this painting as a woman bent on revenge. She also represents several religions, symbolized by the tallith that covers her head (Jewish), the snake armband (Hindu), the *hamsa* amulet (Muslim), and the bullet wound suggesting stigmata (Christian). Benjamin, despite considering Lilith a sacrificing mother, war widow, woman soldier, and rape victim, presents her as a strong woman facing down her opponents and detractors—a survivor and a heroine.

Other paintings in the *Fereshteh* series are unusual if not unprecedented, at least in Jewish American art. Through gesture, dress, and activity, Benjamin comments on contemporary political concerns both national and international. As she explained in a statement written in 2004, she uses women to force "confrontation of unresolved issues." A clear example is *Finding Home #61 (Fereshteh) "Beloved"* (2003) (fig. 34), which portrays Sarah and Hagar embracing each other despite the relevant passages to the contrary in Genesis 16 and 21. Abraham, husband to Sarah, is the father of Isaac, the progenitor of the Israelites and the father of Ishmael, who is the ancestor of the Arabs and whose mother is Hagar, Sarah's servant. Benjamin's painting projects her own desire to see the end of enmity between the women, obvious surrogates for Israelis and Palestinians, but the barely visible figures on the right and left sides indicate that she knows the struggle may never end. Those on the right extend a friendly hand but, intending mayhem, have bombs belted to their bodies. Those on the left, well-intentioned amputee soldiers, already victims, will be unable to stop the expected carnage. As suggested in some of Janet Shafner's paintings, history repeats itself—what did not happen then will not happen now, and what happened then will be repeated now. Nevertheless, Benjamin makes a statement about the potential voice and power of women in contemporary politics. There is always hope that a healing will take place despite the drops of blood splattered across the clothing of both women in *Finding Home #61*. As Benjamin mentioned in an email on September 9, 2010, "I like to make parallels to stories and circumstances today. It's all about bridging and understanding that almost nothing has changed from the myths of old to today." And in regard to her personal life, the painting hints at her own desire to resolve the differences between her original Indian and adopted American selves—minus, of course, the bombs, bullets, and general mayhem. In that sense, she is both Sarah and Hagar.

The painting of Rebecca, *Finding Home #67: "The Immigrant's New Clothes" (Rebecca)* (2006) (fig. 35), a single-figure work, raises more general issues about life in the mid- and late twentieth century. The biblical reference to the jugs at Rebecca's feet indicate that she is at the well, therefore a dispenser of life. She stands in a garden surrounded by pomegranate trees, but she looks into a hand mirror and sees an atomic explosion. And she wears an American flag sari that just misses covering an undergarment that recalls the striped clothing worn by concentration- and death-camp prisoners during the Holocaust. In the figure of Rebecca, then, Benjamin opposes an Edenic garden to total annihilation, freedom to bondage, and ideal existence to devastating real-time events. Her choice of Rebecca to symbolize such unreconcilable opposites is perfect for the painting's purposely ambiguous meaning insofar as Rebecca is a biblical matriarch, but both a morally suspect mother and a manipulator of Jacob, her son, and of Isaac, her husband.

In the following years, Benjamin added several paintings to the *Finding Home* and other biblical series in which she both points out similarities between ancient and modern times and employs biblical figures to comment on contemporary events. In addition, her style grew more complex, and her figures became less earthbound, more surreal in their bodily proportions, and more fanciful in pose or action. Her feminist point of view grew stronger, and her use of myth and mythic figures more inventive. What or who they represent became increasingly veiled through the use of symbolic imagery in response to contemporary events. The result has been a conflation of her memories of Indian culture and its religious imagery and her increasingly imaginative turns with biblical figures. All of these things emerge clearly in a complex set of four paintings she completed in 2014 and titled *The Four Mothers Who Entered Pardes (Paradise)* (fig. 36). The four mothers are, reading from left to right, Rachel, Sarah, Leah, and Rebecca.

One of the surprises here is that Benjamin audaciously substitutes women for men in the famous Jewish legend of the four men who entered paradise. The Four Mothers take the place of four sages who lived in the first

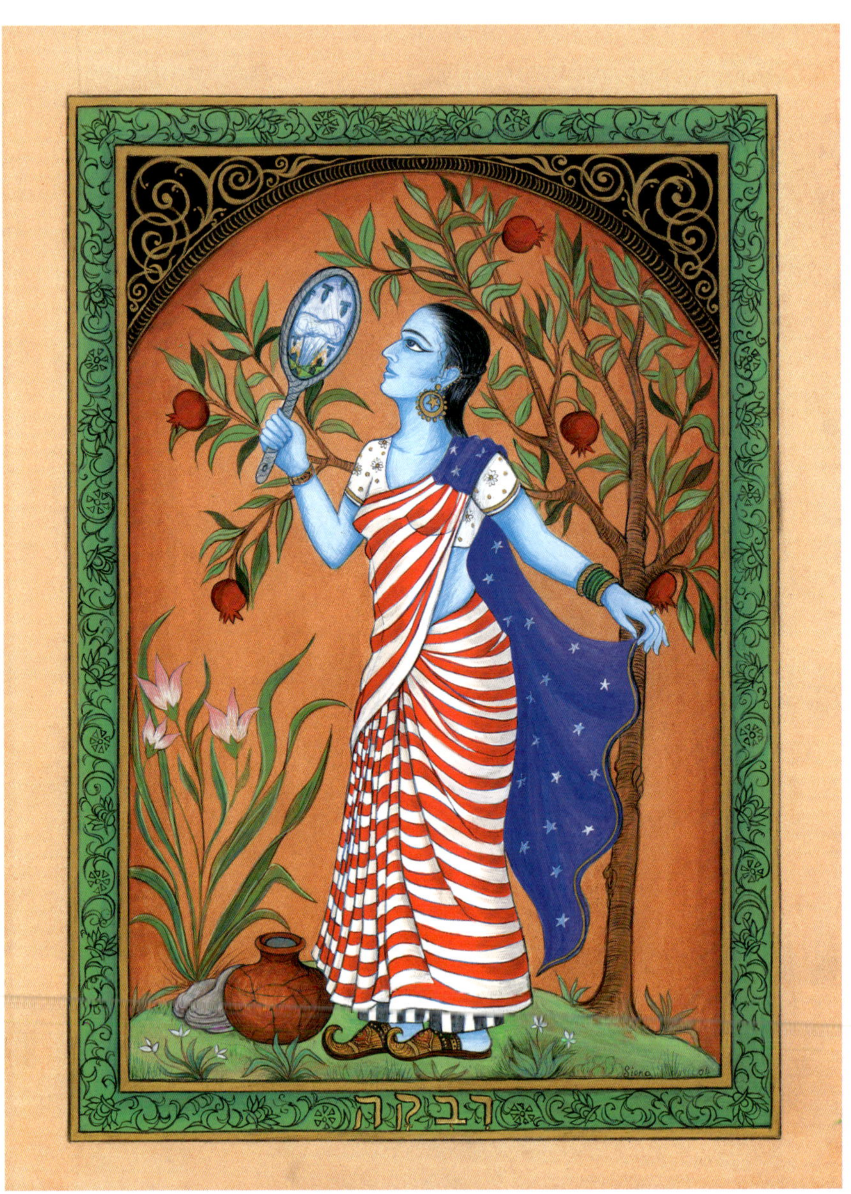


35. Siona Benjamin, *Finding Home #67: "The Immigrant's New Clothes" (Rebecca)*, 2006. Gouache on paper, 10 × 14 in. Courtesy of the artist and ACA Galleries, New York, www.artsiona.com.

century CE and who, as recorded in the Talmud in Hagigah, section 14b, entered paradise with varying results. They were Ben Azzi, who died after looking at the Divine Presence; Ben Zoma, who went insane; Acher (Elisha ben Avuya), who became a heretic and cut down plantings; and Rabbi Akiva, who alone managed to leave paradise in peace.

The painting of Rachel at the extreme left reveals Benjamin at her most pessimistic. In a headlong dive, Rachel dies. An angel lies upon her chest. Around her, other angels, some evil and some good, weep as Rachel mourns the loss of her children (Jeremiah 31:15). Although in the next verse in Jeremiah the children's return is promised, Benjamin associates Rachel's loss with the future catastrophes of the Jewish people.

In the next painting, we see Sarah, mad with worry. She eats money associated with financial scammers as an atomic explosion rises behind her. Beneath her, suppressed angels are set loose as demons. The reversal of the positions of heaven and hell, with heaven below and hell above, suggesting the reversal of our notions of good and evil, call to mind the art

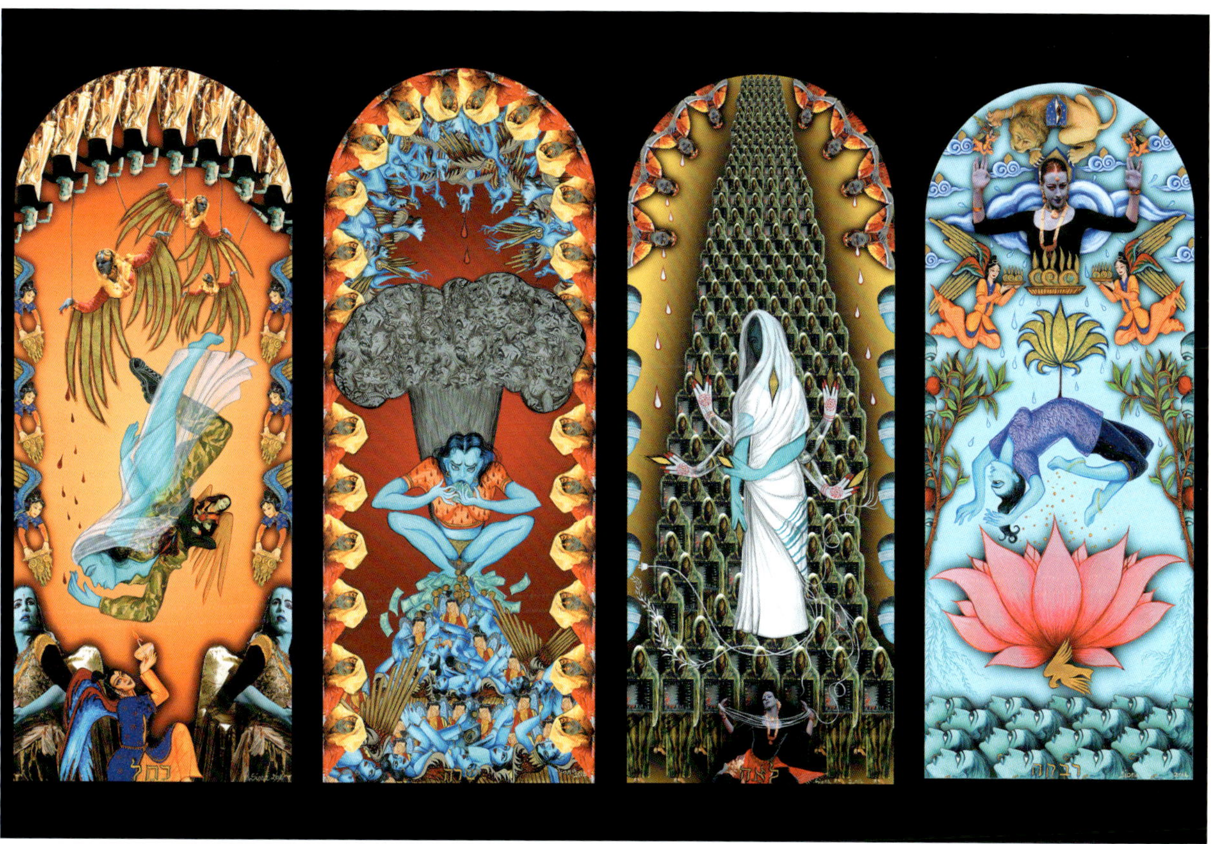

36. Siona Benjamin, *The Four Mothers Who Entered Pardes (Paradise)*, 2014. Gouache and mixed media, each panel 10½ x 24 in. Courtesy of the artist and ACA Galleries, New York, www.artsiona.com.

of Hieronymous Bosch (1450–1516), the early Netherlandish figure in whose works evil could be seen as triumphant. Benjamin is clearly commenting on our contemporary world, and her assessment of our civilization is not different from Janet Shafner's.

The image of Leah shows some signs of redemption for humanity. Benjamin places her in a field of cut grain that in legend Acher destroys after leaving paradise. Leah has weak eyes and, according to Benjamin, has learned to look within herself to find faith. It is a fanciful faith, to be sure, but one that allows her to leave the male world of the patriarchs and embrace a world where her daughters and sons will equally inherit their proper share and thus be an inspiration to humanity. In this regard, Leah finds great strength by seeing with her heart rather than with her weak eyes. At the same time, Benjamin juxtaposes Leah's sense of goodness with the blind figures around the edges of the painting, who suggest loss of faith.

In Benjamin's interpretation of Rebecca in *The Four Mothers*, quite different from the interpretation in *Finding Home #67* (fig. 35), she ascends to paradise like Rabbi Akiva and descends in peace, but, unlike Rabbi Akiva, Rebecca knows that even in paradise there might be problems (Baigell 2016, 20). Showing that peace will not be disturbed in paradise, two lotus flowers, one emerging from Rebecca's stomach, indicate rebirth. At the top, a photograph of a celebratory dancer is collaged onto the surface and painted over. Above the dancer's head, the Lion of Judah, a figure of protection, appears, and in the center of the painting

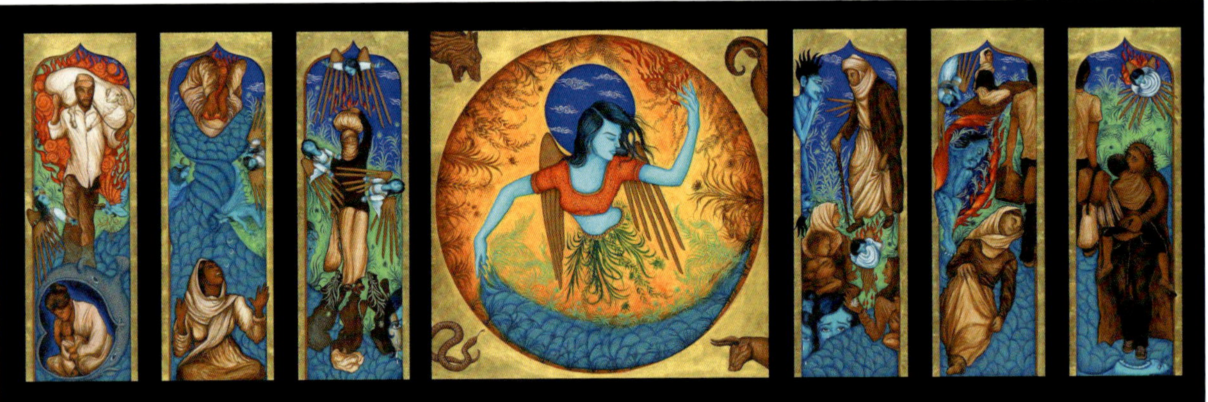

37. Siona Benjamin, *Exodus: I See Myself in You*, 2016. Gouache, acrylic, and twenty-two-caret gold on wood panel, 3½ × 10 ft. with frames. Courtesy of the artist and ACA Galleries, New York, www.artsiona.com.

there is a house that includes a flame, a symbol of hope.

It would seem that a major underlying theme of Benjamin's paintings is the conflict between her desire for peace and cooperation among people and her recognition of the fact that we live in an imperfect world, not unlike the meaning of her painting of Sarah and Hagar (*Finding Home #61*, fig. 34). She is not overly optimistic about the prospects for humanity's future. At best, she seems to say, there is struggle ahead to maintain the veneer of civility in society. It is no wonder that Benjamin often refers to her search for a homeland: a diverse, accepting, and harmonious homeland does not seem to exist on our planet.

This view is made abundantly clear in the series of paintings and drawings that make up *Exodus: I See Myself in You* (2016) (fig. 37). In its final form, the principle part of the series includes seven paintings that replicate the form of a seven-branched menorah. Benjamin describes the seven paintings this way. In the central panel, the figure is an angel in the Garden of Eden. Her arms make a ying-yang shape. Around her are the snake as well as predators and prey. The Garden, then, is not the perfect, hoped-for place for the refugees depicted in the side panels but is only an illusion we carry with us. The flanking panels depict displaced persons whose plight has been well publicized as they try to escape from war-torn and drought-stricken areas in the Middle East and Africa, their brown color symbolizing mud and weariness. In each panel, demons try to hinder or stop their search for refuge. The man in the last panel to the left carries a sheep, which is transformed into the Abrahamic sacrificial ram, or he might also be a version of the traditional image of Jesus as the shepherd of his flock. In other panels, mothers try to protect their children. Beneath the central panel, a golden ram sits in a pool bright red in color, which might be its blood. Benjamin's refugees are homeless and will remain so, rejected by possible host countries—altogether a bleak vision despite the lovely colors and interesting shapes.

When looked at as a total unit, Benjamin's paintings are built around two general themes: feminism and female power, on the one hand, and the unbridgeable gap between reality and the ideal, on the other. Their protagonists might be biblical figures or refugees. Her habit is to allow each work, whether a stand-alone or part of a series, to tell its own story rather than to become part of a continuous narrative about a particular person or event. Much of her output exists at the interesting and ambiguous point of allowing the viewer to see each work both as an individual entity and as part of an ongoing continuum in Benjamin's progression as an artist. It is evident that as Benjamin's interactions with current events broaden and deepen, the more mythical are the forms she includes in individual works. By including biblical figures, contemporary individuals, and mythic beings in her paintings, she invokes the idea that we are in a cosmic battle to define the place we want to call home, the place that embodies safety and security.

# 7 Carol Hamoy

Before becoming "a woman who is an artist," Carol Hamoy (b. 1934) had a successful business career ("Carol Hamoy" 2013). But by the late 1970s, exasperated with some male colleagues' inappropriate behavior, she retired and turned to art. Emboldened by the feminist movement, she decided to make women her subject matter, to acknowledge their presence in both history and in the contemporary world, and to fight discrimination in museum galleries. In 1982, when she was forty-eight years old, she became bat mitzvah (was confirmed) while studying with Rabbi Lynn Gottlieb, a charismatic and inspiring figure in the Jewish Renewal movement. In conversations, they discussed social, political, and economic matters, including issues revolving around the treatment of women in the Bible, not least the fact that so many are unnamed. Rabbi Gottlieb suggested that Hamoy make art based on their lives, a suggestion that marked a turning point in her art making. *Sabbath Bride* (1985) (fig. 4), discussed in the introduction, is an early example of what Hamoy produced in response to Gottlieb's idea.

All of the artists discussed in this book are politically aware. If Hamoy's works are any indication of what occupies her mind, she seems to be the most aware and the most political. In interviews, in her writings, and certainly in her work since the 1980s, she has assumed a strong feminist position in calling attention to the presence of women in American history and to both the better-known and the lesser-known women in the Bible.

In an important declaration included in the catalog accompanying her exhibition *Carol Hamoy/Voices*, she stated that feminism is not just for women: "The issues I address in my work are without gender. It is the sibling, not just the sister who interests me; the child, not just the daughter. Although I illustrate my personal experience as a woman, I want my art to speak to anyone who has ever been a parent, child, sibling, lover, or friend" (Hamoy 1992, 9). Her concerns, then, are not just about women or just for women. Men, she feels, should understand the context(s) in which her subjects are shown. In another comment at that time, she said:

> In fundamental and Orthodox Judaism, there is an edict that men and women cannot pray together, since if they do men may not be able to focus on their prayers due to the distraction of the female presence. So, they pray separately. This edict assumes women would not be distracted from *their* prayer by the presence of men. I just thought it was time the voice of women—"*Kol Ishah*"—was heard. (qtd. in Kresh 1992)

Her observations are important because they assert the importance of women both as subjects for artists and as humans in actual situations as well as the importance of herself as a voice that "presents," which is a more active position than just "representing." On the cover of an issue of the Jewish feminist journal *Bridges* in 1994 featuring Hamoy's work, the following words are quoted: "My work is about life viewed through an acquired feminist lens. Rarely are a wife, mother, daughter, or sister mentioned in Torah. Jewish women's historical importance is not emphasized in our tradition. My work is an effort to change tradition and make visible the invisible part of the children of Israel" (*Bridges* 1994).

In a review of an exhibition in Philadelphia in 1995 titled *Strong Houses*, Hamoy was quoted as saying, "I felt there was a place for me in Judaism as a woman, and it was then I started to do work with Jewish themes. More women would be Jewishly involved if the patriarchal stuff disappeared. I'm a Jewish woman involved in a Judaism that includes women's experiences." Sometimes, for Hamoy, that means "making up my own rules" (Josephs 1995).

In 2001, on the occasion of an exhibition titled *Women of the Book: Jewish Artists, Jewish Themes*, Hamoy showed the construction *Morning Prayer*, in which the words "Thank God For Making Me A Woman Who Is An Artist" are placed in the center of a triptych surrounded by beads, mirrors, pins, and lace. The sentence is, of course, a direct challenge to the prayer Orthodox men say on awakening: "Thank you, God, for not making me a woman" ("Books on View" 2001, 19; Kushner 1998, 4).

In a statement written in 2010, Hamoy explained:

> I feel my job is to identify the unnamed women in the Bible. . . . Although women and girls will find my work of particular personal interest, there is no reason to assume men and boys would not benefit from the knowledge this work imparts. . . . It is my goal to have the viewing public see my art and, while looking, hear the following phrase, "Here we are, women in Torah, and these are our names and know us and remember us as you do our husbands, brothers, uncles, and fathers." What a joy that would be!

And in an email written on November 27, 2011, she said:

> It occurred to me that the Torah is really a his/story—a collection of experiences told by men about men. I decided it would be my job to fill out the population of those five books [Genesis, Exodus, Leviticus, Numbers, Deuteronomy] by telling the her/stories of the women who were in those pages at the very same time. I felt it would be a real bonus to review aspects of this religion from another point of view—a twenty-first-century feminist perspective.

The seeds of Hamoy's attitude were probably planted in her childhood. In reminiscing about those years in an interview on June 22, 2006, she remembered the pain when at an early age she could no longer accompany her father to the bema to take part in religious services reserved only for men. And in various statements, she has said that the expectations that her immigrant parents had for her brothers differed greatly from those held for their daughter. "I am sure their decision in this matter sowed the seeds of my ardent feminism and my need as an artist to reveal to Jewish girls and women a heritage of which they should be proud. Acknowledging and honoring women is [*sic*] the focus and subject matter of my art." She views her work as commentary in the Jewish tradition of midrash by bringing the ancient texts, as she has often said, into the twenty-first century.

But just as Hamoy left the synagogue but not Judaism, so she distanced herself from her family's expectations but not from her family.

Her family worked in various aspects of the garment industry, and as a child she was able to play with textile remnants, beads, lace, buttons, and mirrors. When she became an adult and an artist, these items became the materials for many of her assemblages. Thus, she combines and commemorates in her work personal memories with her interests in religion and feminism. In effect, her work is an amalgam of her personal history and her social concerns.

But something further needs to be said of many artists' desire to maintain some sort of community connection, however loose-jointed it might be. As Hamoy indicated in an email of September 24, 2015, "Although I am what one would call severely secular, I do enjoy some of the traditions and rituals. Mostly that Jews all over the world are observing/saying the same things as I am at one time. There's something about the connectiveness I find alluring." As mentioned in the introduction, for the generation born from the 1930s to the 1960s, connections were no longer based so firmly on communal memories, which were largely forgotten by the now dispersed children of former Jewish immigrant neighborhoods even as they read and studied the ancient texts and participated in religious rituals. So, for better or worse, it is the open-ended "something" that still serves as a binding agent, a felt but difficult-to-articulate "connectiveness" for this generation.

And, finally, in an email exchange dated February 28, 2015, and in an interview on November 6, 2015, Hamoy mentioned that she is a storyteller who wants young girls to know that the women in the Bible are as tough as the men and are often able to take care of themselves by whatever means possible. She wants to bring them to life as real people and to make note that they existed in the world. She wants people to think realistically about what she calls "the children of Israel" as depicted in the Bible. Where would the children of Israel be without the participation of women? She likes to think of her work as feminist education—feminism and education going hand in hand. As a result, she has completed many works both religious and secular themed to emphasize her point of view regarding women's participation in Judaism and in secular activities. These works include assemblages based on the lives of event-making women in the Bible, such as women who were prophets, as well as on the stories of women immigrants who came to America to find a better life.

Tamar, for example, was, along with figures such as Ruth and Esther, an event-making woman (Genesis 38; Baigell 2012, 38–39). After each of Tamar's two husbands die without impregnating her (they were brothers), she becomes an outcast. No longer living under a man's protection, she dresses as a prostitute to seduce Judah, her former father-in-law, in order to conform to the will of God to perpetuate his line. Like the biblical Ruth, Tamar initiates the sexual encounter, driven not by lust but by the goal to survive through conceiving a child. As one observer notes, Tamar "turns the passive victim to the active arbiter of her own fate . . . [;] [her] triumph depends on the total control of her being" (Aschkenasy 1998, 86, 89). And another points out that Tamar is not necessarily the victim of patriarchy forced to act deceitfully but rather "an active agent transforming the social order in which [she] lived" (R. Adelman 2012, 88). After she fills her role by becoming a mother (she gives birth to twin boys, one of whom is the ancestor of King David), she disappears from the Bible and is criticized in legends for her trickery (R. Adelman 2012, 88; Bellis 1994, 69, 91; Klein 2003, 62–70).

In her work *Tamar: A Womb of Her Own* (1990) (fig. 38), Hamoy does not illustrate a particular episode in Tamar's marriages, her seduction of Judah, or his response. Rather, its title indicates how Hamoy clearly supports Tamar's control over her own story and her

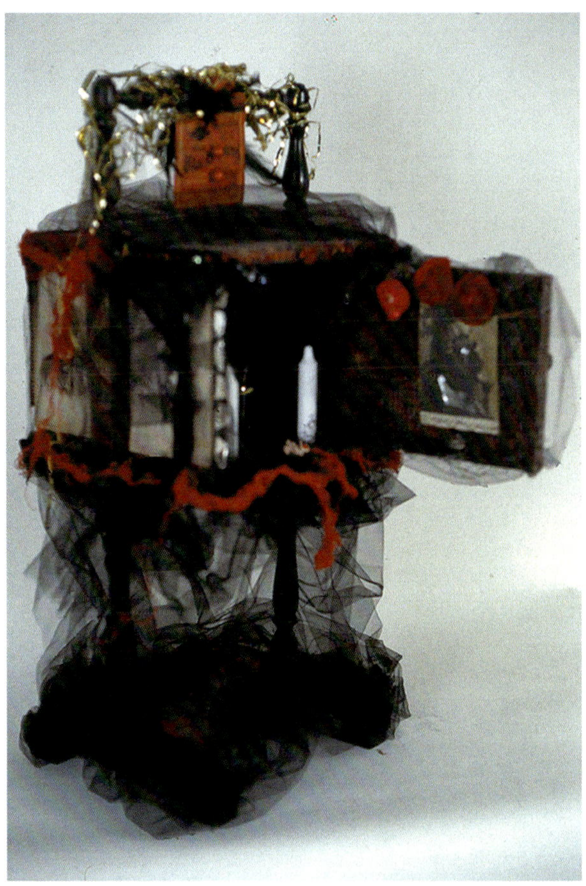

38. Carol Hamoy (American, b. 1934), *Tamar: A Womb of Her Own*, 1990. Mixed media, 28 × 16 × 20 in. B'nai B'rith Klutznick National Jewish Museum Collection of the Skirball Museum, Cincinnati, OH.

own body. The work is about Tamar and the various objects that indicate her place as a woman in biblical history. The black veils suggest her double widowhood, the two candles in the central rectangle (her womb) represent her twin sons, and the red cloth around the rectangle recalls the passage in Genesis 38:28–30 describing how a midwife ties a crimson thread around the hand of the twin Zerah, who emerges first but withdraws into the womb so that the other brother, Perez, can be born first. King David is descended from Perez.

In making this work, Hamoy, thinking of Tamar in contemporary terms, decided that Tamar realizes she has lost her place in the world after the death of her second husband. She does not give up but decides to take responsibility for her life and, given the circumstances available to her at the time, chooses the best way to reestablish herself in society. For Hamoy, it does not matter how Tamar makes this happen. What is important—the message young women should take from Tamar's example—is that she saves herself. She is smart, strong, and tough. Her existence, Hamoy's work insists, should be acknowledged, her story recognized.

In 1994 in an exhibition titled *Wonder Women* (see Vatsky 1994), Hamoy honored the Four Mothers—Sarah, Rebecca, Leah, and Rachel—as well as seven women prophets—Miriam, Deborah, Huldah, Abigail, Bathsheba, Hannah, and, again, Sarah. Rather than employ a free-standing unit, as in *A Womb of Her Own*, Hamoy used wall-mounted, open boxes and mixed-media relief assemblages.

Huldah prophesizes the destruction of the Temple in Jerusalem in 586 BCE, the time of Jeremiah (Second Kings 22:15–20; see also Ginzberg [1909–38] 1917–87, 4:282, 6:377, and Kedar 2004, 390). She tells King Josiah, who fears exile, that misfortune can be averted but that the Temple in Jerusalem will be destroyed after his death. Why is Huldah asked to prophesize? Legends suggest that because she is a kinswoman of Jeremiah, who by sheerest chance is out of town at that time, the task falls to her. Like Tamar, she is criticized and called a hateful woman and the daughter of a harlot.

This is the kind of response to which Hamoy is attracted; she wants to right a biblical wrong and to remind her viewers that women such as Huldah, to whom people looked for advice, should not be forgotten, ignored, or denigrated. Each assemblage in this series, such as *Huldah* (1994) (fig. 39), contains a page from a nineteenth-century book of women's names that also includes a poem about each individual. In *Huldah*, the columns symbolize the

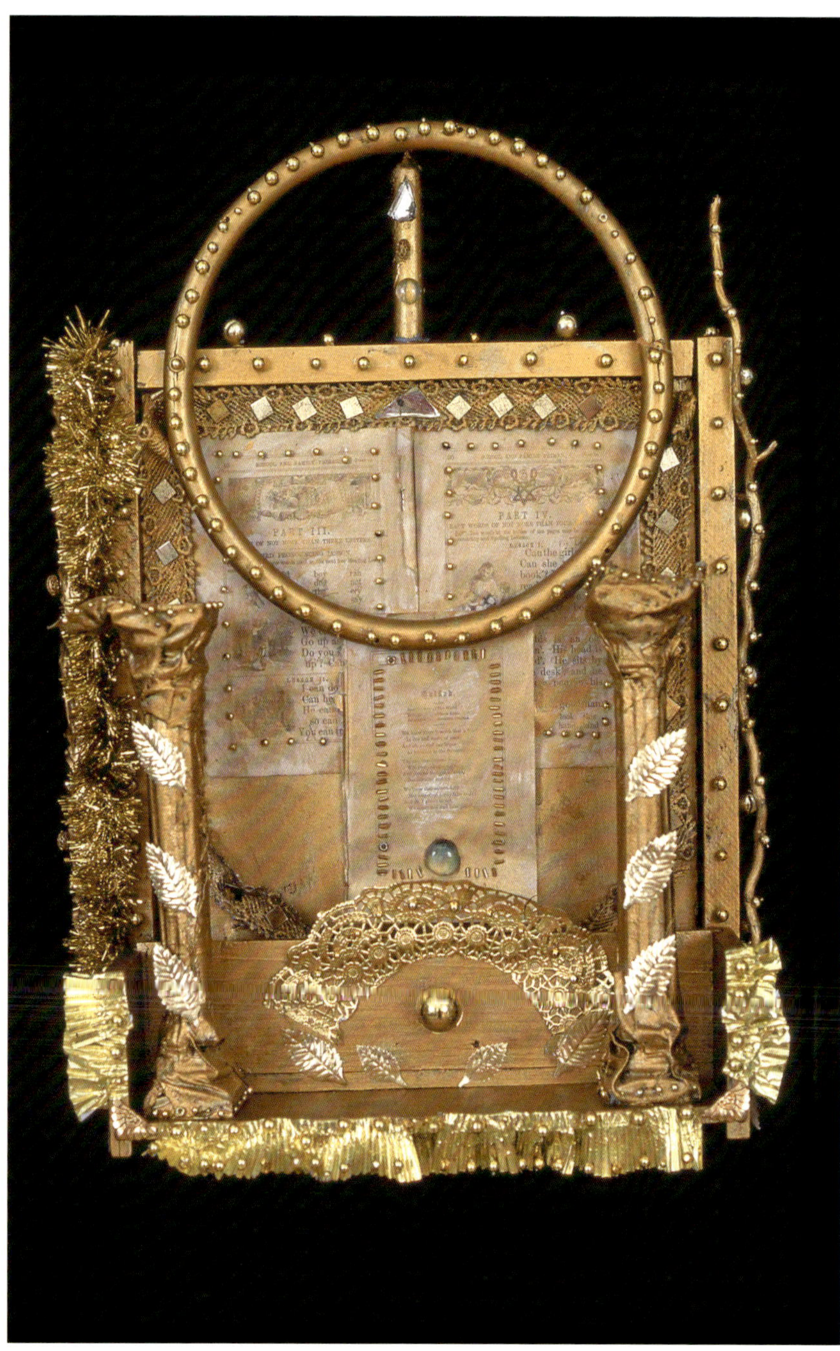

39. Carol Hamoy, *Huldah*, 1994. Mixed media, 22 × 16 × 16 in. Image courtesy of the artist.

Temple in Jerusalem, and the branch attached to the frame refers to the Tree of Knowledge in the Garden of Eden. The circle at the top is the symbol for women as well as for eternity. By adding these iconographic motifs, all of which relate to each prophet's role as portrayed in the Bible, Hamoy in effect is insisting that the women prophets should be attributed the same dignity and seriousness of purpose as their male counterparts. The paraphernalia added to the constructions add meaning to the women's position and bearing and center their place in biblical history.

An insistent materiality is apparent in Hamoy's works because she often uses actual objects in her assemblages, such as clothing or even a pair of shoes. In this regard, *Queen Jezebel* (1992) (fig. 40) is one of Hamoy's slyest

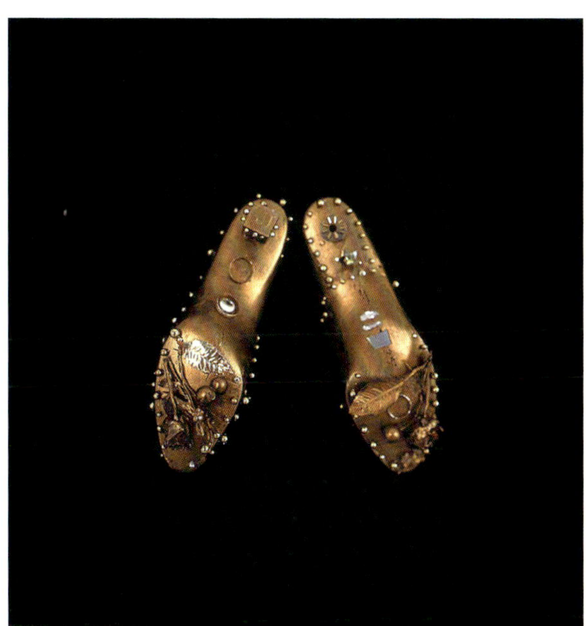

40. Carol Hamoy, *Queen Jezebel*, 1992. Mixed media, 10 × 7½ in. Collection of Eileen and David Peretz. Courtesy of the artist.

inventions. Jezebel, a Phoenician, dominates her husband, King Ahab (r. 874–53 BCE), has prophets murdered, is an idolater, and thinks of herself as an absolute ruler (First Kings 16:31, 18:4, 19:2, 19:223–25; Second Kings 9:10, 30–37). Jezebel is so disliked that the Israelites refuse to bury her when she dies, instead tossing her body over the city wall, where dogs devour her remains except for the soles of her feet.

The great Talmudic scholar Adin Steinsaltz has called Queen Jezebel "perhaps the most perfect representative of evil in the whole of Scripture" (1984, 211; see also Patai [1967] 1990, 42, and N. Rosenblatt 2005, 214). But Hamoy would have none of that. She instead concentrated on Jezebel's good qualities. One legend describes her as quite sympathetic to the joys and sorrows of others. At funerals, she joins the ranks of the mourners, and at weddings she takes part in the festivities by dancing before the bride and groom, an act that is still today considered a good deed, or mitzvah (Ginzberg [1909–38] 1917–87, 4:189). Hamoy therefore honors this aspect of Jezebel's activities by representing her as a pair of gaudy dancing slippers.

Hamoy has also dressed biblical figures in gaudy clothing not unlike the dress worn by the bride in the *Sabbath Bride* (fig. 3), which is understated in comparison. She lessens the demonization of Adam's legendary first wife, Lilith, by dressing her in a fantastical ball gown. (Hamoy has dressed at least two other figures in such gowns—Hokmah, who represents wisdom as one of the ten characteristics [*spherot*] of God in kabbalist thought, and Serah (or Serach), the young woman who told Jacob in song that his son Joseph is alive [see chapter 5 for Shafner's interpretation of Serah]). Lilith, never mentioned in the Bible except in passing (her name given in lower case, "lilith," meaning "she-demon," in Isaiah 24:14), is in legends the first human to talk back to God, the first to be expelled from the Garden of Eden, a known seducer of men who is able to sexually arouse them in their sleep, and even a murderer of children (Ginzberg [1909–38] 1917–87, 1:65, 3:280, 5:148, 6:338; Patai [1967] 1990, 233–36). (See also chapter 6.)

In her work, Hamoy also hangs adult- and child-size dresses from ceiling supports. They usually need titles and descriptive statements attached to them or placed on nearby walls to explain what or who they represent. Composed of just one type of material or of pieces of dozens of cloth, plastic, or paper garments, each piece usually has a polemic intention. (Hamoy is not the only artist in recent years to use garments alone in Jewish-themed works, but she might be the first.)

In *Mourning Coat* (2011) (fig. 41), Hamoy reflects on human mortality and the need to acknowledge and mourn the dead in either private or public space. At first glance, *Mourning Coat* seems little more than crumpled paper cut in the shape of a coat with some writing on it, but it is more than that. It is inscribed

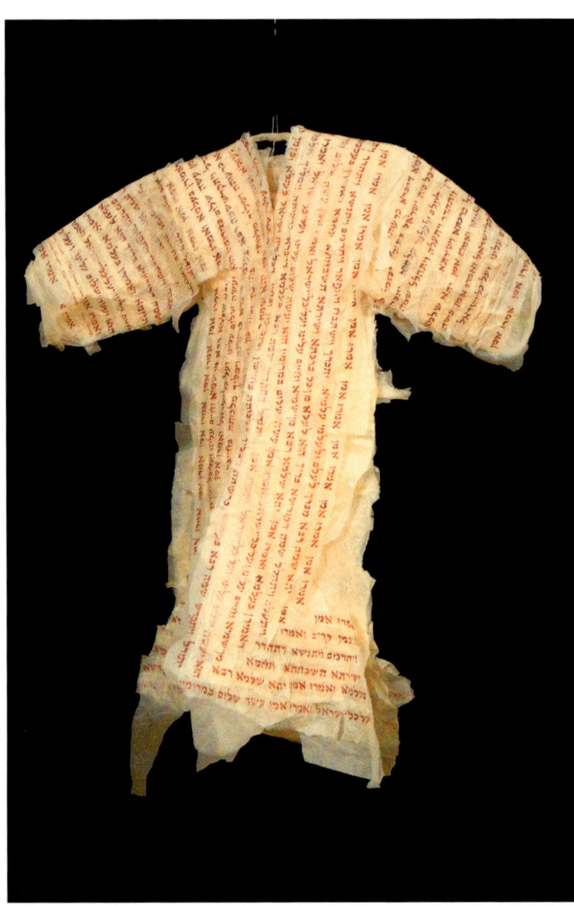

41. Carol Hamoy, *Mourning Coat*, 2011. Mixed media, 39 × 40 × 29 in. Courtesy of the artist.

in both Hebrew with the mourner's prayer and the Latin alphabet with names of many women who have died. Among the Orthodox, women are not allowed to say prayers for the dead in public, including in a synagogue or at a gravesite, even if the deceased is a spouse or close relative. That task is reserved only for men. By creating a mourning coat with names of women, Hamoy symbolically invites all women to don the coat as their symbol of public mourning. Even if Orthodox women cannot say the prayer for the dead publicly, having the prayer written on the coat allows it to be read by others, a wry comment on an outdated tradition rejected by virtually all non-Orthodox Jews.

Dresses and other garments have turned out to be a very flexible medium for Hamoy in secular- and biblical-themed works. The subject of *The Invisible Part of the Children of Israel* (2001) (fig. 42) is the many unnamed women in the Bible. In this installation, one hundred transparent dresses made of clear vinyl are suspended from the ceiling, and more than fifty text pages are displayed listing the names and accomplishments of almost four hundred women mentioned in the Bible, both the named and the nameless, including women such as Lot's wife (Idit), Noah's wife (Amara or Noamara), and Jephthah's daughter (Sheilah), names found only in various legends (Ginzberg [1909–38] 1917–87, 5:241, 4:44; Margolis 2013, 140). Others are identified by their connections to the men in their lives (i.e., "my name is Idit, and Lot is my husband"). Each is honored by a different style of dress.

Two ideas are at play here. First, the title and subject are enhanced by Hamoy's use of Jewish numerical symbolism (see also the discussion of the use of numerology in chapter 9). The number of dresses, one hundred, is significant because ten and its multiples have mysterious qualities in Judaism—the Ten Commandments, the ten qualities (*spherot*) of God as recorded in kabbalah, and ten persons required as a quorum for prayer. The second idea revolves around the contemporary manner in which objects, the dresses, are used to propel the narrative. They create the work's structure; the title of the work and the display of names provide the keys for decoding the work. We understand the content and context by looking and reading. The aesthetic value, important as it is by itself, is meant to enhance what the dresses and texts represent.

Hamoy addressed the matter of numerical symbolism several years later by asking ten questions of female rabbis. Of the more than 200 rabbis she contacted, 125 responded,

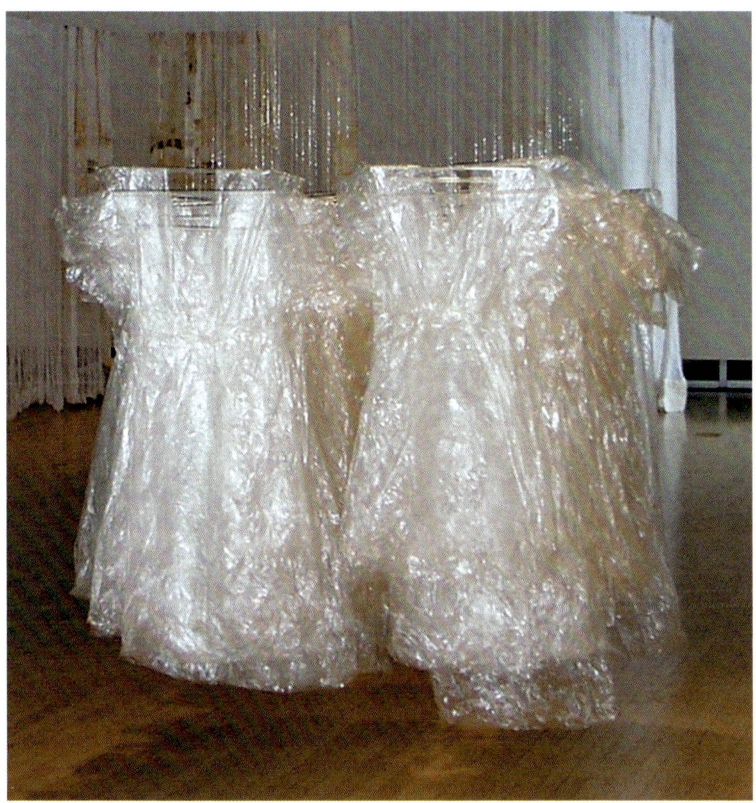

42. Carol Hamoy, *The Invisible Part of the Children of Israel*, 2001. Mixed media, size variable. Collection of the Mishkan Museum of Art, Ein Herod, Israel. Courtesy of the artist.

including an Orthodox female rabbi in Israel, who said her male colleagues refuse to pay her any attention. The questions included the rabbi's age, when she decided to study for the rabbinate, how her family responded to her decision to become a rabbi, and what her motivations, expectations, obstacles, and innovations (such as adding rituals with which she might be involved) were. The answers, incorporated into *Ten Questions* (2015) (fig. 43), are noted on *katan*s, an undergarment worn by Orthodox men. In her usual wry manner, Hamoy used pink, braided threads instead of the usual white and blue for the tzitzit that hang from the corners of the *katan*s.

Among her secular works done in this manner, *Welcome to America* (1994) is derived from the experiences of immigrant women as they arrived in America between 1892 and 1992. Inspired by many personal stories, Hamoy interviewed 200 immigrants or their descendants in preparation for her celebration of those women courageous enough to forge a new life in a strange land. The installation includes more than 150 garments created from wedding gowns, dresses, skirts, bed linens, scarves, and undergarments. Each garment carries a woman's first name, her place of origin, and her arrival date as well as a brief statement about her life excerpted from Hamoy's interviews. All the garments were originally white but then tinted and stained to acquire an antique patina. Suspended from the ceiling, they move ever so slightly when viewers walk among them, as if containing the spirits of those long-departed women who hoped for their piece of the American dream.

Hamoy has said: "The dresses come from a secret place in my soul" (Hamoy 1996, 83). She wanted to invoke these women's physical presence and strength as well as the emotional duress they experienced in adjusting to new

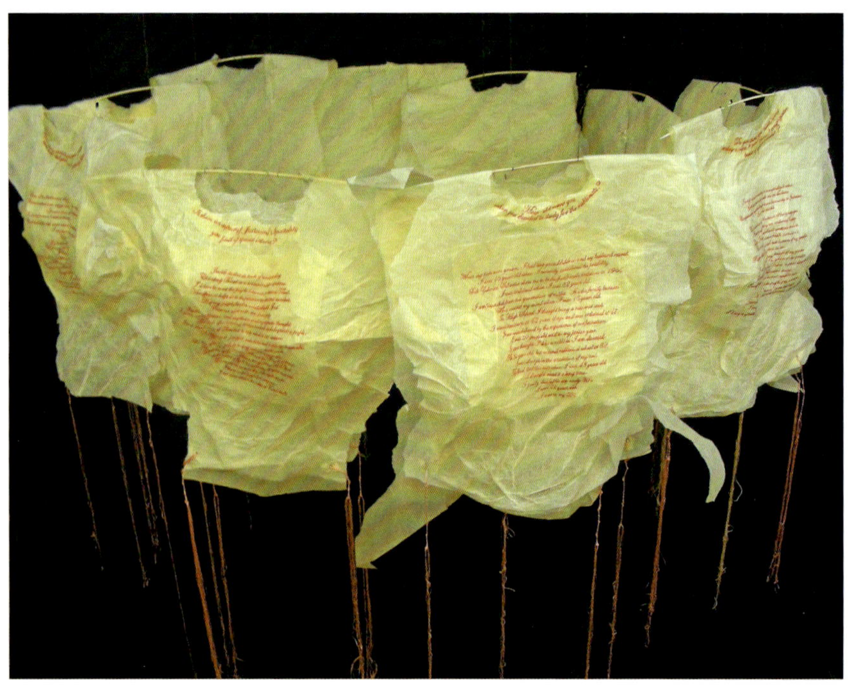

43. Carol Hamoy, *Ten Questions*, 2015. Paper, acrylic ink, and knitting needles, 55½ × 38 in. circumference. Courtesy of the artist.

customs, a new language, and difficult living and working conditions after they bravely made the voyage to America. *Welcome to America* represents the aspirations of ordinary but heroic people. It is history from the ground up, so to speak, rather than a record of a noteworthy event or a famous person, its subjects not unlike those whom Ruth Weisberg honors in *The Scroll* (1986) (chapter 4). For Hamoy, an assemblage like this, recalling the time when her family lived and worked in the garment industry, obviously carries both emotional and visceral overtones for the artist as well as for those descendants of families who were or are still involved in garment work. (In my own family history, my father, who handled linings for fur coats, worked, as he often said, "half a day," which meant from six in the morning until six in the evening, until his last illness.)

Other works of this sort by Hamoy include *The Triangle Shirtwaist Fire* (1996), which honors the lives of 146 mostly immigrant Jewish and Italian women garment workers who perished in a factory fire in New York City on March 15, 1911, and *Portraits of the Artists as Young Girls* (2000), for which she asked many female artists for a childhood photograph and transferred them to the fronts of children-size "dresses" made of paper. In a conversation, Hamoy said she hoped that as light shines through the translucent dresses and illuminates the faces of the young girls, viewers will sense the artistic spirit in those little girls who became artists in adulthood. One critic captured Hamoy's central point when he wrote: "One assumes this radiance represents the visionary characteristic of all the artists cited, while at the same time alluding to a sisterhood built on a shared strength" (Lombardi 2000).

Hamoy's concern for the place of women (and men) in society extends to those who have personal issues and are troubled in some way. For those individuals, she created a nondenominational meditation space, *PsalmSong* (2005) (fig. 44), among the most complex and carefully thought-out meditation spaces by a Jewish American artist, in which every element of its design is focused on spiritual, emotional, and bodily healing—the kind of space where those in mourning might repair for personal

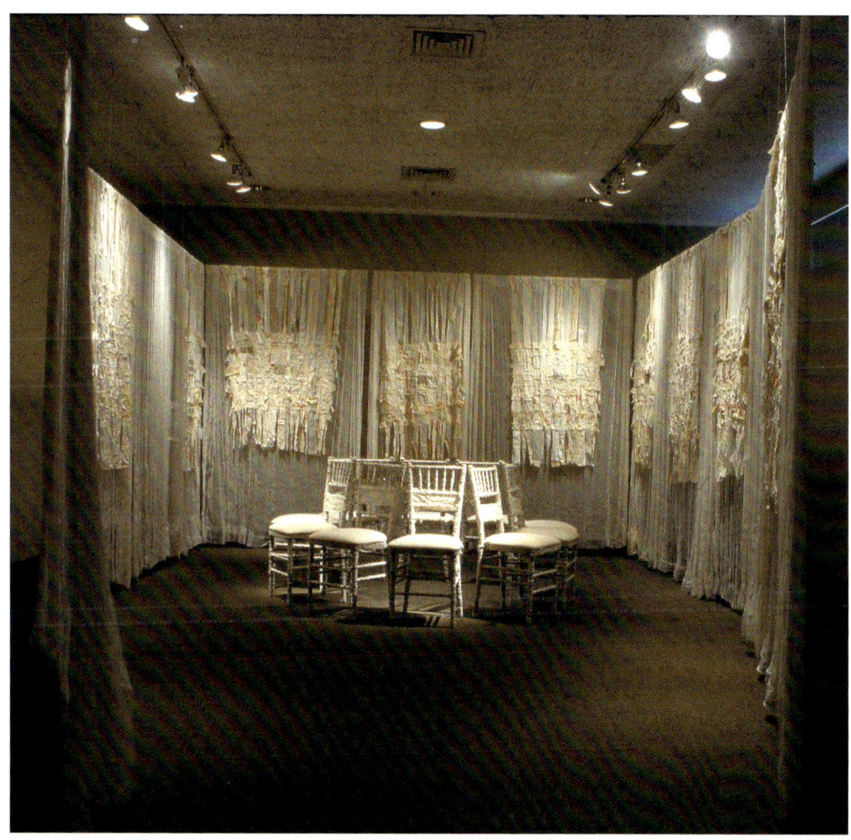

44. Carol Hamoy, *PsalmSong*, 2005. Mixed media, approximately 25 × 18 ft. Courtesy of the artist.

sustenance as well as emotional and physical healing (Rosensaft 2005). (Beth Ames Swartz and Tobi Kahn, among others, have also created similar spaces. Swartz's includes the Arizona Center in Tucson. For Kahn, see chapter 9 and the website for the National Center for Jewish Healing.)

Hamoy and other artists of this generation, such as Swartz and Kahn, have addressed an issue, the creation of sacred and meditative spaces, that has largely been overlooked in the art historical literature. By "sacred spaces," I do not mean places one visits or makes pilgrimages to enlighten the mind, body, or spirit, to desire personal transformations, to connect to the universal being through the mystical stream, or to eat healthful foods. Rather, I mean quiet, transient spaces created in religious buildings, hospitals, private homes, office buildings, and planned outdoor sites where one can sit or stand for short periods of time to meditate on physical, mental, and emotional healing.

Within the Jewish community, the healing and meditation movement gained momentum in the early 1990s. Many sacred spaces are nondenominational, although various techniques and procedures are framed within a Jewish historical context. When asked how *PsalmSong* came about, Hamoy noted in an email on October 29, 2013, that she really could not explain why she decided to create the work in the form of a healing circle that included a Hedge of Herbiage. But its genesis probably lay in passages she read in 2002 concerning Reb Nachman of Breslov (1772–1810), a well-known figure in Orthodox circles who claimed that reading a group of ten psalms in a particular order would promote healing. Hamoy, aware of kabbalistic thought regarding how certain numbers or combinations of numbers are considered to have special strengths, became fascinated with the idea that the ten psalms might actually possess healing power.

The question then became how to illustrate Reb Nachman's belief. Hamoy decided to construct a five-sided meditation chamber (five for the *chamsa*, the hand raised to deter the evil eye), approximately twenty-five feet by eighteen feet and consisting of ten woven and five unwoven panels suspended from the ceiling, the former inscribed with Reb Nachman's ten psalms, rewritten in gender-free language and arranged so that they would be read in the following order by those so inclined: Psalms 16, 32, 41, 42, 59, 77, 90, 105, 137, and 150. Within the ten woven panels, there are thirteen horizontal strips for the thirteen children of Jacob. The Healing Circle consists of ten chairs (the number needed for group prayer, or minyan), the backs of which are embroidered with words designating those in the healing professions—*curandera*, *healer*, *herbalist*, *mansin*, *midwife*, *nurse*, *physician*, *shaman*, *sobadora*, and *yerbera*. Individuals within the circle can meditate or read the psalms for whatever soothing benefits they might provide. A cantor (singer of religious melodies in synagogues) softly sings the psalms in the background. The Hedge of Herbiage, outside the meditation chamber, is embroidered with the names of twenty-two herbs (the number of letters in the Hebrew alphabet) that help the healing process, from aloe (for treating burns and frostbite) to wheatgrass (for increasing stamina).

Although *PsalmSong* might be considered an anomaly in Hamoy's work, it is central to her way of thinking, in this instance calling attention to those in need of psychological and emotional support and, just as important, to men and women in order to remind them about gender equivalence on the street, in the home, in the workplace, and in moments of meditation. When she speaks to an audience about her work with Jewish themes, she concludes with the following statement: "According to midrash, when the Messiah comes (Blessed be She), the spaces between the letters in the Torah will become a new alphabet, and there will be a new Torah. My hope is [that] in the New Torah, if not before, Lilith, Hadassah [Esther], Sarah, Rachel, Leah, Dinah, Vashti, Eve, Tzipporah, Bilhah, Deborah, Elisheba, Hagar, and all the brides, queens, wives, sisters, daughters, and significant others will be included alongside the original cast of characters."

# 8 Robert Kirschbaum

As noted, each artist profiled in this book has arrived at a sense of Jewish self-awareness by a different route. Several have mentioned growing up in a Jewish cultural or religious environment in which certain lifestyles, patterns of behavior, and values are familiar, internalized, and taken for granted. Then, as adults out in the world, they realized they are part of a religious minority. In response to this realization, some artists developed a strong desire to maintain that minority identity as part of their self-identity. In time, they established personal points of view that they reveal in their art and choice of subject matter. For example, Siona Benjamin's concern for *tikkun olam* involves social improvement, gender equality, and personal safety as preliminary to her ideal world, whereas Robert Kirschbaum's notion is more abstract. It is based on the spiritual reconstruction of the Temple in Jerusalem, twice destroyed in ancient times (586 BCE and 70 CE), which symbolizes spiritual reconstruction as well as individual spiritual restoration and repair. This is not to say that Benjamin is not spiritual or that Kirschbaum cares little for social issues. She is, and he does, but their interests have followed different trajectories.

This chapter is a revision of my article "Robert Kirschbaum's Art: Abstract, Spiritual, Intellectual," *Ars Judaica* 11 (2015): 79–90. I thank the publishers of *Ars Judaica* for permission to use parts of that article here.

Robert Kirschbaum (b. 1949) felt very comfortable growing up Jewish in New York. He received undergraduate degrees from the University of Rochester and the School of the Museum of Fine Arts in Boston and a master of fine arts degree from Yale University in 1974. He taught at the Nova Scotia College of Art and Design from 1974 to 1976 and Southern Illinois University at Edwardsville from 1976 to 1978, and he is currently professor of fine arts at Trinity College in Hartford, Connecticut. He has also traveled in Israel (1985, 1995, and 1997) and India (1988 and 1996–97).

In the 1970s, when he left his home environment, he began to explore his relationships to both American and Jewish cultures. At Yale, his teachers, Gabor Peterdi and Al Held, both Jewish, suppressed conversations about Judaism. And the farther away Kirschbaum traveled from New York—to Boston, to Nova Scotia, to southern Illinois—he felt the need to assert his Americanness, almost, as he has said, as an act of defiance, especially in Canada, where he experienced some anti-American feeling. In these communities, he did not feel an anti-Jewish bias as much as being an outsider because many people he met had never previously talked to a Jewish person. In such circumstances, Kirschbaum, aware of the then emerging identity movements in America, also felt empowered to figure out what it meant to be Jewish.

With each move geographically and culturally more distant from New York and with the greater isolation in increasingly homogeneous Christian environments, his Jewish identity became progressively more important to him. Acting on his sentimental attachment to eastern European Yiddish culture and his sense of profound loss because he never learned to speak Yiddish, the language of his elders, he developed a desire to discover more about the Judaism he had not learned as a child or when as a young adult he had searched for spiritual sustenance in the desiccated synagogue services he encountered (or endured) during the 1960s and 1970s. In a letter dated May 20, 1992, he wrote, "I felt different, more Jewish[,] and chose to assert my Jewish personality and explore my Jewish origins through art." He began his first Jewish-themed works, *The Portal Series*, in Illinois in 1976.

But at the same time Kirschbaum also responded to current events as an American. An issue he was not alone in contemplating was how to retain one's sense of optimism in late-twentieth-century America as one lived through the unpopular, stalemated war in Vietnam as well as the decline of cities and the vulgarization of culture. The promise that America held for many had begun to dissipate if not disappear completely.

One way today to imagine this state of affairs is to compare the view of the nineteenth-century philosopher Ralph Waldo Emerson, who in the flush of American optimism indicated that endless horizons lead to farther horizons, with that of the earth artist Robert Smithson (1938–73), who found instead that the "horizon [was] closing in . . . around [him]." For Emerson, "The eye is the first circle; the horizon which it forms is the second, and throughout nature this primary figure is repeated without end. . . . Every action admits to being outdone" ([1841] 1983a, 403). Smithson, to the contrary, in discussing his work *Sites/Nonsites* of the late 1960s, stated that "no matter how far out you go, you are always thrown back on your point of origin. . . . You suddenly find the horizon is closing in all around you. . . . In other words, there is no escape from limits" or, furthermore in Smithson's universe, from entropy (qtd. in Lippard 1981, 32; see also Baigell 2015a).

Smithson's ever-constricting universe was not acceptable to Kirschbaum. He countered it by his idealization of the Temple and the Temple Mount in Jerusalem, which reflected a feeling that a virtual ideal universe could be imagined through Jewish thought and in a Jewish place and that Judaism provided a way to compensate for the failures he found in the American present. This point of view did not mean that he turned pious or religious or anti-American, but that aspects of the religion meaningful to him gave him an Emersonian sense of a positive futurity and some sense of moral and spiritual elevation. As Emerson wrote in his essay "The Poet," "Nature has a higher end . . . , namely *ascension*, or, the passage of the soul into higher forms" ([1844] 1983b, 458, emphasis in original).

For Kirschbaum, this sense has led to a forty-year interest in the Temple and the Temple Mount in Jerusalem—the site of two destroyed temples, but especially the initial Solomonic Temple, which became central to his ever-growing interest in biblical history and kabbalah—as well as in Israel as the site of spiritual redemption and fulfillment. Kirschbaum's art warrants special attention here because of his sustained and determined search for forms symbolic of worldly perfection in an imperfect world, which he has based on the shape and meaning of the Temple Mount. He calls the search an ongoing spiritual reconstruction in that it reflects his own profound meditations on both his art and his identification as a Jew. As he has said in conversation, he feels "at once rooted in the depth of Jewish history but definitely cast adrift in the sea of modernity. My art was a way to fish these waters. The deeper you go, the deeper you want to go."

In a letter written on October 25, 1992, Kirschbaum remembered that he first encountered kabbalah as an undergraduate when reading about South Asian art and culture. In time, he was excited to discover that certain mystical aspects of kabbalah resemble facets of Hinduism and to find parallels between aniconic geometric imagery used in Tantric worship and diagrams of the ten kabbalist *spherot*, the ten emanations of God. But it was his trips to India that finally pointed him in a direction from which he has not wavered. He was especially impressed by simple roadside temples and altars that suggested to him primary religious experiences, and he was quite moved by the ways in which the Indian sites took on a sacred character by the simplicity of the temples' architectonic forms. His sense of the spiritual emanations given off by these simple structures was reinforced by texts such as the Vastusutra Upanishad and the Mayamata, which address Hindu religion, philosophy, and especially the symbolism and composition of architectural forms (see *Mayamata* 1985; *Vastusutra Upanishad* 1982). He especially noted that one could express profoundly complex ideas through geometry.

His interest in these forms was also prompted, he has said, by his preference for abstract rather than representational forms or narrative themes. His life-long attraction to, as he puts it, "abstraction and to esoteric and even hidden knowledge" was also greatly enhanced by his study of two modern Jewish artists he considers role models, the Russian Lazar Lissitzky (1890–1941), known as "El Lissitzky," who developed an entirely nonrepresentational style, and the American Louis Lozowick (1892–1973), who favored architectural forms. Lozowick was instrumental in introducing Lissitzky's art to America in the 1920s.

Kirschbaum chose not to imitate closely the Indian structures he saw in that country but rather to connect them intellectually and spiritually to his Jewish heritage. Their forms suggested to him the importance of doorways and portals as metaphors for one's passage to a more spiritual state of being, and, as he has said, they "evoked in me the origins of the Jewish Temple's architecture in a simple tent (the Tabernacle) and of the biblical altar of burnt offerings." (In many religious Jewish books, an image of a doorway precedes the first pages.) Acting upon that insight after returning from his first trip to India, he began to invent designs based on the Temple, which then became his principle symbol for conveying Jewish content and a sense of perfection in the world.

The Temple Mount, or Har haBiyit in Hebrew, is arguably the holiest site for Jews today, more sacred than Mt. Sinai, where Moses received the Tablets of the Law. (I mention its Hebrew name here despite the two United Nations General Assembly Resolutions of November 31, 2018, ignoring Jewish ties to the Temple Mount.) It also figures more often in Jewish history and legend than Mt. Sinai. Solomon's Temple was built upon it around 947 BCE and destroyed in 586 BCE. The Second Temple was erected in 516 BCE and destroyed in 70 CE. In legends, the Temple Mount is considered to be the location of the Foundation Stone used in the creation of the world, the place where Adam brought the first sacrifice, Cain and Abel offered gifts to God, Noah built an altar after leaving the ark, the Binding of Isaac took place, and God told Abraham that a temple would be erected and then destroyed (Ginzberg [1909–38] 1917–87, 1:285). An appropriate midrash says,

> The land of Israel sits at the center of the world; Jerusalem is in the center of the land of Israel; the sanctuary is in the center of Jerusalem; the Temple building is in

> the center of the sanctuary; the ark is in the center of the Temple building; and the foundation stone, out of which the world was founded, is before the Temple building. (*Midrash Tanchuma* 1996, Kedoshim, Siman 10)

Ezekiel refers to the Israelites as "living at the center of the earth" (38:12).

Two related series mark the beginning of Kirschbaum's mature works: *The Portal Series* and *Jerusalem Gates Studies.* In a letter on May 20, 1992, Kirschbaum explained how the Temple affected him. He reasoned that the Temple is the most potent symbol of Judaism and that it stands in the mind's eye both as a shelter for the spirit and as a model of heaven in the days of the coming of the Messiah. In other words, the Temple is an object for broad-based contemplation as well as for meditation on the completion of Creation (Scholem [1941] 1961, 273–74). Obviously knowing that we live in an imperfect world, Kirschbaum was aware of Gershom Scholem's suggestions that the destruction of the Temple contributed to the delay in the arrival of the Messiah and that, according to the *Zohar*, the principle kabbalistic text written at the end of the thirteenth century, Israel "now stood at the period of transition which proceeded the beginning of redemption" (Scholem 1978, 164, 232).

But, for Kirschbaum, "[the Temple] stands as a symbol for artistic creation (in creating we are symbolically re-building the Temple)" (qtd. in *Temple* 1997). In other words, he allies his artistic concerns, especially his preference for abstract forms, with his religious interests, making them one and the same (Kirschbaum c. 1998). The paintings in *The Portal Series*, begun in 1977, represent his initial attempts to visualize these complex thoughts. Individual works in this series invoke the names of places in Israel rather than the Temple Mount, although one of the paintings is in fact entitled *Moriah*, using a name for the Temple Mount. Their forms ultimately derive from his readings of Ezekiel's description of God's presence in the Temple (Ezekiel 43).

Certainly, these passages could trigger different kinds of responses. In any event, Kirschbaum was less concerned with the appearance of the Temple and the activities therein as recorded in Ezekiel 43 than with imagining what it might be like to be in the presence of the Lord and to be borne along with the spirit that carried Ezekiel into the inner court (verses 4–5), a powerful set of images of holiness that might certainly prompt meditation if one were so inclined. For Kirschbaum, the Temple also projects a symbolic physical and metaphysical presence. Historian Bernard Goldman pointed out several years ago that the portal was in ancient Judaic art a primary symbol of the mundane counterpart to the heavenly residence of God, his regal palace on earth (1966, 31). And Kirschbaum, through his readings of kabbalah, connected the Temple with the Torah, finding the latter to be both like a human body and like an entire building, thus intimating that the Temple is a physical embodiment of the Torah as well as an evocation of Adam Kadmon, or primordial man (not to be confused with the Adam of the Garden) (Kirschbaum 1990; Matt 1995, 136; Scholem [1941] 1961, 269, 279, and 1965, 104).

Kirschbaum was also taken by the ideas of Rabbi Isaac Luria, the major sixteenth-century kabbalist. According to Rabbi Luria, God withdrew into himself to provide space for the creation of the world. *Kidron Valley #3* (1990) (fig. 45), a painting in *The Portal Series*, is Kirschbaum's interpretation of Rabbi Luria's cosmology. Composed of complex grids, it symbolizes the "primordial world of points" that expand as "circle and line" in the process of creation (Kirschbaum 1990, 45; email, May

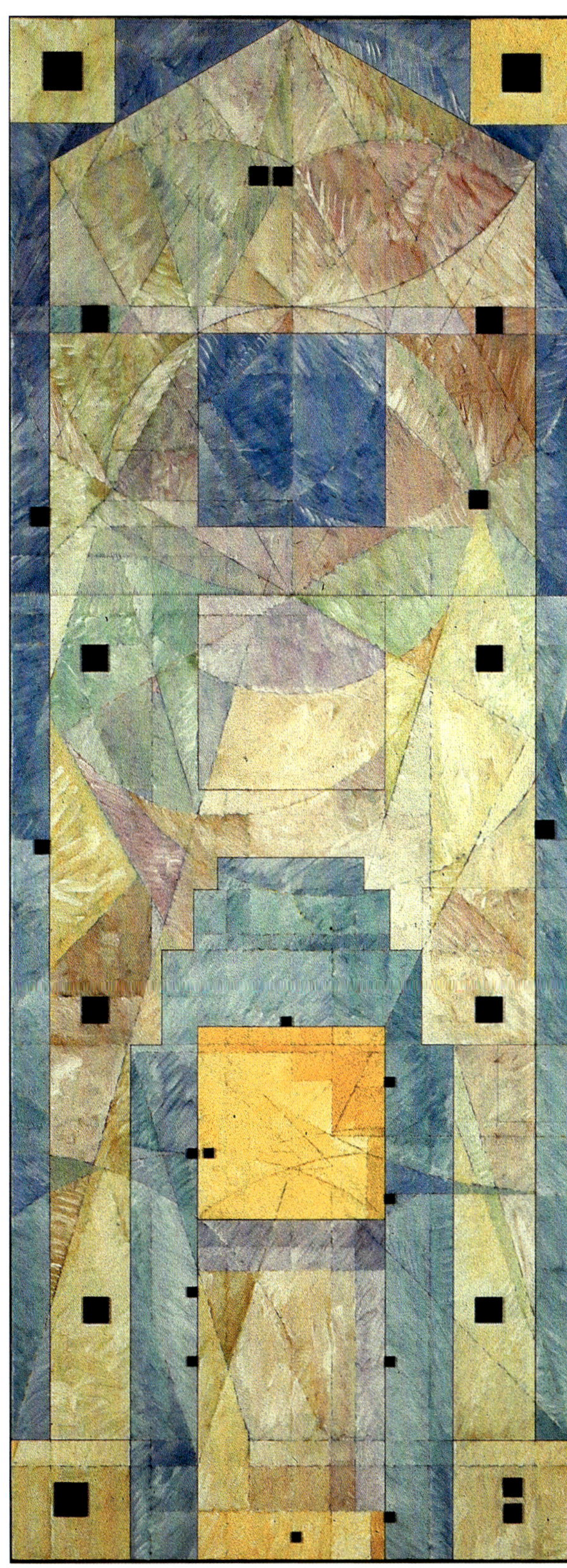

45. Robert Kirschbaum, *Kidron Valley #3*, 1990. Oil on wood, 80 × 30 in. Courtesy of the artist.

5, 1992). In the artist's thoughts, circles relate to the perfection of the Ein Sof (God, the Creator, the One who is known only to itself), and lines refer to the first human who represents the ideal of perfect structure. Further, the juxtapositions and superimpositions of circles, lines, and points on a grid pattern covered with diaphanous layers of paint suggest the ineffable simultaneous appearance and disappearance of forms within one's imagination.

Underlying Kirschbaum's image of the imagined portal of the Temple's facade is his desire to suggest God's perfection as it intersects with the ideal of human perfection, which lies beyond our grasp. He seeks what he imagines might lie on the other side of the Temple portal: "the ineffable, an attempt to glimpse the unattainable" (qtd. in *Temple* 1997), certainly an understandable if unreachable goal for a person on a spiritual quest.

To complicate matters in a good way, the light and bright colors characteristic of each of the paintings in *The Portal Series* symbolize the initial light of Creation as set forth by the Ein Sof. Three passages from sacred texts help explain Kirschbaum's intentions. The first, from the *Zohar*, considers the importance of light: "The primal center is the innermost light, of a translucence, subtlety, and purity, beyond comprehension. That inner point extended becomes a 'palace' which acts as an enclosure for the center, and is also of a radiance translucent beyond the power to know it" (*Zohar* 1977, 28). We humans are not capable of fathoming that translucent radiance, but we can nevertheless meditate upon it as something indefinable that lies beyond our grasp. And two additional passages, suggested by Bernard Goldman, call upon the viewer to think of the portal as an ideal symbol of transformation, metamorphosis, revelation, rebirth, and regeneration. On the other side of the portal lies the hope of "perfect understanding, transfiguration, and eternity." Passing beneath the lintel becomes "an act of consecration." The portal, however, can be considered as an opening both for entering and for leaving. Divine figures symbolically pass in reverse direction into human space from the other side of the portal. "It is between the door-leaves that the epiphany is to be beheld. When the doors of the palace-shrine are thrown wide at the appropriate moment, the theophany is made manifest" (B. Goldman 1966, 21, 73).

When one reads these passages, the issue is not suspending disbelief. Rather, it is contemplating the imaginative possibilities of portal and Temple. In whatever ways Kirschbaum considers portal and Temple, he thinks of them as sacred, ideal spaces, as shelters for the spirit, as symbols of Creation, and as spiritually charged spaces through which one wants to pass in order to access higher realms of being and spiritual enlightenment, not unlike the Emersonian ascension of the soul into higher forms. In short, Kirschbaum seeks access to the never-to-be-reached mystical stream.

But Kirschbaum is also an artist and, as such, moves from idea to idea based on visual clues elaborated upon in succeeding works. For example, in *Kidron Valley #3* we can see intimations of three-dimensional architectural forms in the Temple steps, gates, column bases, and squares that suggest cross-sections or ground plans of column bases. These hints led to a series of sculptural works, including *Temple and Altar* (1991–95) (fig. 46). The temple includes stepped pyramid forms above a templelike form, and the altar is a hollow-centered, stepped pyramid. But these forms lacked the mystery Kirschbaum sought; he realized that each sculpture described the appearance of a structure without necessarily insinuating further meaning. This combination—a structure with spiritual overtones—was to come to him later.

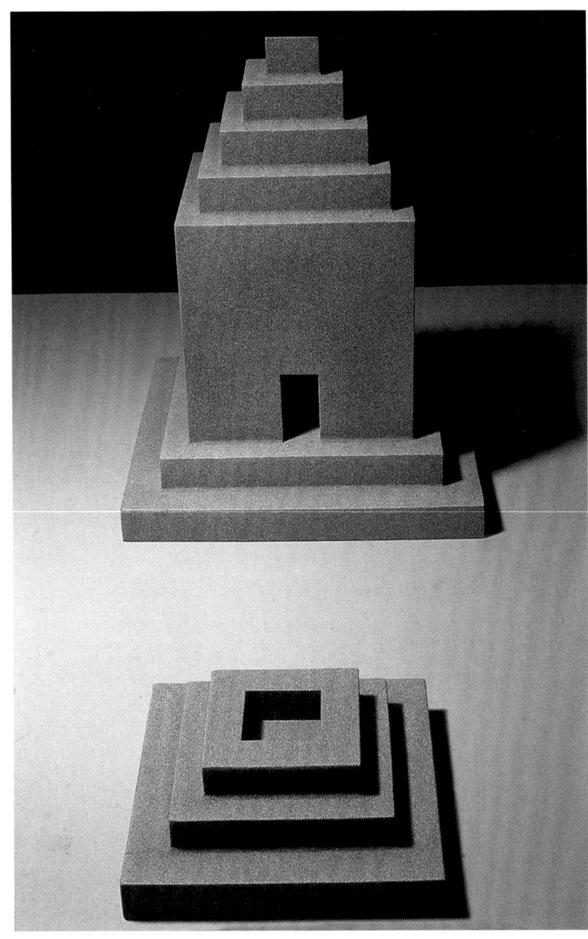

46. Robert Kirschbaum, *Temple and Altar*, 1991–95. Flame coated steel, 20 × 16 × 16 in. and 4 × 20 × 10 in. Courtesy of the artist.

The subsequent series, entitled *Squaring the Mount #2* (1997) (fig. 47), is, by comparison, loaded with meaning. Kirschbaum turned literally to the Mount itself, its underlying irregular shape, and the possibility of shaping it into an ideal configuration so that it would be congruent with the measurements of the Temple platform, which included the Temple itself and the altar, in order to suggest an image of perfectibility and stability (Ezekiel 41:1–15, 43:17). The resulting series, composed of four etchings, each etching containing three individual drawings, are to be read from right to left. The plan of the Mount is a reasonably accurate indication of how it exists today. Kirschbaum

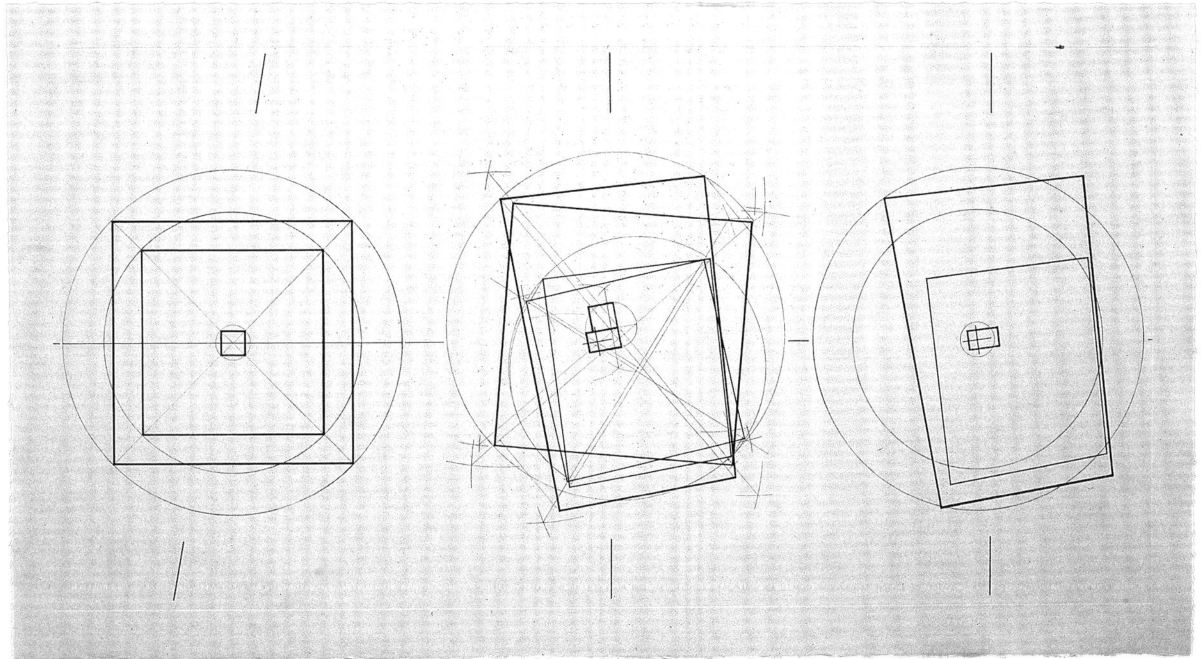

47. Robert Kirschbaum, *Squaring the Mount #2*, 1997. Intaglio, 36 × 72 in. Courtesy of the artist.

then indicated the plan for each of the historical temples on the site, transforming the quadrilateral plans of each temple and the irregular quadrilateral of the Mount to a perfect square equal in area to each quadrilateral. By the time Solomon's Temple was built, the Mount had become square. Thus, on the left of *Squaring the Mount #2* the squares are set inside circles, which for Kirschbaum indicate the integration of the material within the spiritual, the earth within the cosmos. Theoretically, each of these sets can be redrawn an infinite number of times, creating a ritual activity that, in the artist's words, provides a context for "meditations on the meaning of the Temple, its earthly destruction, and its heavenly re-creation" (Kirschbaum n.d.).

Kirschbaum's line etchings, which look like an architect's notes, are also layered with unfulfilled emotional and messianic connotations. In the brochure published for the permanent installation of these works in Trinity College's Hillel House, he appended the following passage from Ezekiel 43:7: "This is the place of My throne and the place for the soles of My feet, where I will dwell in the midst of the people of Israel forever." He also included his own comments:

> I . . . absorbed the fundamental idea that we Jews are a people whose experiences have been shaped by exile; that our return to our most sacred space awaits the miracle of redemption. Aware of our dispersion, I have found a need to internalize this ideal, to contain my sense of the sacred center, and to carry a sacred space within the precincts of my imagination. . . . My art has been a means for me to reconcile the existence of tangible architectural elements in the home and in the synagogue with the broader significance of the Temple, its destruction and mythic re-construction. (Kirschbaum n.d.; see also Kirschbaum c. 1998)

When the line etchings were exhibited in Jerusalem, Kirschbaum added the following thought to the catalog—that the exhibition's presence in that city was akin to an artistic aliyah (permanent return to Israel), "one which I hope will invest my work with new meaning. In bringing my work 'home,' I feel that I am completing the circle, fusing symbol and object, spirit and substance, in a personal act of repair and restoration" (Kirschbaum c. 1998).

For Kirschbaum, the Temple Mount is obviously not just a piece of property. So at a time of his own personal and professional losses around the year 2000 (clearing out his childhood home after the deaths of his parents, the ruin of his own home and studio by fire, and the loss of friends in the attack on the Twin Towers at the World Trade Center in New York City in 2001), he found a healing process in the creation of a series of images associated with the Temple Mount that he called *Akedah*, using the name by which the binding of Isaac by Abraham is known. In Kirschbaum's mixed-media drawings, in which he purposely avoided narrative focus for open-ended meditative possibilities, there are intimations of biblical events and legends associated with the Mount that overlap each other through poetic connections (McBee 2011). One of the most significant events for this series is the legend that Isaac was reported to have been sacrificed and burned, his ashes forming part of the foundation of the Temple; in another legend, the ashes from the ram sacrificed in place of Isaac were included in the foundations for the inner altar of the Temple (Graves and Patai 1963, 178; Spiegel 1993, 4, 35, 37). In other words, Kirschbaum appropriately included death and rebirth in this series, not unlike their inclusion in events that had recently transpired in his own life.

In a letter dated April 1, 2009, Kirschbaum explained, not unexpectedly, that he used ash—or carbon from charcoal and graphite—as the dominant pigment in the *Akedah* images. The

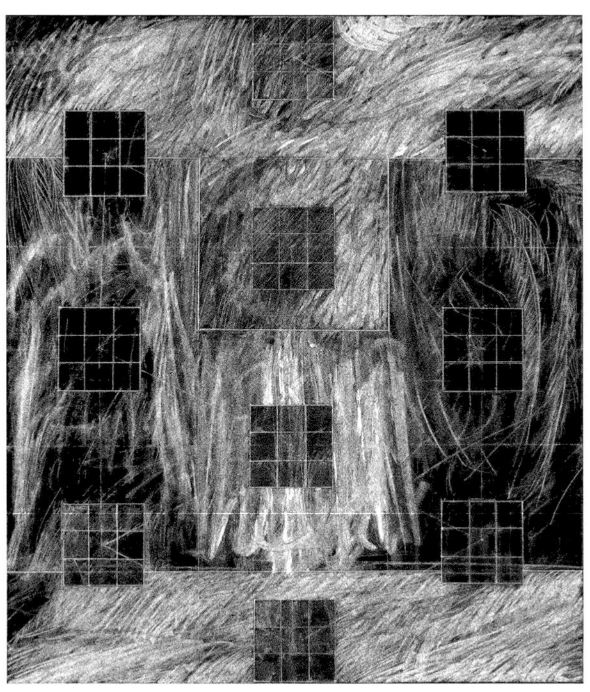

48. Robert Kirschbaum, *Akedah #53*, 2008–9. Digital drawing, size variable. Courtesy of the artist.

work here illustrated, *Akedah #53* (2008–9) (fig. 48), includes square grids, each composed of nine smaller squares arranged in the traditional manner of illustrations in kabbalist literature of the ten *spherot*, or essences of God (variously translated as Wisdom, Understanding, Knowledge, Kindness, Strength, Beauty, Victory, Splendor, Foundation, and the Shekinah). And the scratchy lines have been likened to a ram's head or an angel beating its wings, both creatures associated with the Binding of Isaac (see also Wecker 2009). In other works in this series, a few, faint strokes of colors associated with Israelite priests—purple, blue, ochre, red—can be seen, along with glimpses of ground plans of the Temple Mount, an approximation of the Temple entrance, chariot wheels, and painted-over Hebrew letters. The letters, according to the *Sefer Yetzirah*, one of the oldest kabbalist texts and a book familiar to Kirschbaum, serve as the underlying building blocks for the universe, just as they serve symbolically as the hidden building blocks for the works in the *Akedah* series. Further, an array of small circles representing the constellation Draco might also appear in some drawings; Draco, as stated in the *Sefer Yetzirah*, is "the overseer and director of all the other stars" (*Sefer Yetzirah* 1997, 234).

Despite Kirschbaum's research underlying these iconographic motifs, Richard McBee has suggested what might be the real meaning of the *Akedah* series, particularly in his observations about the last drawing in the series, which includes a very visible rectangle approximating a doorway. Why a doorway? McBee asks. He answers that because we cannot interrogate or question God's intentions, the portal provides the possibility of entry not to find answers but to serve as an opening to the Divine through mystical speculation (McBee 2011). In short, as with *The Portal Series* and the *Squaring the Mount* series, the associative elements Kirschbaum brings to the *Akedah* series attest to the artist's vision of the Temple on the Temple Mount as a mystically speculative ideal of and serious engagement with notions of wholeness, perfectibility, and redemptive communion with the Divine that might also include ways to deal with both personal and worldly catastrophes.

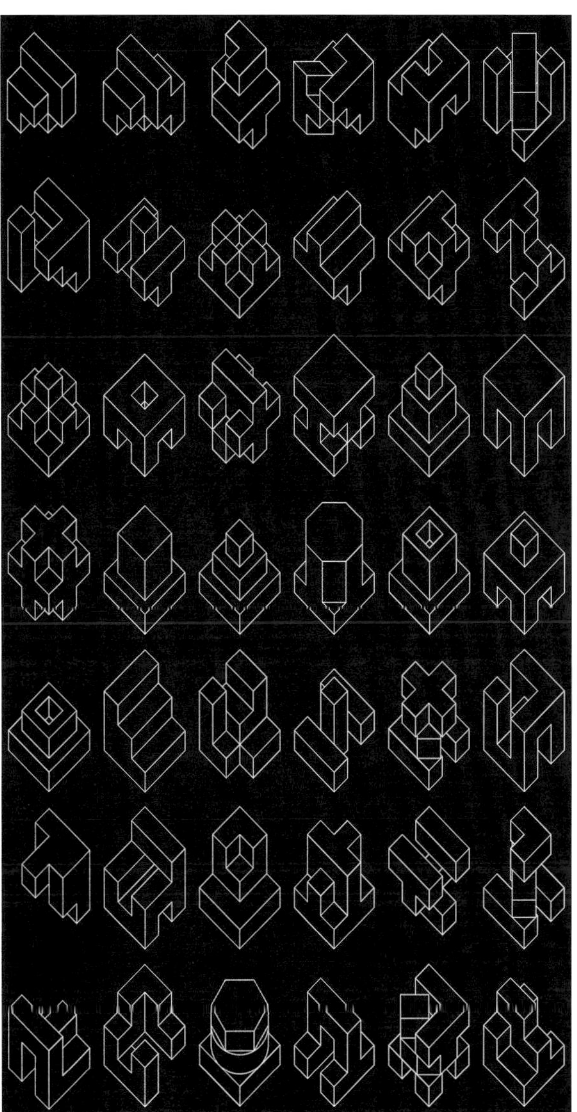

49. Robert Kirschbaum, *The 42-Letter Name Matrix*, 2012. Digital drawing, size variable. Courtesy of the artist.

Negotiating the split between reality and desire (or the experiential with the ideal) seems to have been the motivating force behind Kirschbaum's next project as well, the *Devarim* series, from which he selected forty-two drawings to form the suite of prints entitled *The 42-Letter Name*, begun and completed around 2012 (figs. 49 and 50). This suite also sums up much of Kirschbaum's thoughts about the Mount. Here, too, the associations—and there are several—are poetic and complex rather than straight-line logical. The imaginary Temple suggested in Ezekiel was once again central to the artist's thoughts. Within a square wall, as indicated in the text (50:5), the Temple complex (42:15–20) and the Temple itself (41:13) would also be square in shape. Kirschbaum was probably reminded of Stanley Tigerman's observations that reconstructions of the Temple based on Ezekiel's descriptions were usually organized around a nine-square, geometrically simple grid in order to remove it "from the particularities of a site. This act of displacement allow[ed] for exploration without regard for [a] realistic setting" (1988, 96). Otherwise, anything close to even a symbolic

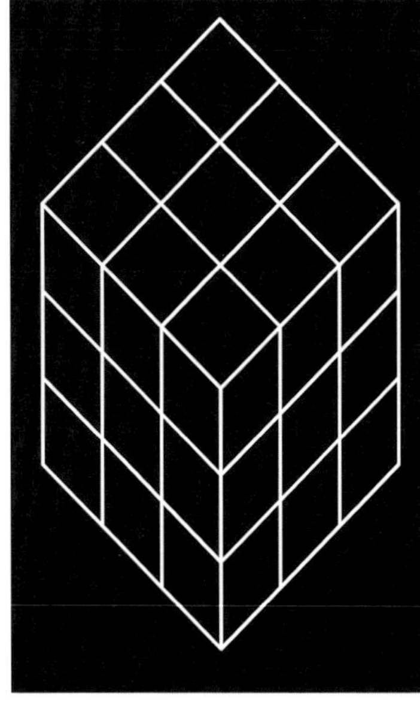
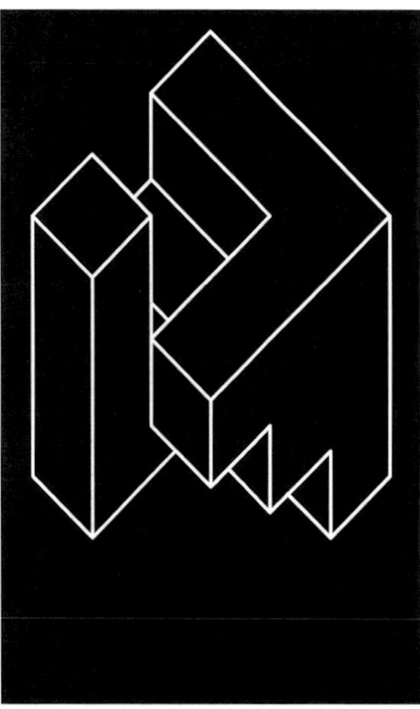

50. Robert Kirschbaum, from *The 42-Letter Name*, left: *Cube*, right: *The 42-Letter Name #7*, 2010. Digital drawings, size variable. Courtesy of the artist.

representation of the Temple would appear as if it were in our physical world, our space.

Kirschbaum chose to represent Ezekiel's Temple vision, not an actual temple. We see in figure 50 a three-dimensional cube, each face divided by a nine-square grid, and another cube from which individual units have been removed. The full cube symbolizes the ideal, completed form—the Temple—and the incomplete cube stands for the fragmented world we live in. By subtracting one or more squares from the cube, Kirschbaum could show "fragments" of the cosmos, which when reassembled would become the whole or complete cosmos, symbolic of the Temple rebuilt in messianic times, an image of perfection and of *tikkun olam*, finally the repair of the world.

To prevent the imaginary Temple from appearing as if it were in a realistic setting that duplicates our human space, Kirschbaum decided to use axonometric projections for *The 42-Letter Name*, a device often used by architects. In this kind of projection, receding lines remain parallel and do not meet at a vanishing point. As has been noted, axonometry represents "an unrepresentable infinity . . . [;] axonometry makes one reflect on (and no longer *see*) infinity" (Bois 1988, 172, emphasis in original). So all spatial representation is eliminated, thus denying the viewer the ability to fathom near or far, here or there. Further, Kirschbaum knew that one of the artists whom he greatly admires, El Lissitsky, wanted to invert space in order to abolish any sense of physical location and even gravity.

With the addition of a forty-third print that shows the complete cube, Kirschbaum created the forty-two works with white lines on black grounds that can be read both two and three dimensionally. Some prints, each a fragment of the completed creation or of the whole, take on aspects of portals, of cubic leather boxes, of phylacteries, and of hollowed-out plazas. In these works, the improvisational-seeming gestures of *Squaring the Mount* (fig. 47) are given precise order and more rigorous definition. But their various permutations suggest that Creation is not yet whole and complete. The "removed" squares reveal an incomplete cosmos (as in the shattered vessels of Rabbi Luria's version of Creation). Each of the removed units would have to be reinstated in order to complete *tikkun olam*. For Kirschbaum, until restoration and repair actually happen, all of life is an ongoing process of seeking God and imagining a completed and whole cosmos (the full cube). In *The 42-Letter Name*, as he has said, "I seek to link Creation—an act of divine construction—within the Temple as a model of the universe" (qtd. in McBee 2010).

Why the title *Devarim*? *Devarim*, which translates as "words and things," is the Hebrew designation for Deuteronomy, a book thought to be composed primarily of three discourses by Moses, the first one actually called *devarim*. Moses's authorship is alluded to in Deuteronomy 31:24. In addition, a scroll found on the Temple Mount during the renovations sponsored by King Josiah in the late seventh century BCE has been associated with the Deuteronomic text and therefore with Moses as its author. (See the discussion on the side panels of Second Kings 22:4 and 22:8 in the *Jewish Study Bible* [1985] 2004, 770–71; see also Mazar 1975, 12.) The word *devarim* is also associated with the Shekhina, one of the kabbalistic *spherot* most closely associated with humans (*Zohar* 1988, 224). In addition, Rabbi Kenneth Brander, dean of Yeshiva University's Center for the Jewish Future, has noted that, according to the Talmud, Deuteronomy is a Second Torah because Moses, not God, presumably wrote it. Rabbi Brander (2010) then suggests that because of this connection, Jews, like Moses, must play an active role in their relationship with God. One way this can be accomplished is to write a Torah of one's own, combining the sacred and the mundane, in order to repair the world and complete Creation. This is precisely what Kirschbaum has done in his own way by suggesting in visual terms his idea of perfection.

Earlier in this chapter, I alluded to the centrality of the Temple Mount within Judaism. At this time and at the risk of providing too much information, I want to give the reader a sense of why that is so; the amount and complexity of some explanations, or rather elaborations, of that location as well as the events thought to have occurred there in biblical times; and, not least, Kirschbaum's preoccupation with the Temple Mount. An abridged passage of a midrash states:

> As the navel is set in the center of the human body, so is the land of Israel the navel of the world. And the foundation of the world comes out of it. The land of Israel sits in the center of the world and Jerusalem is in the center of the land of Israel and the sanctuary is in the center of Jerusalem, and the Temple building is in the center of the sanctuary, and the ark is in the center of the Temple building, and the foundation stone out of which the world was founded is before the Temple building (*Midrash Tanchuma* 1996, Kedoshim, Siman 10.)

God created the Foundation Stone, and on it there appear the forty-two letters that serve as the basis for the Ana B'koach, the prayer reputed to have been written by Rabbi Nehunya ben ha-Qanah in the second century CE (the prayer is in *The Complete Art Scroll Siddur* 2005, 314). The importance of the prayer is as follows: First, God created the world from forty-two letters, which are "the initial letters of the forty-two words constituting the prayer." Second, the forty-two letters are one of the lost secret names of God, which cannot be transmitted except by a discreet, humble, middle-aged, mild-mannered person. Such a person, it is said in the Talmud, will inherit both worlds—this one and the world to come. Third, in one myth the Holy of Holies of the Temple was built on the stone. Fourth, altars erected or gifts brought to the site have been associated with Adam, Cain and Able, Noah, and Abraham. Fifth, there is also the suggestion in the *Zohar* that the name "consists of the first forty-two letters of the Torah" (see Alexander 1984, 120–25; Idel 1988, 89; *Midrash Tanhuma: S. Buber Recession* 1989, 319; Patai 1947, 57–58; *Talmud*

*Bavli* 1993, 2:sec. 71a; Tishby 1989, 2:361; *The Zohar: Pritzker Edition* 2009, 5:sec. 2, 175b). But these letters can be understood only through a process of encoding that, lost to succeeding generations, was known only to the ancient "academy" that flourished from about 10 to 210 CE. What all of this adds up to is an endlessly rich field for the exploration of an unrivaled holy ground rich in history, myth, and legend that appeals to archaeologically, religiously, and spiritually minded individuals, which certainly includes Kirschbaum.

But to return to the physically present, the Temple existed in real time, and the Temple Mount exists in real space. Kirschbaum had earlier translated his multilevel abstract ideas into material forms with the *Temple and Altar* series of 1991–95 (fig. 46), but, as mentioned, he found these forms to be too realistic. In a series titled *Devarim (Sculpture Series) #41, #29, #23* (2010–16) (fig. 51), he found a way to suggest more nearly the abstract shapes of his digital drawings.

In another series begun in 2010 titled the *Ashlar Series*, Kirschbaum created a group of paintings evoking the Western Wall (the Kotel), the cut stone blocks that rise up to the Temple Mount from the plaza floor. It is the place closest to the Mount itself where Jews can pray without harassment. The Wall can be touched. It is solid stone, a place for prayers and religious celebrations, a place for leaving notes in the interstices between the stones in the hope that they will be read in heaven. Kirschbaum, who had shied away from representing the Kotel itself, finally found a way to portray its physical presence commensurate with his abstract style and spiritual concerns.

It took him about twenty-five years to do so. His first visit occurred at midnight in 1985. Kirschbaum remembers, after he was led through the narrow alleyways by an Orthodox young man who insisted that he was performing a mitzvah (a good deed done from religious duty), the way the Kotel, brilliantly illuminated, opened up cinematically before him as he walked into the plaza. His response was partly sensuous—the texture of the stones, their weight and mass, and the soft sounds of the few people praying there—and partly personal in that his father and grandfather had been house builders. Between the stones, he sandwiched *kvitlach*, or notes, that included his grandparents' names. He has told me that on that early visit, overwhelmed by the men in the midst of prayer in what he calls "raw devotional Judaism," he became bonded to the site as the physical and spiritual heart of Judaism.

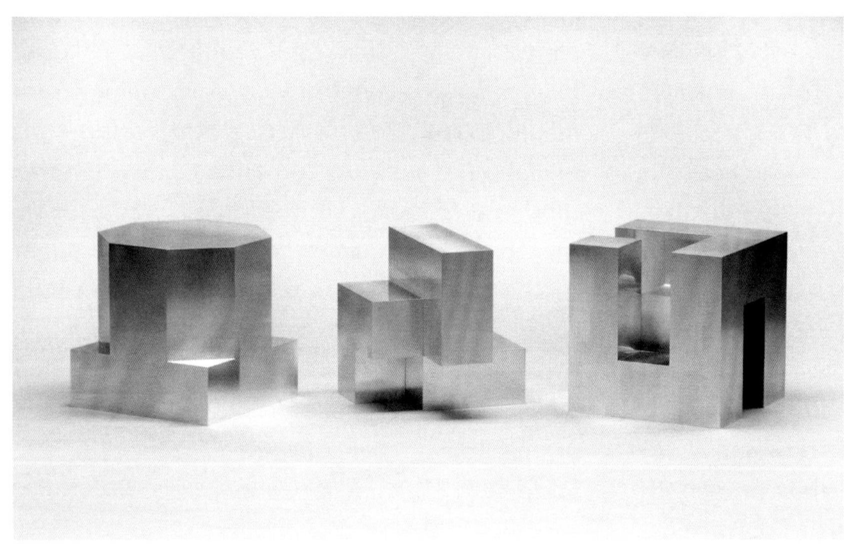

51. Robert Kirschbaum, *Devarim (Sculpture Series) #41, #29, #23*, 2010–16. Machined aluminum, each 6 × 6 × 6 in. Courtesy of the artist.

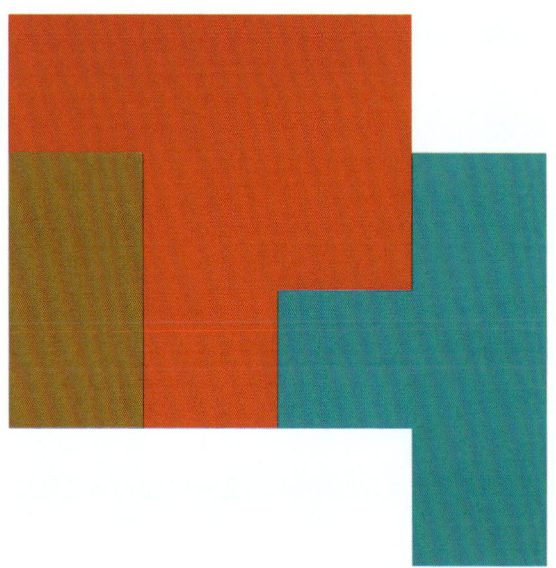

52. Robert Kirschbaum, *Ashlar Series #1*, 2010. Acrylic on wood, 30 × 30 in. Courtesy of the artist.

As is evident in the chapters of this book, each artist's identification with his or her religion is personal and quite varied. In the broad spectrums of style, subject, and attitude, Kirschbaum, an abstract artist, is concerned with imagining an ideal world based on the most sacred place in Judaism, a place that allows for both private meditation and a kind of spiritual grace and that encourages the imagination to roam variously through sacred portals, to contemplate perfect geometrical forms, and to glide easily back and forth between the intangible and the temporal as well as between the intellectual and the emotional. With his abstract ideal forms, he asks us in a gentle, nondirective way to think about the unreachable. Not an easy project for the viewer to grasp, but one that helps distinguish the admittedly open-ended parameters of contemporary Jewish American art from the more text-bound sources that motivated and, arguably, limited many earlier artists.

The manner in which Kirschbaum approaches and works to realize his aims is both rare in its extreme abstract/spiritual concerns and typical of artists of his generation, who are willing to express their religiosity without embarrassment. He and they know that others of their generation are also negotiating or, better, navigating their way in hopes of attaining both artistic and spiritual fulfillment. In this sense, Jewish history and their Jewish present are for these artists less a series of events in physical time than a succession of metaphysical engagements in a spaceless expanse.

# 9 Tobi Kahn

Of his generation of artists, Tobi Kahn (b. 1952) is among those who have explored the aesthetic possibilities of many mediums. He is a painter, a sculptor, a creator of objects used in religious rituals, as well as a designer of synagogue, multifaith, hospital, and hospice interiors as well as of spaces intended for personal meditation. He is also an observant Jew and the most religiously knowledgeable among a group of religiously knowledgeable artists. Having attended equivalent elementary and high school yeshivas in New York and then devoting himself to religious study in yeshivas in Israel for three years, he has often said that he cannot separate his art from his life and beliefs. Each infuses and is infused by the other (see Van Biema 2016).

Kahn views himself as a conceptual artist whose work is influenced by fractal geometry, color theory, and the power of sacred space. He explained his way of thinking and working when interviewed on July 25, 2013, for the Public Broadcasting Service program *Religion & Ethics Newsweekly*: "I believe that everyone is made in *tzelem elokim*, meaning we are all created in God's likeness. When I see something beautiful, I see God's presence imbued in the world. I want my work to evoke that feeling" ("Artist Tobi Kahn" 2013).

To put this assertion in a slightly different, more secular context, Kahn would probably agree—profoundly agree—with statements made by the twentieth-century American artist Charles Sheeler (1883–1965): "The highest phase of spiritual life has always in one form or another implied a consciousness of it, and its greatest moments, a contact with, what we feel to be the profound scheme, system, or order underlying the universe: call it harmonies, rhythm, law, fact, God, or what you will" (Sheeler 1916), and "The thing I deplore is an absence of spiritual content" (qtd. in Wight 1954, 28).

During a conversation on January 16, 2018, as Kahn searched for words that would link his work and life to his idea of holiness, he mentioned that even though his entire being is steeped in Jewish traditions, he believes that he can live both within his heritage and as an artist in the world. Kahn feels that he wants his art to communicate on a spiritual level to his viewers by whatever words they might use or by whatever religious beliefs they might have. As he once said, "I am very proud to be Jewish . . . but I don't think Judaism is the only path. . . . My lens is as a god-fearing person, Judaism is the religion I know, but I am very interested in all the others" (qtd. in Van Biema 2016). He then added that all people are chosen, and he counts not only rabbis but also priests and ministers among his close friends.

Aware that there are many ambiguous passages in the ancient texts, he initially conceives a work in somewhat realistic abstracted forms so that multiple meanings and a sense of

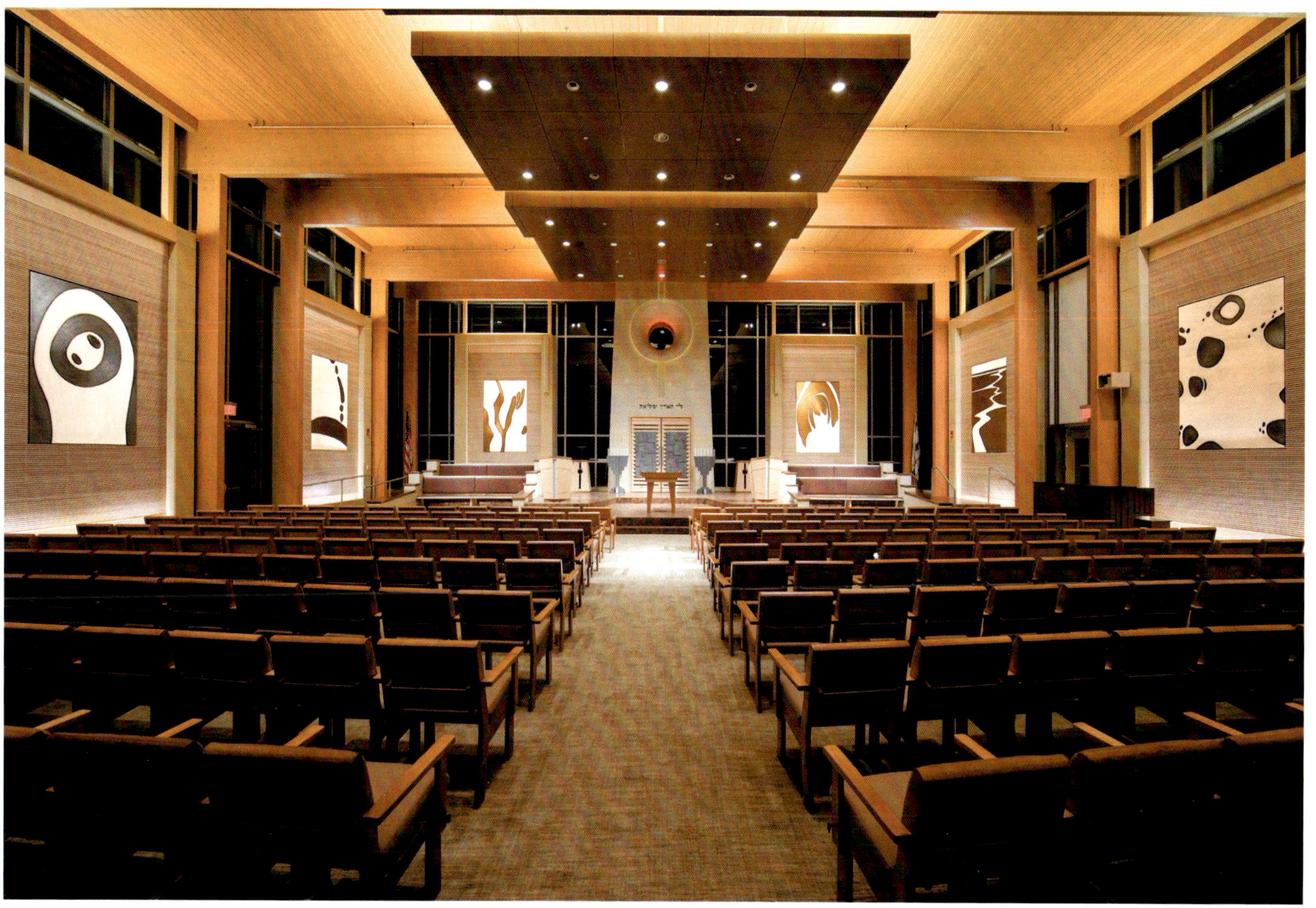

53. Tobi Kahn, interior, Temple Emanu-El B'ne Jeshurun, Milwaukee, WI, 2009. By permission of the temple. Courtesy of the artist.

timeless history can be read into them. That is, in the best sense of what he feels is his obligation to his faith, he projects his vision through a religious passion that is at once traditional, adventurous, celebratory, contemporary, and knowledgeable, and at the same time he invites his viewers, whatever their religious background and heritage, to interpret his works in ways relevant to their own lives. His ritual objects are the single exception because they are crafted for particular purposes, but he might give even them antic forms or shapes that can be read other than in a religious sense.

One of the easiest ways to grasp fully Kahn's artistic intentions is to look first at the interior of the Temple Emanu-El B'ne Jeshurun in Milwaukee, Wisconsin, completed in 2009, which includes eight paintings by Kahn on the walls and some of the ritual objects and decorations he has made—the panels for the Ark holding the scrolls, the Eternal Light, and the mezuzah (fig. 53). It needs to be said that for Kahn the commission was not just a matter of furthering his career but rather an incredible opportunity to put into practice his belief that "the life of the spirit is integrally bound to the beauty of the world" (Kahn 2009, 11); that is, he wanted to create a beautiful space for the human spirit to flower and flourish. As he wrote,

> In the Jewish way, the divine presence is abstract, incorporeal, without beginning or end. How, then, can God be made manifest in the material world? The infinite and mortal can meet in spaces designated as liminal, dwelling places that invite our spirit, made in the image, to encounter the ineffable God in both splendor and intimacy. (Kahn 2009, 11)

For Kahn, the numerous synagogue and interfaith spaces, hospice and hospital interiors, and exterior spaces represent for him "holiness in use. The life of a community within these sacred spaces encompass[es] ardor and despair, turbulence and tranquility, sorrows and elation" (2009, 12)—in short, the stuff of life infused with spirit, the most completely lived life possible. If one were to chart a graph of how Kahn's works reflect his intentions, these synagogues, interfaith spaces, and hospitals are an important development and, by their very nature, the most complete embodiment of his most ardently held aspirations.

Born in New York, Kahn graduated from Yeshiva University High School in New York and then studied at a yeshiva in Israel in the early 1970s before attending Hunter College and Pratt Institute, from which he received his master of fine arts degree in 1978. By that time, he had begun to make what he called "shrines" in addition to paintings that evoke landscape scenes without depicting them realistically (for additional biographical information on Kahn, see Baigell 2006a, 186–200, and Kahn 2004). Over the years, his paintings have grown more abstract and concerned with the fragility of our environment. The shrines, their concomitant sacred spaces, and their implied holiness have become more central to his career. In this regard, he adheres to that point of view expressed by several Jewish theologians, such as Samson Raphael Hirsch (1800–1888) and the Talmudic scholars Adin Steinsaltz (b. 1937) and Abraham Joshua Heschel (1907–72), who believed that spiritual values are paramount and that traditional Judaism is compatible with Western culture.

For example, some of Hirsch's aphorisms describe Kahn's attitude quite closely. Hirsch wrote that there should be "exaltation and sanctification of spiritual life by symbolic words and acts" and that you should "strive . . . in emulation of the Deity to do all your deeds in love, and thus become a blessing to yourself and to your surroundings" (1969, 75–76, 80). Steinsaltz stated: "The Jewish attitude is that life in all its aspects, in its totality, must somehow or other be bound up with holiness" (1980, 154). To bring this notion into one's daily life, Heschel wrote: "We are a community that maintains that a table in the home is an altar" (1996, 29).

Heschel's precise meaning is not entirely clear, but his words suggest that an altar can be used for self-determined sacred purposes, whether they are specific religious purposes or not. In fact, in recent years a broad-based nondenominational literature has appeared that emphasizes the fact that most sacred spaces and shrines are embedded with personal meaning rather than with religious dogma. It has been stated that "the experience of the sacred, more primordial and more resistant to erosion than religious experience, seems fundamental to man as a cultural being or 'symbolic animal' and that remains even within our secularized condition, a basic *factum*—a weight" (Verschaffel 2012, 50; see also Clines 1998, 2:544.) Accordingly, virtually any space can be made sacred by those who create, shape, and provide it with a sacred content in order to commune with the divine as a symbol of "the unity between the Self and the universe [and to] provide a sacred and holy place amid the ordinary reality of life" (Linn 1999, 11). For instance, a shrine composed of selected objects can be arranged in an altar placed, say, in a corner of one's living room or backyard garden and can be defined as "an ordered arrangement of objects with symbolic meaning." Such an altar can be "displayed in a way that evokes inspiration, memory, respect, or reverence" (McMann 1998, 9; see also Chidester and Linenthal 1995; Keder and Werblowsky 1998; Scott and Housley 1991). In effect, one can transform private or public spaces into sacred spaces as one so desires rather than according to fixed notions of what a sacred space is supposed to entail.

The amount of fluidity between spaces called "sacred," "religious," "holy," and "personal" can then be determined by the person or persons creating such spaces. As a consequence, the distance between the mundane and the holy can be imperceptible for individuals such as Kahn because what he calls shrines and sacred spaces blend one into the other. All contain some degree of holiness for him. He remembers, "[As a child] I loved *Kol Nidre* [intoned at the start of the Yom Kippur service] because I remember everything being white [in some congregations dressing in white clothing is traditional in order to suggest an angelic state free of sin]. It was my first sacred space" (qtd. in Wise 2009). And during an interview on December 21, 2011, he mentioned that he was very impressed by the amount of space in Exodus devoted to the building of the Mishkan, the Tabernacle in the Desert, because of its importance as a holy space. Wanting to create such spaces, he said, was one of his reasons for becoming an artist. To walk into such a space, he believes, changes the way one feels. It slows one down; it becomes a space for meditation, for a spiritual journey. "That's what holiness is to me" (qtd. in Wise 2009). The visual component in designing a sacred site is therefore obviously of great importance to him. He has said: "What we see can be a benediction" (qtd. in Wulkin 2002, 7; see also Bilski 2004, 16; Moorman 2001, 116; Nahas 1987, 14–15; Selz 1997, 14).

The intensity of feeling and piety behind his words and his insistence that *art* and *holiness* are virtually interchangeable terms are certainly rare and probably unique in the history of Jewish American art. On another level, it is worthwhile noting that he is not alone among artists of his generation who so openly project and express their religious feelings in their work, a characteristic much more guarded in previous generations of Jewish American artists, as noted in chapter 1.

In the late 1970s, Kahn began to make shrines and sacred spaces initially from discarded objects. These works soon evolved into devotional objects composed of small figures within protective architectural enframements. Emily Bilski has called these table-top creations "household structures harboring small expressive sculptures" (2004, 16). The largest and most famous of Kahn's shrines is titled *SHALEV* (fig. 54), a thirteen-foot-tall, forty-thousand-pound granite sculpture commissioned by Jane Blaffer Owen in 1993 for an outdoor site in New Harmony, Indiana. (Khan makes up wordlike titles for his works so that their potential meanings are universal, timeless, and open-ended rather than specific or anecdotal.)

Whatever their size, these shrines and their immediately surrounding sacred spaces do not literally enclose people. But as early as 1981, Kahn had planned such a space to be erected in an outdoor setting or in a large room. He called it *Poles for the Dwelling*, and it was based on the design and dimensions of the Tabernacle in the Desert, as described in Exodus 25:36–38. Three temporary walls were to be formed by poles that symbolically connected earth and sky. The open space within, Kahn suggested, would radiate holiness and a sense of peace.

This project, although not completed, might have been the pivotal inspiration for much of his subsequent work. He previously had wanted to "replicate the aura of a chosen

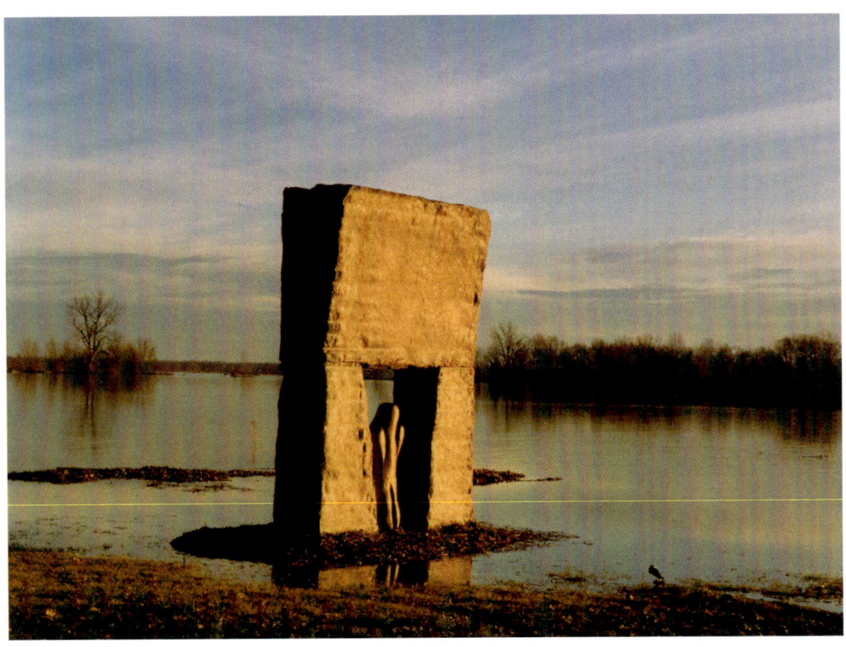

54. Tobi Kahn, *SHALEV*, 1993. Granite exterior, 150 × 98 × 44 in. Bronze interior, 60 × 20 × 14 in. Blaffer Owen Trust, New Harmony, IN. Courtesy of the artist.

object in communion with its own constructed space" (Nahas 1987, 14), but with *Poles* he wanted to hold the viewer visually and conceptually within a created space. A second space never constructed, titled *Creation and Re-Creation*, was less a meditative space than one for reflection on ways people have damaged the world and how it might be fixed. As he stated in an undated, typed sheet, "In the rabbinic tradition, we are mandated to continue God's work, partners in renewing the world." In other words, *Creation and Re-Creation* was intended as a place to contemplate *tikkun olam*. Kahn imagined a series of paintings and sculptures that would form "a sacred space that explores that continuum from the eden of birth and the beginning to the possible loss of our world. Whether we redeem or abandon the world that is our gift—as artists, as citizens—in our hands. This environment is meant to inspire both a reverence for the breadth of the created world and a terror of our record of stewardship."

By such statements, Kahn implies that the spirit within a person together with the spirit revealed within a space or an art object can create a sense of holiness and a spiritual experience. There is a kind of religious intensity here described by Jennings Tofel (mentioned in chapter 1) with which Kahn, of all the artists of his generation, might agree. In a journal entry dated January 5, 1944, Tofel wrote that the story of the design and construction of the Tabernacle (Exodus 25–27) illustrated for him the place of spirit in an artwork. The quality of the materials used are "intended to glorify the One who dwells within the sanctuary and is hidden from view—the spirit. To me this is the most telling parable of a work of art. . . . The spirit of a work of art dwells unseen within and is to be perceived otherwise than by the physical senses" (qtd. in Granick 1976, 222).

One might ask at this point if the nondenominational Rothko Chapel in Houston and the paintings created by Mark Rothko (1903–70) between 1964 and 1967 influenced Kahn, insofar as he has often mentioned Rothko as well as the Jewish artists Chaim Soutine (1893–1943), Louise Nevelson (1899–1988), and Eva Hess (1936–70) as important influences. The chapel, popularly designated a sacred space, is certainly known to Kahn. But his concerns are different from Rothko's. Dominique de Menil, who commissioned the chapel, is reported to have said that Rothko's paintings evoke "the mystery of the cosmos, the tragic mystery of our perishable condition [and] the silence of God, the unbearable silence of God" (qtd. in J. Goldman 2003). Kahn in effect seconded de Menil's observation when he said that the Rothko Chapel is best suited for reading Lamentations (Wise 2009).

In contrast, Kahn, Carol Hamoy, and others think in terms of positive emotional and physical healing rather than in terms of mystery or the silence of God. Kahn once observed: "I want to transmute the darkness, salvage it for meditation without denying its power, revealing the spirit of our inner lives—mysterious, resonant, a sanctuary in a still struggling world" (qtd. in Wulkin 2002, 7). On another occasion, he said, "I want to create environments in hospitals and synagogues and places of worship because I really hope that the art I create brings one's soul to a higher place" (qtd. in Wecker 2010).

In spite of Kahn's more optimistic disposition, he has sometimes mentioned his fear of unforeseen loss and security, of the fact that anything can happen at any moment. In a typed statement dated January 1995, he wrote: "I am always conscious of time's passing, of the possibility of loss, an abrupt reversal of safety." Such thoughts are undoubtedly prompted by the fact that he was named after an uncle who in 1933 was among the earliest casualties of Hitler's murderous anti-Semitism. So it is not surprising that Kahn lavished considerable attention on two gardenlike environments he designed as sacred sites to memorialize those murdered in the Holocaust: the Avrum and Yocheved Holocaust Memorial Garden at the Holocaust Educational Institute of the Jewish Community Center on the Palisades in Tenafly, New Jersey, completed in 1997, and the Holocaust Memorial Garden of the Lawrence Family at the Jewish Community Center of San Diego, completed in 2000 (fig. 55).

For the center in Tenafly, Kahn designed a traffic island in front of the main entrance of the Holocaust Educational Institute. It contains four figures set among trees and two figures placed near the front door. In a typed sheet dated June 1996, he wrote that he wanted to engage

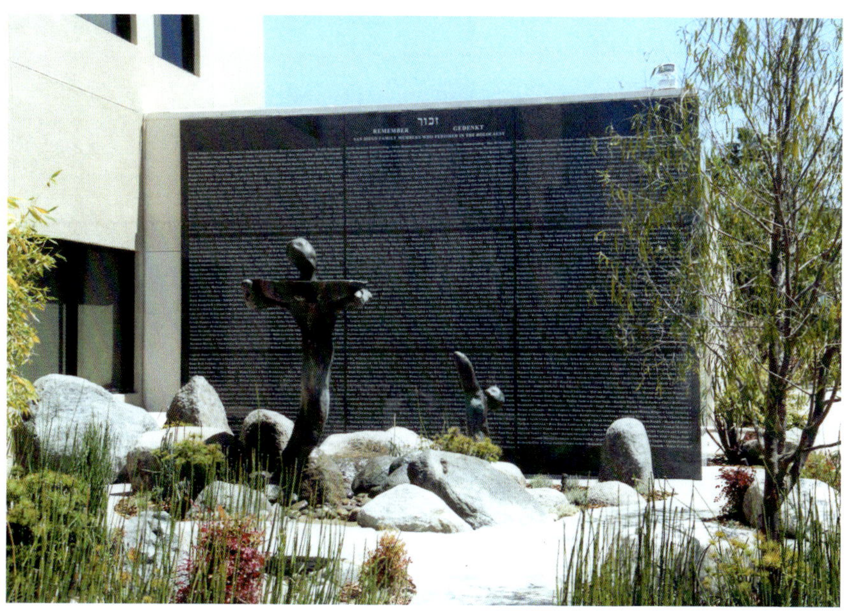

55. Tobi Kahn, Holocaust Memorial Garden in Memory of All Who Perished, 2000. Mixed media. Given in honor of Irene and Eric Racz by Merle and Theresa Racz Fischlowitz. Courtesy of the artist.

> those who are living after them [the murdered] in a way that allows each person who approaches, strolling to a lecture, hurrying to swim, dropping off a child, to encounter the possibility of memory. . . . I hope that this work will be a meditative place. . . . I hope it will be brought to life by people sitting on the rocks circling the images translating them into meaning for their own journeys, linking their imaginations with the people who preceded them. . . . And I hope that through this work, each viewer can locate his or her unique Jewish story in our shared identity.

There it is, his artistic purpose in a nutshell: the desire to move people spiritually, emotionally, intellectually and to provoke personal and community memory.

The memorial in San Diego includes sculptures of a large adult bringing a basin of overflowing water to a child, whose arms are raised in supplication. Names of the murder camps and of the Righteous Ones, those Christians who risked their lives to save Jews, are cut into the stones. The names of members of San Diego families who perished in the Holocaust are chiseled into the dark granite wall. The word *Remember* at the top of the wall is written in Hebrew, Yiddish, and English. In a typed statement dated 1999 and signed by Kahn and his wife, the author Nessa Rapoport, they noted: "Here in this meditative space we can stroll or sit, reflecting on what can never be repaired and on what continues, despite all we have undergone, to persist and flourish."

More than a decade later, in 2011, Kahn created what he called a sacred space, a healing space, titled *M'AHL, Embodied Light: 9-11 in 2011* (fig. 56) in the Educational Alliance building in New York's Lower East Side to commemorate those killed in the terrorist attack on the Twin Towers in New York in 2001 (Kahn 2011, 11). Maya Benton called it "a sanctuary for intimate acts of elegy, meditation, and reflection" (2011, 21). It is impossible to reproduce the entire space in a single view, but it includes a floor panel composed of thousands of wood remnants that suggest an aerial view of the city, seven memorial lights, and seven small shrines, each encompassing an abstract figure and two charity boxes, lacking names of the dead because, as Kahn wrote,

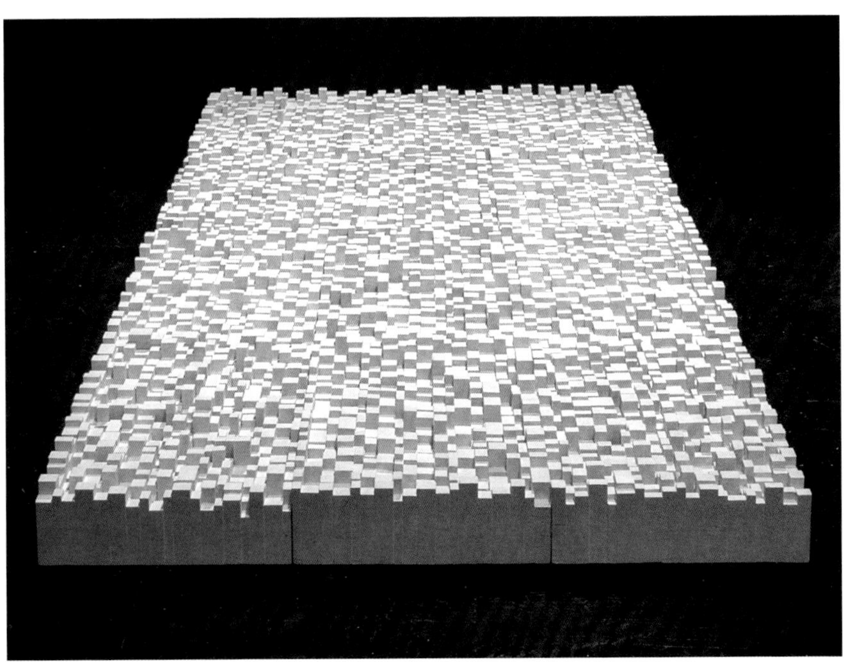

56. Tobi Kahn, *M'AHL, Embodied Light: 9-11 in 2011*, 2011. Acrylic on wood, twelve panels, each 20 × 14 × 5 in; total size 80 × 42 × 5 in. Courtesy of the artist.

their death is an "unnamable sorrow" (Kahn 2011, 11). As Maya Benton noted, "Mourning and destruction are interpreted through Jewish tropes" and include shrines, Jewish ritual objects such as the memorial lights and the charity boxes, with seven being significant because it is the number of days of Creation and the number of days one mourns immediately after a death in the family (2001, 21). In addition, Kahn gave 220 individuals a small wooden block, the total number of floors in the two towers, and asked them to write or draw their responses to the attack.

Despite the severity of the event and the effect on individuals who lost friends or relatives, Kahn also invoked in his statement the traditional Jewish sense of community, here enlarged to include the entire city: "Here we are, bound to each other in remembrance, pledged to transmuting darkness, to creating a sanctuary in a struggling world." But as he has explained about other works that might be initiated by Jewish values, they invariably morph into universal values. He also noted in regard to this memorial space that "grief ruptures meaning. Art can be a small, still voice that begins to mend it . . . by inviting all of us who live after [the victims] to our own imaginative encounter with the possibilities of memory" (Kahn 2011, 11).

In the years before and after making the memorial at the Educational Alliance, Khan completed other meditation spaces as well as the *Sky and Water* paintings, which when exhibited turned galleries into meditation spaces. But before discussing the latter, I should mention at least one additional meditation space titled *EMET, Meditation Space* (fig. 57), created for the Health Care Chaplaincy in New York in 2002, because this space's painted walls are of a piece with the *Sky and Water* paintings. The room was designed as a place of refuge and refreshment for the chaplaincy staff, whose service to those who suffer can become overly stressful. *EMET* was Kahn's first permanent installation for which he provided the designs. In an undated typed statement, he described the room in this way: "[It] joined my interest in sacred space to my exploration of sky, water, and timelessness. I hope the room offers not an

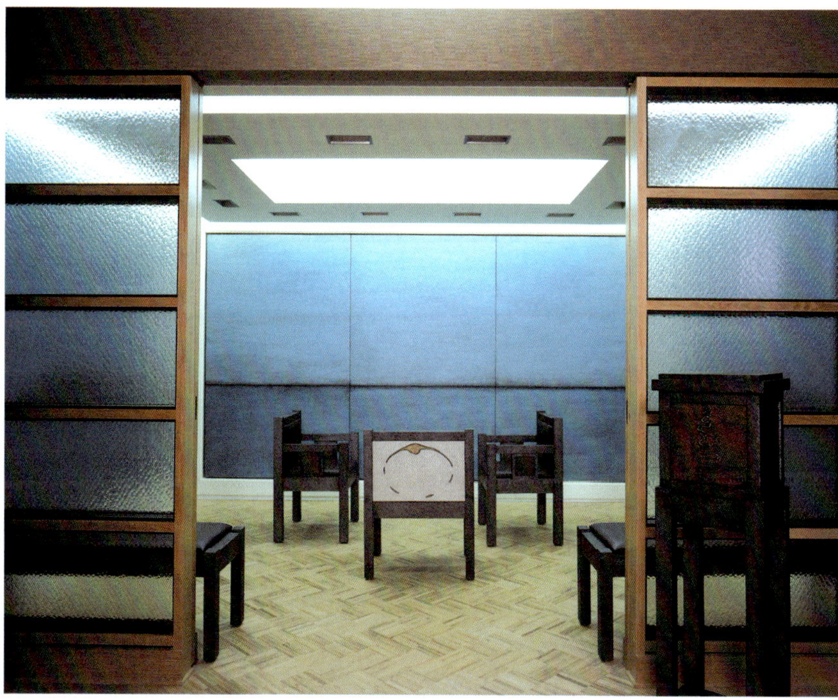

57. Tobi Kahn, *EMET, Meditation Space*, New York Health Care Chaplaincy, 2002. Mixed media, acrylic on canvas over wood. Courtesy of the artist.

escape, but a respite from the staccato pace of contemporary life [and allows the individual] to reenter the world restored, consoled, and engaged" (see also Prescott 2001).

On entering the room, one feels immersed in both sky and water. Each of the three walls there has three vertical sections, forming nine sections altogether composed of a light-blue sky set on a darker-blue body of water. In the softly lit room, one has the feeling of looking down at an infinite distance of water and straight ahead at an equally infinite sky. As one observer noted, "It gives us the sense of peace that can often bring healing, regardless of who we are, or whether we have a spiritual or religious faith" (Bowness-Park 2013).

Kahn, a religious Jew, based the number of panels not on the size of the room and the scale of the objects relative to it, but rather on the notion of bringing some traditional Jewish ways of thinking into consideration. He mentioned in a conversation that he designed each wall to house three vertical units, the number 3 symbolizing the three pillars of the faith, as mentioned in the Pirkei Avot (Wisdom of the Fathers) 1:2—Bible study, worship, loving deeds or charity. And further, Kahn purposely planned three panels for each wall; placed three chairs, two benches, one bookstand within the room; and designed three separate light sources. Altogether, these features add up to eighteen individual decisions on his part. The number 18 carries great weight for Jews. In Jewish numerology, each Hebrew letter is given a number. The letters that spell the Hebrew word for "life," *chai*, add up to eighteen. So Kahn, using Jewish numerology and the life-enhancing associations with the numbers 3 and 18, honored the chaplaincy's extraordinary devotion to its creed and its concern for sustaining human life.

The *Sky and Water* paintings, from which the chaplaincy's meditation room evolved, turned galleries into meditation spaces. (For one of these paintings, see *RIFA: Sky and Water* [2011], fig. 58.) Kahn decided on the format as early as 1985 and on the arrangement of forms by 1987, and he conceived the idea of a series of works exhibited together in 1997. The first exhibition of the works as a group occurred in 1999 at the Albright-Knox Art Gallery in Buffalo, New York, and was titled *Landscape*. The purposeful arrangement of paintings was intended to induce meditations that might evolve or become transformed as the viewer's eyes moved from surface to surface—an active type of contemplation, as it were.

Critics who viewed exhibitions of the *Sky and Water* paintings at other venues ventured the following observations about the paintings' effects on them. At Yeshiva University Museum in New York, the thirty-six paintings shown "fill[ed] two large rooms with the subtle and yet unmistakable aura, the delicate and yet bold and overwhelming instigation, of a meditative and distinctly spiritual incursion" (M. Cohen 2003). Of the installation at the Neuberger Museum of Art in Purchase, New York, a critic noted that "while [I was] staring at them [the paintings] over long periods of time, a wave of great calm swept over me. . . . [The place] looks and feels like a chapel, or at least somewhere you might associate with the veneration of gods" (Genocchio 2003). Another critic suggested that the paintings offered vistas of the "'Beyond' as inscape, a sacred inner space—a sanctuary from the outer world it appears to represent. Taken together, they turn mundane space into meditative space" (Kuspit 2003, 6). And yet another critic thought that the paintings transformed the gallery into "an integrated space for looking, self-reflection, and consciousness" (Young 2003, 7).

The critics clearly understood Kahn's objectives. In a typed sheet, he had noted that he wanted the paintings to turn galleries into contemplative oases. When some of the paintings were installed in the Evansville Museum

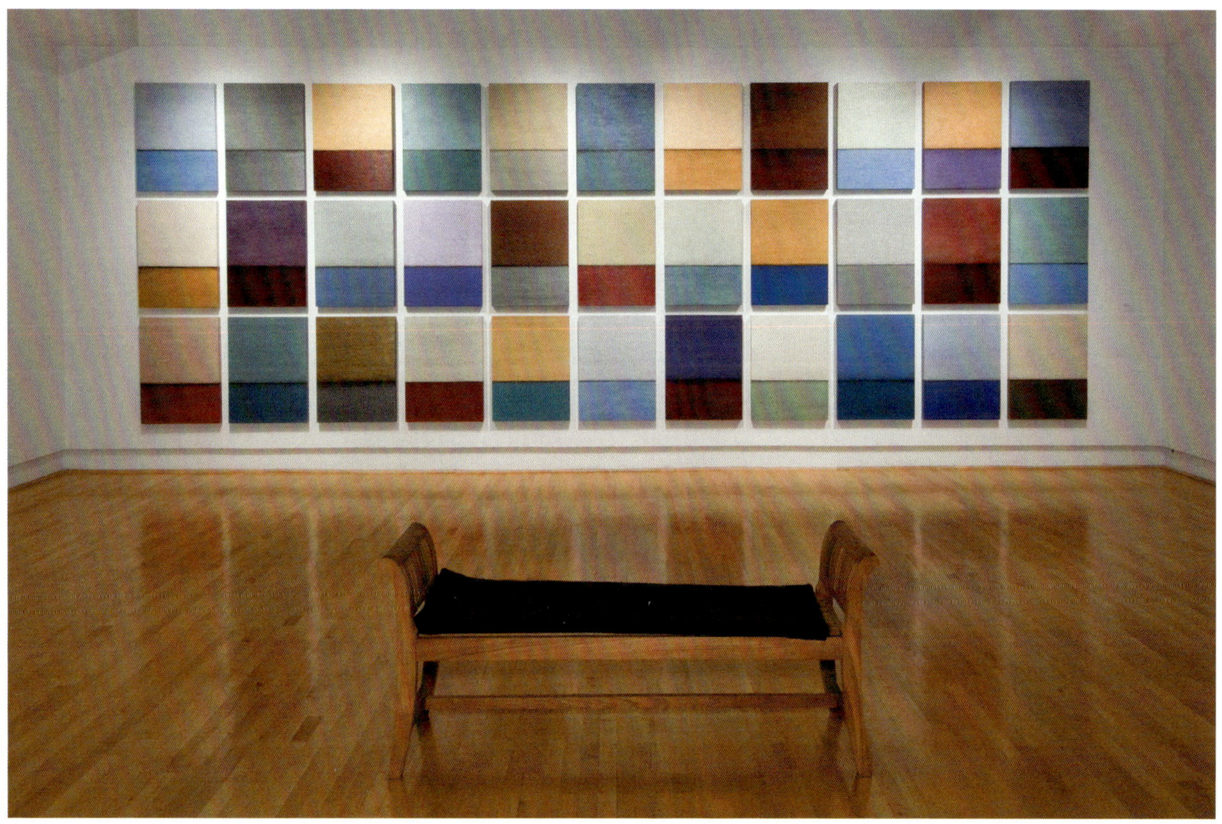

58. Tobi Kahn, *RIFA: Sky and Water*, 2011. Thirty-three acrylic on wood panels, each 32 × 24 × 2½ in. Installation at the University of Maryland Art Gallery, College Park. Courtesy of the artist.

in Indiana in 2010, a yoga class moved into the gallery space. Kahn was delighted. "I know many people have meditated in my spaces," he said, "but I don't know if anyone has ever actually done yoga in one. I'm thrilled" (qtd. in McBain 2010). The yoga instructor and class members also understood Kahn's objectives.

Over the years, Kahn has made at least four sets of works concerned with women of the Bible—two sets of chairs, a mural series, and a set of sculptures. The first set of chairs, titled *NATYH* (1987), was created for a baby-naming ritual when Kahn and his wife, Nessa, had their first child. The chairs, intended for Nessa, her mother, and Kahn's mother, are similar to the later *Shalom Bat Chairs* (2008) (fig. 59), except for the images on the chair backs. Kahn intended the rounded, swelling forms to suggest body parts described in the Song of Songs, but when the chairs are placed close together, the forms on each chair seem to reach over to the adjoining chairs but do not quite connect or properly line up, suggestive of the line, according to Kahn, "I sought but found him not" from the Song of Songs.

The *Shalom Bat Chairs* were commissioned for ceremonies naming baby girls (G. Rosenblatt 2007, 7; see also Wertheimer 2018, 46, for the history of Shalom Bat rituals). Created to honor the Four Matriarchs—Sarah, Rebecca, Leah, and Rachel—the panels are abstract in design, as is Kahn's usual intention. (In figure 59, the panels are arranged in the following order from left to right: Rachel, Rebecca, Sarah, Leah.) During a visit to his studio, he indicated how he balanced his aesthetic concerns for color and form with his desire to suggest in each panel a minimal narrative that

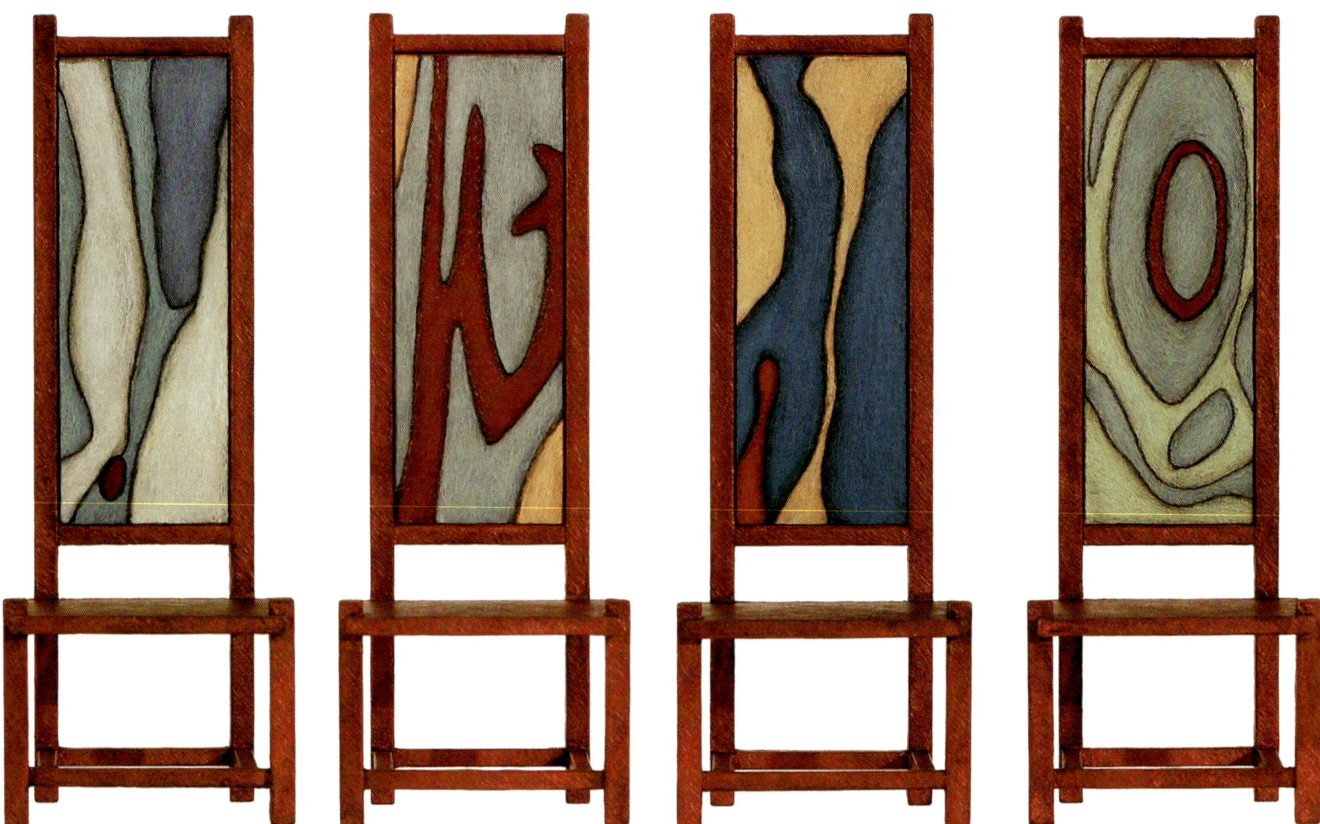

59. Tobi Kahn, *AHMA: Shalom Bat Chairs—Rachel, Rebecca, Sarah, Leah*, 2008. Acrylic on wood, 70 × 21 × 26 in. Commissioned by the Shaykin Family Foundation for the Abraham Joshua Heschel School, New York. Courtesy of the artist.

defined each matriarch's behavior and character. But Khan did not reveal the narrative clues, always preferring his viewers to interpret his works as they so choose. My interpretations follow.

In biblical chronological order, in the panel honoring Sarah (third from left), the two large blue forms separated by a thin yellow line signify the closeness yet distance between Sarah and Hagar. Sarah is the form on the left. Her head is thrown back because when she found out at the age of ninety that she would have a child, she laughed inwardly (Genesis 18:12). The red area between her legs suggests blood symbolizing life, the birth canal, or her son, Isaac. The upper part is slightly enlarged as if it might be a head. The blue color of the two women might also symbolize water, continuity, purification, and the flow of time. In comparison to Hagar's figure, Sarah's upright posture gives her a noble, royal bearing, appropriate to the mother of the Israelite people and, with Abraham, the parent of a nation (Genesis 17:4).

The spiky, red-brick forms in the Rebecca panel (second from left) probably symbolize the personal difficulties Rebecca encountered in raising two quite different sons, Jacob and Esau, as well as her personal turmoil because she convinced Isaac to bless Jacob in place of Esau. After all, it was she who planned to substitute Jacob for the first-born Esau when Isaac in his old age wanted to bless his sons: "Your curse, my son [she said to Jacob], be upon me" (Genesis 27:13). The open mouthlike form on the upper right might suggest Rebecca's interference in the lives of her sons. The vertical form rising the length of the painting probably alludes to Rebecca's desire to keep the boys apart. The triangular, sharp-edged wedge in the upper left might be a stand-in for Esau, and the softer rounded form in the lower right might represent Jacob. In any event, of the four paintings, this one elicits the greatest sense of turmoil, an appropriate response by Kahn to the most complicated of the founding mothers.

Leah's power lay not in her devious actions but in her fertility. Kahn represents, Leah (fourth from left), the unloved wife of Jacob who gave birth to four sons, by the large womblike form in the center. The thin form at the bottom that traverses the painting represents an umbilical cord, and the curving forms between the center form and the thin form suggest amniotic fluid. And Rachel (first on left), Jacob's beloved, is represented by one of Kahn's most erotic creations—if one imagines that the red circle at the bottom of the painting is an egg within Rachel's body and the darker-blue form descending (or penetrating) from the upper right is Jacob's penis. If we can call these works narratives of indirection, then the painting of Rachel is a marvel of discretion.

In the years between creating the sets of chairs, Kahn was commissioned to make seven large paintings based on the stories of Esther, Deborah, Sarah, Rebecca, Rachel, Leah, and the daughters of Zelophehad for the Yeshiva University of Los Angeles Girls High School. They were completed in 2004. Kahn typically sought open-ended readings in each work, but a viewer knowledgeable in Hebrew might find enough clues to identify each of the figures. The painting of Deborah, for example, based on an earlier work, *AAPHA* (2001) (fig. 60), can be described in the following way: on a white field, a flattened, tan flowerlike form extends its petals out to the painting's edges. A thin blue ring outlined in black circles the center of the flower.

Now, a possible reading of the painting of Deborah. Deborah prophesied the Israelite victory in the battle with Sisera (Judges 4–5). In the painting, she is symbolized by the tan circle within the blue ring, the center and heart of the painting. The blue ring that surrounds her signifies her allegiance to her people as well as the army that surrounds her. The radiating petals suggest the disposition of the army in battle formation. At the same time, the circular tan form at the painting's center might symbolize the sun, and therefore the petals might indicate the sun's rays reaching outward. If so, then Kahn also intended to make an indirect reference to the last line of the hymn marking the victory prophesied by Deborah: "So may all Your enemies perish, O Lord! But may his friends be as the sun rising in might!" (Judges 5:31). And their might and strength are such that a few of the petal's edges are not contained by the painting's borders but reach beyond the framing edges.

Yet another interpretation is derived from the legend that Deborah, a prophet, dispensed judgment outdoors because of the prohibition on men visiting a woman in her house (Ginzberg [1909–38] 1917–87, 4:35–36). In the painting, then, Deborah is represented by the central circle, and the petals that reach out to and beyond the borders suggest the limbs and leaves of a tree under which she sits. The white background is simply the sky. Finally, Kahn, familiar with the works of many American painters, might also have had in mind the allusive language of the surrealist artist Dorothea Tanning (1910–2012): a flower is a "map of possible geography" (Tanning 1998, cited in White 2003, not paginated).

The fourth work by Kahn in which women are the principle subjects is his rendering of the

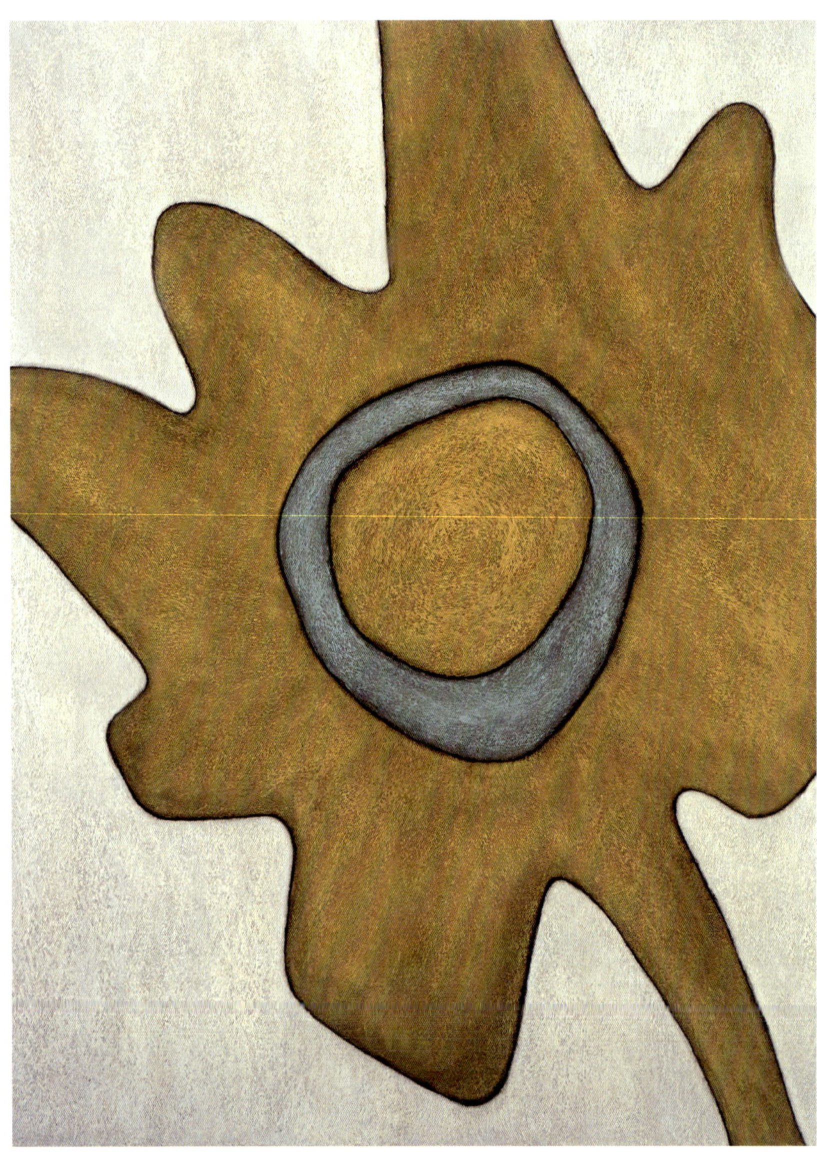

60. Tobi Kahn, *AAPHA*, 2001. Acrylic on canvas over wood, 60 × 44 × 2½ in. Courtesy of the artist.

Women of Valor described in Proverbs 31:10–32, represented by three figures. The figures in *YAFAH II, Women of Valor* (2011) (fig. 61) are composed of simple volumes—svelte, curvaceous, devoid of clothing, and at the same time de-sexed. Knowing that the lines in the proverb concentrate on women as helpmates, Kahn minimized a patriarchal point of view by choosing the three figures to represent three roles he finds basic to women: as inspirations, judges, and parents.

The final works to be considered here are the *Omer Counter*[*s*], the earliest dated 2002 (there are more than twenty versions). Each contains forty-nine removable blocks of wood; the interior spaces, as seen in *SAPHYR III, Omer Counter* (2015) (fig. 62), are painted gold to suggest purity. Each block is a ritual object that can also stand as an independent sculpture. Together, the blocks are intended to aid in counting the Omer, the forty-nine days between the second day of Passover and Shavuot, the day when the Israelites received the Torah at Mt. Sinai. (An omer is a sheaf of barley given during biblical times as an offering in the Temple.) This is the period between

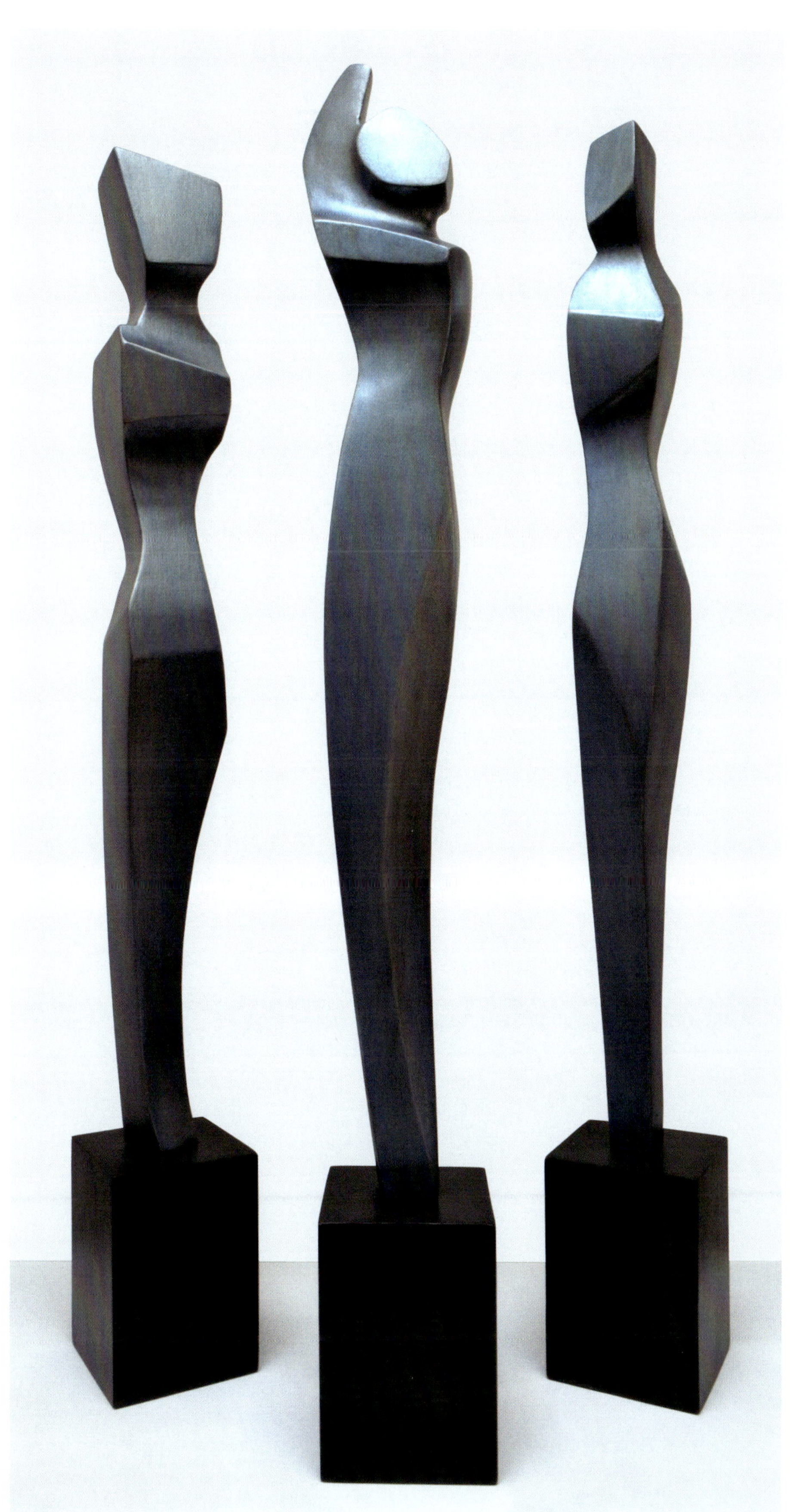

61. Tobi Kahn, *YAFAH II, Women of Valor*, 2011. Acrylic on wood, three figures, each 72 × 10 × 9 in. Courtesy of the artist.

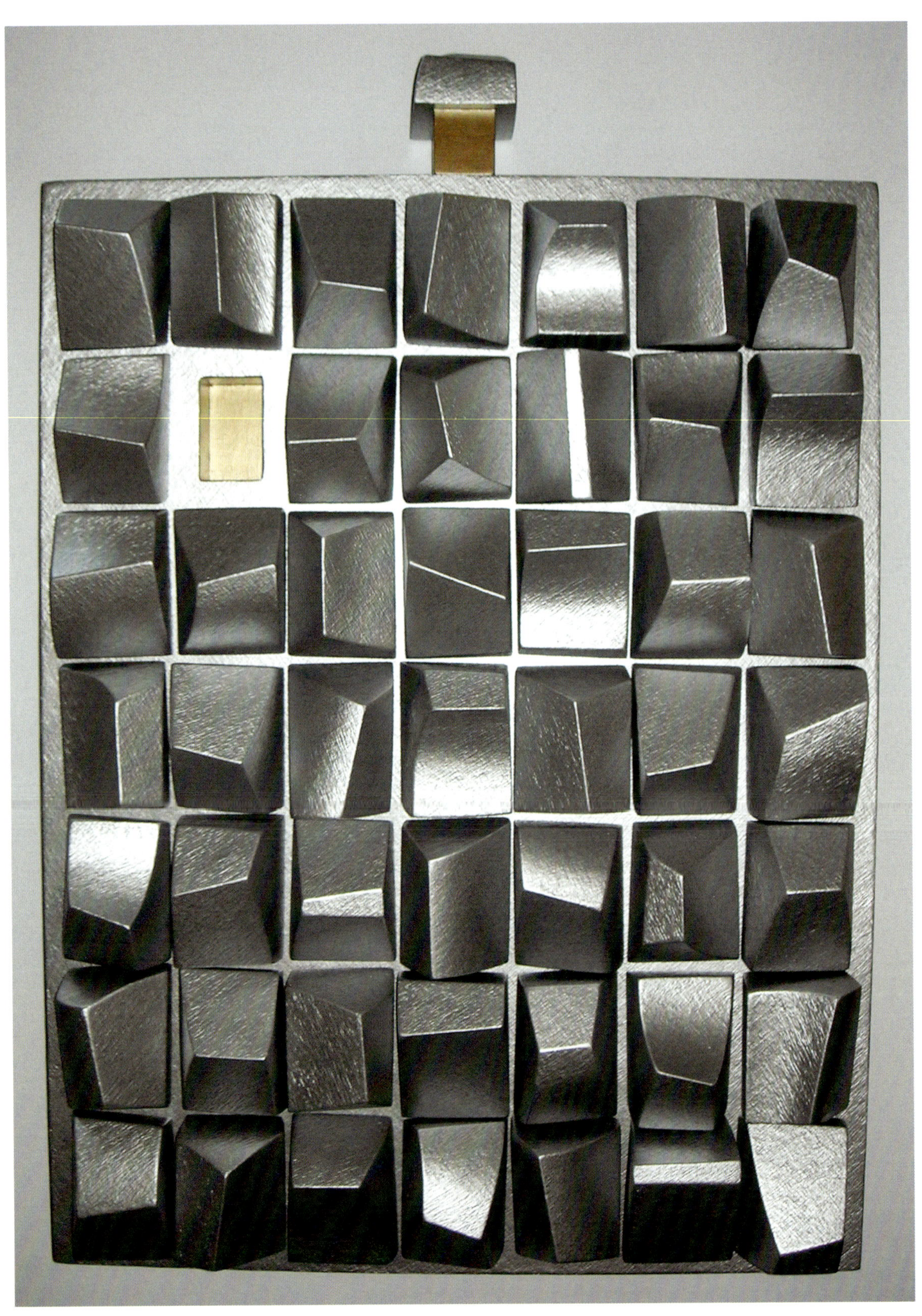

62. Tobi Kahn, *SAPHYR III, Omer Counter*, 2015. Acrylic on wood, 24 × 18 × 2 in. Courtesy of the artist.

the Exodus from Egypt, marking the physical redemption of the Israelites from slavery, and the day denoting spiritual redemption at Mt. Sinai. The forty-nine days are considered a time for personal reflection and improvement as well as for mourning. During this period, the deaths of the martyred students of Rabbi Akiva, murdered by the Romans for studying Torah in ancient Israel, and the many pogroms that have occurred since that time are remembered (Rotberg 1983, 1–20).

The forty-nine differently shaped blocks are also meant to symbolize the different kinds of personality traits we possess. Removing one block each day or, if all blocks have been removed, adding one each day is meant to keep track of time because the specific number is not to be said out loud until the appropriate blessing is offered. At the end of the forty-nine days, all the pieces having been removed or fitted together, symbolize the goal of becoming a complete person in all possible ways.

The literal hands-on aspect of this ritual also reminds us that Judaism ideally and actually is a performative religion that includes lighting candles on the Sabbath and other special occasions, saying annual prayers for those who have passed, adhering to certain dietary restrictions, intoning a particular prayer on awakening each day, and, especially for men, saying three lengthy daily prayers—among several other ritual and social observances beginning with births and continuing after the deaths of loved ones. The *Omer Counter* exemplifies Kahn's overall philosophy of life—to celebrate the sacredness of life by making useful and beautiful works of art and to lead a life that in both its religious and its secular aspects contributes to the overall betterment of humankind. As he stated simply, "[I want to] take people on a journey visually . . . , but I want it to be a positive journey, one of contemplation and beauty. . . . I believe we [Jews] are losing people who do not connect as easily to an ancient text without linking it to the visual world" (qtd. in Eisenberg 2009, 172, 173).

# 10 Richard McBee

Each artist has different reasons for exploring the ancient texts. The reasons that prompted Richard McBee (b. 1947) are probably the most circuitous, and, unlike Tobi Kahn's, his art, life, and belief were initially distinct and separate. Born to parents for whom religion was largely irrelevant, McBee did not know he was Jewish until he was twenty years old, and it was not until the mid-1980s that he committed himself entirely to an Orthodox way of life as well as to the exploration of Jewish themes, an essentially full-time commitment. His immersion in his religion and his art was not a revolt against a particular situation or the result of an epiphany but a gradual realization of his desire to learn as much as possible about Judaism.

This central development in McBee's life can be traced to the 1970s, when he began to make paintings with a group of secular-minded artists who shared a common background in politics of the left and a preference for figural rather than abstract art. By the middle of that decade, they turned to biblical subjects, in particular the Hebrew Bible rather than the Christian Gospels because it was a narrative of a people rather than of a single individual and therefore the range of subject matter was much broader. His group, he has said, considered the Hebrew Bible only in a sociological context as part of the creation of Western culture. As he recalled in an email of March 21, 2018, he was not consciously intending to become religious, nor was he attracted to "religiosity" (his word) at that time, but, as he wrote,

> what gripped me was an inescapable LOGIC, i.e. if these Jewish texts and the ideas contained [there] had in some way fueled much Western culture, and the conundrums they posed still confronted contemporary humankind, it became imperative that I adopt the practice of those Jewish people who equally considered these ideas important and central to their lives; the Orthodox Jews.

McBee began to find religious subjects vital to explore through his art. By 1978, he switched exclusively to Jewish subjects and began to find subject matter in the Book of Ezekiel that year and then in the life of Isaac in 1979, the Binding of Isaac in 1982, and the Book of Ruth in 1982.

By 1988, he became observant as a consequence, he says, of his involvement with the Jewish subjects of his paintings. In that same email of May 21, 2018, he noted that "the primacy of Jewish ideas found in my artwork demanded that these ideas become primary in living my daily life." He then began to live as a Jew, observing the many laws and traditions pertaining to diet, synagogue attendance, ritual activities, daily study, and strict Sabbath observance.

But at the same time he reserved the right to raise serious questions about the Jewish God. For example, how does one reconcile the moral values inherent in the Ten Commandments with an unknowable and unpredictable God who asks Abraham to sacrifice his son? How can one reconcile rational thinking with terror? Why would God ask Abraham to sacrifice his son? Why was Sarah, who is not involved in the sacrifice, the only person to die as a result of it? As McBee wrote in a statement dated December 2, 1996, "After working with this subject for 18 years, I still don't understand, but now I don't understand in a deeper and more troubling way." He answers the same questions with similar words (and a wry smile) today.

So in his art McBee began to push back against the text and sought answers to unanswerable questions. Or, like David Wander, he learned to live with imponderables. Doing so required a leap of faith that allowed him both to continue to raise questions and to follow rituals that provided a kind of day-to-day order as well as a sense of completeness to his life. He had, in effect, established a framework within which to conduct his life on a daily basis, but he also insisted on complete intellectual freedom to question and dispute the framework even while not abandoning it. One might say that his journey became one in search of reconciliation and fulfillment. He would prefer to say, as he told me, that he "stumbled into a corner of the modern world that shared a set of beliefs."

McBee and the other artists profiled in this book live in this world, not, as George Steiner would have it, in the Jewish texts (see the introduction). Judaism is a performative religion awash in rituals that, depending on one's religiosity, begin the moment of awakening in the morning and continue throughout the day. For McBee, it provides a centering for his life, a home, and an anchor in the world. His relationship with Judaism is, as he has said, an intellectually and emotionally active, exploratory, and committed one.

But, as he has also pointed out, his art is not religious art, art about belief. True, it is based on religious texts, but his images grow from passages that disturb him, that lead to the questioning of the incidents described in the texts, or that trigger comparisons to contemporary events. By exploring the ramifications of various passages—what they might suggest or imply—McBee might then create imagined scenarios in sequences of narrative paintings that fill out the stories under consideration, not necessarily to his complete satisfaction but aimed at a better understanding of the stories' meanings, purposes, or values.

Because McBee's attitude toward religious belief is neither confrontational nor totally accepting but rather inquisitive and questioning, he sees himself as an outsider who is not as comfortable as those raised in the religion, even though he has been president of his congregation for years (where he is definitely an insider). But because of his late arrival to Judaism, as it were, he raises significant issues not usually addressed, speculates where others do not venture, and, as seen in his painting of the relationship between Abraham and Isaac discussed in the introduction, *After* (1994) (fig. 5), he searches for understanding when others might simply accept. (He reminds me of one of my black-hatted, black-suited, ultra-Orthodox nephews, who showed up red-eyed one morning at a family gathering. When asked what's up, this nephew said that he was awake all night arguing with God. I asked him who won the argument, and he answered: "We're still arguing.")

McBee's position has also influenced his choice of subject matter. Like Siona Benjamin, he is aware of the outsider status of his subjects, in particular the women. But rather than explore issues related to feminist opposition to male patriarchy, he accepts their situations as

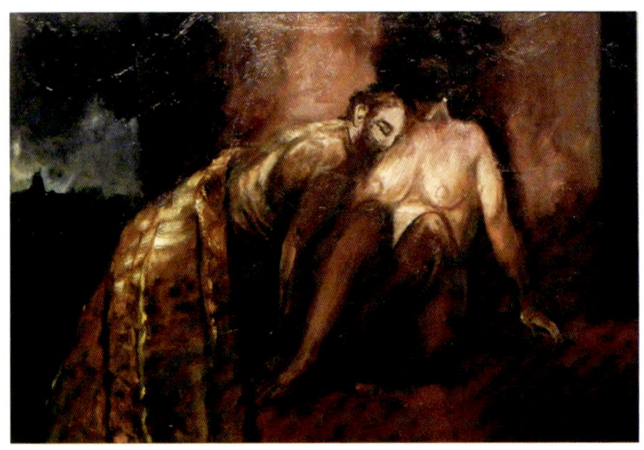

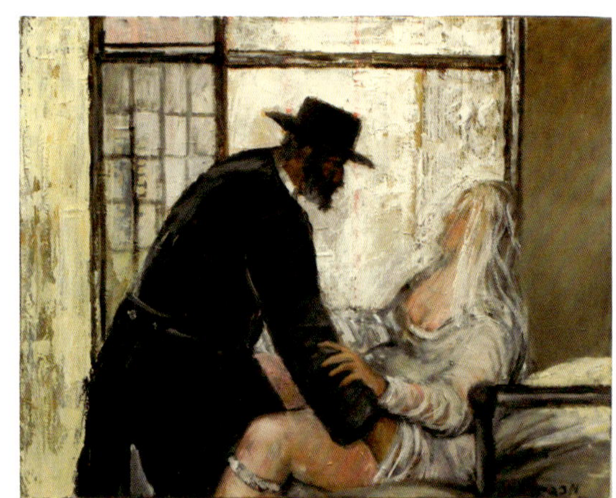

63. Richard McBee, *Judah and Tamar*, 1982 and 2006. Oil on canvas, 30 × 40 in., and oil on canvas, 24 × 30 in. Courtesy of the artist.

vehicles for advancing the Israelite narrative—Hagar's presence in Abraham and Sarah's life; Lot's daughters' incestuous relations with their father; Tamar's seduction of Judah, her father-in-law; Ruth making Boaz aware of her presence, all ultimately contributing to the birth line leading to King David and the coming of the Messiah—and then he, McBee, will invent multiple scenarios based on their situations. Through the images he creates, he enters the narrative to see where these men's and women's actions might lead.

When transposed to our contemporary world, such actions might prompt us to understand that elements in our individual histories do not always fit together neatly. As in modern life, biblical events can seem to be similarly quite discordant. It is these untold stories that McBee invents and tells. They give us imagined glimpses into the private lives of the biblical figures. In a manner both similar to and different from Ruth Weisberg's approach in *Sisters and Brothers* (figs. 21–22), for example, he explores the lives of his subjects but does not necessarily draw moral lessons from what is given in the Bible and the legends.

McBee's developing religious concerns affected over time his painting style and the manner in which he presented his subjects, as we can see in two views of Judah and Tamar, the earlier dated 1982 and the later 2006 (fig. 63). The earlier work, like others completed at the time, is based on Renaissance or Baroque models. The latter is a more realistically styled painting in which Judah, an all-too-human leader of one of the twelve tribes of Israel and from whom the Davidic line descends, is recast as a Hasid, presumably a religious man, who is also involved with a prostitute. Both Judah and Tamar are shown acting in roles far beneath their social positions.

McBee's mature works are in the later style, and no biblical figure escapes his scrutiny. He finds contradictions in their stories, and so as he enters their narrative, he finds it necessary to explore those contradictions in multiple series of paintings because one single painting cannot sum up what he finds interesting and disturbing. In a typed statement dated July 2008, he explained his motivation:

> In the heart of monotheism, I had discovered the impenetrable chasm between God and Man. God is unknowable. Just as we impute what amounts to human meanings to the workings of God's universe, so, too,

> we proclaim the human attributes that God is just, merciful, and full of kindness. . . . The Creator is not limited by His creation or the consciousness He placed in man.

Among his many multipaneled series to which he has often returned, he has explored especially the ramifications of the Akeida (McBee's preferred spelling), or the Binding of Isaac, for which he has made about one hundred paintings, imagining generational, family, literary, and anthropological aspects of the relationships between Abraham, Isaac, Sarah, and Hagar. For example, he wonders about the psychology of Abraham and about what was on Isaac's mind as he and his father proceeded to the site of sacrifice. How was the altar built? Was Isaac traumatized afterward, and, if so, could he ever fully recover? Where did he go afterward? Could he ever trust his father again? What about Sarah, who in both the Bible and the various legends at first had no idea of the event that was to take place? How did she find out? Why and how did she die?

The Binding is told succinctly in nineteen verses in Genesis 22, with no apparent explanation. To McBee's way of thinking, God, in an act of terror, commands Abraham to sacrifice his son, which Abraham then proceeds to plan and carry out. At the last moment, an angel tells him to stop. God then promises Abraham that his descendants will be "as numerous as the stars in heaven and the sands on the seashore" (Genesis 22:17). Abraham then returns to Beersheba without Isaac.

The entire episode is included in daily morning religious services and is an important part of Rosh Hashanah services. Why in the lives of the first Israelite family do God and Abraham appear to be irascible, inscrutable, difficult, and arbitrary figures? What can it all mean? To this day, this event still generates books and articles laden with interpretations (of the many, see Agies 1988, 30; Arieli 1981, 56; Auerbach [1946] 1953, 8–11; Boehm 2007, 17; M. Brown 1982, 103, 105–11; Ginzberg [1909–38] 1917–87, 1:274–86, 5:256, 5:292; Kierkegaard [1843] 1985; Milgrom 1988, 2, 24; Wellisch 1954, 9–24, 74–77).

In an email dated November 16, 2006, McBee asked the following question: "How can we live with a God who demands such a sacrifice?" His answer: "We go on living. We have a rough relationship with God. We challenge God by engaging Him, not by abandoning him. We have received a gift with thorns on it."

In the introduction, I discussed one of McBee's paintings in a series concerned with the relationship between Abraham and Isaac and the latter's probable rejection of his father. In another series, one concerning Abraham's actions, McBee based his interpretation on material he found in Julian Jaynes's book *The Origin of Consciousness: The Breakdown of the Bicameral Mind* (1976, 69–99, 295, 304). This book explores the human mind before it becomes aware of itself, before self-consciousness, subjectivity, and free will. McBee calls this series *Akeda* [*sic*] (1982) (fig. 64). Jaynes notes that none of these qualities of mind exist in the figures in *The Iliad*. He calls this absence the action of the bicameral mind, according to which an external force—the gods in the case of ancient Greece—controls an individual's activities. Jaynes sees Abraham as having a bicameral mind and even goes so far as to assume that Abraham hallucinates voices that direct his activities.

In *Akeda*, McBee portrays Abraham as unreachable, inhuman, unselfconscious, and monstrous, towering over Isaac, seemingly following the dictates of a force beyond his awareness and control—an example of the bicameral mind at work. Abraham drops the knife not because he loves his son but at the behest of the hallucinated voice of an angel. Isaac's cry cannot be heard; it is the cry without sound. The

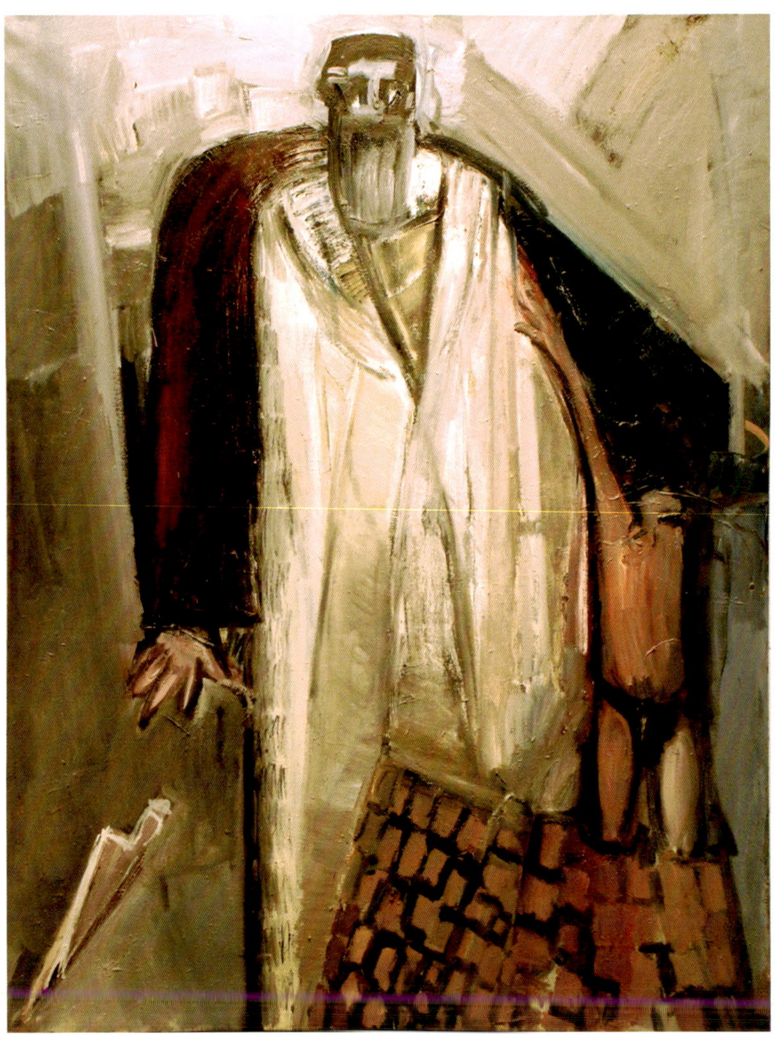

64. Richard McBee, *Akeda*, 1982. Oil on canvas, 90 × 70 in. Courtesy of the artist.

tiles that McBee added in the lower right play a role in several paintings. Meant to indicate the presence of a rational pattern, they often appear to be on the verge of falling apart, thus indicating anything but rational patterns of behavior (Baigell 2009b).

Jaynes also suggests that the Book of Amos, dated to the eighth century BCE, is an example of the bicameral mind, whereas Ecclesiastes, which might date from the second century BCE, reveals a subjective, reflective consciousness that is entirely postbicameral. (This understanding is not unlike Bruno Snell's thought in *The Discovery of Mind in Greek Philosophy and Literature* [1982] that Euripides's Medea marks the first time in literature that an individual is self-willed rather than performing at the insistence of the gods—that one's limbs, for example, are moving because of human agency, not at the direction of the gods.)

Whether McBee actually accepts Jaynes's thesis is moot and perhaps beside the point, but in comparing figure 64 and figure 5 we see the demonstration of the bicameral mind at work. To state this in more Jewish terms, one can follow a line of thought from Abraham through the prophets in which God appears to and, in effect, speaks through humans. And then at a certain point God is removed from human contact and becomes an omniscient force beyond human understanding, a remote figure without physicality. In Ecclesiastes and in our own lives, as Arnold Eisen and Rabbi Neil Gilman have pointed out (see the end of chapter 1), we exercise our individuality by making our own decisions. We live in a postbicameral state of mind.

McBee seems to have explored this idea through his paintings with a "let's see if this explains anything" attitude. As he said in an interview by Judith Margolis, the driving force behind his art is his struggle with "the divine imperative" (Margolis 2011a, 203). This struggle can be seen in his portrayals of the relationship between Abraham and Isaac. For McBee, "That we attempt to relate to and comply with the divine imperative flies in the face of our alienation from God" (2011). Nonetheless, McBee's struggle continues not so much as a battle but as a desire to understand the nature of God.

Like Siona Benjamin, Janet Shafner, and David Wander, McBee is also attuned to correlations between biblical times and contemporary events. Each makes connections in her or his own way. McBee, rather than indicating direct correspondences, finds instead echoes of the ancient stories in contemporary events and individual behaviors. Abraham evokes in his mind contemporary despots, and Isaac has become a symbol of the survival and revitalization of the Jewish people after the Holocaust. In paintings McBee made before the various Akeidah series, he connected the story of raising of the dead in Ezekiel 37, in particular the words of verse 12, to the survival of the Jews after the Holocaust and the establishment of the State of Israel. God says to Ezekiel, "Prophesy, therefore, and say to them: Thus said the Lord God: I am going to open your graves and lift you out of the graves, O My people, and bring you to the land of Israel."

McBee's paintings call to mind such passages. Whether he believes they are the literal truth is irrelevant and also entirely personal. Rather, it is important to note here that some Jews assume that such prophecies will in time be fulfilled. Others believe instead that such events and other markers recorded in the Bible are ways to connect to Jewish history, to join or remain united with those who share long-standing traditions, and to be part of an inherited common cultural language and legacy. Knowing these stories is a way to affirm one's heritage. I suspect that except for those entirely deracinated, most Jews live somewhere on the same point of the religious spectrum as McBee, who, as suggested earlier in this chapter, is well aware of that spectrum. I call attention to this state of mind lest we forget that he and the other artists, whatever else they believe or might have read, choose to view the world, even to make life decisions, through a Jewish lens.

McBee soon realized that the stories of Sarah and Hagar were connected to and extensions of the stories of Abraham and Isaac. Like other artists, he chafes at the paucity of explanation in the Bible:

> The extremely terse nature of the biblical narrative cries out for the kind of textural deconstruction that the rabbis in *midrashic* literature pursued. In the course of explaining, elaborating, or exploding thorny theological moral or practical issues the biblical texts present at practically every turn, the ancient rabbinic minds have provided a plethora of diverse strategies for contemplating these stories. (McBee 2013–14, 49)

To enter Sarah's and Hagar's narratives and to better understand their experiences, McBee decided to invent his own midrashim. Although sensitive to the feminist movement and to the outsider position of women, he based his paintings less on feminist critiques and more on his own point of view as a person who accepts the parameters of the ancient texts and then conjures the kinds of responses that women could manage within those constraints.

In *Sarah's Trials* (2006–8), composed of sixteen paintings in eight diptychs, McBee "created an imagined paraphrase of Sarah's observations" (Margolis 2011b, 192; see also *Sarah's Trials* 2010). Sarah's comments are attached to each panel. In addition, McBee prepared an exhaustive summary of the appropriate passages in Genesis, the midrashim, and various commentaries. He indicated that the relationship between Abraham and Sarah was not normal, that Sarah "was the fatal victim of Abraham's piety," and that he, McBee, could not "escape his gendered thoughts about a woman . . . who had struggled with fulfilling God's will and suffered for it" (qtd. in Margolis 2011b, 192). As he noted, "Sarah introduced another woman, Hagar, into her marriage bed, seriously complicating their relationship, and Abraham as a husband seems at best self-centered and non-communicative with his wife Sarah" (in Margolis 2011a, 202).

The first diptych shows the shop of Abraham's father, Terach, filled with nude female idols, which Abraham is in the midst of destroying. Sarah's comment for the first painting is "Terach, my father-in-law, made idols and had an idol shop." For the second painting, she says, "My husband, Abraham, discovered God, transcendent, without substance, or gender. While working at his father's shop, he decided to smash the idols to show how powerless they were." The story then follows the biblical text. The third diptych includes Abraham, in formal, modern clothing, taking Hagar, in a minidress, into their home as Sarah, in ancient garb, watches from a distance. In the caption for the paired painting, Sarah says, "Just like that, Abraham went and had sex with her and she conceived a male child, Ishmael."

In one of the paintings in the seventh diptych, *Isaac Returns* (fig. 65), Sarah dies. The caption reads: "I worried about my missing son and husband. Then Isaac returned, shaken. He told me Abraham almost slaughtered him on an alter to God. I cried out." Almost immediately, Sarah died, but how? According to one midrash, Isaac returned and told his story, and

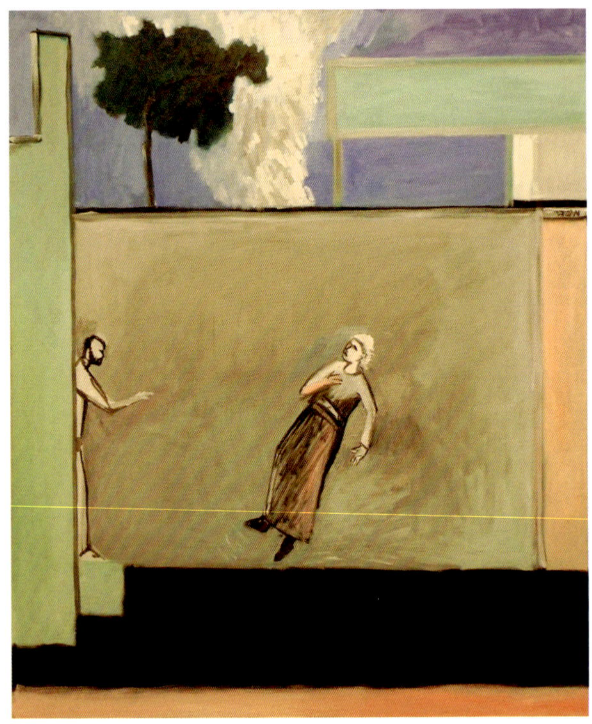

65. Richard McBee, *Isaac Returns*, from *Sarah's Trials*, 2006–8. Oil and collage on canvas, 72 × 60 in. Courtesy of the artist.

Sarah screamed and died. In another, when Sarah realized Isaac was still alive, her reaction was so excessive that "her soul went out through joy" (Ginzberg [1909–38] 1917–87, 1:287; *Midrash Rabbah: Leviticus* 1983, 253–54; Zornberg 1995, 123–28).

In the final diptych, the first painting shows Isaac taking Rebecca, a child bride, indoors. Abraham looks on. The caption reads: "After Abraham buried me [Sarah], he sent to his family in Haran for a child bride for Isaac." The second painting shows Abraham, an old man with a cane, looking at Hagar, still in her minidress. The caption ends on a note of tragedy for Sarah: "Men have needs . . . so again Abraham took a wife and her name was Keturah. This was Hagar. They had six children. When he died, he was buried next to me in the cave of Machpelah." End of story.

But for feminist historian Phyllis Trible, the story of the Binding of Isaac in Genesis 22 is, plain and simple, an example of biblical patriarchy: "[It] has given us not the sacrifice of Isaac (for that we are grateful) but the sacrifice of Sarah (for that we mourn)" (1999, 287; see also Mark 2010; Schneider 2004, 101–6; Tuchman and Rapoport 2004, 67–77).

There are no close-ups in any painting in this series, no revealing of emotions—anger, sorrow, or glee—on any of the characters' faces. They are, after all, acting out a drama not of their own making but one imposed upon them by the "divine imperative," and they are personalized instead by their clothing. Abraham is well dressed in either modern or biblical-style garb; Hagar is the miniskirted, seductive neighborhood floozy; Sarah is the neat but slightly boring housewife resigned to her assigned role and station in a patriarchic society.

When McBee completed this series, he realized that he could not end it with Sarah's observation that men have needs—meaning sexual needs. This would imply that Hagar might be considered merely a concubine. Was there something special about Hagar that might lift her above this kind of role assessment? Yes, according to McBee. In an interview on December 21, 2018, he said that he realized that in this dysfunctional family, in which Abraham does not tell Sarah where he is taking Isaac and in which Sarah has nothing to do with the sacrifice but is nonetheless the only person who dies as a result of it, Hagar is a survivor.

She is also a royal princess, a slave, a concubine, a mother, a proud, strong, abandoned woman of color who founds a nation and in legend subsequently gives birth to five more children. With lots of material to work with, McBee then turned his attention to completing a set of sixteen paintings, *Hagar* (2010–13), based on his thoughts about Hagar's life. (On her life, see Chheenah 2012; Ginzberg [1909–38] 1917–87, 1:223–37, 5:232, 5:264–65; *Pirke de Rabbi Eliezer* 2004, 287–88; Teubal 1997, xxi; Tuchman and Rapoport 2004, 13–21, 129; Williams 2006, 172–73. Needless to say, the approaches taken by Savina Teubal, a feminist; Muhammad Ashraf Chheenah, a Muslim; and Dolores Williams, who in her article discusses Hagar from an African American point of view, differ considerably from McBee's.)

In the eight diptychs, McBee presents a rather anodyne version of Genesis 16, 21, and 23. But, as he has often said, he never tries to tear down or debunk the biblical text or the commentaries. In comments attached to each scene, McBee tells how Hagar leaves Egypt with Sarah as her maid or slave. When Sarah proves barren, she gives Hagar to Abraham so that he might have a son. Hagar becomes pregnant and says that after sex Abraham was very tender and affectionate. "I think he fell in love with me." Sarah, jealous, has Abraham expel Hagar from the household. Hagar returns and believes that Abraham is happy to see her. After she gives birth to Ishmael, Abraham is overjoyed with Ishmael and in one painting holds his son close to his chest. Expelled once again, Hagar returns to Egypt to find a mate for Ishmael. In the last set of paintings, she returns to an old and decrepit Abraham, and when he dies, both sons, Ishmael and Isaac, mourn him (fig. 66).

Another instance of a woman poorly treated in the Bible is the Sotah, the presumed adulterer. Although the event and the punishment as described in Numbers 5 and the Talmud might never have taken place, they are nevertheless still discussed in considerable detail. A wife suspected of adultery by her husband must submit to a degrading test that will prove or disprove her innocence. She must drink bitter, dirty water concocted from pure water in the Temple, earth from the Temple floor, and the erased letters of a curse. (In the Talmud version, she is stripped to the waist, and her hands tied.) If she is guilty, her stomach and thighs will distend, a euphemism for repellent genitalia. If innocent, she can return home to her

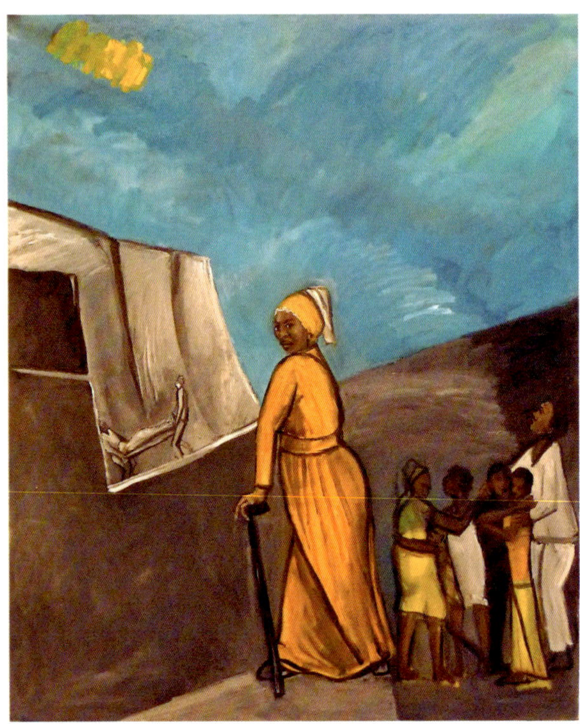

66. Richard McBee, from *Hagar*, 2010–13. Oil on canvas, 72 × 60 in. Courtesy of the artist.

jealous husband who charged her with adultery and resume a normal marital life, which might even include having more children with him.

Perhaps there are paintings based on this story. If so, they are exceedingly rare. But two artists, Janet Shafner and McBee, have imagined scenes focused on the sequence of events and outcome of the trial of the accused adulterer. In Shafner's painting, *Broken: The Sotah* (2005), the husband and wife sit naked on opposite sides of a bare room painted in icy-blue colors. They look away from each other. In each of two lunettes at the top of the painting, one above the husband, the other above the wife, Shafner has placed an enormous arm with outstretched fingers that reach toward the center of the painting. The fingers, of course, will never touch, let alone entwine. The marriage is over despite whatever legal arrangements force the couple to remain together.

In 2009, McBee decided to create four paintings set in an urban environment that encapsulate the story. Because the Torah is reread each year, his primary motivation was his "anger and frustration as we encounter this [episode] each year when reading Numbers. The accused wife's ordeal seems so cruel and unjust as embedded in the holy Torah. . . . I was compelled to depict it in as disturbing a way as possible to convey my distress with its contents." And, as he added, he felt the need "to depict the narrative in contemporary terms" that "reflect the unchanging reality of the contemporary subjugation of women" (qtd. in *Richard McBee* 2016).

The first painting in the series, a rear-window view, shows the presumably adulterous couple entering a room of an apartment house. The second painting, a street scene in front of McBee's synagogue, shows the Sotah's upper body exposed to the public. In the third and fourth paintings (fig. 67), she drinks the liquid in front of the synagogue, and then, in another rear-window view, having been judged innocent and now at home, she sits in a separate but adjoining room from her husband, he in a chair and she on a bed, as physically distant from him as possible.

One has to ask: What were McBee's narrative choices in creating these series, and how does he raise the matter of God's intentions? None of the women fares well. Sarah is not told about Abraham's plans for Isaac and, although uninvolved in the attempted sacrifice, dies. Hagar is a sexually exploited slave and then an abandoned single mother. The abused wife, the Sotah, returns to live with the man who does not trust her. If McBee has previously asked, "What does God want?," he does not ask in anger, as some contemporary critics might, nor does he blame God, who is, after all, inscrutable. Rather, he deflects those kinds of questions and the uncomfortable answers they might demand to the biblical scholar who might find them worth exploring. As he has said, he is interested in sexuality in the Torah. "We tend

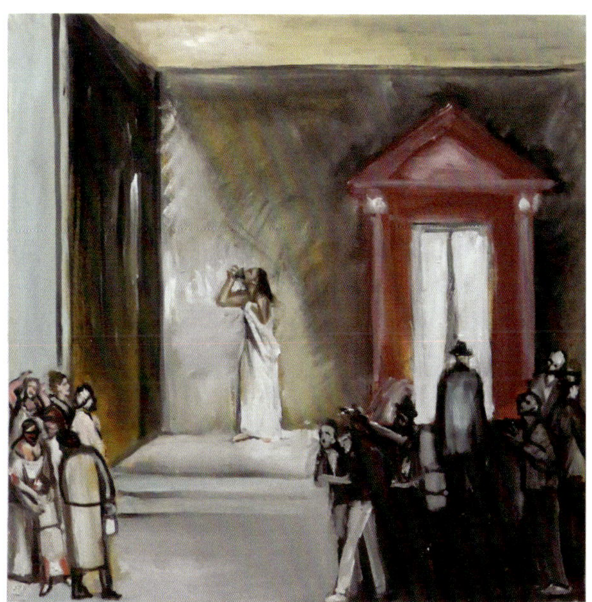
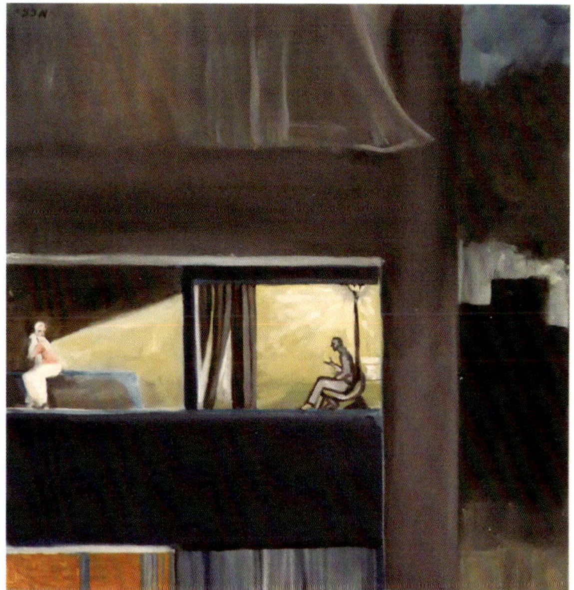

67. Richard McBee, from *The Sotah*, 2009. Oil on canvas, 24 × 24 in. Courtesy of the artist.

not to notice or hear the women," he says. "I believe we don't have a misogynous religion but we have a misogynous history." Movement or direction in the Torah is often driven by women. They are protagonists in their stories even if their primary function is to provide male children. He cites, as previously noted, Lot's daughters' incest, Abraham and Hagar, Judah and Tamar, and Ruth and Boaz (Margolis 2011b, 192, 193). He admits that "the male gaze, as a middle-aged male['s] fantasy[,] is definitely present in regard to Abraham and Hagar" and that feminists have attacked him for picturing Hagar as a sex object. He is not impervious to such criticism, but in response he has placed the female actors in roles central to the Torah narrative (Margolis 2011a, 202, 203). Or as Rachel Adelman suggests, the women are not necessarily victims of patriarchy forced to be deceitful but can be considered "active agents transforming the social order in which they live" (2012, 88).

McBee's other narratives also raise questions and provoke the kinds of responses that indicate the contemporaneity of the Bible. The same can be said for narratives by Weisberg and Wander. But because McBee visualizes the biblical figures' possible actions as if stills in a motion picture or television series, the viewer can identify not only with the moral issues he raises but also with the actual activities his subjects might have engaged in. In effect, we can agree or disagree with his projections onto their characters, but that is precisely one of the merits of his series—that they engage his viewers in what the Bible and the legends state or imply. The desire to bring the Bible into everyday conversation is, as mentioned, these artists' goal. One can argue, then, that McBee's paintings are among the most provocative in the entire history of Jewish American art.

On a different level, McBee is not alone in his questions about God, especially among those who want to have a close and, at whatever level possible, reciprocal relationship with God. For example, the biblical scholar Avivah Zornberg has raised several issues on this point, including how one can believe in God in the face of so much enormous evil in the world. "I think that the only way we can live in a world

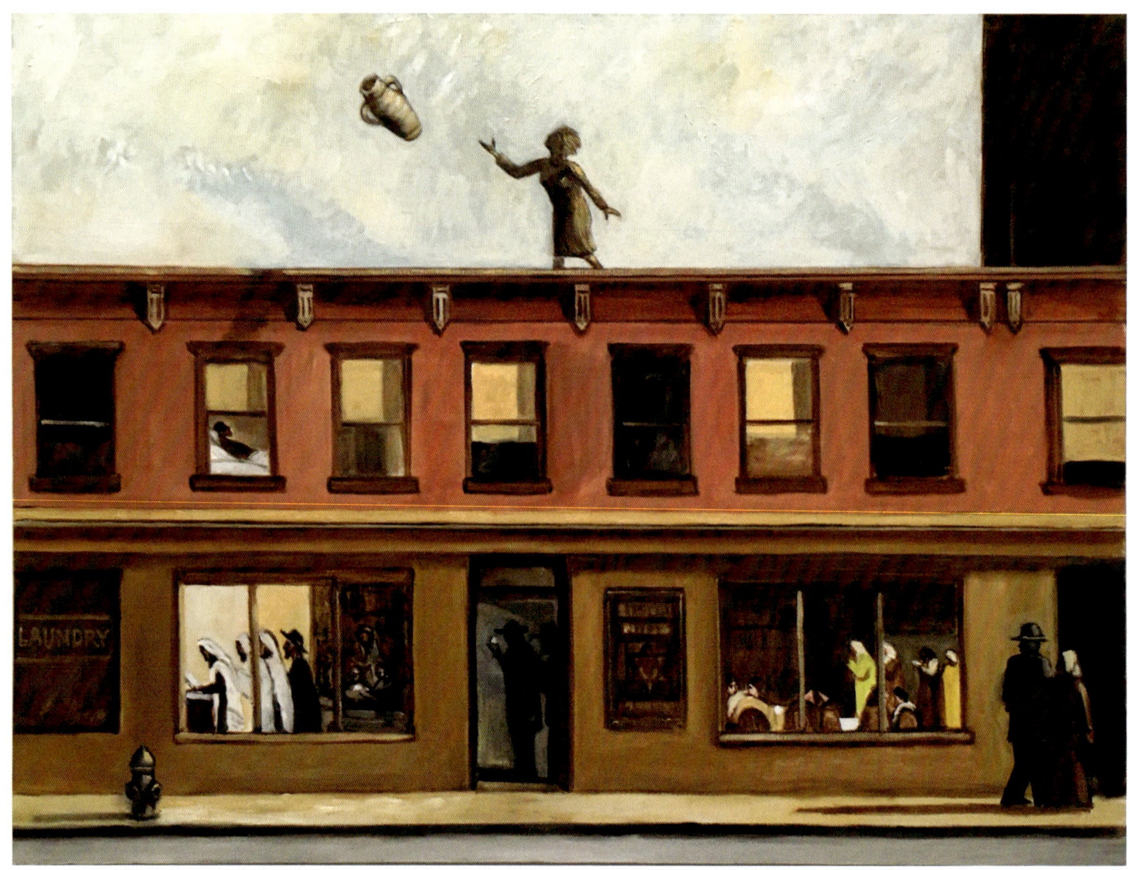


68. Richard McBee, *Rebbe's Maid*, 2016. Oil on canvas, 30 × 40 in. Courtesy of the artist.

that is connected to God is by openly acknowledging brokenness . . . [,] that nothing is whole and that our understanding of God is never complete" (2018, 52). And as the Orthodox rabbi Sara Hurwitz has indicated, "Today we have to see God and our belief system through a world that includes great challenges and destruction" (2018, 53). In other words, McBee is in good company and not alone in searching for answers or in acknowledging that these answers might always remain beyond reach.

Yet another facet of McBee's art deserves comment. Observing ritual can be either unthinkingly automatic or central to the ways one conducts one's life. Sometimes there is confusion between the two, even with the best of intentions. McBee's painting *Rebbe's Maid* (2016) (fig. 68) is an example of what I mean. McBee appropriated Edward Hopper's (1882–1967) famous painting *Early Sunday Morning* (1930) to help set an appropriate dramatic tone based on an event described in the Talmud: Ketubot 104a.

The rebbe is Rabbi Yehudah, the prince who lived from 135 to 217 CE. He is shown through an upstairs window lying in bed, very ill and in great pain, and his students are on the ground floor praying fervently for his recovery. The intensity of their prayers prevent him from dying, much to the chagrin of the rebbe's maid. McBee shows her on the roof throwing a jar down onto the street. According to the story, the explosive sound of the crash surprises the students, whose praying ceases for a moment, and in that moment the rebbe is able to die.

McBee interprets the maid's action in the following way. He knows that many, but not all, experts of Jewish medical ethics hold that if a person is dying and suffering but is prevented from dying by some agent or process, it is permissible to remove that agent and allow the person to die peacefully. In modern terms, we might say the maid took it upon herself to pull the plug. Her intervention, an act of charity, allows the hopelessly ill rebbe to die peacefully.

But a larger and important point of which this tale and the painting are an example is the tale's relevance to the concept of *derech eretz*, usually translated as "the way of the world." In both a Jewish and nondenominational context, it refers to the importance of conducting one's self in an ethical way, of acting with a sense of common decency and with respect to others, and, of equal importance, of balancing traditional teachings with modern notions of behavior (Wertheimer 2018, 64, 259). In the particular instance of the rebbe's maid, it refers to doing the right thing by releasing the rebbe from his unendurable pain and allowing him to pass away quietly.

# 11 David Wander

Needless to say, Richard McBee is not alone in choosing subject matter with moral value—about doing the right thing, acting responsibly, and, in a religious sense, seeking the "religiously responsible act" (Borowitz 1961, 38). Of the artists considered here, David Wander (b. 1954) is most intent, but only by degree, in seeking out stories in the ancient texts that have positive moral value. For example, he recently came upon a short story in the Talmud about a very ugly man who teaches a rabbi an important moral lesson (Taanit 20 a–b; see also Genesis 1:27, Leviticus 19:18, and Dorff 2002, 5, 2003, 21). The story reminds the reader to treat all individuals equally or, in religious terms, to remember that we all are created equally in God's image.

The entire story is told in the three panels of figure 69, *The Rabbi and the Exceedingly Ugly Man* (2018). A rabbi, who is alternately walking and riding his donkey, comes upon an exceedingly ugly man. The rabbi asks if all people from the man's town are so ugly. The man advises the rabbi to tell the Craftsman (God) who made the ugly man and his fellow townspeople how ugly the vessels are that he made. The rabbi, realizing that he has sinned against God and also insulted the man, who might be the Messiah, apologizes and prostrates himself before the ugly man. They then continue to the rabbi's community, where the ugly man explains what transpired. He tells the rabbi's congregation that he forgives their leader but only if the rabbi "accepts upon himself not to become accustomed to behave like this." The moral is then suggested that individuals should not be so stiff-necked, which can lead to sin, but rather adopt a flexible, understanding, and humane attitude, which is the appropriate religious response.

Wander has also created several other narrative series, preferring to improvise only minimally beyond the text and sometimes updating particular events in the story for contemporary relevance. His usual mode of presentation is some variant of a comics format, such as a foldout accordion book or a rolled-out scroll with a continuous narrative, as a way to modernize the ancient stories as well as to make them approachable and more comprehensible (see Baskind and Omer-Sherman 2008; Waldman 2005; and Wander's website, davidwanderart.com, entries under "Book Art"). His many works include *The Jonah Drawings*, works on the Five Megillot or Scrolls (the Books of Esther and Ruth, the Song of Songs, Lamentations, and Ecclesiastes); works on the lives and activities of biblical figures such as Judith, Joseph, and King David (five scrolls); and scrolls on the biblical flood as well as on life in the Auschwitz murder camp during the Second World War. He also created a Holocaust Haggadah in the late 1970s (Wander 1985 or *Wolloch Haggadah* 1985), replacing the exodus from Egypt with the voyage from Auschwitz to Jerusalem at a time when artists of his generation were

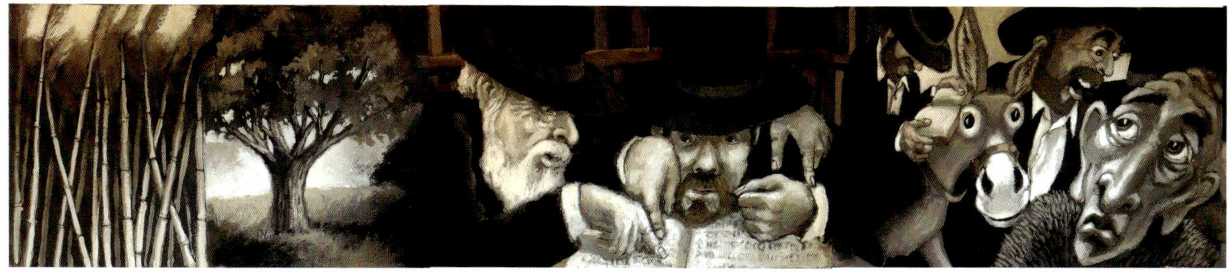
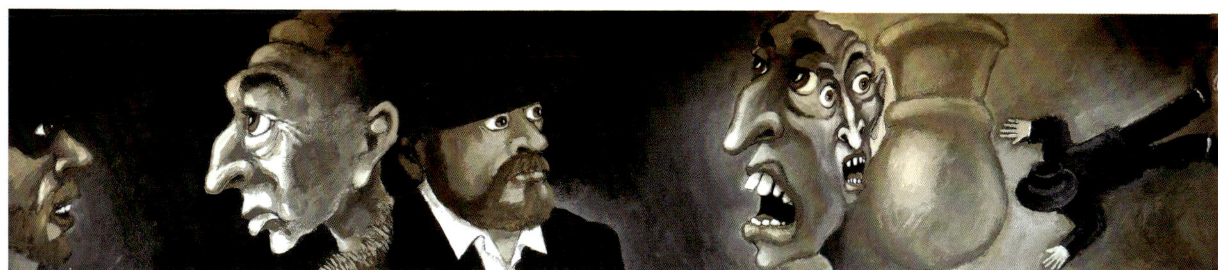
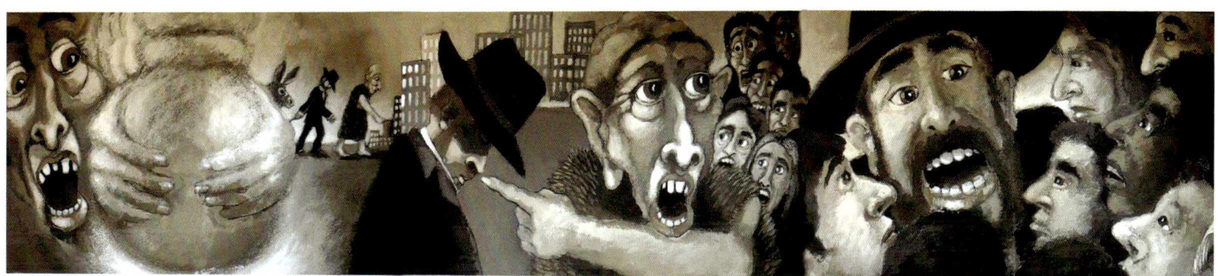
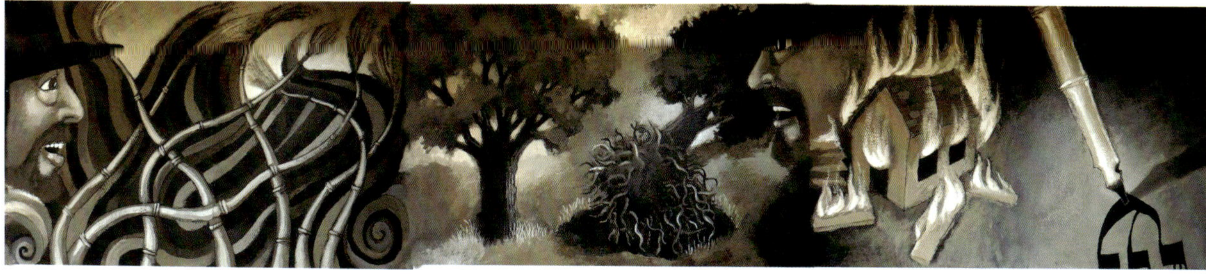

69. David Wander, *The Rabbi and the Exceedingly Ugly Man*, 2018. Acrylic and ink on paper accordion book, 11 in. × 18½ ft. Courtesy of the artist.

just beginning to come to terms artistically with the destruction of European Jewry.

Wander grew up in a semiobservant household knowing that most of the members of his father's family were murdered during the Holocaust. And like other Jewish youngsters, he was the target of anti-Semitic remarks in schools but did not respond gently to them, in comparison to, say, Abraham Rattner (1895–1978), an artist of an earlier generation who as an adult could only complain bitterly, still upset about the anti-Semitic abuse he experienced when growing up in Poughkeepsie, New York ).[1]

1. Abraham Rattner to Jennie (his sister), Feb. 1954, roll 1212, frames 972–77, and Apr. 14, 1955, roll 1212, frames 1056–57, Abraham Rattner Papers, AAA. See also Baigell 2006a, 144, and Bandes 16, 1997.

Always proud of his religious heritage, Wander studied at the Rhode Island School of Design and Pratt Institute and as a student explored Jewish subject matter to fill the religious vacuum that he felt existed in art instruction in both schools. He was also able to study Hebrew calligraphy. Like others of his generation, he struggled to find ways to interact and pray to the Jewish God, who did not protect Jews from the Holocaust. And finding minimal spiritual nourishment in organized Judaism during the 1970s and 1980s, he became involved with Zen Buddhism, Kung Fu and Tai Chi martial arts, as well as Native American rituals. A spiritual teacher, knowing that Wander was a born student, suggested that he stop shopping the world's religions and philosophical systems and turn to his own religion for metaphysical and spiritual enlightenment. Wander did so and, immersing himself in Jewish lore and history, began a course of study with Rabbi David Kraemer of the Jewish Theological Seminary that continues to this day.

In several conversations, he has explained why he reads biblical and Talmudic texts as well as their ancient and modern interpretations: to fathom God's word, to study sources of morality in the Western world, to learn about the society of ancient Israelites, to understand the nature of the Jewish religion, to assert his Jewish identity, to achieve some measure of self-awareness and self-definition, to ensure and sustain Judaism's contemporary vitality, to fulfill ritual obligations that he has assumed as part of his self-identity, to attain personal comfort and solace, and to find a spiritual anchor in a frightening world. That is to say, religion beyond its various rituals is not something to which he pays lip service but is an active element in his life.

In the late 1990s, he found an outlet for his studies and his spiritual feelings in the making of accordion books, scrolls, and one-of-a-kind artist books. Overall, he likes narratives, folklore, and folk tales and calls himself a storyteller. He identifies with the characters in the stories he illustrates by placing himself in their situations as a way to understand their actions better and, by extension, himself. But unlike Richard McBee, he does not augment and amplify the stories as told in the Bible and the legends but remains reasonably close to the texts. Creating such works also allows him, he says, to become part of a long tradition of Jewish art and artists, to make the Bible come alive for himself and his viewers, and to tell in pictures "our Jewish stories." And, most of all, he wants to find contemporary relevance in those ancient stories in order to make religion meaningful in his own daily life.

But there are layers beneath layers, and during our conversations he has revealed specific motivations for the kind of art he makes. Shocked by the Holocaust—his Holocaust Haggadah (Wander 1985 or *Wolloch Haggadah* 1985) was commissioned by a family member who survived the murder camps—he feels the need to fill the void within his own soul caused by that event and to understand what it means to be a Jew today, well aware that anti-Semitic outbursts never lie far beneath the surface of normal daily life, increasingly so in recent years. He feels that such massive destruction can happen again, that an overwhelming Other can murder him at any time—a point of view revealed in some of his images and clearly stated by Archie Rand (see chapter 12).

In another but related register, he finds the stories that attract him, which he calls the "wisdom stories," provide no definitive answers to issues they raise. As a result, he thinks that one simply does the best one can to make sense of what life has to offer through the insights one finds in the stories. He feels that as he thinks about these stories, he is able to understand better and to record to the extent possible the measure of his life and what he has so far accomplished. As an artist, he wants to live

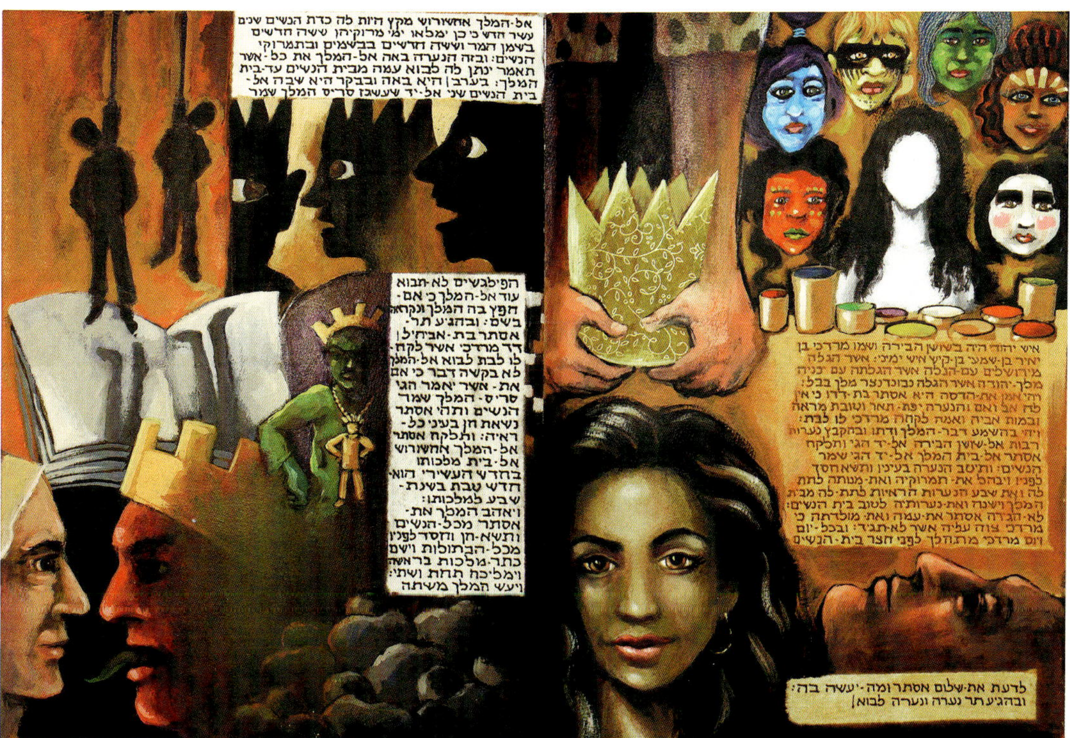


71. David Wander, from *The Book of Esther*, 2007. Acrylic-ink and rice-paper collage on paper accordion book, 19 in. × 50 ft. Courtesy of the Herbert & Eileen Bernard Museum, Temple Emanu-El, New York.

upon her son, Darius, to allow the Israelites to return to their country (Ginzberg [1909–38] 1917–87, 4:363–448). Each panel of Wander's accordion book contains several episodes of the story. To get some idea of how Wander proceeded, we will look at one of the thirteen panels (fig. 71). At the upper right, we see a number of women brought to King Ahasuerus's court, one of them to be chosen as his next wife because the king had ordered the murder of Queen Vashti when she would not perform a dance unclothed for his guests. In the center of this group, Esther, who is described as very reserved and who reveals nothing about herself, is seen as a faceless woman. She becomes, therefore, a mirror of the viewer's desire. The horizontal head in profile on the lower right is that of Mordechai, usually considered to be Esther's uncle, who watches over her like a hawk.

In the center, we see Esther crowned after she becomes Ahasuerus's queen. Wander has been quick to note that he thought of this image as both a teaching point and, in his own mind, a folk tale of mothers telling their daughters that they, too, can dress up as Queen Esther on Purim, the holiday on which Esther's story is read, and that they, too, can be a queen and save the world. The slightly greenish cast to Esther's complexion refers to the myrtle, an evergreen shrub that symbolizes piety; Esther's Hebrew name, Hadassah, means "myrtle." The myrtle also has a pleasant scent but a bitter taste, just as Esther was pleasant to the Jews but bitter to the subsequently vanquished archenemy, Haman (Esther Rabbah 6:5). The haunted look in her eyes is Wander's way of invoking a survivor's memories, whether they recall ancient threats such as Haman's desire to kill all Jews or modern ones such as the Holocaust.

This connection is not an idle one. Jewish tragedy is never far from Wander's mind.

In biblical terms, the descendants of Amalek, enemies of the Israelites (Exodus 16:8–14), might still be alive today and must be fought. In a subsequent panel of *The Book of Esther*, the sons of Haman are killed by hanging, and Wander covers the head of one son with a Ku Klux Klan hood and the others with pillow cases, symbolizing faceless enemies to make the point that if you attack us without open-faced confrontation, we retaliate in kind.

Haman is ultimately vanquished, and his edict to kill all Jews is rescinded. Both the biblical and legendary accounts state that the feast of Purim, honoring Esther's successful defense of the Jewish people, will be celebrated forever. The last panel of Wander's scroll *The Book of Esther*, based on legendary accounts, testifies to that belief by showing the return to Jerusalem (Ginzberg [1909–38] 1917–87, 4:352, 366). That Wander ends his graphic novel with legendary material rather than with the biblical account in which there is no mention of Jerusalem attests to the importance of Israel in the imagination of Jewish American artists, a topic yet to be studied in depth.

Another accordion scroll, *The Book of Ruth* (2010) (fig. 72), tells the story of Naomi and her Moabite daughter-in-law Ruth, both widows. Ruth follows Naomi and accepts the God of Israel as her own when Naomi returns to her home. It is then arranged for Ruth to meet Boaz, Naomi's kinsman, while Ruth gleans in his fields. They marry, and King David is one of their descendants.

Because Ruth was, in effect, a convert, Wander's text is in English, but his pages read from right to left in the Hebrew manner. Like other artists who see connections between the ancient past and the present, he dresses his characters in both ancient and modern clothing. Ruth appears early in the story in Middle Eastern garb, her head covered, but later as a blond bombshell when she arrives in Bethlehem with Naomi. The middle-aged Boaz, not a handsome man but honorable, wealthy, and knowledgeable in business practices and the law, wears modern clothing. As Wander, Benjamin, and Shafner have said to me in conversations, "What happened then also happens now."

Wander does not turn the story into a modern May–December romance, but he does intertwine some modern images, ideas, and a few extras with the ancient text. In that part of the scroll when Boaz first speaks to a demure Ruth, Wander has added an image of the Shekinah, variously the Divine Spirit and the feminine aspect of God, who envelopes both Boaz and Ruth. The Shekinah calls our attention to the divine plan for Ruth as the progenitor of the line that will lead to King David and, ultimately, to the Messiah. Wander then places side by side images of a bar scene and the moment when Ruth uncovers Boaz's feet on the threshing-room floor as instructed by Naomi, her mother-in-law (fig. 72). In the midst of this scene, a ghostly King David plays a harp, which provides Ruth's actions with a spiritual glow, further emphasizing her role in God's plan. A traditional-minded viewer might object to the scene of men pouring drinks down their throats in a bar, but Wander updated the following lines from the Book of Ruth (2:8):

> Boaz said to Ruth, "Listen to me, daughter. Don't go to glean in another field. Don't go elsewhere, but stay here close to my girls. Keep your eyes on the field they are reaping, and follow them. I have ordered the men not to molest you, and when you are thirsty, go to the jars and drink some of [the water] that the men have drawn."

One obvious place to go today would be a bar.

At the end of *The Book of Ruth*, Boaz and Ruth disappear from the story. Naomi raises their child, her grandson, Obed. Wander gives him a slightly frightened look, as if to say that whether in biblical or modern times, parents

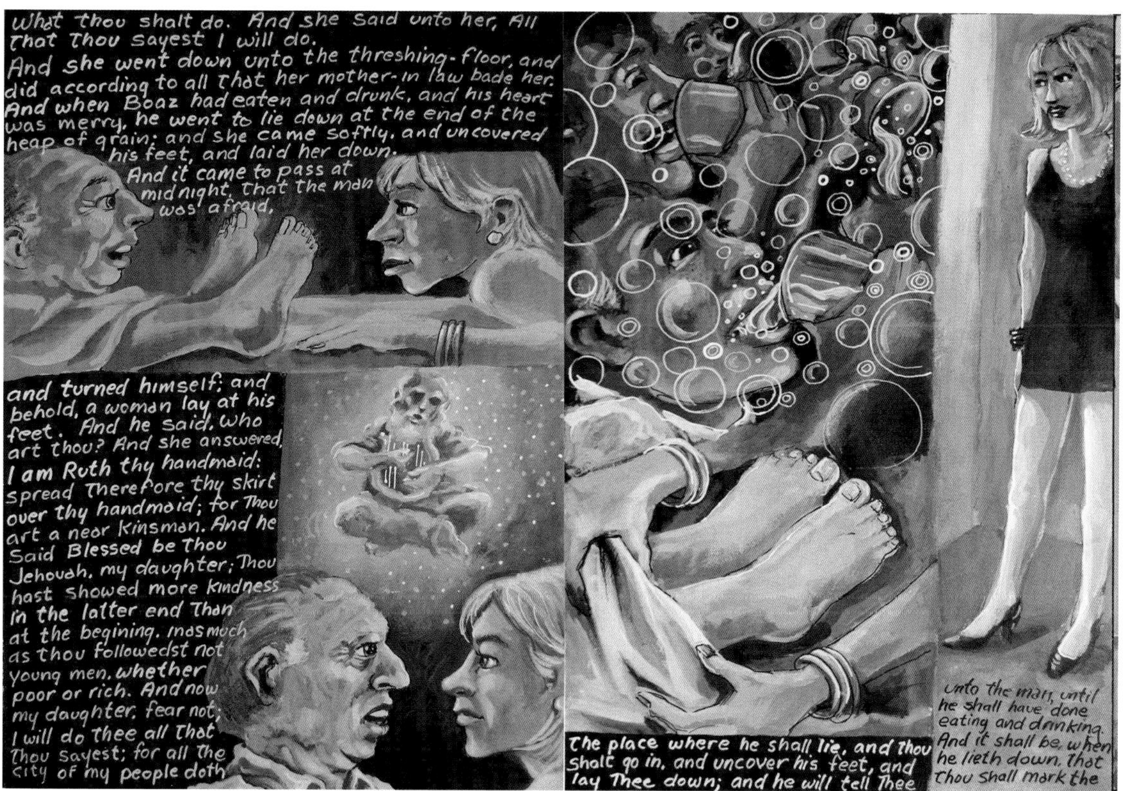


72. David Wander, from *The Book of Ruth*, 2010. Acrylic ink on paper accordion book, 25 in. × 25 ft. Courtesy of the artist.

are not always able or available to raise their children.

By comparison, when Wander planned his illustrations for his work *The Song of Songs* in 2011–12, he decided to emphasize the erotic aspects of the poem or the sexual connections between the lovers. He reasoned that even though the poem could be read as an allegory of the close relationship between Israel and God, he found the lovers' words and their descriptions of their actions too obvious to ignore. This interpretation is made quite clear with the images he placed literally behind the name of the poem and its opening lines written in Hebrew (fig. 73). The slightly open mouth with its exaggerated and presumably smoldering lips refers directly to the opening passage, "Oh, give me of the kisses of your mouth, for your love is more delightful than wine." And the man, perhaps completely nude (not just his torso) and lying in a diagonal position, appears to illustrate the next few lines: "Draw me after you, let us run! The king has brought me to his chambers. Let us delight and rejoice in your love" (1:4). Whatever interpretations have been developed of these lines, Wander suggests that we are intruding on a very personal moment between two people. That is, he has chosen to emphasize the physical rather than the spiritual both here and throughout his scroll. Further, Wander also makes the viewer quite aware that the woman is "dark, but comely" (Song of Songs 1:5), perhaps a countrywoman of Hagar's.

Some of the images are quite erotic but not sensationalist because Wander literally covers several bodies with the text passages. Thus, he teases the viewer, whether a Hebrew reader

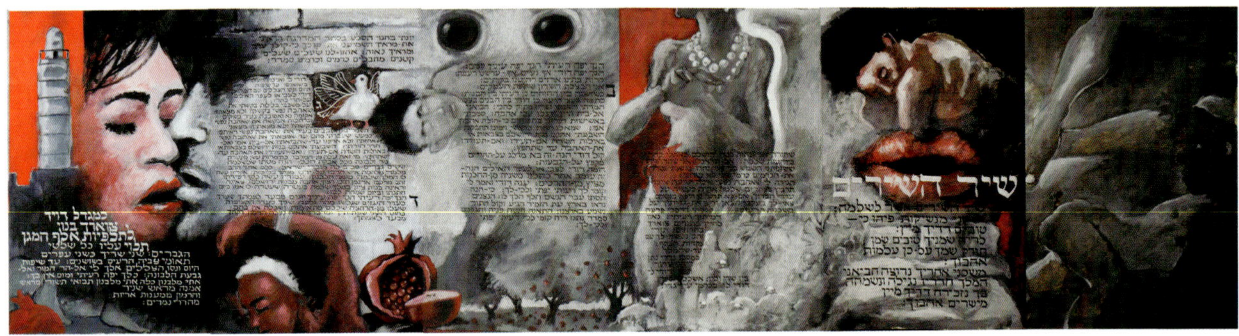


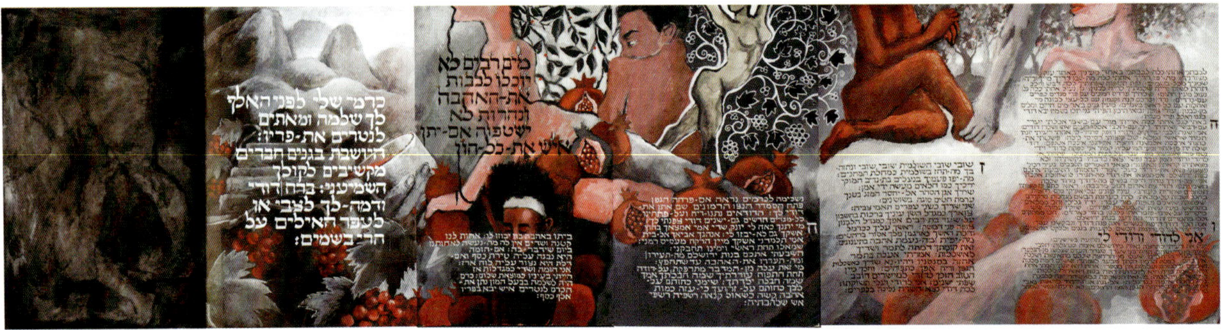

73. David Wander, from *The Song of Songs*, 2011–12. Acrylic ink on paper accordion book, 24 in. × 18 ft. Courtesy of the artist.

or not, and only hints at some of the images the text might suggest, a clever way to control the strong sexual overtones of the language and at the same time to provoke the viewer's imagination.

Unlike the stories of Jonah, Esther, and Ruth, there is no precise narrative arc to *The Song of Songs*. As a result, images might be based on a conflation of verses from different chapters. Pomegranates, a symbol of sexuality and fertility, appear throughout. Wander seems to have been especially enamored by chapter 7 of Song of Songs, which contains some of the most explicit sexual language in the entire poem. His image of the dancing woman whose body is superimposed on the man's back recalls the language of chapter 7:1: "Turn back, turn back, O maid of Shulem. Turn back, turn back, that we may gaze upon you. 'Why will you gaze at the Shulemite in the Mananaim dance?'" Another image showing the man holding his lover's foot is coupled with a nude woman whose body is hidden behind a text passage. It includes lines from chapter 6:3, "I am my beloved's and my beloved is mine" (similar wording appears in chapter 2:16), and is coupled with a passage from chapter 7:2 in which the man itemizes, "How lovely are your feet in sandals . . . , your rounded thighs are like jewels," and so on. In a nearby image, the viewer sees the lovers' heads, their eyes closed as in sleep, which recalls these lines: "And your mouth like choicest wine. 'Let it flow to my beloved as new wine gliding over the lips of sleepers" (7:10).

Wander's work *Echa* or *Lamentations* (2011–12) (fig. 74), a story in a different key and mood, required a different style of presentation. Because it describes the destruction of Jerusalem and the Temple as well as the grief and suffering of exile that followed, it is among Wander's most expressionist works. Just as he

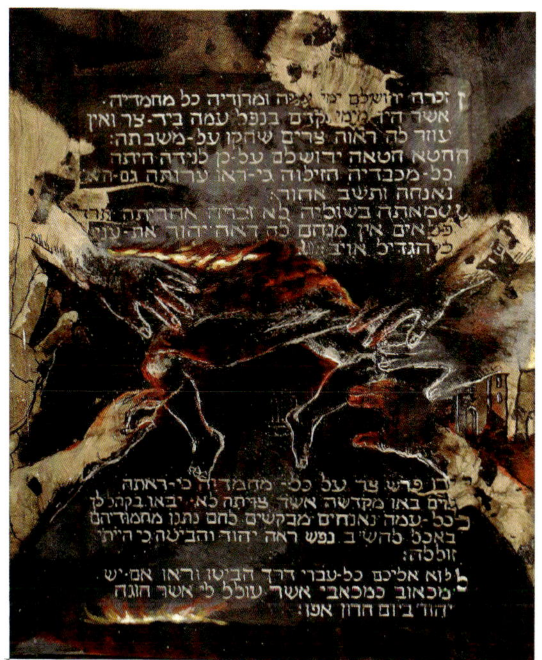

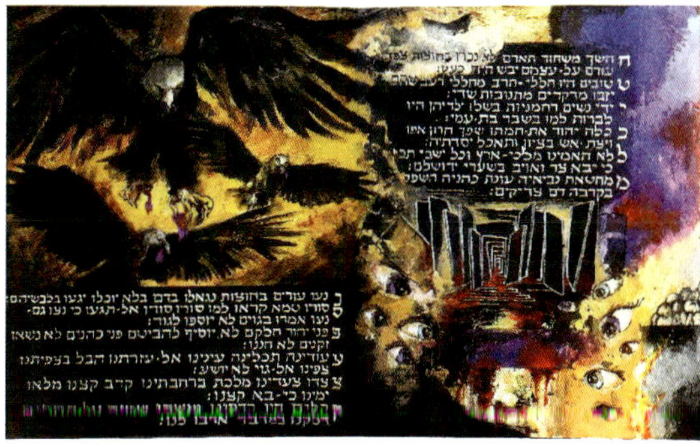

74. David Wander, from *Lamentations*, 2011. Acrylic ink and burned rice paper on paper accordion book, 13 in. × 24 ft. Courtesy of the artist.

did not soften the eroticism of *The Song of Songs*, so he insisted on emphasizing the horrific events described in Lamentations. He did so in part because he found in the text the same persistent, underlying anti-Semitism (or anti-Israelite sentiment in the biblical story) that prompted him to put a Ku Klux Klan mask on one of Haman's sons in *The Book of Esther.*

Lamentations is read each year on the ninth day of the month of Av in the Jewish calendar to commemorate the destruction of Jerusalem and Solomon's Temple in 586 BCE as well as other disasters experienced by the Jewish people in ancient, medieval, and modern times. Wander keeps asking himself, as does Richard McBee, Why remember the horrors of the past and the forces of oppression and degradation that have plagued Jews through the centuries? Why subjugate ourselves to thoughts of endless outrages as we reread the text year after year? He answers his own questions: we reread Lamentations perhaps as an assertion of presence and continuity as well as a constant sense of rebirth in a hostile world.

His answers are borne out by the last images of his scroll, which show two rabbis on the Temple Mount who see foxes, a sighting symbolic of the return to Jerusalem by the Israelites and the rebuilding of the Second Temple destroyed by the Romans in 79 CE (Talmud Makkot 24b). This is a departure from the biblical text, which ends instead on a more hesitant note with the plea to "renew our days as of old. . . . Take us back, O Lord, to Yourself, and let us come back; renew our days as of old" (Lamentations 5:21–22). In effect, Wander ends the story with a positive vision rather than with a plea.

But before we arrive at the last affirmative image, Wander offers some of his most startling, even demonic forms, and his emphatic brushstrokes are most evocative, especially in the ragged superimpositions of colors that bleed into each other. To capture the anxiety, despair, and imminent catastrophe inherent in the text, he first wrote it in white ink on black parchment paper, then burned some passages and attached white parchment paper on which he wrote the missing words with black ink. The interchange between white and black ink was ultimately based on the midrash that states: "How was the Torah written? It was written with letters of black fire over a surface of white fire" (*Midrash Tanchuma* 1996, Bereshit, Siman 1; see also Ginzberg [1909–38] 1917–87, 1:3). The black fire obviously refers to the printed letters, the white fire to the spaces between and around the letters. The black letters tell the reader what happened; the white spaces are meant to provoke thoughts about the events taking place. In the white letter–black letter reversal, the black paper with the white letters almost forces the viewer to contemplate the devastations recorded in Lamentations and the horrors Jews have experienced in the succeeding centuries. In the annual reading of Lamentations, the horrors are to be remembered, but the survival is also to be celebrated—both human depravity and the strength to prevail are acknowledged.

Wander visualizes the lines describing God's fury (Lamentations 4:1), showing the destruction of Jerusalem and the violation of the inhabitants. "Our pursuers were swifter than the eagles in the sky" (4:19). Hands grab and pull apart the legs of a woman (1:9–13), emphasizing in his illustration lines such as "her uncleanness clings to her skirts . . . , the foe has laid hands on everything dear to her." The streets of Jerusalem appear as a series of propped-up screens or doors that open into an infinite distance, as if nothing can block the invading army's march through the city. "The Lord has acted like a foe, He has laid waste Israel" (2:5). "He has made wall and rampart to mourn, together they languish. Her gates have sunk into the ground" (2:8–9). The staring eyes that form a depressed arc in the lower-right portion recalls the line in chapter 2:11: "My eyes are spent in tears."

Along the lower-right edge, a cauldron appears to contain children being boiled, a clear reference to chapter 2:20, "Alas, women eat their own fruit, their new-born babes!" A deranged-seeming mother eyes her terrified children. All of this is given before the image of foxes on the Temple Mount. It is as if Wander himself calls out to God the famous passage from chapter 3:55–56, "I have called out Your name, O Lord, from the depths of the pit. Hear my plea; do not shut your ear to my groan, to my cry," and is assured in his last image that his cry has been heard.

As if in recoil from the horrors he depicted in *Lamentations*, Wander sought in *Ecclesiastes* (2013) an elegiac tone rather than the kinds of observations on life that would be all too easy to depict. Virtually the entire scroll is composed of flowers. As he said in a taped interview in August 2013, this scroll "is about how beauty is fading and all is vanity. We bring beautiful flowers to all occasions, and they ultimately fall apart and die." While illustrating this scroll, Wander imagined the thoughts of an old king who, knowing that he would die soon, let his reminiscences of youth and old age glide gently back and forth, one into the other. We can well imagine Wander and the old king heeding the opening lines of Ecclesiastes chapter 12: "So, appreciate your vigor in the days of your youth, before those days of sorrow come and those years arrive of which you will say, 'I have no pleasure in them, before sun and light and moon and stars grow dark, and clouds come back again after the rain.'"

In recent years, Wander's style of storytelling has evolved. Although he still portrays events, he has come to rely on facial close-ups, showing individual reactions surrounded by textual passages. These passages propel and at the same time allow individuals greater latitude of emotion and agency. This is most evident in his five-book compendium of the life of King David (2012–13), one of the sections of which is illustrated here (fig. 75).

Based on First Samuel 28, this section describes King Saul's visit to the Witch of Endor to find out if he will be victorious in battle against the Philistines. The images going from left to right, Saul appears at first masked before revealing himself. The words in the upper left, beginning with "Do you want . . . ," are said by the witch, fearful that Saul is trying to trap her

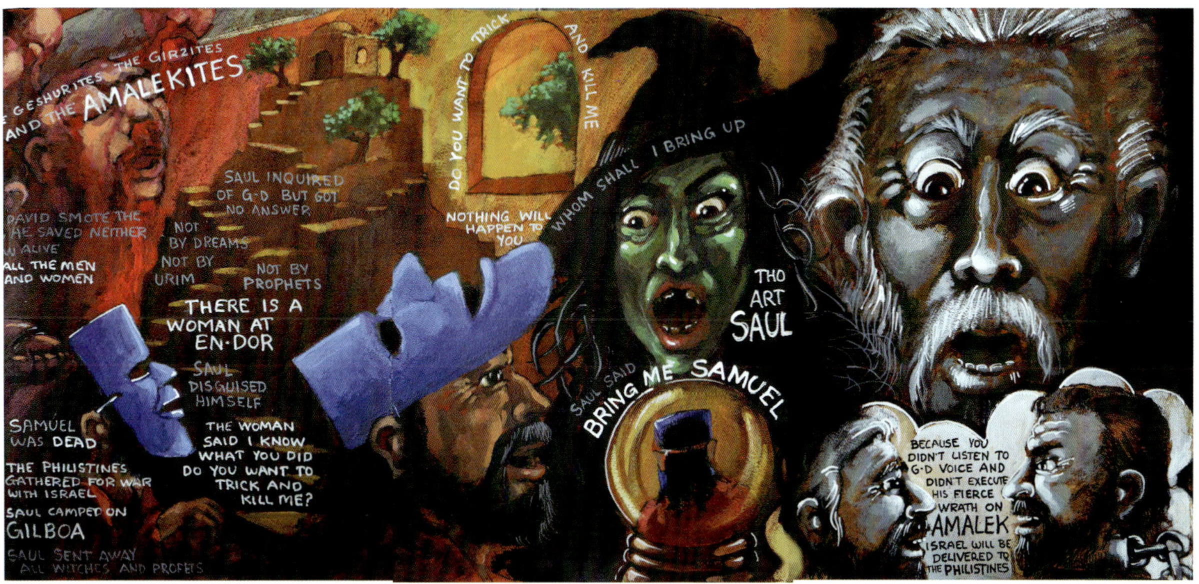


75. David Wander, from *The Five Books of King David*, 2012–13. Acrylic ink on paper accordion book, 17 in. × 16 ft. Courtesy of the artist.

because he previously banned the use of ghosts and spirits. Saul asks her to raise the spirit of the recently deceased prophet Samuel, who is shown emerging from a jar. Samuel predicts disaster for Saul, whose enormous face, ashen with fear, dominates the scene. Just below the close-up of Saul, the reason for predicting Saul's defeat is seen in the face-off between Saul and Amalek: in a previous battle Saul did not obey God's order "to execute His wrath upon the Amalekites" (28:18).

I have described at some length the images in these scrolls and accordion books because Wander, who calls his work "visual midrash," has tried to illuminate in them a universe of emotions and feelings while adhering closely to the ancient stories. They describe a range of human actions and emotions, including not only fear based on the artist's knowledge of the Jewish past and more recent present but also inspiration provided by some individuals' actions, valor and morality, civic responsibility, matters of individual spiritual concern, and the carrying out of God's commands. In this way, Wander provides his viewers with a range of responses as well as with the possibility of adding their own interpretations to the scenes presented.

Of course, the same can be said of the other artists considered here. Because the development of narratives among Jewish American artists is still a relatively recent phenomenon, there has not yet developed specific iconographical canons—in contrast to, say, the life of Jesus—and perhaps no such canons will ever be devoted to the lives and actions of individuals such as Jonah, Esther, and Ruth or events of Jewish historical importance. As one can readily imagine, an enormous range of images—in effect, visual midrashim—are possible, limited only by the artists' and viewers' imaginations, concerns, and interests. Wander brings his texts to life by using pictures, graphic designs, and innovative formats so that he can enter into, as he says, the secrets of a book or story. He reimagines these stories through sketching and what he calls "cinematic visualization techniques" that reveal their wisdom and the intricacies of relationships otherwise potentially inaccessible without further textual elaboration. In addition, he feels that he is translating the stories into an engaging contemporary language. In this regard, Wander's art is an art of personal discovery that invites viewers to respond in kind and to become involved in an intellectual and spiritual dialogue with that art's images. As with the other artists, for Wander the past is always in the present tense.

# 12 Archie Rand

Without question, Archie Rand (b. 1949) has produced more Jewish-themed and secular works of art than any other member of his generation. I would guess at least one thousand. Their styles range from abstract to representational, the latter including cartoons and comics. Mediums include paintings, murals, stained-glass windows, and a variety of graphics techniques. He is religiously knowledgeable, but his attitude can range from reverent to irreverent. Treatment of subject matter extends from pious to laugh out loud. His sources include just about anything he has seen in person or in reproduction. His many series of works might be about a particular subject (e.g., a specific psalm or a particular prayer) or about something open-ended (the seven days of Creation, the entire Torah). Finally, he is the only artist discussed here who has explained his reasons for and his processes of creating the forms and shapes that constitute his subject matter. They add up to a personal and intensely committed kind of art theory.

Like other artists discussed in this book, Rand needs to be the subject of a monographic study, especially because he is arguably a unique figure within the history of Jewish American art. Through the 1970s and 1980s, he was a rising mainstream figure who favored abstract forms. His willingness to add representational figures to his repertoire and to explore Jewish-themed subject matter was based in part on friendships with several mainstream figures such as Philip Guston (1913–80), who had abandoned abstraction for representation in the late 1960s (Baigell 2006a, 201–19, 2009a; Cameron 1984, 3; Lane 1979, 133–35; Schwabsky 1987, 23–24). As Rand asks in a brochure titled *Archie Rand Iconoclast* (2004), "What does it mean to identify as Jewish now? Here? It is a question that Philip Guston and I talked about in his last days. Locating oneself within the community, rather than repeating conventions ascribed to the community, is a form of personal research which has not been enjoyed by many painters," a point I discuss later in this chapter.

Equally important, Rand's growing preference for Jewish-themed subject matter and his responses to the loss of approbation by many in the mainstream art community could form the basis for a case study analyzing the reluctance of Jewish art-world figures to acknowledge, let alone support, artists who feel the need to explore this subject matter. (See the discussion of this issue in chapter 3.) Despite rejection, Rand persisted and in 1988 offered an explanation that might have represented at that time the feelings of other artists discussed here: "It seems that my insides were more Jewish than I thought. . . . I believe there are other Jewish artists who actually feel more of a tie to their Jewishness than they are willing to admit. I've chosen a different way, and it has given me a great deal in return" (qtd. in Lester 1988).

Of course, this explanation is too simple and needs further explication. Suffice it to say here that Rand's family was involved with Jewish organizations and that he attended synagogue as a youth. He grew up in a Brooklyn neighborhood where youngsters of different ethnic and religious backgrounds had to assert and defend their heritage. He remembers (because one never forgets such things) that by the time he was in junior high (middle school) in New York, anti-Semitic taunts were a commonplace experience for him. In the ensuing years, whatever else he was then absorbing from the art world, he began to identify with marginalized racial and other minority groups, including his own religious community. He still recalls quite vividly store owners in his neighborhood with concentration- and death-camp numbers on their arms. This sense of identification prompted him at the age of eighteen to begin the creation of *The Letter Paintings* (1969–71), in which on scrolls (reminiscent of Torah scrolls) he wrote the names of African American jazz, blues, and rock-and-roll musicians. These paintings are paradoxically celebratory and tragic insofar as he brought to attention the names of many known and unknown musicians who helped define the popular music of their culture and at the same time prompted worry that it might soon be lost, absorbed into mainstream culture. Rand called these paintings "tombstones." (He included the largely forgotten Amos Milburn and the Chicken Shack Boogie Cats, a band that in the late 1940s was the only gut-bucket rock-and-roll band that played in the midtown New York jazz club I frequented.)

In addition, in a taped interview on December 27, 2017, while reminiscing about those early years, Rand said he believed that different cultures needed to invent their own histories, quite the reverse of the kind of modernism espoused by art critic Clement Greenberg (1909–94), according to which paintings are to be composed only of flat patterns of forms and colors, revealing no depth or story line, in great measure erasing the personality and history of the artist as well as any sense of a past except as these things relate to other paintings. One of the other great art critics of the post–Second World War period, Harold Rosenberg (1906–78), did allow for the presence of an artist's individuality but only in the interaction between the artist and the canvas, according to which the particular stroke of the brush is made in response to the previous stroke (in the context here, see Baigell 2005a and 2015b, 186–96). Rand felt at the time that he had to place himself in history, that he wanted to concern himself with issues in his own time and in his own way, which Greenbergian modernist art discourse did not encourage or find relevant.

When asked in 1974 to decorate the interior of the B'nai Yosef Synagogue in Brooklyn, Rand was ready for the challenge (Feld 1977; Jablons 1978; McBee 2004; Schwabsky 1986). Completed in 1977, Rand's designs initially covered 8,000 square feet of wall surface, to which he added another 3,000 square feet soon after. The subject matter ranged from the Creation to the messianic age, and the design included images derived from the Holocaust, the Bible, various holidays, the Passover Haggadah, kabbalah, the Pirkei Avot (Wisdom of the Fathers), religious rituals, and a variety of symbols and abstract shapes of Rand's own invention (fig. 76). His sense of personal piety provided focus for his artistic imagination and where it might take him, but he always respected religious and midrashic parameters concerning acceptable subject matter. On completion, the murals marked an epochal achievement in the history of Jewish American art matched only by Ruth Weisberg's *The Scroll* (1986), discussed in chapter 4. Rand's murals are considered to be the first set of thematic murals to cover so

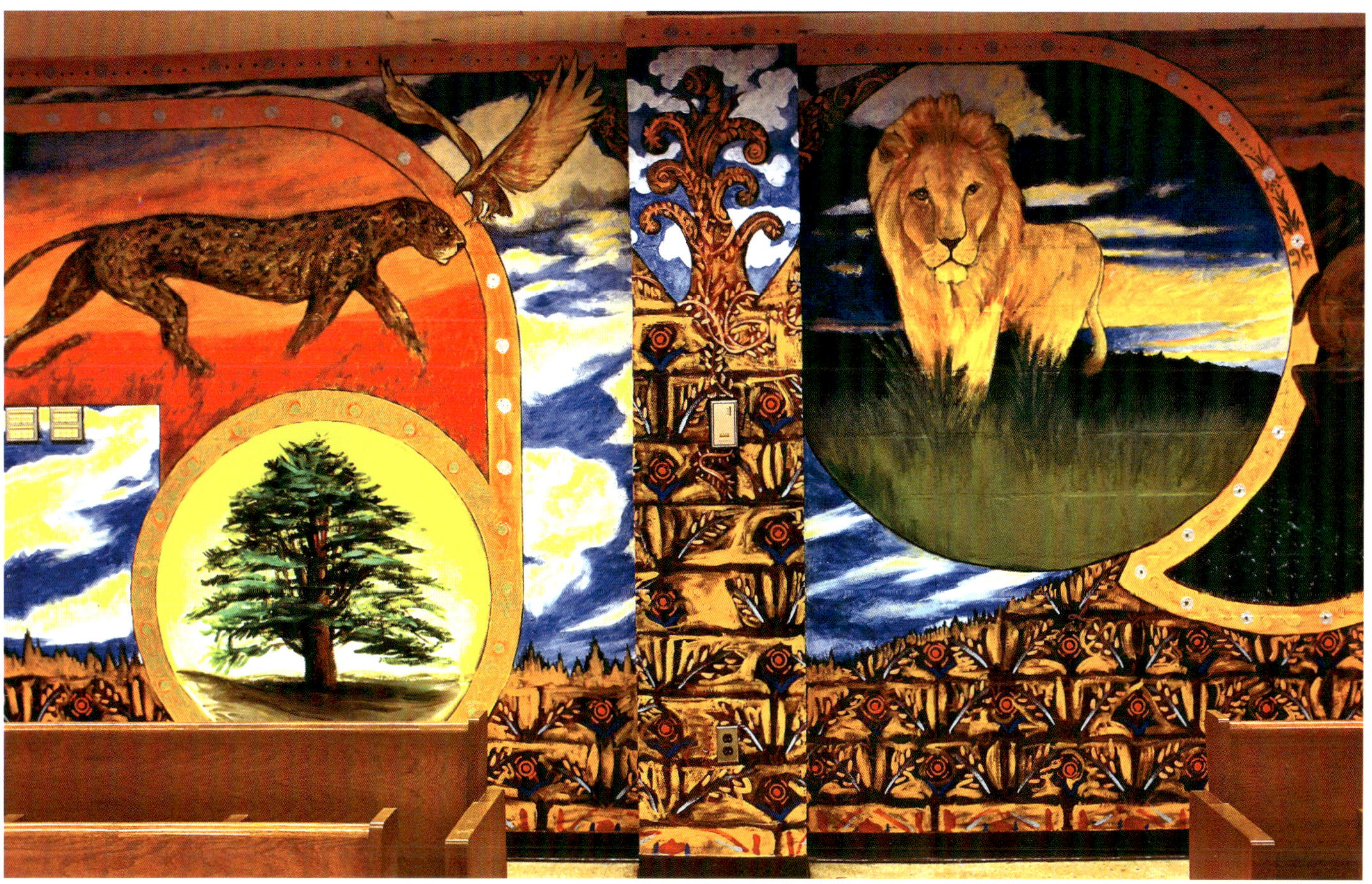

76. Archie Rand, interior, B'nai Yosef Synagogue, 1974–77. Courtesy of the artist.

much space in a synagogue since the murals at the synagogue in Dura Europos in Syria in 244–56 CE.

Rand's efforts upended tradition by his insistence on personal freedom of invention. He respected the Bible and other texts, but he was the arbiter and authority of what might or might not be included in his work, how it was to be treated, and where it might be placed. This is an important point because he came to his material unlike earlier artists, who, whatever their political beliefs, grew up within traditional boundaries of Jewish life and customs and who evidently could not and did not take the kinds of liberties in their work that Rand took and continues to take in his. After the B'nai Yosef murals, almost anything became possible for artists of his generation—and certainly for Rand. As he said, after B'nai Yosef "I had 2,000 years of unillustrated rabbinical commentary to draw on, which sent me into an explosion of joy" (qtd. in Shluker 1996).

But "draw on" in what ways? How illustrative of the story line should his work be? How abstract? Over the years, Rand has considered his approach to his subject matter and has explained it on several occasions, perhaps the only artist of his generation to formulate a mode of presentation within a Jewish context. His explanation allows his viewers to make sense of his abrupt changes from sketchlike to more finished passages and from figurative to abstract images in his paintings, sometimes all within the same work. At the risk of simplifying what is a complex relationship between text, image, and the connections Rand feels to the Jewish community, it is possible to condense his position to a series of propositions. He believes that cultures should invent and reinvent their own histories without the burden of tradition, nostalgia, and old symbols. Art need not be illustrational because the visual effect is more important than the textual. There is often a need to invent a new iconography that the artist might arbitrarily designate—for example, in this instance a Jewish iconography especially for assimilated Jewish Americans. The bottom line is that an image does not have to make narrative or storytelling sense but merely suggest something to the viewer in order to provoke a dialogue through shapes and colors—much like the many unresolvable interpretations in Talmudic disputations.

Some underlying factors should also be mentioned. Rand feels that when he is in the midst of creating a work, he is merely the passive vessel through which his inspiration flows. He does not know where the inspiration comes from; perhaps it is from God. He feels that all artists want to believe that their work is more than just random strokes of the hand and arm, so that the belief in some external force provides the work with a sense of gravitas. He therefore chooses not to edit his strokes or marks because he is merely the transcriber of the first draft, as it were. Otherwise, as an editor, he would be disturbing the initial inspiration that came from another source. As he has said, "[I] had the feeling that it [creating Jewish-themed works] had not come from me, but through me—that I had been an instrument of God. I think every good artist who ever lived gets that feeling when he does the work he really has to do" (qtd. in Lester 1988).

For Rand, the personal is at the center of his art and provides access to his desired intimacy with God, a point of view he shares with several artists, who emphasize both the spiritual aspects of their art and the meditative aspects of their art-making processes (Baigell 2006b). In fact, Rand holds that art provides a window for prayer, "across which meaningful devotions can be mediated toward Heaven. One doesn't pray to an image, but through it. . . . Art serves to act for the greater glory of God" (Rand 1999a). (It is impossible to imagine figures such as Mark Rothko [1903–70], Barnett Newman [1905–70], Jack Levine [1915–2010], and Leonard Baskin [1922–2000] making such an assertion.)

Rand also worries about the lack of a visual Jewish legacy and wants his art to rise above being *about* Jewishness and instead *become* Jewish. What he means is that he pursues this goal by exercising both his insistent individuality and by acknowledging the traditional Talmudic habit of raising questions about the issue at hand. In this regard, he chooses not to indulge in a predictable iconography, but for a particular work or a series he decides "to construct a visually cohesive, not textually obedient iconography" (Rand 2003). This does not mean that his choices of forms are entirely arbitrary. In an email of March 12, 2018, he stated: "All images have some reference to some text or commentary regardless of how obscure but I allow myself an almost infinite topography of potential narrative selections." In this sense, the art comes first. He feels that "Judaism even against its will must have its own paintings. Judaism needs to offer up a painted language, a visual manifestation. This evidence is a required component of any operating culture" (Rand 2006; see also "Archie Rand" 2016). Each work he completes, then, becomes a contribution to the vibrant operation of that culture through his viewers' open responses without the limitations of precise or traditional expectations.

Like other artists, Rand is aware of the need to create and maintain a Jewish culture appropriate to the now decentered Jewish American scene, as mentioned in the introduction. He is also aware of the threat that more traditional works—such as Grandma lighting the Sabbath candles, dancing Hasids—are static images that will pass into history unreflective of life in modern America. He is anxious not to let that happen. As he said in 1984, "At a certain point, I have to function on faith. There is a synapse after your intellect stops and you have to make a jump that is completely blind. And that jump is based on—if I honestly think that something is important enough to preserve, then there must be something in it that maybe others can relate to" (Rand 1984, 6). He appeals to the audience who believes, as he does, that "for religion to function, it's got to be real, it's got to be believed, and it's got to be independent of the very community that it maintains its association with. By arriving independently at one's need for use of Judaic heritage, you become a community in absentia" (qtd. in Rosen 2001, 60). That is, he is willing to rattle tradition, to confront moribund complacency, in his desire to sustain a living Jewish culture.

His attitude toward the art-making process and his brash undertaking to cover the walls of a synagogue in Brooklyn with paintings prepare us to follow the career of an artist who obviously has no fear of whatever project is at hand. Following the synagogue murals, Rand has made many multipaneled series, the largest one so far is *The 613* (2001–6), 613 paintings based on the commandments a Jew is supposed to complete in a lifetime. In a generation of artists for whom creating narratives or a continuing series of one type or another is quite normal, this series is an unprecedented achievement.

One of Rand's most popular series, *The Fifty-Four Chapter Paintings* (1989) was included in the Jewish Museum's exhibition *Too Jewish? Challenging Traditional Identities* (1996), which marked the first large-scale recognition of contemporary artists who explore Jewish themes (Kleeblatt 1996b; see also *Jewish Themes* 1986). Based on the fifty-four divisions of the five books of the Torah—Genesis, Exodus, Leviticus, Numbers, Deuteronomy—each panel of *The Fifty-Four Chapter Paintings* is labeled in Hebrew at the top. Painted simulations of an open Torah scroll frame each panel. The subjects of the paintings are approximately evenly divided between the five books and describe different kinds of activities both sacred and mundane as well as supernatural and ordinary. The images range from figurative to abstract, from the obvious to the obscure, and include individuals as well as representations of God as creator, instructor, performer of miracles and blessings, as well as the One who established the covenant, rituals, and rules of behavior for the Israelites. Some panels include objects that do not necessarily convey relevant content, indicating that Rand intended them to act as points of departure for thought rather than as places for easily digestible information. But—an important "but"—as in the synagogue murals, in *The Fifty-Four Chapter Paintings* Rand kept his imaginative flights well within appropriate religious parameters. As he noted in an email of March 22, 2018, "I expanded my inclusions to give myself as much breathing room as possible but still maintained threads to what I felt had to be obligatory connections."

Some panels are easier to strike up a dialog about than others. For example, the panel titled *Chaya Sarah* is based on Genesis 23:19: "And then Abraham buried his wife Sarah in the cave of the field of Machpelah facing Mamre—now Hebron—in the land of Canaan." Even though Sarah is the first of the Four Matriarchs, Rand does not indulge in hagiography. His panel includes a cave in the side of a hill, with some scraggly greenery haphazardly scattered about. There are no easy means of access, no steps, no path, no monumental entrance for the mother of the Jewish people—just a hole in the side of a hill. One wonders, then, what the artist thought about Abraham's feelings for Sarah

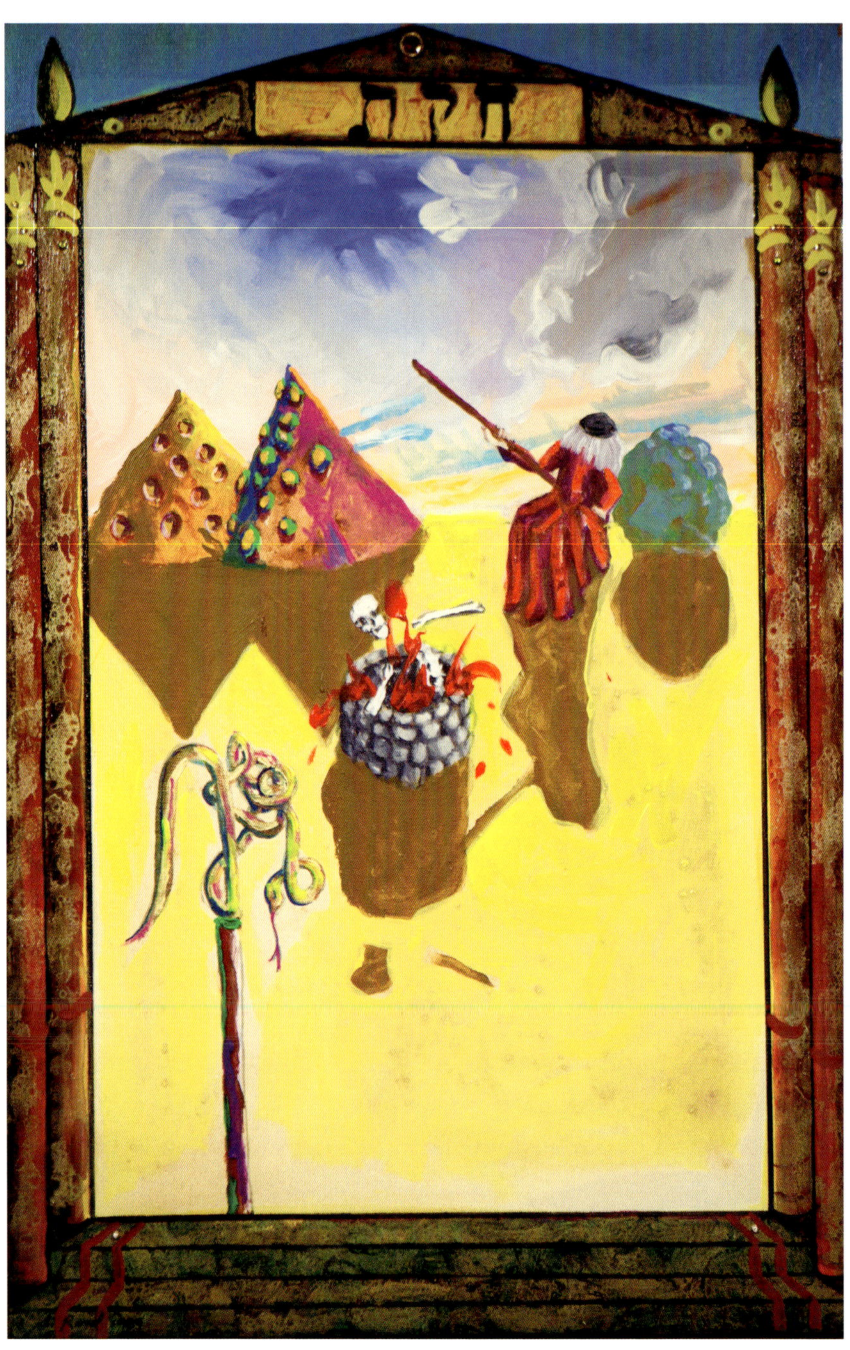


77. Archie Rand, *Hukkat*, from *The Fifty-Four Chapter Paintings*, 1989. Mixed media on canvas, 36 × 24 in. Courtesy of the artist.

insofar as Abraham lies twice about their relationship by calling her his sister (Genesis 12:13 and 20:2) and, according to legends, lies again when he takes Isaac away to be sacrificed, telling Sarah that he wants Isaac to study the ways of God. After Sarah's death (Genesis 23:2), Abraham remarries and has several more children, perhaps with Hagar (Ginzberg [1909–38] 1917–87, 1:274–75).

One of the most difficult panels to fathom is titled *Hukkat* (fig. 77), the name of the weekly Torah portion that includes Numbers 19–22. The viewer needs to do some homework to figure out what this panel is about, but I include it here because the Bible reveals Moses as a complex, imperfect human being given to temper tantrums and questionable activities, not unlike individuals we might know or qualities we might share. In addition, at least one legend offers an explanation of why God allows Moses to die after all the years Moses wanders in the desert and before he reaches the Promised Land.

The passage Rand chose to illustrate, Numbers 20:11, refers to a miracle. "And Moses raised his hand and struck the rock twice with his rod. Out came copious water, and the community and their beasts drank." God told Moses only to order the rock to yield its water, not to strike it. But Moses strikes the rock instead of speaking to it, and so the implication is that Moses is taking credit for the water. God, angry at Moses's lack of trust and usurpation of miraculous power, tells Moses that he will not lead his people into the land promised to them. The moral lesson of this passage, then, is to give credit where credit is due, especially if you are dealing directly with God.

There is a legend, however, that softens the severity of God's decree concerning the death of Moses. God evidently decides that Moses will die in the desert because if he leads his people into the Promised Land, it might be thought that those who died along the way, their bodies buried in the desert, will have no share in the future world. But if Moses were to be buried with them, he would be able to lead them into the Holy Land after the Resurrection (Ginzberg [1909–38] 1917–87, 3:43, 52, 310–12, 481). Thus, Moses dies while still in the wilderness, as God has intended. The moral messages here are that you might think you are in control of your destiny, but you are not, so be humble and thankful for what you have and what you can do and believe that there might be a reasonable explanation for a seemingly inexplicable act.

Rand also included two miracles in *Hukkat*, items for additional contemplation. The first concerns the serpent wrapped around the pole in the foreground. Several Israelites had died from serpent bites because they had spoken against the Lord. Moses interceded, and God then told Moses to create a serpent mounted on a rod. Anyone who had been bitten would be cured by looking at the rod (Numbers 21:8–9).

The second miracle lends itself to the kind of lively research Rand described after completing the B'nai Yosef Synagogue, quoted earlier in this chapter: "I had 2,000 years of unillustrated rabbinical commentary to draw on, which sent me into an explosion of joy." Who is the skeletal figure emerging from the well, and what is its meaning? In an email dated December 18, 2018, Rand wrote that he remembered the passage in Exodus 13:19, according to which during the Israelites' departure from Egypt Moses takes Joseph's bones for subsequent burial (see also Joshua 24:32). So the skeletal figure might indicate Joseph's presence.

A few days later, on December 22, Rand wrote that he had just read a midrash that Moses knows he cannot leave Egypt without Joseph's bones. So, clearly, the bones are Joseph's. A quick check proved that Louis Ginzberg describes this episode in greater detail in *The Legends of the Jews* ([1909–38] 1917–87, 2:179–81). Now the question: Who discovers the bones? According to legend, it is Serach (or Serah), daughter of Asher. Jacob's sons are afraid to tell him that Joseph is alive. So they ask Serach to sing the news to him in a song, which she does. Her other good deed is to remember where Joseph's coffin was dumped in the Nile River (Ginzberg [1909–38] 1917–87, 2:115–16, 181–82).

There's more. In good Talmudic fashion, Rand also accepts the following interpretation. When Hagar and Ishmael are traveling in the desert after leaving Abraham's home, they consume all of the water they are carrying. Ishmael is quite ill. God hears his prayers, and Miriam's well, which was created on the sixth day of Creation, appears to them (Ginzberg [1909–38] 1917–87, 1:265). God admonishes Moses for hitting the rock—"Thou shouldst have learned from the life of Ishmael to have greater faith in Me" (Ginzberg [1909–38] 1917–87, 3:312)—so perhaps the figure emerging from the well in the painting might also be considered the ghost—or the bones—of Ishmael. We might interpret the skeletal figure as evoking both positive and headstrong aspects of Moses's character.

In any event, Rand chose an extraordinarily rich and complex passage that describes the presence of God, miracles, human weakness, and a community that challenges its leader. It speaks to Robert Kirschbaum's point that the deeper you explore the ancient texts, the deeper you want to go (see chapter 8). And as Ruth Weisberg comments on midrashim, they "tend to enliven the archetypal stories for successive generations" (2004a, 138). Rand would certainly agree and probably add that midrashim can both reinforce tradition and provide an autonomous perch for an artist, that cultural memory does not have to be narrowly delineated but can accommodate multiple viewpoints—again, a very Talmudic attitude. "Judaism," Rand has said, "has to accept its diversity or it will cease to flourish" (qtd. in Rosen 2001, 60).

In 1992, Rand completed *Sixty Paintings from the Bible* in a cartoonlike style, elements of which had appeared in his work as early as 1985 in a thirty-five-foot-long painting titled *Garden Party* and in his series of portraits of rabbis of that year (fig. 3). In *Sixty Paintings*, several statements issuing in text bubbles from the subjects' mouths are by turns pithy, outrageous, even blasphemous, but they provide the biblical figures with a humanity they otherwise rarely display. Rather than mythic beings, they become ordinary people who react in less than ideal ways, their all-too-human melodramas revealing the Bible to be a book filled with interesting human stories that also convey moral values. By combining word and image in what he terms a "more accessible and user friendly" manner, Rand wanted to present biblical episodes in a more down-to-earth way than, as he said, they are given in the "off-putting academic . . . rabbinic literature" (qtd. in Wecker 2004). His great concern in this regard reflects his belief that Jewish artists must force-feed their "work into the digestive system of a community that is visually anemic" (qtd. in Wecker 2004).

In one of the most startling panels in *Sixty Paintings*, *We're Naked* (fig. 78), a nude Adam and Eve are in the Garden separated by the Tree of Knowledge, around which the serpent is coiled. They are surrounded by an array of real and mythical animals. The image refers to Genesis 3:7: "Then the eyes of both of them were opened and they perceived that they were naked and they sewed together fig leaves and made themselves loin clothes." In Genesis 3:11, God asks: "Who told you that you were naked? Did you eat of the tree from which I had forbidden you to eat?" Obviously, neither Adam nor Eve actually says, "We're naked," but Rand would have known of other biblical expletives said at key moments. At least two of these moments occur in stories associated with King David. First, Bathsheba says to King David, "I am pregnant" (Second Samuel 11:5), and, second, Amnon, after raping Tamar, his half-sister, in his tent, says, "Get out" (Second Samuel 13:15; see also Alter 1981, 76).

Rand included the phrase "We're naked," as he said, to "get past the standard English translation and find the eye catching 'punch' of the original Hebrew" (qtd. in McBee 2004). The "punch" also includes the lines immediately following Genesis 3:7, in which God asks Adam, heretofore an innocent in the Garden of Eden, how he knows he is naked. Adam has no answer other than to pass the buck to Eve, who in turn blames the serpent. Rand indicated in an email of June 17, 2010, that the matter is more complicated:

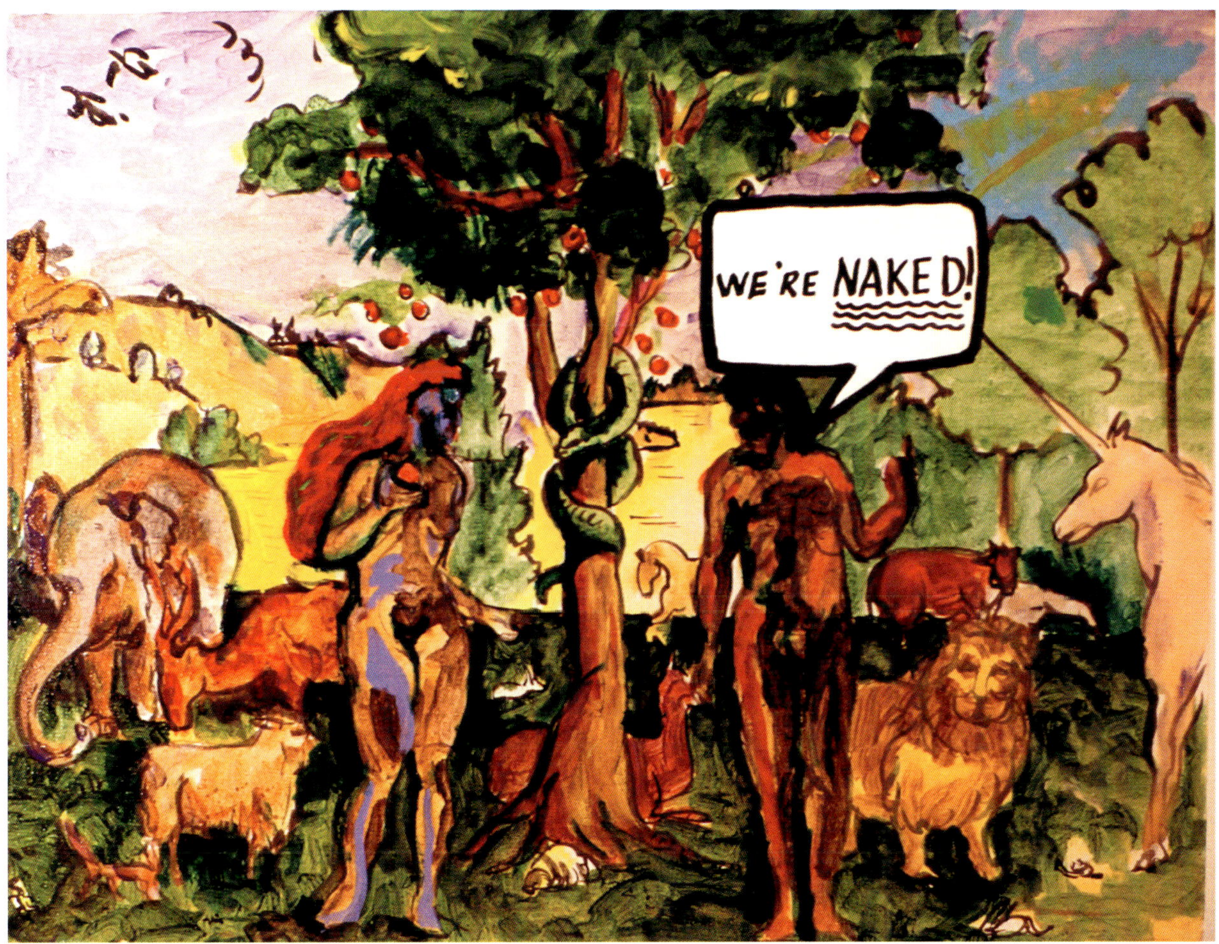


78. Archie Rand, *We're Naked*, from *Sixty Paintings from the Bible*, 1992. Acrylic on canvas, 18 × 24 in. Courtesy of the artist.

> Adam at once realized that he blew his contract and THEREFORE he is on his own. I don't think that he's happy that he is "free" from God but he's now a quick read because he now has knowledge and he's a realist and quickly switches into survival and continuance-planning mode. Adam's posture is "conscious." Many of the protagonists in this series [of paintings] have realized that SOMETHING is up. (emphasis in the original)

Another interpretation of Adam's exclamation revolves around the idea that humans alone, among all the animals, possess acute self-awareness. Adam's first act in his desire for freedom is disobedience, an act that throws him into history, having to live in the world rather than in paradise. That is what makes him human. One can imagine that had Adam been American, he would have expressed realization of his nakedness by saying, "OH MY GOD, we're naked."

Feminists spin the encounter with God differently (Aschkenasy 1998, 122–29; *The Five Books of Moses* 2004, 24–25 [Genesis 3:6–13]). In his translation (*The Five Books of Moses* 2004), Robert Alter clearly suggests that Eve is intellectually more advanced than Adam. In Alter's version, "the tree was good for eating and a delight to the eyes, and that the tree was desirable as a source of wisdom" (Genesis 3:6). Aschkenasy translates that passage as "the tree was good for food, that it was pleasant to the eyes, and a tree to be desired to make one wise," and then she explains that with these words Eve has the ability to differentiate between three areas of human experience—the physical, the aesthetic, and the intellectual (1998, 126). In contrast, Adam simply takes the fruit from Eve without comment. When questioned by God, Adam blames God for giving him *that* woman, who then gave him the fruit. When Eve is questioned by God, she says that she was "beguiled" (Alter's word) by the serpent, not "duped," as in the usual translations (Genesis 3:13), "beguiled" being a more active, participative response than being merely "duped." She also admits responsibility for her actions. In Rand's painting, Adam can do no better than muster an OMG response. However one chooses to evaluate these passages in Genesis or even just to think about them, Rand's painting is successful because we begin to wonder: Just who is this Adam who in the Bible is father to the world of people?

Other paintings in the series *Sixty Paintings* carry text bubbles. King Solomon, when deciding the fate of a child claimed by two mothers, says (based on First Kings 3:25), "Cut the kid in half!! And give one half to each mother!" The most ribald comment is from the wife in *Potiphar's Wife*, who in a vain attempt to seduce Joseph calls after him as he runs from her chamber, "Fuck me!" (based on Genesis 39:12). But in addition to the earthly, corporeal, and mundane activities of some biblical figures in *Sixty Paintings*, Rand also included images of the heavenly, the incorporeal, and the immaterial, thereby providing a visual immediacy that textural passages do not always convey.

One such painting, *Elisha Watches Elijah Depart* (fig. 79), visualizes Elijah's assent to heaven. Elisha sits on a hill under a tree overlooking a seaside scene. In the sky, a chariot flies off into space. The bubble text next to Elisha reads: "Can I have a double portion of your spirit?" It is based on Second Kings 2:9. "As they were crossing [a miraculous dry path through water], Elijah said to Elisha, 'Tell me, what can I do for you before I am taken from you?' Elisha answered, 'Let a double portion of your spirit pass on to me.'" In subsequent verses, we learn that Elisha's request will be granted if he sees Elijah ascending. Rand shows Elisha witnessing the event, Elijah's mantle fluttering to earth, and Elisha retrieving it (Second Kings 2:13). The spirit of Elijah has indeed settled upon him (Second Kings 2:15).

If *The Chapter Paintings* and *Sixty Paintings from the Bible* represent the public Rand, then two sets of paintings completed within the next two years, from around 1992 to 1994, represent the private, more intimate Rand, in which, as he might say, his heart led his hand. One set, *Psalm 68* (1994), is composed of thirty-six paintings small in scale and abstract in style, and the other set, *The Eighteen* (1994), includes eighteen mostly abstract paintings based on the Amidah, the central prayer of every religious service. Neither conveys the slightest hint of the type of over-the-shoulder comments found in *The Sixty Paintings from the Bible*, and neither, with a few exceptions in *The Eighteen* series, suggests depth or deep space. Forms tend to hug each picture's surface because of the even saturation of the colors. It appears as if Rand wanted to keep the subject matter of both series close to him as he painted each canvas. As he said of *The Eighteen*, "I tried to find out how the prayers made me feel rather than what they were specifically although not exclusively saying" (qtd. in Belitsky 1998).

The same can be said about *Psalm 68* (fig. 80). He chose to illustrate this psalm because it has thirty-six stanzas (Rand 2014, 19).

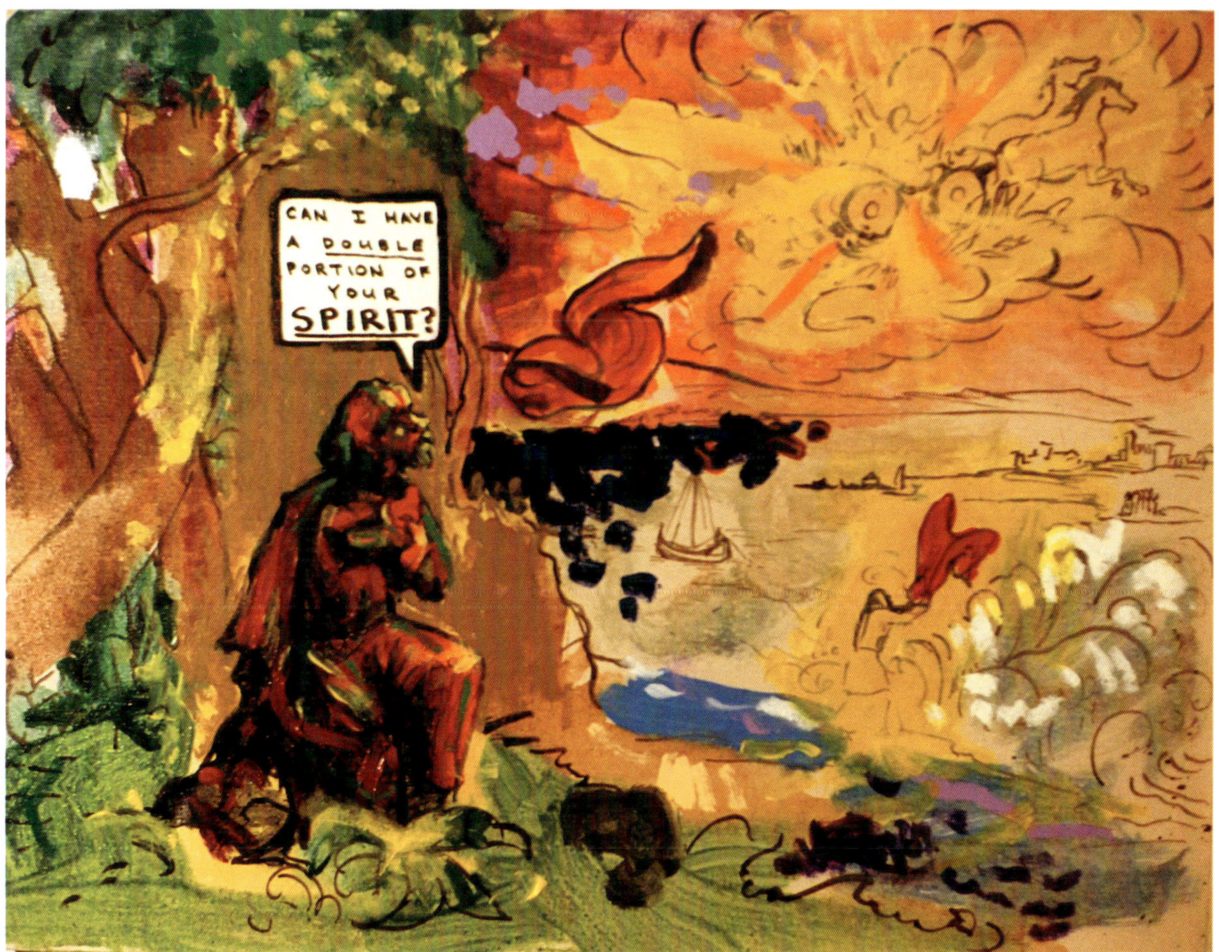


79 Archie Rand, *Elisha Watches Elijah Depart,* from *Sixty Paintings from the Bible*, 1992. Acrylic on canvas, 18 × 24 in. Courtesy of the artist.

In Jewish numerology, thirty-six is double eighteen. As mentioned in chapter 9, each letter in the alphabet has a numerical equivalent. The letters that spell the Hebrew word *chai*, "life," add up to eighteen. Thirty-six, then, signifies double life. Despite the clear letter/number connection, this psalm has been called the most difficult of all the Psalms, "a collage of citations from a variety of old poems" (commentary by Robert Alter in *The Book of Psalms* 2007, 229; see also Dahood 1968, 133–52, and the side-panel comment to Psalm 68 in *Jewish Study Bible* [1985] 2004, 1353). Some passages invoke triumphal hymns; others recall events described in Exodus concerning the defeat of the Egyptians, the deliverance of the Israelites, the escape into the wilderness, the theophany at Sinai, and the settlement in Canaan. Several verses have puzzled scholars for centuries and remain open to many and even contradictory interpretations.

But Rand, adventurous and wildly imaginative, accepted the challenge of confronting Psalm 68, letting its moods wash over him, reveling in them, allowing their contradictions to remain unresolved, and responding to their aural-tone vibrations. A journey into the unknown? The desire to let his brush lead him

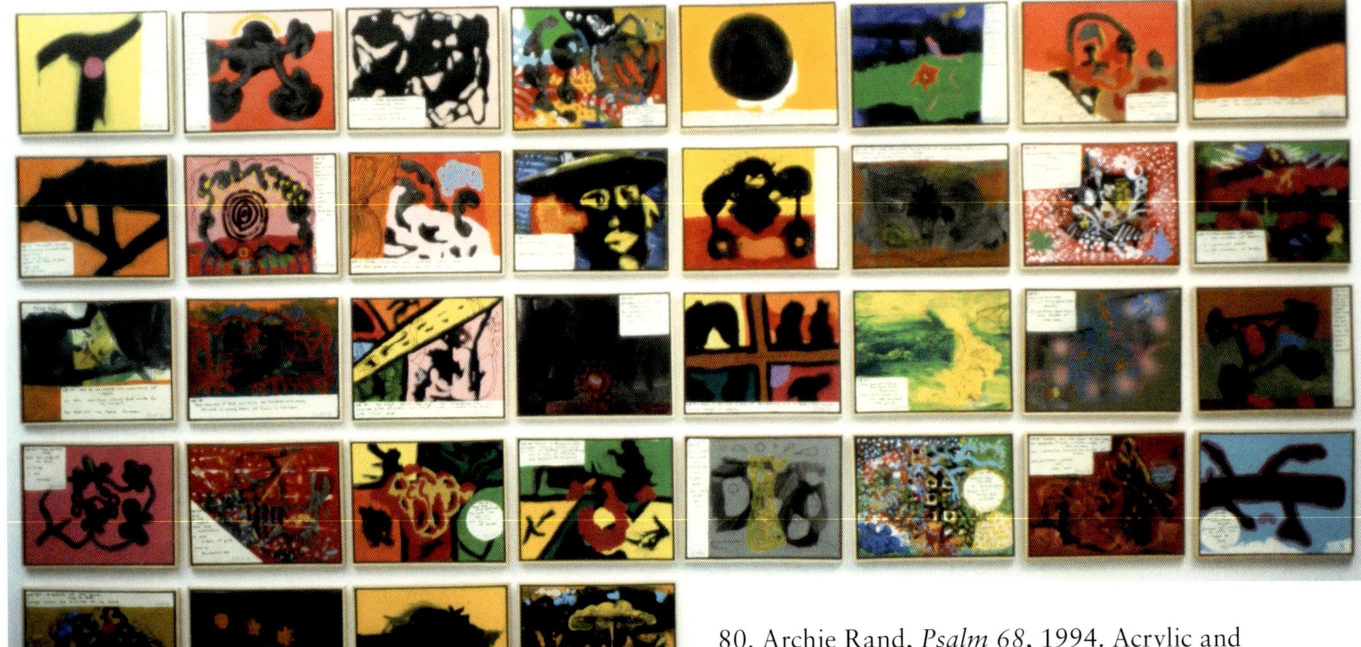

80. Archie Rand, *Psalm 68*, 1994. Acrylic and marker on canvas, each panel 12 × 16 in. Courtesy of the artist.

in the spirit of the moment? Certainly. Colors might approximate the mood of a stanza, ranging from black suggesting wickedness to riotous mixtures of color expressing happiness or spots of color indicating rain. Particular passages might invoke certain forms, such as the blunt, awkward shapes in verse 32, which suggest the arms and legs of an African sculpture (fig. 81). But rather than assign such obvious meanings to colors and forms, Rand would rather have his work awaken in the viewer a nonverbal feeling parallel to but not descriptive of the written text. Ideally, eyesight and language, what one sees and what one reads, are brought into harmonious balance, a kind of visual-spiritual adventure that might even be devoid of narrative meaning or quite simply might be a Jewish kind of visualization.

About *The Eighteen*, Rand noted that "the artist has often functioned as an intermediary between God and us. These 18 represent that belief in visual terms. I believe I was given a special mission. These paintings are unabashedly spiritual" (qtd. in M. Greenberg 1998). He channeled his feelings through three primary motifs: the circle, the gateway, and the six-pointed Star of David (fig. 82). The circle symbolizes both God, who according to Jewish belief has no beginning and no end, and the earth in constant rotation. The gateway symbolizes a transition to a higher level of being, as noted in Robert Kirschbaum's *The Portal Series* (chapter 8). And the Star of David represents Jewish peoplehood and the six days of Creation (as discussed in Kaufman 2003 and Kessler 1998, 9; see also Hoffman 1997, 2:11). As with *Psalm 68*, Rand wrote the appropriate words on each painting for *The Eighteen*, using Hebrew instead of English this time. Creating this series was a nervy thing to do because it is based on the eighteen sections (a nineteenth was added in the second century CE) of the Amidah, the

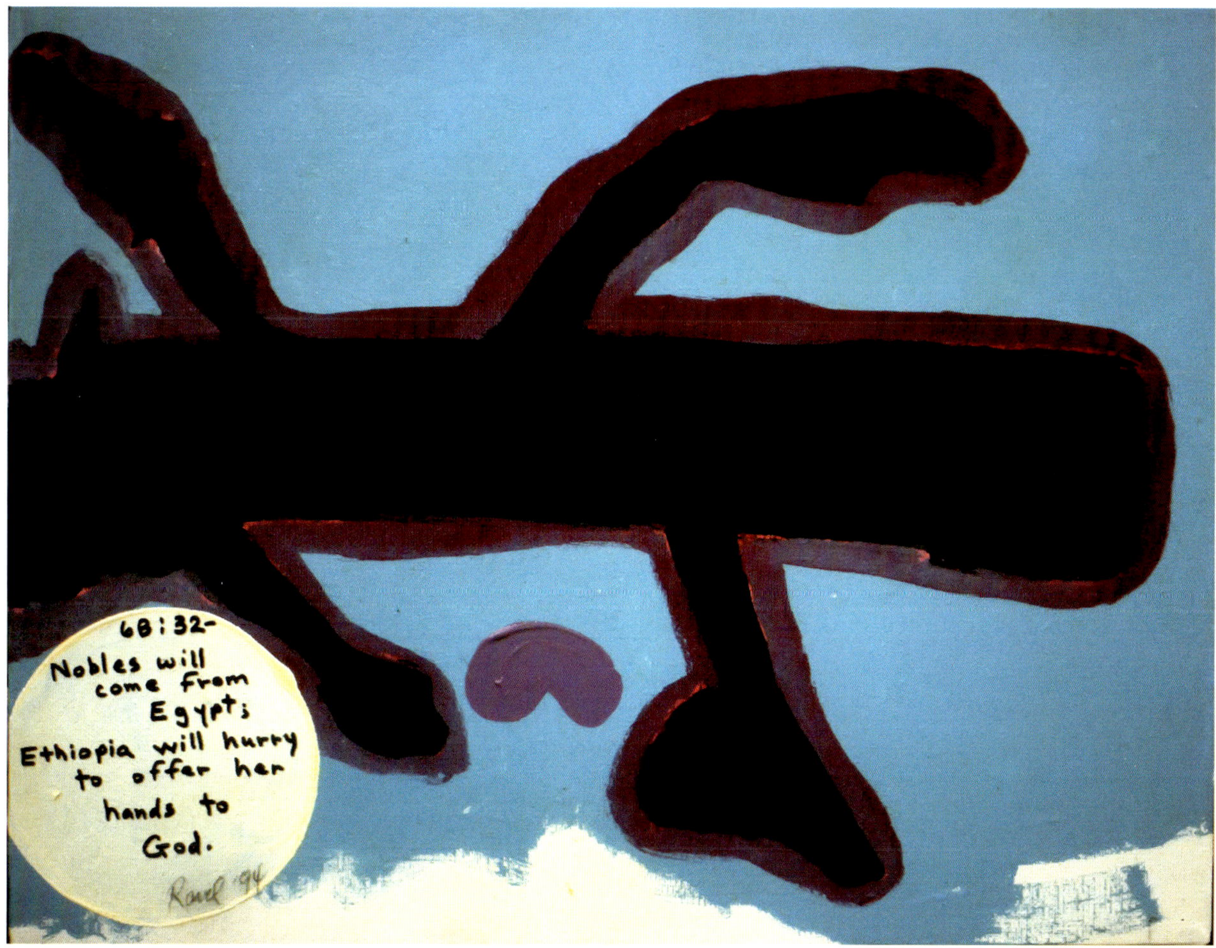


81. Archie Rand, detail from *Psalm 68*, 1994.
Courtesy of the artist.

central prayer of Judaism repeated three times a day, with slight variations for the Sabbath and holy days. It is said silently and is perhaps of all Jewish prayers the one in which Jews commune most directly with God.

The sample from *The Eighteen* illustrated here, *Number Fifteen* (fig. 82), is the most unusual of the series because it is not a flattened circle filled with abstract shapes or a design based on the six-pointed star but instead has narrative elements and is therefore the most easily comprehended. It is based on the fifteenth benediction of the Amidah, concerned with redemption and the coming of the messianic age. It reads in part: "Speedily cause the offspring of David Your servant to flourish and raise up his glory through Your salvation, for Your salvation we await the day."

In the painting, two columns supporting the arch are covered with the scales of the primordial leviathan. Rams' horns forming the capitals symbolize the trumpetlike sounds announcing the Messiah's arrival and suggest glory or majesty. The three columns, two on the picture plane and one in the distance, represent the three foundations of the Jewish world—Torah, worship, and loving deeds—mentioned in the Pirkei Avot (Wisdom of the Elders). Their presence in the painting conveys the notion that religious observation and good

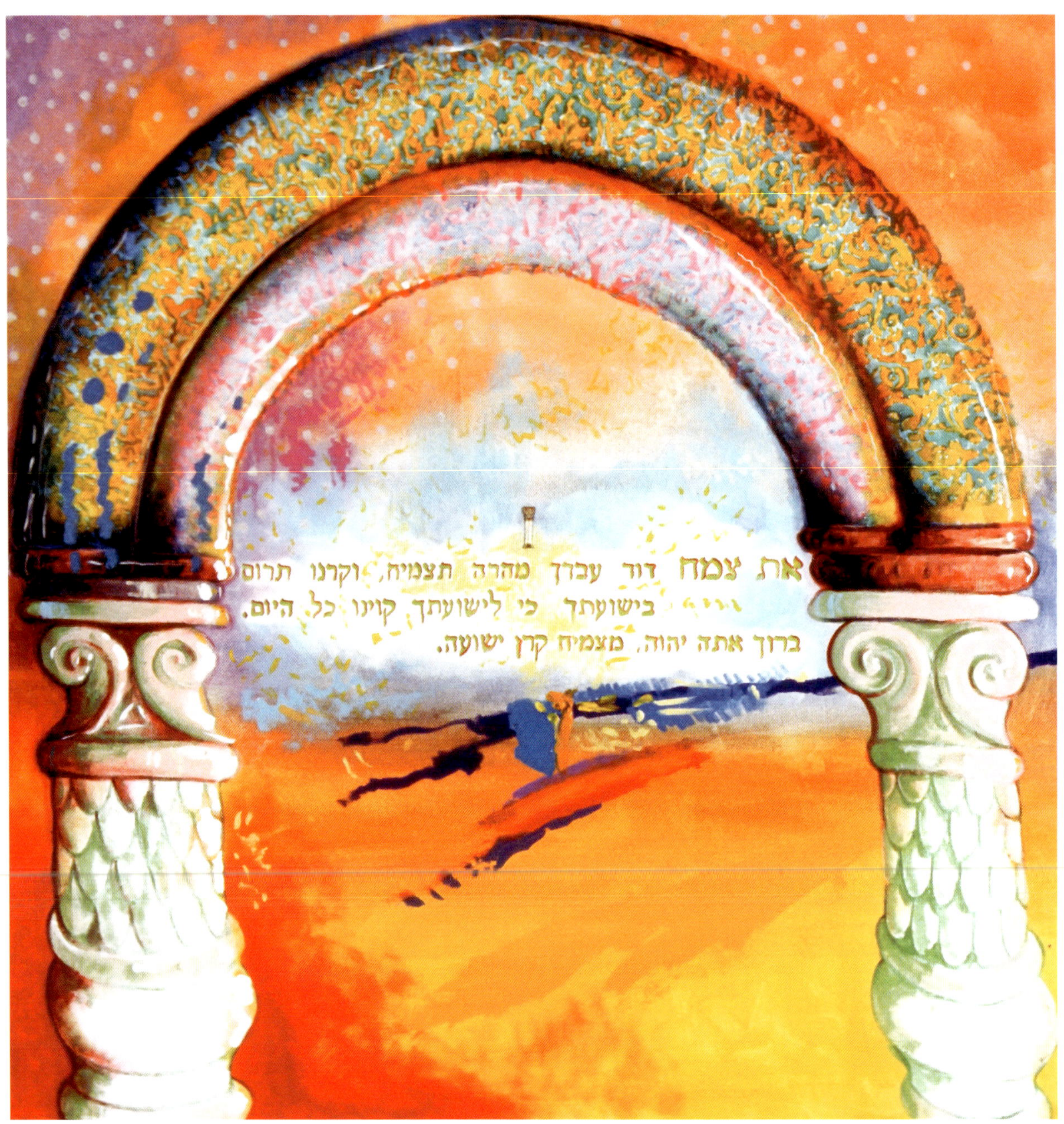


82. Archie Rand, *Number Fifteen*, from *The Eighteen*, 1994. Acrylic on canvas, 54 × 54 in. Courtesy of the artist.

deeds (*tikkun olam*) will hasten the arrival of the Messiah and complete the Creation.

Rand returned to the Bible in 2002 with *The Nineteen Diaspora Paintings*, a much less spiritual series of paintings that if published in book or brochure form might appeal to those who prefer a nontraditional approach to biblical stories, one that speaks in contemporary visual terms (Rand 2003; see also Finkelshteyn 2003). He explained his method for creating this series: "I placed blocks of scriptural fragments, each of which addresses a pivotal point in the story of the Jewish people, into each painted chapter. These scenes are arranged to tell a story in a restructured chronology about the rise of Israel, its internal dissolution and exile—with the last pictures reflecting on the hope of continuance" (Rand 2003).

With their comics style of presentation, these nineteen paintings are among the most approachable in Rand's entire oeuvre. "I wanted to . . . break from stereotyped Yiddishized nostalgia," he said, "so I looked at guys I looked at as a kid" (qtd. in Finkelshteyn 2003), meaning he read comic books, which were often written and illustrated by Jewish artists and writers (see also Rosensaft 2004). Needless to say, Rand aimed his paintings at a Jewish American sensibility free of eastern European sentimental and *Fiddler on the Roof* associations.

In terms of biblical chronology, the *Eve* panel is the first, the pivotal point being the arrival of the initial biblical family and the problems they faced and created. The text from Genesis 1:31 states: "And God saw all that He made and found it very good. And there was evening and there was morning, the sixth day." In the painting, Eve, in a dress and therefore living outside of Eden, confronts a dinosaur in what is now an incredibly dangerous world. The juxtaposition of the human and the terrifying creature from the ancient past invokes science fiction and therefore calls to mind a contemporary way of focusing on what the expulsion really meant and means. Clearly, Rand wants to shock us into rethinking the shattering implications of what was gained and lost by human entry into the material world.

Another panel, titled *Cain and Abel*, its pivotal point suggesting familial problems, shows the murder in an urban setting, complete with an attending medic, a policeman restraining Cain, another policeman comforting Abel's wife (or partner), and a photographer. The text from Genesis 4:10 reads, "The voice of your brother's blood is screaming to me from the ground."

But for our purposes the panel most interesting to consider is *Elijah* (fig. 83). The text is the same as that for *Elisha Watches Elijah Depart* (fig. 79) in *Sixty Paintings from the Bible*, Second Kings 2:11–12. The panel's pivotal point is, as noted in Malachi 3:23, Elijah's association with the messianic age and presumably the rebuilding of Jerusalem. Instead of a cartoonlike image set in an imaginary landscape, Elijah is now shown, eleven years after Elisha watched him depart, as an astronaut in an updated comics style and updated way of thinking about travel through the heavens, this time by modern rocketry rather than by miraculous means.

It needs to be stressed here that the comics style is not meant to be playful or superficial. It is instead meant to help those who lack knowledge of their religious heritage but who are hungry for such knowledge and who want to connect to their heritage. In these panels, Rand provides the viewer with a painless way to enter into a biblical discourse that might not occur with just the text or traditional imagery.

With a copy of the book *The 613* in hand, in which all 613 paintings of the commandments are in color, a viewer has that many chances to start a discourse. The paintings date from 2001 to 2006. The word *commandment* denotes law, obligation, and deed, while connoting goodness, value, piety, and even holiness (Isaacs 1996, xi; see also Chill 1974). Today, it is impossible to perform all the commandments, nor did Rand intend to illustrate each one's precise "command." He instead looked at old comics, children's books, posters, and newspapers. "I would riff on these," he said, "pulling something at random off the wall and then saying that this image could be that commandment" (qtd. in Somerstein 2006), meaning that interpretation would be personal and intuitive rather than doctrinal and authoritative.

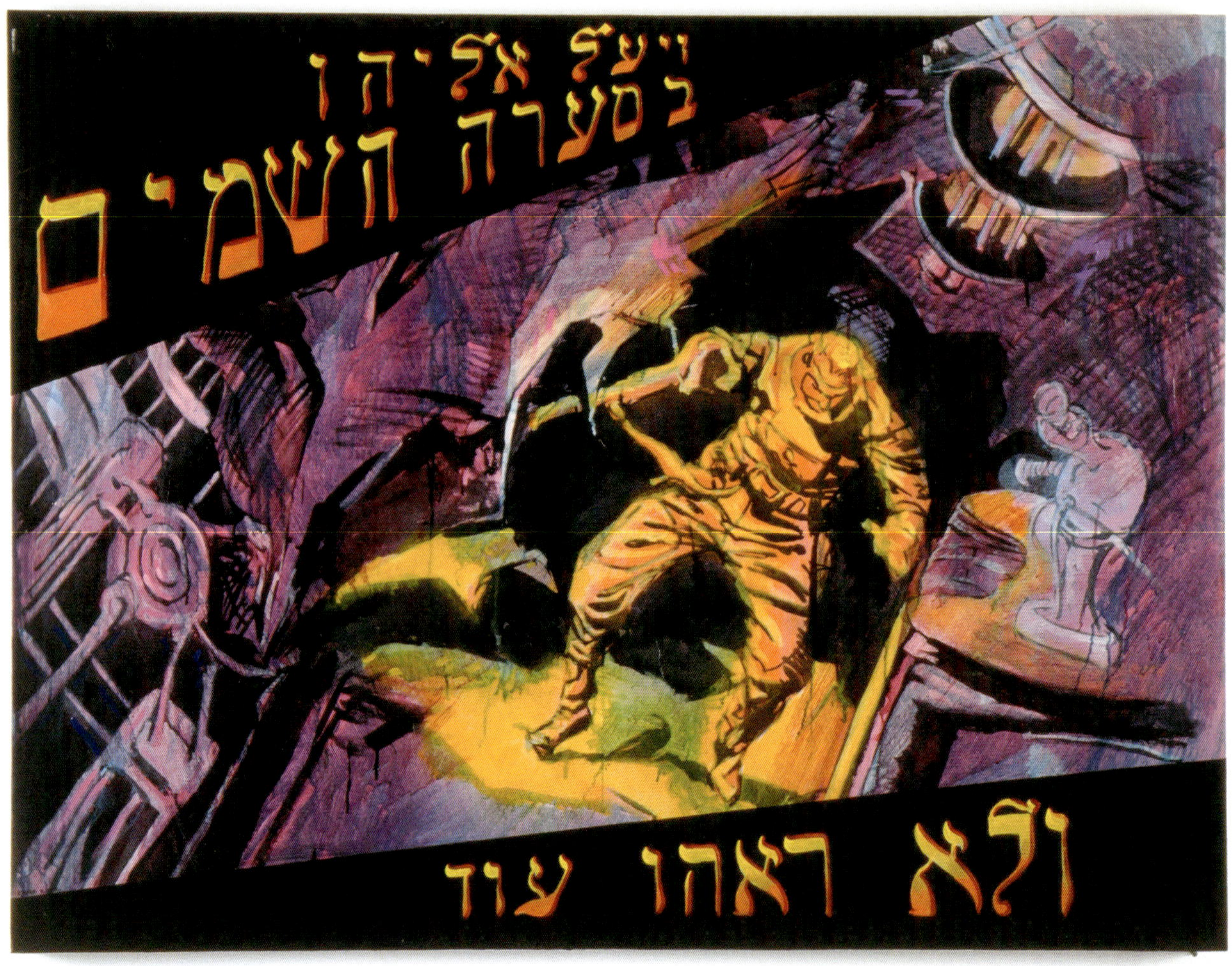


83. Archie Rand, *Elijah*, from *The Nineteen Diaspora Paintings*, 2002. Acrylic on canvas, 48 × 64 in. Courtesy of the artist.

Some of the text sources accompanying each image make no sense to me, at least not yet, but many images open up new and unexpected ways of interpreting the meaning(s), lesson(s), and value judgment(s) implicit in a particular commandment and therefore adding to my knowledge about Jewish ethics and moral concerns. For example, Rand associates four of the commandments with Leviticus 19:17, which tells us not to hate, embarrass, hold a grudge, or take vengeance against relatives. Commandment 17 instructs us not to embarrass others (fig. 84). That is straightforward. Some images, purposely crude, are entertaining to look at but have an underlying seriousness that Rand clearly intended. In this series and in his other series, he prefers evocation to simple illustration because the former offers "avenues that are not worn and provides the viewer with more stimulating fare" (qtd. in a brochure for Temple Shalom, Chicago, 1982). The goal, he feels, "is to reach the unstable realm of analogies, free association, and constant metamorphosis. The realm of unrestricted thinking" (qtd. in Yau 1989, n.p.).

As indicated earlier, Rand holds that such an interaction is essential to the development of a modern Jewish art because it reflects the vibrancy and health of the culture. And if that interaction is a little uncomfortable and

left to right, the biblical time sequence is wrong; for those who normally read from right to left, the sequence is correct, even if the included figures do not appear in the biblical story.

What is one to say about such a painting? A few things. First, the secular and the sacred inhabit the same space. Second, if one insists, according to an Orthodox belief that nothing much matters, that time is really timeless between the giving of the tablets at Sinai and the coming of the Messiah, then one can say that Silverstein populates this painting accordingly—the religious is neither better nor worse than the secular. But a more socially relevant contemporary observation would hold that worshiping the Golden Calf symbolizes the desire for material goods and the elimination of restraints placed on one's life, whether economic or moral. This is not a painting about delayed gratification or sublimation. In this way, Silverstein gives this biblical story contemporary relevance as a possible example of principled or unprincipled uplift and at the same time notes that people probably have not changed in the intervening years. So at one extreme the painting might be considered scandalous by the mixing of the secular and the sacred, and at the other it provides an astute observation of a particular set of human traits that has biblical precedent.

Such multivalent interpretations are characteristic of Silverstein's paintings. He says that years ago he was particularly impressed by two lines he read in William Blake's poem "Proverbs of Hell" from *The Marriage of Heaven and Hell* (1790–93): "The road to excess leads to the palace of wisdom" (line 3), and "You never know what is enough unless you know what is more than enough" (line 4) (Blake 1970, 35, 36). I would add the line "Without Contraries is no progression" (Blake 1970, 34). In paintings such as *The Golden Calf*, Silverstein hopes that both the congruities and the incongruities within a scene can lead to greater understanding, if not appreciation, of both sacred and secular elements and that one can shade off to the other slowly or abruptly.

The idea of combining sacred and secular elements as well as their actual and potential interactions, Silverstein remembers, was also prompted by his close reading of Thesis Nine of Walter Benjamin's "Theses on the Philosophy of History" (Benjamin 1969; see also Boyarin 1992, 34–35). Musing on a painting by Paul Klee, *Angelus Novus* (1920, Israel Museum, Jerusalem), Benjamin noted that the angel appears ready to look away from his object of contemplation. Imagining that the figure is the angel of history looking at the past, Benjamin explained that it sees the wreckage of the past and wants to fix it. But a storm blowing from paradise is so strong that the angel is instead pushed into the future. "This storm is what we call progress," Benjamin wrote (1969, 259–60). In Silverstein's own interpretation, the past, paradise, includes Jewish memory as well as paintings from previous centuries. The wreckage includes scenes from everyday life. Broadly speaking, the past and the present represent, respectively, the sacred and the profane, which, joined together, are the "collage" from which Silverstein finds his subject matter. He offers no value judgments, just blunt observations.

On occasion, Silverstein will place two different images so close together that they seem to mesh rather than be juxtaposed. Another work painted in 1999, *The Tower of Babel* (fig. 86), shows the Tower of Babel and a government-subsidized, low-rent, high-rise apartment tower leaning against each other. Again, logical time and place are ignored to make the point that a multiplicity of languages existed in a mythical biblical building and still exists in an actual multiethnic modern structure common to inner-city living. Human diversity then as now. But Silverstein also slyly raises the matter of the futility of erecting a structure to

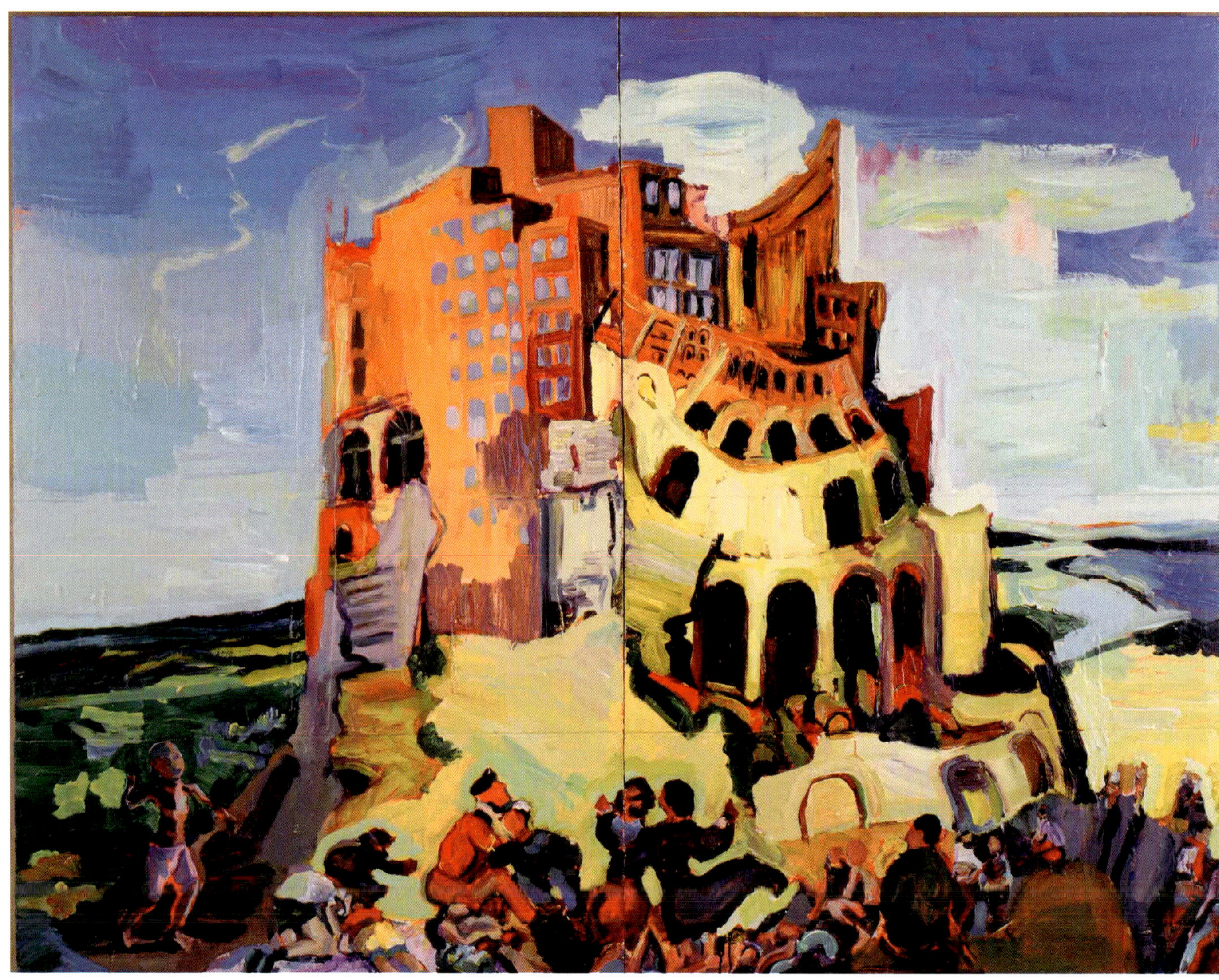

86. Joel Silverstein, *The Tower of Babel*, 1999. Acrylic on wood panels, 96 × 60 in. Courtesy of the artist.

reach to the heavens so that its inhabitants will become godlike (Genesis 11:5) and the issue of how those living in a modern building are unable to communicate effectively with each other because they speak many languages. Both structures are comments on the possibilities and failures of human aspirations. The figures in the lower part of the painting, based on Francesco Goya's prints *Los Caprichos* (1797–98), suggest darkly the follies and therefore the failures of humankind.

One of the more intriguing large-scale works by Silverstein is *Brighton Beach Exodus* (2008) (fig. 87), which mixes personal with biblical history. Brighton Beach, many miles in length, occupies the eastern end of Coney Island (no longer an island because the channel has long since been filled in) on the southern shore of Brooklyn directly facing the Atlantic Ocean. Silverstein grew up near the beachfront and spent many summers on the beach. One can see several stone breakers reaching out into

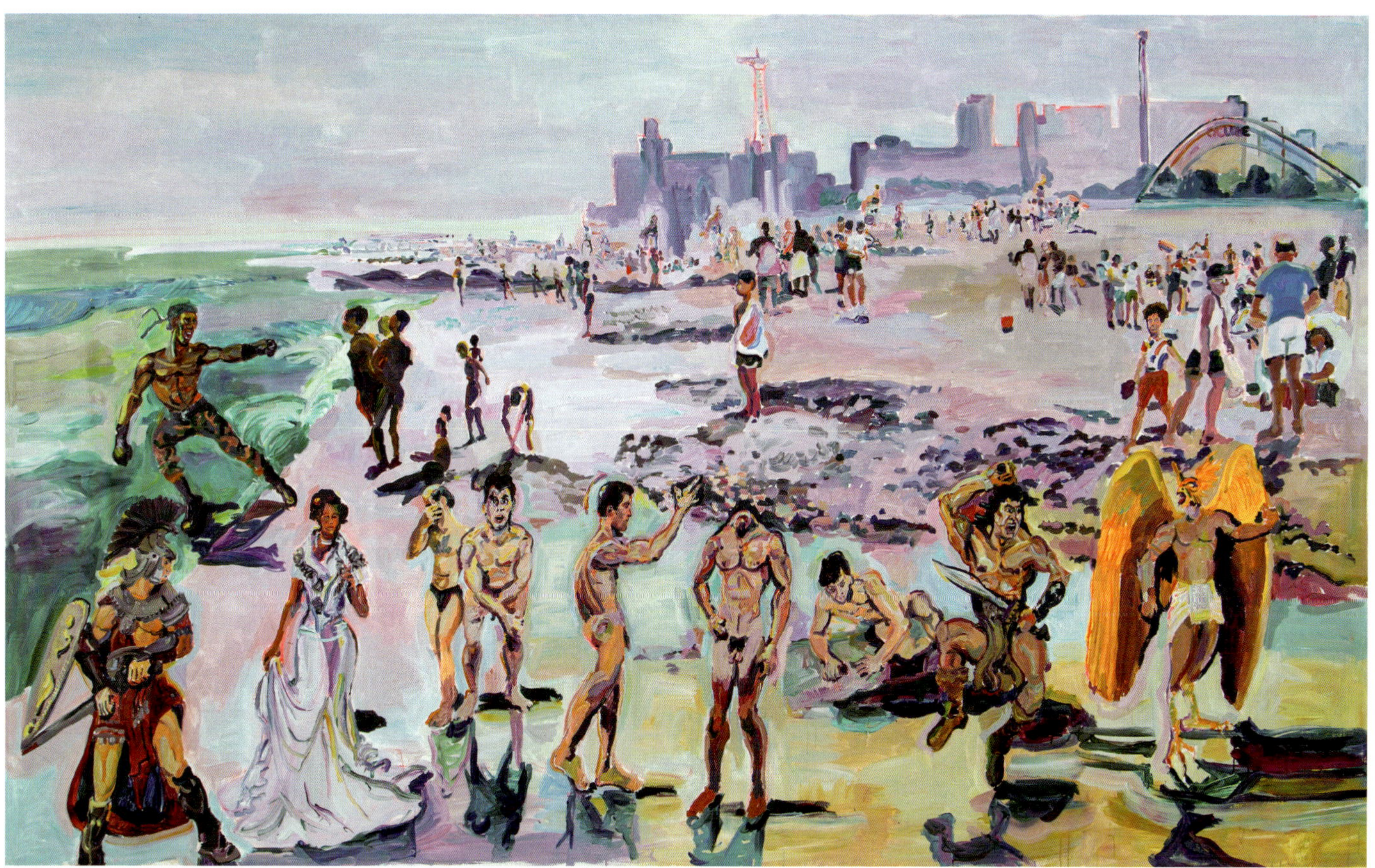

87. Joel Silverstein, *Brighton Beach Exodus*, 2008. Acrylic on canvas, 120 × 60 in. Courtesy of the artist.

the sea to break the incoming waves and in the distance the Parachute Jump and the roller coaster, famous attractions closer to the western end of Coney Island.

Especially on hot summer weekends, the beach is packed with people, swarming with activity: children playing war games, weightlifters flexing their muscles before their friends, varying kinds of ball games in progress, people walking and running and working on their suntans—a place for an imaginative, well-read youngster to fantasize any activity into something of mythic or even biblical proportions. And so in *Brighton Beach Exodus* the two central nude figures represent Moses and the Egyptian taskmaster whom he slays (Exodus 2:12).

Silverstein is not certain just how he decided that this encounter should take place at Brighton Beach, but there is a retelling of the story in Louis Ginzberg's magnum opus *The Legends of the Jews* that might be a source. With God's approval, Moses slays the Egyptian, who is not treating the Israelites properly. "Neither physical strength nor a weapon was needed to carry out his purpose. He merely pronounced the Name of God and the Egyptian was a corpse" ([1909–38] 1917–87, 2:280–81). Silverstein shows the Egyptian's head as exploded. Ginzberg goes on to say: "To the bystanders, the Israelites, Moses said: 'The Lord compared you unto the sand of the sea-shore, and as the sand moves noiselessly from place to place, so I pray

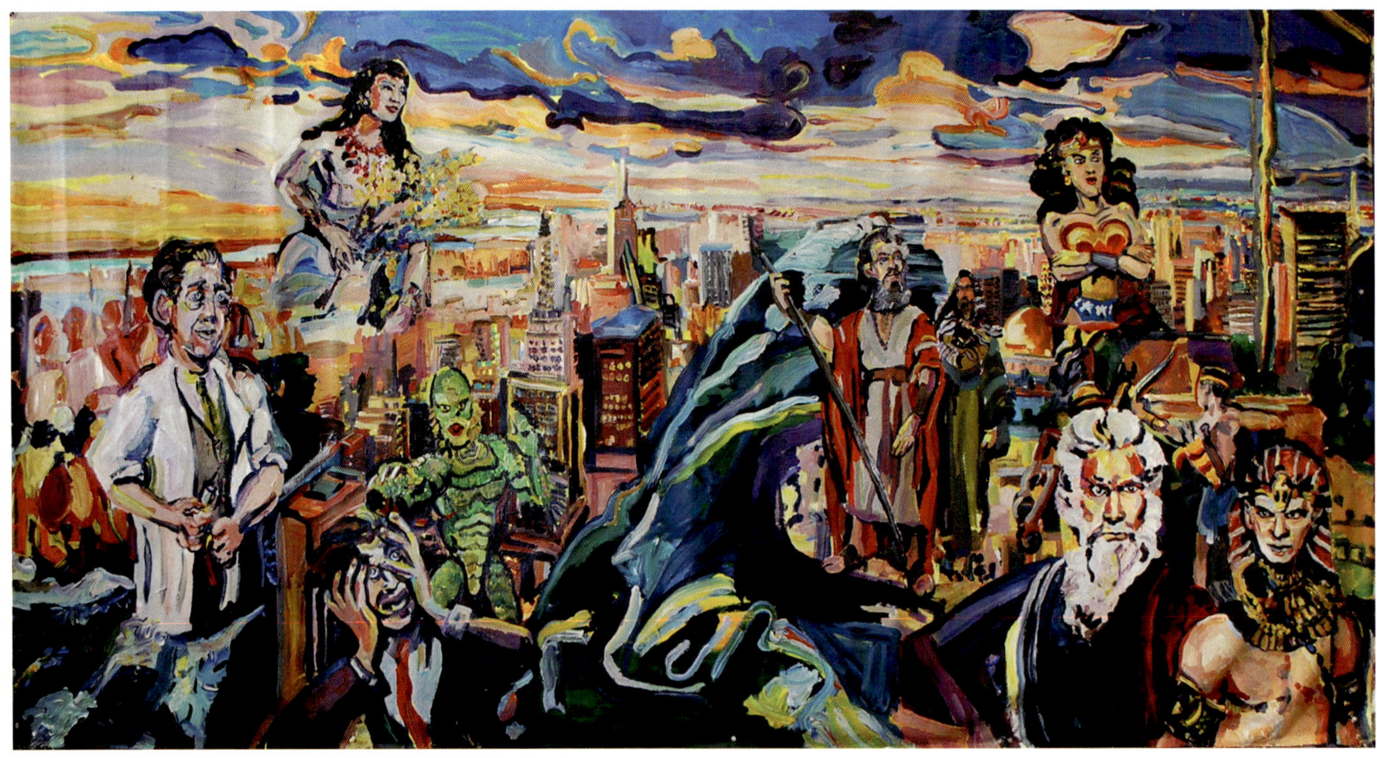

88. Joel Silverstein, *Ten Commandments and a Question*, 2016. Acrylic on canvas, 118 × 60 in. Courtesy of the artist.

you to keep the knowledge of what hath happened a secret.'"

They did not, but memory of the reference to sand might have prompted Silverstein to place the action on a beach. A Roman soldier and Conan the Barbarian flank the central scene, the latter figure based on the movie of the same name starring Arnold Schwarzenegger (John Milius, 1982). Conan sought vengeance for the death of his parents by recovering his father's sword.

In the artist's imagination, violence in history, the Bible, and the movies plays out on just another day on the beach in Brooklyn. The people there seem to be unaware or just ignore the action taking place in the foreground. Paintings such as this one can be called postmodernist because of the mixture of the real and the not real, present time and past time, actual time and biblical time, dislocation and de-familiarization. But *Brighton Beach Exodus* can also be thought of as post-postmodern in that Silverstein's social conscience warranted his highlighting the fact that violence is constant in both what we personally experience in the present and what we have read about in the past. There is a message here, not just a bunch of strange juxtapositions.

Among Silverstein's large paintings, *Ten Commandments and a Question* (2016) (fig. 88) is one of the most crowded. It juxtaposes New York on the left with Jerusalem on the right, the two cities separated by the parting of the Red Sea. On the New York side, Silverstein has included a drug-addicted doctor, Ann Baxter as Princess Nefertiti in the movie *The Ten Commandments* (1956), and the creature from *The Creature from the Black Lagoon*

(Jack Arnold, 1954). On the Jerusalem side, Silverstein has included Moses and Aaron, based on the two central figures in the wall painting *Exodus and Crossing the Red Sea* at the Dura-Europos synagogue (244 CE); Wonder Woman; Charlton Heston and Yul Brynner from the film *The Ten Commandments*; and a pillar of smoke representing the Shekinah.

The artist is not necessarily comparing the two cities in praise or condemnation but freely associating ancient and modern buildings as well as real and imagined figures. Such random association, however, reflects upon the values assigned to the different figures, with the biblical figures receiving no more and no less emphasis than the others. They all are of equal value. One imagines that Silverstein would have included different figures and assigned different values if the question implied in the title had been answered. But the question remains: Why did God bother giving Jews the Ten Commandments and then subject them to such a punishing history?

Silverstein, quite familiar with that history, knows the necessity of protection from punishment. As a result, over the past few years, he has made a few paintings on the theme of the golem, the mythic figure made of clay to protect Jewish people. He celebrates the most famous golem, a symbol of Jewish creativity and its maker, Rabbi Judah Loew (c. 1510s or 1520s–1609) of Prague, in *The Golem Maker* (2017) (fig. 89). But insofar as the golem is soulless, Silverstein also recognizes the spiritual dangers in relying on its potential powers. The painting includes both Jewish and non-Jewish elements. The two figures in the upper left behind the machine gun are taken from a science-fiction magazine. The gas-masked figure, a self-portrait of the artist, stands over a model of the Temple in Jerusalem, a double reference first to the protection of Israel from its hostile neighbors and second to the artist, aware of God's injunctions of unacceptable behavior, particularly with regard to dress when entering the Tabernacle (Exodus 28:35, 40–43). The implication here, as also suggested by the title *Ten Commandments and a Question*, is that Jews need protection from above as well as from beyond.

On the right side, the golem, turned on its side and hanging with its head down, is based on the figure of Jesus in *The Dead Christ with Angels* by Rosso Fiorentino (1494–1540, Museum of Fine Arts, Boston). A model of the Altneuschul in Prague sits on the golem's chest, and Dr. Frankenstein and the monster he created stand over the golem. Architectural elements from New York's Eldridge Street Synagogue fill out the background. Built in 1887, this synagogue is among the grandest synagogues in New York's Lower East Side, a building Silverstein holds sacred.

The comic-book hero Superman is also a mythic creature, but one that resonates more with Americans than the golem does. Artists such as Andy Warhol (1928–87), Roy Lichtenstein (1923–97), Mel Ramos (1935–2018), and Philip Pearlstein (b. 1924) have included Superman in their works. It is also a long-standing joke that Superman is Jewish. One author has stated without qualification that Superman is Jewish (Tye 2012, x, 30, 65–69, 73; see also Bogaerts 2013, 92; Engle 1987, 86; Arie Kaplan 2008, 209; for the counterargument, see Berlatsky 2018). Briefly, here are the reasons for this assertion. The creators of Superman, Jerry Siegel (1914–96) and Joe Shuster (1914–92), were Jewish. Superman first appeared in comic-book format in 1938 as a fantasy savior figure when Hitler's anti-Jewish laws, initiated in 1933, were attracting worldwide notice. He comes from Krypton, a disintegrating planet (Europe), to Earth (the United States) to fight for truth, justice, and the American way, a trio of activities not unrelated to the three foundational activities of Judaism—Torah, worship,

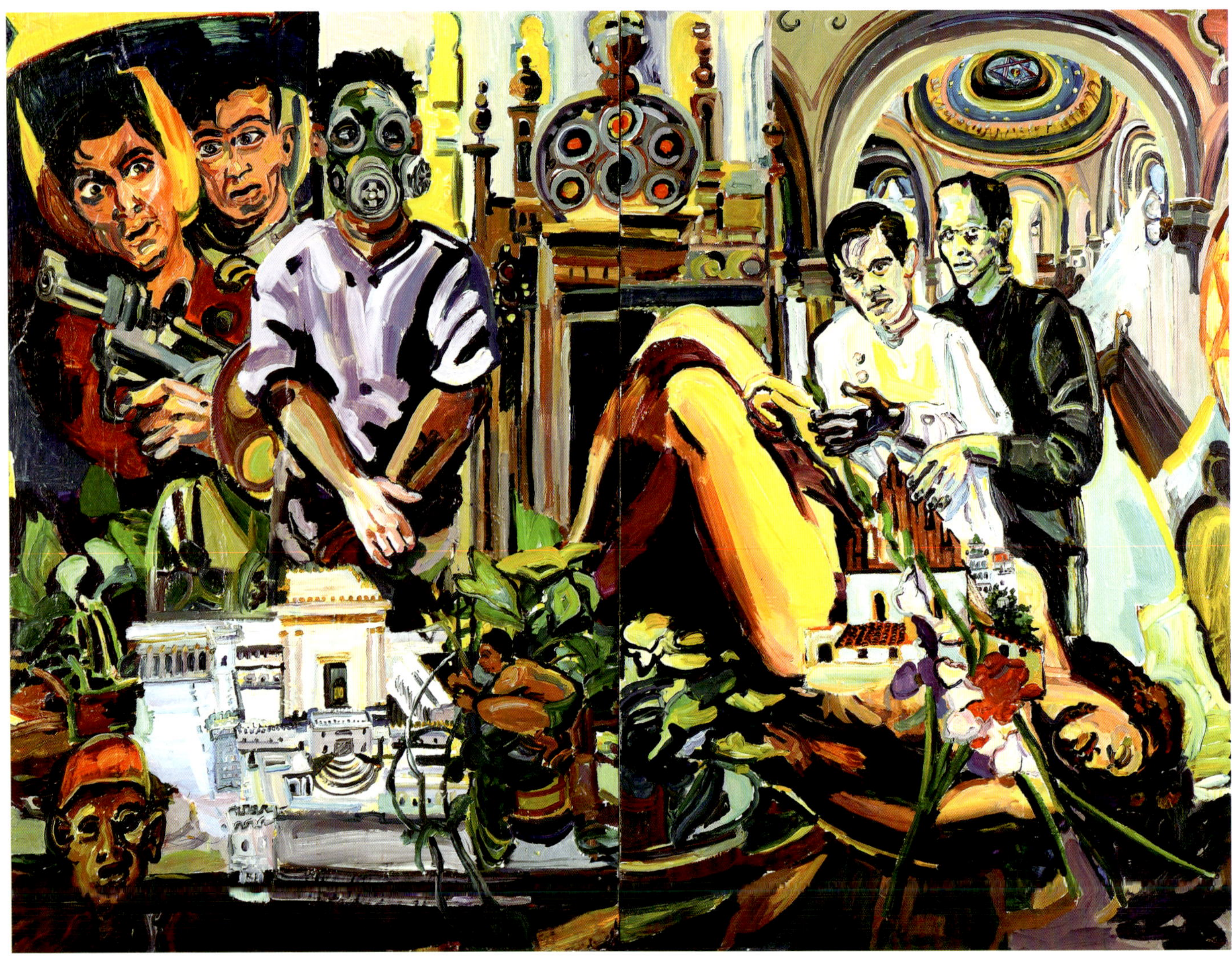

89. Joel Silverstein, *The Golem Maker*, 2017. Acrylic on wood panels, 96 × 84 in. Courtesy of the artist.

and loving deeds, as mentioned in the Pirkei Avot (1:2). His father, Jor-El, a name variously translated from Hebrew as "God Teaches" and "Heavenly Father," dispatches his son on a spaceship to America, an interplanetary version of the *kindertransport* that took children from central Europe to safety in Great Britain in the late 1930s. The Kryptonite child is adopted by the Kent family. Superman, whose Kryptonite name is "Kal-El," translated as "Voice or Vessel of God" as well as "All That God Is," takes the name "Clark Kent," an obviously WASP (white Anglo-Saxon Protestant) name that only a Jew would pick for himself, as Michael Chabon notes in his novel *The Amazing Adventures of Kavalier and Clay* (2000) (Arie Kaplan 2008, 209).

For Silverstein, as for others, Superman, whatever his true identity, is a revered figure, a role model, a defender of those in need of protection, a fighter for good and against evil. Of the several paintings Silverstein has created around the subject of Superman, one of the most interesting is *House of El* (House of God)

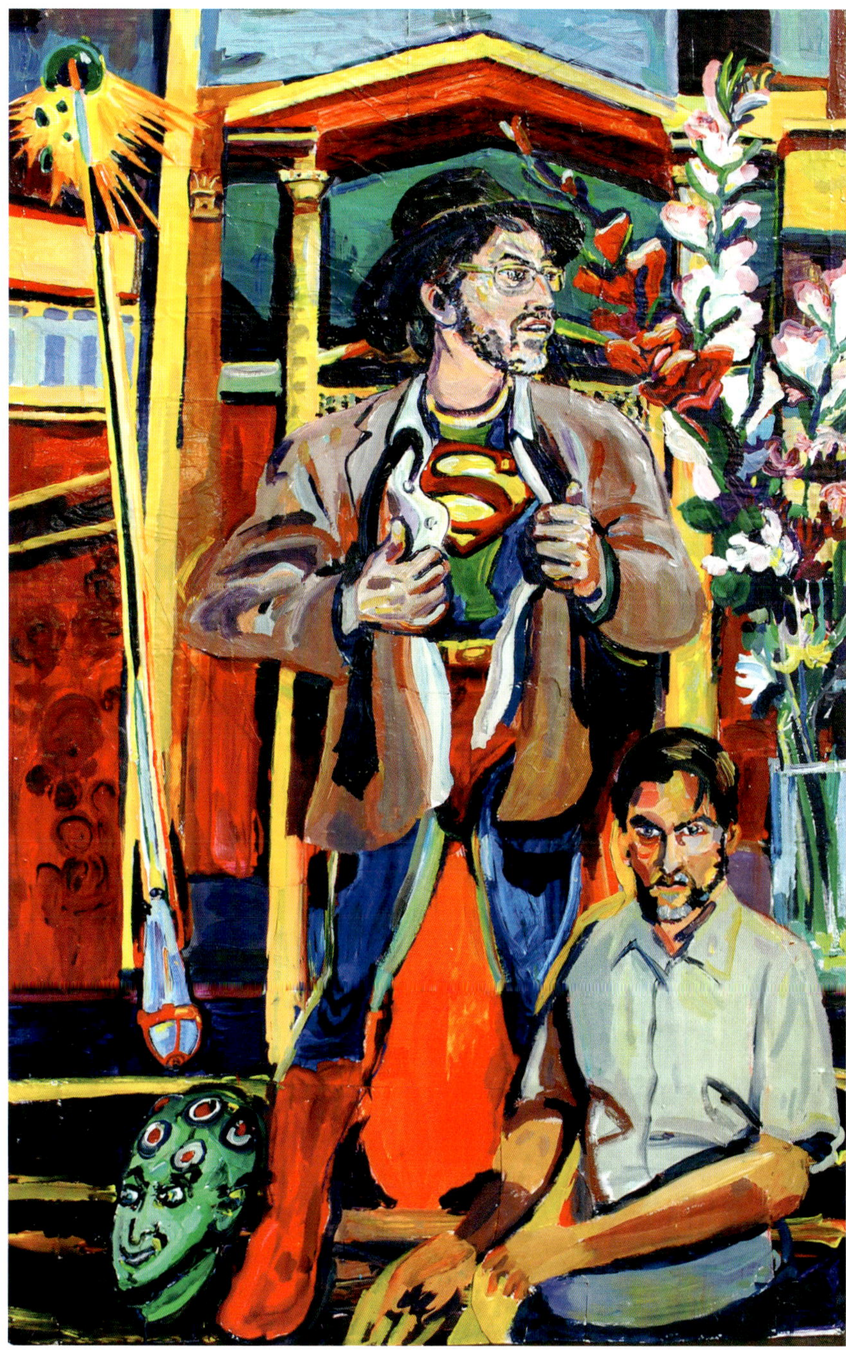

90. Joel Silverstein, *House of El*, 2012. Acrylic on canvas with collage, 48 × 84 in. Courtesy of the artist.

(2012) (fig. 90), in which he literally identifies himself (Joel) with the imaginary person. He reasons that humans, like superheroes, can also change the world but only through their art—that is, through their imagination (see *Jo-El/Jore-El* 2014). He finds powerful comic-book characters such as Superman, many created by Jews, closer in manner, intention, and values to the biblical prophets than to the warrior-heroes of Greco-Roman literature.

In this double self-portrait, Silverstein portrays himself both as himself and as Superman, who happens to be wearing the kind of fedora favored by many ultra-Orthodox and Hasidic men. That kind of hat was also worn by the Clark Kent character in the American

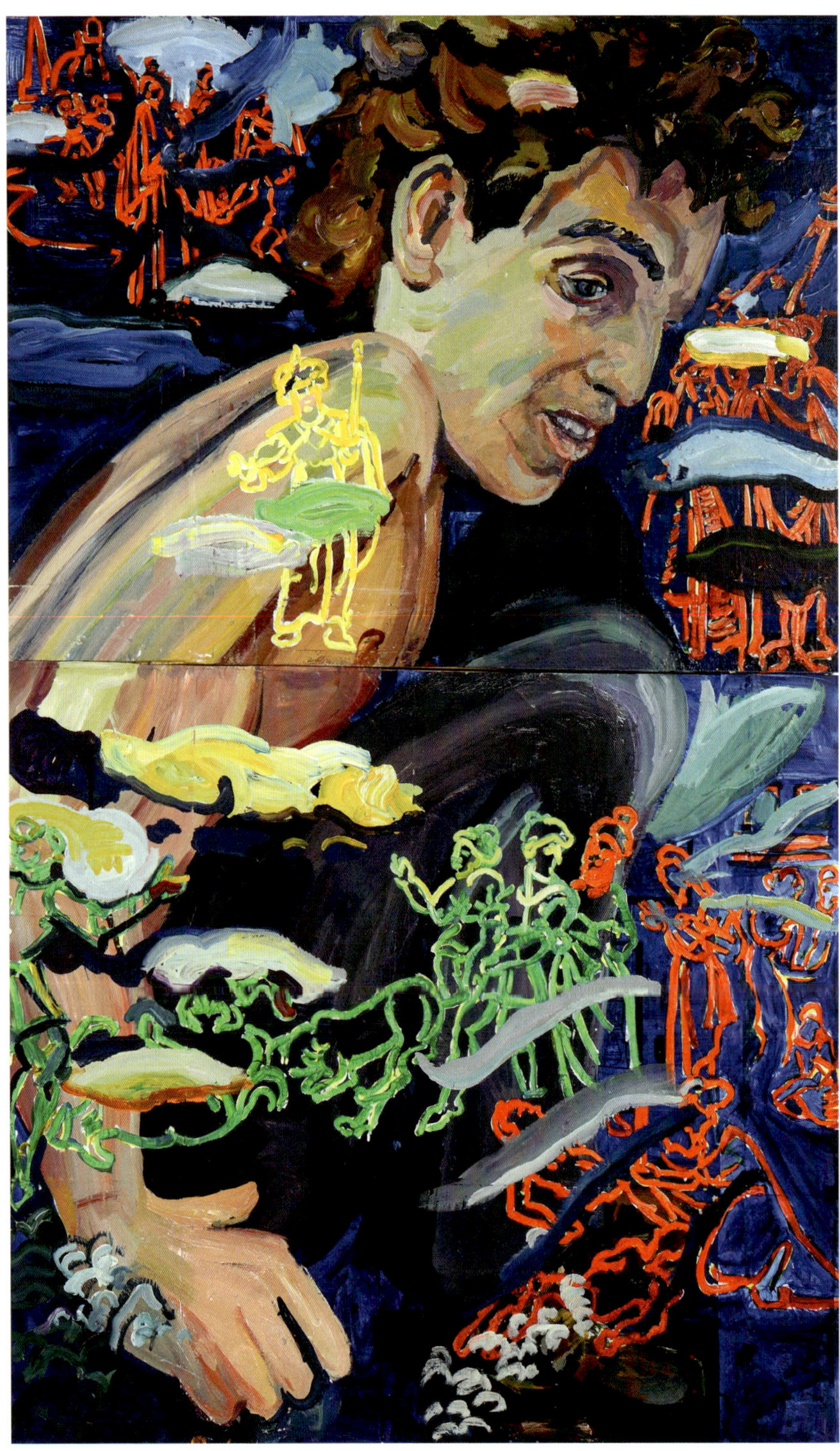

91. Joel Silverstein, *The Plagued Man*, 2017. Acrylic on canvas with collage, 60 × 96 in. Courtesy of the artist.

television program *The Adventures of Superman* (1952–58). Thus, Silverstein hints at his own sense of alienation while assuming the guise of another much more powerful individual, an ideal secular messianic figure. The double portrait signifies altogether what the artist (and humans in general) are in actual fact, what they would like to become, what powers they have and would like to have, and what their fantasies might be, but also how in the end they must, as Silverstein has often said, wake up in the morning and go to work. I would also add that in our conversations Silverstein has more than hinted at the need for protection from race baiting and at the rise of anti-Semitism in America and Europe.

As is his habit, Silverstein included elements of various artworks in *House of El*. The altarlike arrangement is based on Titian's *Pietà* (1576, Venice Accademia), and the head of the robotic Brainiac in the lower left is derived from Caravaggio's *David with the Head of Goliath* (c. 1610, Borghese Gallery, Rome).

One of Silverstein's most recent paintings, *The Plagued Man* (2017) (fig. 91) speaks to this matter in both biblical and existential terms. As the artist explained in an email of January 15, 2019, the subject is a victim of the plagues visited upon the Egyptians during the Exodus narrative; he is a stand-in for any person who has suffered from both physical and spiritual horrors. Because the Haggadah is read during the seder meal celebrating the departure from Egypt, the small figures Silverstein added to this painting are taken from the 1695 edition of the Amsterdam Haggadah (Seidman 1969). By emphasizing the large figure's physical unease, Silverstein questions God, who exacts terrible retribution against the Egyptians when perhaps there might be a better solution. Unlike, say, David Wander's Jonah, who chooses to accept and make peace with God's intentions, Silverstein's man seems to exist alone in a state of perpetual existential crisis and physical pain that lacks any foreseeable resolution.

It is a disquieting image for our contemporary moment, one tied to the secular present yet couched in a biblical event. Perhaps the painting suggests the end of an era of good feeling in which this generation of artists thrived. More so than several artists considered here, Silverstein does not find the sacred religious sources and traditional hierarchies of unimpeachable value. This attitude suggests at least two possible directions for the next generation of Jewish artists who work with Jewish themes and who choose to remain within a Jewish cultural orbit: first, mixing secular with traditional religious imagery and symbolism and, second, questioning traditional readings of the ancient texts, as seen, for example, in Helène Aylon's *The Liberation of G-D* (1990–96) and Siona Benjamin's *Finding Home #61* (2003) (figs. 8 and 34).

But there is also the possibility of taking a much different direction. Among artists of the next generation, Eden Morris (b. 1971), is already part of that possible future. In her email of July 9, 2013, Morris stated a position that Silverstein would certainly understand: "Although I was raised Jewish and am proud of being a Jewish woman, my attitude toward the Bible is not one of reverence so much as of reference. I do not feel constricted by traditional explanations; it is my intention to give voice to the women who came before me and empower me."

It is the phrase "not one of reverence so much as reference" that catches the eye here and that suggests an orientation and direction different from those exhibited by the artists of the 1930s–1960s generation. Obviously, other artists will continue to revere more than merely refer to the ancient texts, but it would appear that a new chapter is waiting to be written in the history of Jewish American art.

# 14 Conclusion *The Generation Summarized*

In the early 1940s, crisis years when millions of Jews were being murdered in Europe, the editors of the *Contemporary Jewish Record* asked several younger writers for their opinions about Jewish literature and Jewish life in general (Greenberg [1944] 1986). The responses, as one can imagine, were laden with fear for the present and future, weighed down with profound humiliation, shock, paralysis of spirit, and even the desire to abandon a religion that had brought and would probably bring the respondents nothing but grief.

More than half a century later, for its January–February 2018 issue *Moment* asked several authors to assess the current state of Jewish American literature, which could not help but mirror the position of Jews in America ("American Jewish Literature" 2018). The responses were entirely different. Although anti-Semitic attacks were rising, there was not yet worry of an international or national emergency in 2018. The authors felt comfortable with their lives in America and were not shy about discussing their interest in and connections to Judaism. In fact, many answers are similar to and parallel the thoughts articulated by the artists considered here, and some observations are not unlike those of particular artists.

For example, although nobody would find too many similarities between Nathan Englander's writings and Tobi Kahn's works, the author stated: "The fact that my world ends up being a Jewish world or that my metaphors are Jewish metaphors or that my logic is Talmudic is because that is a complete and whole universe to me" ("American Jewish Literature" 2018, 43). Most members of the Jewish Art Salon in New York and the Jewish Artists Initiative in Los Angeles would agree with Ruby Namdar's thought that the current generation of writers "wants to know what it means to be a Jewish writer or a Jewish artist" (45). Gal Beckerman noted that Jewish writers are interested in questions of Jewish identity and a willingness to explore Jewish traditions as well as the Hebrew Bible (47). Allegra Goodman observed that in comparison to older writers such as Philip Roth and Saul Bellow, younger authors "have become much more comfortable writing about Judaism in a more spiritual way, not just culturally." She found *that* to be "a big shift." Authors, she added, now write about Jewish identity, search for ways to be Jewish, and are interested in tradition and the appeal of ritual. They "are more willing to talk about their personal spiritual connection to Judaism and Jewish history" (44). Mohsin Hamid feels that writers are "interested in recapturing a meaningful spirituality" (51). And Alicia Ostriker noted that much contemporary Jewish American poetry is midrashic and includes "poems that openly question Jewish traditions." Such poems, she wrote, are often composed by women (46).

The artists, then, are not alone in mulling over issues that challenge, bedevil, and at the same time inspire. They do not imagine themselves staggering into an unknown future, as was the case in 1944, but are concerned with figuring out and reflecting on ways to maintain a viable religious and cultural identity worthy of cultivation in the broad space between retreating into parochial, well-guarded enclaves at one extreme and abandoning their heritage completely in an assimilative America at the other extreme.

That said, how can their generation—a generation that includes many more artists than featured here—be profiled in general? First, although it is impossible to say how many artists of this generation explore Jewish-themed subjects, it is safe to say that there are more than one would have imagined in, say, 1960. They live in communities across the country. I have interviewed artists who live in coastal cities such as Boston, New London, Connecticut, Seattle, San Francisco, New York, and Los Angeles as well as in interior cities such as Detroit and Minneapolis–St. Paul. Second, their attitude is very positive, and they feel that they are creating important and worthwhile art. Third, because most do not live in virtually all-Jewish neighborhoods, they have not passively absorbed their religious interests and historical knowledge from the street, the home, or the family synagogue but often have acquired them through self-education, *havura*s (study groups), and even private lessons. As a result, these artists do not fall back on traditional ways of thinking or create traditional scenes that merely illustrate or render visual equivalents of stories found in the ancient texts. Fourth, they find in the traditional texts aspects of stories that help them clarify or reflect their own ways of thinking. The important point here is that they often choose to explore their own minds through the ancient texts. So their desire to learn is not an ongoing exercise in piety (although it might be that as well) but a way to apprehend the world, a way to find or maintain and sustain community attachment as well as a healthy spiritual outlook. Fifth, such an outlook is not meant to be only self-serving. All have expressed the desire to see their art as making a contribution to societal improvement and continued Jewish presence. Through their art, they announce their own sense of morality and civic responsibility.

An observation offered in a totally different context about the art of Leon Golub (1922–2004) is relevant here because it is concerned with opinions and feelings viewers bring to a work as well as with the effects that work might have on them: "Paintings help make us aware that looking is not a neutral process but is invested with the psychic and social determinants of the subject's history and formation" (Bird 1982, 17, qtd. in Rifkin and Gumpert 1984, 56). This observation is certainly basic to the purposes of the artists considered here, with Archie Rand being the most vocal about the effects works might have and their ramifications in the viewer's mind.

Taken altogether, the artists explore their material within different frameworks and often bring out the human qualities in those distant and sometimes remote biblical figures pertinent to the present. Ruth Weisberg tends to view her subject matter from an empowered feminist position and as a matter of course will include women in key roles and present women's experiences heretofore neglected by male artists. And like the other artists, she hopes her art contributes to a better world, and she is certainly aware of the concept of *tikkun olam.*

But wishes and reality clash in the works of some of the other artists. Janet Shafner does not seem to hold out much hope for humanity. Social problems that existed in biblical times, as she pointed out, seem to be with us still. A continuous theme in Siona Benjamin's work seems to be the impossibility of feeling safe and secure and at home anywhere in the world. Unlike the immigrants in Weisberg's mural (fig. 23), Benjamin's figures might always feel the impact of her own sense of displacement. So, too, might Carol Hamoy's women, but more because they are living in societies defined and controlled by men than because they are individuals living in foreign cultures.

At the same time, Hamoy's women are politically active fighters who assert their place in society, who make their presence known, who demand equivalence with men, and who define themselves as they so choose. In contrast, women in works by Richard McBee and David Wander accept their places as expressed in the Bible. But Wander, more explicitly than others, will sometimes directly address moral issues within a Jewish framework.

Benjamin can be linked with Robert Kirschbaum and McBee in their realization that perfection, or a sense of the ideal, is intellectually knowable but unattainable. Benjamin's concerns focus on finding home and all that it implies. Kirschbaum contemplates perfection in the world and the completion of Creation when the Temple on the Temple Mount in Jerusalem is spiritually restored (but not physically restored because he does not hold to fundamentalist beliefs). McBee wants to understand and be able to accept completely the unknowable and remote God of the Jews, an attitude that does not seem to engage Tobi Kahn. Kahn accepts without question, and David Wander accepts but only after serious existential questioning. Archie Rand, in contrast, appears to be less concerned with religious frameworks than with finding ways for Jewish-themed art to appeal to assimilated Jewish Americans. His concerns are less about an imperfect world than about one in which Jewish life is absorbed into the American mainstream. And Joel Silverstein, whose subject matter mirrors an artist most integrated into American life and mainstream culture, seeks Jewish inflections rather than Jewish values, although, of course, Jewish values are central to his life. Of the work of all these artists, his work forecasts a direction the next generation might take.

One difference between the artists and the literary figures quoted earlier needs further clarification, although my awareness of it might be the result of having spent so many hours with the artists and hearing their personal stories. The artists seem to be a bit more edgy about their place as Jews in America because of increasing numbers of overt anti-Semitic statements and actions and desires of some white Christians to maintain cultural, social, and political hegemony in the country. And they are aware of the increasing threats to women's rights in this and other countries (see, for example, Beinart 2018).

Even so, the artists continue to explore their subject matter in the same manner they did in the late twentieth century. So far their attitude is that they are Americans and that nobody will bully them or force them into altering their points of view. This attitude is not necessarily a matter of conscious reasoning. It stems from the relatively friendly religious climate in which they grew up. It is what they know.

Because we still assume the friendly climate to be a given, I want to tell a personal story here to make the point that current levels of tolerance cannot be taken for granted in the United States and certainly not in some European countries. During a recent summer evening, my wife and I were walking with a visiting Polish Jewish couple, she a sociologist, he a journalist. We wanted some coffee and dessert. I said I would ask in a nearby restaurant if we could order only dessert rather than a full meal. After I made the necessary inquiry and returned to our group, the journalist had tears in his eyes and said that a Jew never could ask such a question in Poland. It had not occurred to me that I might get an anti-Semitic response or that I was not entitled to ask. Granted, we live in the

United States rather than a less-tolerant country, but this fear nevertheless lurks somewhere in the minds of the artists featured here.

So, at the end of the second decade of the new century, these artists concern themselves with issues that mark their generation as the first assimilated generation of Jewish artists but also as a generation that does not want to lose or renounce its heritage. The artists, as I hope is clear, do not feel tied to traditional interpretations or illustrations of the ancient texts or to traditional religious boundaries. They might burrow into a particular passage to extract certain meanings, or they might use a passage as a palimpsest for a flight of individual fancy or for political purpose. They might invoke what they feel are Jewish values that they have absorbed within the culture—helping, supporting, contributing, assisting, aiding—with or without using obvious Jewish subject matter to do so. They might, as the feminist artists do, question and discount patriarchy without apology, asserting that it is their right to do so.

Granted, these artists are motivated to create Jewish-themed works, but when they are asked if there might be one idea or thought that propels them to create their images or what their "ur-motivation" is, so to speak, their answers vary. There is general agreement that by exploring the ancient narratives of a people, a family, or an individual, they might be able to make some sense of the seeming chaos of life. In this regard, the Bible remains their central source if not of stability then at least of some sense of balance. Its stories tend to be memorable and larger than life. Individuals are described as both heroic and vulnerable or less than perfect, their actions sometimes disturbing but also incredibly generous, their complex interactions providing insights into contemporary life. Nothing is determinate for the artists, but rather the ancient texts have served as a guiding force in the creation of their art and in the manner they conduct their lives.

Because those who attend services reread the Bible every year in weekly portions, its stories are very familiar to them and have a cumulative effect on their thought processes. This annual ritual breeds both a sense of loyalty to and identification with the religion as well as a way modern history and current events can be better understood. What this ultimately means is that the Bible and the ancient texts do not stand separate from life but in both obvious and subtle ways are part of each artist's worldview and therefore self-identification. It is not as if the artists share a secret and have a secret handshake, but they do share a core set of values as well as a "family" history and continuity that have provided them with a fund of life-enhancing values, a sense of community however vague and ill defined, and the important feeling that they are not alone in the world.

They are well aware that their youthful experiences are not the same as those of the next generation of artists, that times change, and that they grew up in rare and extraordinarily positive and optimistic circumstances. In the long view, they know that things cannot remain the same. So it is with good wishes that they look forward to what the next generation will accomplish with regard both to their connections to their religion and life in America and to what degree Judaism and the kind of Judaism will remain viable motivations for artistic creativity in a secular society (contemporary newspaper and magazine articles aside, see Weisman 2018).

I have saved until this point, as a kind of coda, a consideration of the elephant in the room—Ronald Kitaj (1932–2007), very much a part of the generation considered here. I have great respect for the battles he fought against anti-Semitism in England, where he lived from 1957 until he relocated to Los Angeles in 1997; the hostile responses of English critics, about which he often commented; and his intense efforts to become a Jewish artist and to develop a Jewish art. I visited him on one occasion for what he said would be a twenty-minute interview but that lasted more than two hours. As interesting and important as he and his art certainly are to both mainstream and Jewish-themed art, he does not belong in this book. In fact, any discussion of his concerns reveals how distant they are from those of the artists considered here, a position I have held for many years (see, for example, Baigell 2006a, 217–34, and 2007a, 139–41).

My reasons for believing so can be stated simply and briefly here. First, as much as Kitaj wanted to be Jewish, as he repeated constantly in many statements over the years and emphasized again and again in his memoir *Confessions of an Old Jewish Painter* (2017), I do not believe he truly understood what it means to be Jewish. Yes, he read voraciously the ancient texts as well as books by Jewish philosophers, historians, and novelists, and he listened to music composed by Jewish musicians, yet he always seemed to be on the outside looking in. As much as he searched for emotional connections, he wrote as if he were engaged in a series of intellectual exercises—on the nature of anti-Semitism, the place of Jews in the modern world, whether there can be a Jewish art, and, if so, what its nature in the Jewish Diaspora might be.

He seems to have missed the essential point that Judaism, as mentioned, is a performative religion to whatever degree individuals choose to honor the Sabbath, follow dietary laws, observe religious rituals, traditions, and moral commitments, or engage in acts of *tikkun olam*. As more than one ultrareligious person has said to me, it is not a matter of believing in God but of living as a Jew. This, Kitaj did not do. As he once stated, "It is the case, for now anyway, that Jews and what happens to them fascinate me more than Judaism does. *We* more than the God of the Jews; the phenomenal history of anti-Semitism tantalizes me more than a faith I never knew" (qtd. in Livingstone 1995, 29; see also D. Cohen 1997, 30). And as he writes in *Confessions*, "All my Jewish life, Jewish religious buildings and rituals would fail to interest me, a disinterest I shared with dozens of my Jewish heroes" (2017, 168). All well and good, but the artists I have considered here do live as Jews and in this sense lead Jewish lives.

In effect, Kitaj chose not to participate in being Jewish. He was instead a student of Judaism. He thought that creating disjunctive narrative images, juxtaposing fragments, was diasporic. As he once wrote, "People are always saying the meanings of my pictures refuse to be fixed, to be settled, to be stable, *that's* Diasporism [*sic*], which welcomes interesting, creative misreading" (Kitaj 1989, 37, emphasis in original). He considered this "diasporism" to be Jewish, but he was commenting rather on the modern condition of alienation, a topic often written about in the years after the Second World War. Kitaj might have read the comments of Clement Greenberg, one of the most important art critics of that period, who held that because prejudice prevented Jewish writers from feeling integrated into mainstream society, they had to create their own identities by understanding the nature of their own experiences. He blamed capitalism for this situation because it universalized this Jewish predicament. "Thus his [the Jewish writer's] plight becomes like every other plight today, a version of the alienation of man under capitalism; all plights merge, and that of the Jew has become less particular because it turns more and more into an intensified expression of a general one" ([1944] 1986, 1:178; also qtd. in Baigell 2005a, 656). Greenberg chose Jews as the representative modern, alienated persons—alienated from themselves and from traditional and mainstream cultures. In effect, their efforts were directed toward ascertaining their place in society. The artists discussed here do not feel alienated in Greenberg's sense but work at relating positively to both their traditional culture and their mainstream culture, sometimes critically but mostly with a sense of affirmation and a desire to actuate changes they hope will be for the better.

A third point of difference concerns Kitaj's responses to anti-Semitism, certainly a stronger presence in daily life in England during the years he lived there than the kinds of hostility artists found in America. As a result, Kitaj identified much more strongly with twentieth-century figures such as Franz Kafka and Walter Benjamin, who could never identify positively, if at all, with the countries of their birth. Living *in* a country was not the same thing for them as being *from* a country. In that sense, Kitaj was involved in rear-guard battles more common to those living in Europe in the first half of the twentieth century than to those living in America in the latter half. This is not to say that important figures such as Kafka and Benjamin are irrelevant to the American artists I spotlight here, but one need not invoke their names to explain the artists' choice of subject matter or status in and feelings about America. For the artists, it is not necessary or essential to assert so aggressively and defiantly and therefore defensively their Jewishness or to write about it so incessantly. Rather, just as Janet Shafner can be associated with Serach (see the end of chapter 5), so the artists discussed here are perpetuating Jewish memory materially through their religiously themed art. They are doing it. They are living it. They do not worry it. Unlike Kitaj, they also live comfortably with both their Jewish and their American identities, which makes them members of a unique generation in the history of Jewish American art. So far.

*Works Cited*

*Index*

# Works Cited


"Aaron Goodleman." 1947. In *100 Contemporary American Jewish Painters and Sculptors*, edited by Louis Lozowick, 66. New York: Yiddisher Kultur Farband Art Section.

Adelman, Penina. 2005. *Praise Her Works: Conversations with Biblical Women*. Philadelphia: Jewish Publication Society of America.

Adelman, Rachel. 2012. "Seduction and Recognition in the Story of Judah and Tamar and the Book of Ruth." *Nashim* 23 (Fall–Spring): 87–109.

Adler, Rachel. 1998. *Engendering Judaism: An Inclusive Theology and Ethics*. Philadelphia: Jewish Publication Society of America.

Agies, Aharon. 1988. *The Binding of Isaac and Messiah: Law, Martyrdom, and Deliverance in Early Rabbinic Religiosity*. Albany: State Univ. of New York Press.

Alexander, Philip S., ed. and trans. 1984. *Textual Sources for the Study of Judaism*. Manchester, UK: Manchester Univ. Press.

Alter, Robert. 1981. *The Art of Biblical Narrative*. New York: Basic Books.

"American Jewish Literature Dead or Alive: A *Moment* Symposium." 2018. *Moment* 43 (Jan.–Feb.): 40–53.

Amishai-Maisels, Ziva. 1993. *Depiction and Interpretation: The Influence of the Holocaust on the Visual Arts*. Oxford: Pergamon.

Anand, Aswati. 2018. "India Jews in America: Finding Self in World of Transitions." *Sephardi World Weekly*, Jan. 26.

Applehof, Ruth Ann. 1981. "Interview with Beth Ames Swartz." In *Israel Revisited: Beth Ames Swartz*, not paginated. New York: Jewish Museum.

*Archie Rand Iconoclast*. 2004. Brochure. Copy in Archie Rand's files.

"Archie Rand with Barry Schwabsky." 2016. *Brooklyn Rail*, Feb.

Arieli, Silvano. 1981. *Abraham and the Contemporary Mind*. New York: Basic Books.

"Artist Statement, Bill Aron." 2007. Jewish Artists Initiative of Southern California, Los Angeles, May 19. At http:www.jaisocal.org/artists_directory.php?user_id=43&PHPSESSID=ebcd5c7eb2fc1a4.

"Artist Tobi Kahn." 2013. *Religion & Ethics Newsweekly*, PBS, aired July 25. At https://www.pbs.org/video/religion-and-ethics-newsweekly-artist-tobi-kahn/.

Aschkenasy, Nehama. 1986. *Eve's Journey: Feminine Images in Hebraic Literary Tradition*. Detroit: Wayne State Univ. Press.

———. 1998. *Women at the Window: Biblical Tales of Oppression and Escape*. Detroit: Wayne State Univ. Press.

Auerbach, Erich. [1946] 1953. *Mimesis: The Representation of Reality in Western Literature*. Princeton, NJ: Princeton Univ. Press.

Aviv, Caryn, and David Shneer. 2005. *The End of the Jewish Diaspora*. New York: New York Univ. Press.

Aylon, Helène. 2012. *Whatever Is Contained Must Be Released: My Orthodox Girlhood, My Life as a Feminist Artist*. New York: Feminist Press.

Bach, Alice. 1999. Introduction to *Women in the Hebrew Bible*, edited by Alice Bach, xiii–xvii. New York: Routledge.

Baigell, Matthew. 1999. "Contemporary Jewish American Artists and Kabbalah." *Tikkun* 14 (July–Aug.): 42–53.

———. 2001. *Artist and Identity in Twentieth-Century America*. New York: Cambridge Univ. Press.

———. 2002a. "Hyman Bloom's Jewish Paintings." In *Color and Ecstasy: The Art of Hyman Bloom*, edited by Isabelle Dervaux, 33–41. New York: National Academy of Design.

———. 2002b. "Yefim Ladyzhensky." In *Yefim Ladyzhensky*, 1–28. New Brunswick, NJ: Jane Voorhees Zimmerli Art Museum, Rutgers Univ.

———. 2003. *Jewish Artists in New York: The Holocaust Years*. New Brunswick, NJ: Rutgers Univ. Press.

———. 2004a. "Archie Rand: The Nineteen Diaspora Paintings." In *Archie Rand: The Nineteen Diaspora Paintings*, not paginated. New York: Hebrew Union College–Jewish Institute of Religion.

———. 2004b. "Soviet Artists, Jewish Imagery: Selections from the Norton and Nancy Dodge Collection of Nonconformist Art." *Zimmerli Journal*, Fall, 30–49.

———. 2005a. "Clement Greenberg, Harold Rosenberg, and Their Jewish Issues." *Prospects* 30:651–64.

———. 2005b. "What's Jewish about Jewish Art: Some American Views." *Art Criticism* 20, no. 1: 76–85.

———. 2006a. *American Artists, Jewish Images*. Syracuse, NY: Syracuse Univ. Press.

———. 2006b. "Spiritualism and Mysticism in Recent American Art." *Ars Judaica* 2:135–50.

———. 2007a. *Jewish Art in America: An Introduction*. Lanham, MD: Roman and Littlefield.

———. 2007b. "*The Scroll* in Context." In *Ruth Weisberg Unfurled*, 14–25. Los Angeles: Skirball Cultural Center.

———. 2008. "Abstraction and Divine Contemplation in Jill Nathanson's Paintings." *Sh'ma* 39 (Dec.): 14–15.

———. 2009a. "Archie Rand: American Artist with a Judaic Turn." *Images* 3:57–79.

———. 2009b. "Richard McBee's Akedah Series: Re-imagining and Reconfiguring Jewish Art." *Ars Judaica* 5 (2009): 107–20.

———. 2012. "Carol Hamoy's Art: Religious and Secular Passions." *Woman's Art Journal* 33 (Fall–Winter): 35–41.

———. 2013a. *As Subject and Object: Contemporary Book Artists Explore Sacred Hebrew Texts*. New York: Museum of Biblical Art.

———. 2013b. "Biblical Narratives in Contemporary Jewish American Art." *Shofar* 31 (Spring): 1–24.

———. 2015a. "Robert Kirschbaum's Art: Abstract, Spiritual, Intellectual." *Ars Judaica* 11 (2015): 79–90. At https://jewishartsalon.files.wordpress.com/2015/04/baigell-re-kirschbaum_ars-judaica-vol-11.pdf.

———. 2015b. *Social Concern and Left Politics in American Art, 1880–1940*. Syracuse, NY: Syracuse Univ. Press.

———. 2016. "A Feminist Midrash." In *Siona Benjamin: Beyond Borders*, edited by Elizabeth Greenberg, 16–21. Albany, NY: Opalka Gallery, Sage Colleges.

Ball, Maudette W. 1979. "Collected Histories." *Artweek* 10 (Nov. 17): 1.

Bandes, Susan. 1997. *Abraham Rattner*. Tampa, FL: Tampa Museum of Art Collection.

Barrett, Robert. 1990. "Conversation with the Artist." In *Ruth Weisberg Prints: Midlife Catalogue Raisonné, 1961–1990*, 9–19. Fresno, CA: Fresno Art Museum.

Baskin, Leonard. 1961. "To Wear Blood Stain with Honor." *Judaism* 10 (Fall): 294.

———. 1974. *A Passover Haggadah*. New York: Central Conference of American Rabbis.

Baskind, Samantha. 2007. *Encyclopedia of Jewish American Artists*. Westport, CT: Greenwood, 2006.

Baskind, Samantha, and Ranen Omer-Sherman, eds. 2008. *The Jewish Graphic Novel: Critical Approaches*. New Brunswick, NJ: Rutgers Univ. Press.

Baskind, Samantha, and Larry Silver. 2001. *Jewish Art: A Modern History*. London: Reaktion.

Bearman, Rabbi Rachel. 2018. "Don't Mansplain Vashti to Us." *Forward*, Feb. 28. At https://forward.com/opinion/letters/395230/dont-mansplain-vashti-to-us/.

Beinart, Peter. 2019. "The Global Backlash against Women." *Atlantic*, Jan.–Feb.

Belitsky, Helen Mintz. 1998. "Rand Brings 18 Canvases to 'Life.'" *Washington Jewish Week*, n.d. Copy in Archie Rand's files.

Bellis, Alice Ogden. 1994. *Helpmates, Harlots, and Heroes: Women's Stories in the Hebrew Bible*. Louisville, KE: Westminster, John Knox Press.

Benjamin, Walter. 1969. "Theses on the Philosophy of History." In *Illuminations*, edited by Hannah Arendt, 253–64. New York: Schocken.

Benton, Maya. 2011. "A New Yorker's Kaddish." In *Embodied Light: 9-11 in 2011: An Installation by Tobi Kahn*, 21–23. New York: Educational Alliance.

Ben-Zion. 1963. "An Artist's View of a Jewish Museum." *Jewish News*, Sept. 13.

Berger, Alan L. 1985. *Crisis and Covenant: The Holocaust in American Jewish Fiction*. Albany: State Univ. of New York Press.

Berlatsky, Noah. 2018. "Superman May Not Tell a Jewish Story—but It's Not the One You'd Think." *Forward*, Apr. 2.

Berlind, Robert. 1999. "Helène Aylon: Deconstructing the Torah." *Art in America* 87 (Oct): 142–47.

*Beth Ames Swartz: Inquiry into Fire*. 1978. Scottsdale, AZ: Scottsdale Center for the Arts.

*Beth Ames Swartz: Israel Revisited*. 1981. New York: Jewish Museum.

Bilski, Emily. 2004. *Objects of the Spirit: Ritual and the Art of Tobi Kahn*. New York: Hudson Hills.

Bird, Jon. 1982. "Leon Golub: Fragments of Public Vision." In *Leon Golub, Mercenaries, and Interrogations*, 17. London: Institute of Contemporary Art.

Blake, William. 1970. *The Poetry and Prose of William Blake*. Edited by David V. Erdman. Garden City, NY: Doubleday.

Bloom, Lisa. 2006. *Jewish Identities in American Feminist Art: Ghosts of Ethnicity*. New York: Routledge.

Boehm, Omri. 2007. *The Binding of Isaac: A Religious Model of Disobedience*. New York: T&T Clark International.

Bogaerts, Arno. 2013. "Rediscovering Nietzsche's Übermensch in Superman as Heroic Ideal." In *Superman and Philosophy: What Would the Man of Steel Do?* edited by Mark D. White, 85–100. New York: Wiley-Blackwell.

Bois, Yve-Alain. 1988. "El Lissitzky: Radical Reversibility." *Art in America* 76 (Apr.): 172–74.

*The Book of Psalms: A Translation with Commentary*. 2007. Translated and with commentary by Robert Alter. New York: Norton.

"Books on View." 2001. *Minneapolis Star Tribune*, Apr. 13.

Borowitz, Eugene B. 1961. "Crisis Theology and the Jewish Community." *Commentary* 32 (July): 36–46.

Bourne, Randolph. 1916a. "The Jew and Trans-National America." *Menorah Journal* 2:277–84.

———. 1916b. "Trans-national America." *Atlantic Monthly*, July.

Bowman Park, Anna. 2013. "Owning Our Health: Art Can Bring Peace to Hospital and Hospice Spaces." *Vancouver Sun*, Sept. 2. Copy in Tobi Kahn's files.

Boyarin, Jonathan. 1992. *Storm from Paradise: The Politics of Jewish Memory*. Minneapolis: Univ. of Minnesota Press.

Boym, Svetlana. 2001. *The Future of Nostalgia*. New York: Basic Books.

Brander, Rabbi Kenneth. 2010. "Scribing Our Covenant: A Vision of Orthodoxy." In *Sukkot to Go*, not paginated. New York: Yeshiva Univ. Center for the Jewish Future.

*Bridges*. 1994. 4 (Winter–Spring): cover.

Broude, Norma, and Mary D. Garrard, eds. 1994. *The Power of Feminist Art: The American Movement of the 1970s, History and Impact*. New York: Harry Abrams.

Brown, Betty Ann. 1991. "Ruth Weisberg." *Lilith*, Spring, 20.

Brown, Michael. 1982. "Biblical Myth and Contemporary Experience: The Akedah in Modern Jewish Literature." *Judaism* 31 (Winter): 100–111.

Brown, Milton W., and Stephen Robert Frankel. 1989. *Jack Levine*. New York: Rizzoli.

Byrne, Debra J. 2001. "A Conversation with the Artist." In *Heightened Realities: The Monotypes of Ruth Weisberg*, 1–17. Seattle: Frye Art Museum.

Cameron, Dan. 1984. "Archie Rand." *Arts Magazine* 58 (Feb.): 3.

"Carol Hamoy." 2013. ART CART Oral History, Teachers College Research Center for Arts and Culture, Columbia Univ. Libraries. At https://academiccommons.columbia.edu/doi/10.7916/D8ZK5DNZ.

Carvalho, Solomon Nunes. [1853–54] 1953–54. *Incidents of Travel and Adventure in the Far West*. Reprint. Philadelphia: Jewish Publication Society of America.

Cembalest, Robin. 1994. "Taking an Air Gun to the Eyes of Jesus." *Forward* 6 (May). Copy in Archie Rand's file.

Chamberlain, Mary L. 1914. "East Side Street Types in Color and Clay." *The Survey* 32 (May): 193.

Chheenah, Muhammad Ashraf. 2012. *Hagar, the Princess, the Mother of Arabs, and Ishmael, the Father of Twelve Princes*. Edited by Abdus Sattar Ghauri. Islamabad, Pakistan: Interfaith Study Research Centre.

Chicago, Judy, and Miriam Schapiro. 1973. "Female Imagery." *Womanspace Journal* 1 (Summer): 11–14.

Chidester, David, and Edward T. Linenthal, eds. 1995. *American Sacred Space*. Bloomington: Indiana Univ. Press.

Chill, Abraham. 1974. *The Mitzvot: The Commandments and Their Rationale*. New York: Bloch.

Christ, Carol P. 1979. "Why Women Need the Goddess: Phenomenological, Psychological, and Political Reflections." In *Womanspirit Rising: A Feminist Reader in Religion*, edited by Carol P. Christ and Judith Plaskow, 273–87. San Francisco: Harper and Row.

———. 1980. *Diving Deep and Surfacing: Woman Writers on Spiritual Quest*. Boston: Beacon.

Cipolla, Benedicta. 2006. "Mark Podwal: A Vision Vaster Than Words." *Religion & Ethics Newsweekly*, PBS, episode no. 925, aired Feb. 17.

Clines, David J. A. 1998. *On the Way to the Postmodern: Old Testament Essays, 1967–1998*. Vol. 2. Sheffield, UK: Sheffield Academic Press.

Cohen, David. 1997. "In Search of Kitaj." *Art Criticism* 12, no. 2: 25–35.

Cohen, Deborah Nusbaum. 1997. "Artist: 'I Want to Liberate Torah.'" *Jewish Bulletin of Northern California*, July 11, not paginated.

Cohen, Mark Daniel. 2003. "The Visual Chant: The Prayer for the Eye in the Art of Tobi Kahn." *New York Arts*, July 11. Copy in Tobi Kahn's files.

Cohen, Steven. 1983. *American Modernity and Jewish Identity*. New York: Tavistock.

Cohen, Steven, and Arnold Eisen. 2000. *The Jew within Self, Family, and Community in America*. Bloomington: Indiana Univ. Press.

*The Complete Art Scroll Siddur*. 2005. Edited by Rabbi Nosson Scherman and Rabbi Meir Zlotowitz. New York: Mesorah.

Dahood, Mitchell, SJ. 1968. *Psalms II: 50–100*. Garden City, NY: Doubleday.

Dinnerstein, Leonard. 1994. *Anti-Semitism in America*. New York: Oxford Univ. Press.

Dorff, Elliot N. 2002. *To Do the Right and the Good: A Jewish Approach to Modern Social Ethics*. Philadelphia: Jewish Publication Society.

———. 2003. *Love Your Neighbor as Yourself: A Jewish Approach to Modern Personal Ethics*. Philadelphia: Jewish Publication Society.

Eisen, Arnold. 1997. *Taking Hold of Torah: Jewish Commitment in America*. Bloomington: Indiana Univ. Press.

———. 2008. "Rethinking American Judaism." In *American Jewish Identity Politics*, edited by Deborah Dash Moore, 119–38. Ann Arbor: Univ. of Michigan Press.

Eisenberg, Evan. 2009. "Nessa Rapoport and Tobi Kahn." In *Jewish Sages Today: Profiles of Extraordinary People*, edited by Aryeh Rubin, 168–79. New York: Devora.

"Elizabeth Greenberg in Conversation with Siona Benjamin." 2016. In *Siona Benjamin: Beyond Borders*, edited by Elizabeth Greenberg, 27–57. Albany, NY: Opalka Gallery, Sage Colleges.

Emerson, Ralph Waldo. [1841] 1983a. "Circles." In *Ralph Waldo Emerson: Essays and Lectures*, edited by Joel Porte, 401–14. New York: Library of America.

———. [1844] 1983b. "The Poet." In *Ralph Waldo Emerson: Essays and Lectures*, edited by Joel Porte, 445–68. New York: Library of America.

Engle, Gary. 1987. "What Makes Superman so Darned American?" In *Superman at Fifty: The Persistence of a Legend*, edited by Dennis Dooley and Gary Engle, 79–87. New York: Colliers.

Ezekiel, Moses Jacob. 1975. *Memories of the Baths of Diocletian*. Edited by Joseph Gutmann and Stanley F. Chyet. Detroit: Wayne State Univ. Press.

Farago, Jason. 2018. "A Flag Is a Flag Is a Flag." *New York Review of Books*, Mar. 22.

Feld, Ross. 1977. "On the Hook: The Work of Archie Rand." *Arts Magazine* 52 (Dec.): 136–39.

Finkelshteyn, Leah. 2003. "Old Story, New Telling." *Hadassah Magazine*, June–July. Copy in Archie Rand's files.

Fischer, Irmatraud. 2005. *Women Who Wrestled with God: Biblical Stories of Israel's Beginnings*. Collegeville, MN: Liturgical Press.

Fishman, Sylvia Barach. 1993. *A Breath of Life: Feminism in the American Jewish Community*. Hanover, NH: Brandeis Univ. Press.

———. 2000. *Jewish Life and American Culture*. Albany: State Univ. of New York Press.

*The Five Books of Moses: A Translation with Commentary*. 2004. Translated and with commentary by Robert Alter. New York: Norton.

*The Five Scrolls*. 1984. Edited by Herbert N. Bronstein and Albert H. Friedlander. Illustrated by Leonard Baskin. New York: Central Conference of American Rabbis.

Fuchs, Esther. 2000. *Sexual Politics in the Biblical Narrative: Reading the Hebrew Bible as a Woman*. London: Sheffield Academic Press.

Funkenstein, Amos. 1993. *Perceptions of Jewish History*. Berkeley: Univ. of California Press.

Gass, Alison. 2000. "The Art and Spirituality of Helène Aylon." *Bridges* 8, nos. 1–2: 12–18.

*A Gathering of Sparks*. 2011. Los Angeles: Jewish Artists Initiative of Southern California.

Gefen, Nan Fink. 1999. "The Nature of God, Torah, and Art." *Tikkun* 14 (Mar.–Apr.): 72.

Geller, Laura. 1995. "From Equality to Transformation: The Challenge of Women's Rabbinic Leadership." In *Gender and Judaism: The Transformation of Tradition*, edited by T. M. Rudavsky, 243–54. New York: New York Univ. Press.

Genocchio, Benjamin. 2003. "Nature's Majesty." *New York Times*, Connecticut ed., Aug. 3.

Gillman, Rabbi Neil. 1990. *Sacred Fragments: Recovering Theology for the Modern Jew*. Philadelphia: Jewish Publication Society.

Ginzberg, Louis. [1909–38] 1917–87. *The Legends of the Jews*. 7 vols. Translated by Henrietta Szold. Philadelphia: Jewish Publication Society of America. Vol. 1, [1909] 1917; vol. 2, [1929] 1948; vol. 3, [1911] 1939, 10th impression, 1987; vol. 4 [1913] 1941, 13th impression, 1987; vol. 5, [1927] 1953, 13th impression, 1987, vol. 6 [1930] 1956, 9th impression, 1987; vol. 7 [1938] 1966.

Glanz, David. 1977. "An Interpretation of the Jewish Counterculture." *Jewish Social Studies* 39, nos. 1–2 (Winter–Spring): 117–28.

Goldman, Bernard. 1966. *The Sacred Portal: A Primary Symbol in Ancient Judaic Art*. Detroit: Wayne State Univ. Press.

Goldman, Julia. 2003. "A Landscape for Contemplation." *Jewish Week*, July 11.

Gottlieb, Lynn. 1995. *She Who Dwells Within: A Feminist Vision of Renewed Judaism*. San Francisco: Harper San Francisco.

Gouma-Peterson, Thalia. 1988. "Passages in Cyclical Time: Ruth Weisberg's *Scroll*." *Arts Magazine* 62 (Feb. 1): 56–59.

Graetz, Naomi. 2005. *Unlocking the Garden: A Feminist Jewish Look at the Bible, Midrash, and God*. Piscataway, NJ: Gorgias.

Granick, Arthur. 1976, *Jennings Tofel*. New York: Harry Abrams.

Graves, Robert, and Raphael Patai. 1963. *Hebrew Myths: The Book of Genesis*. Garden City, NY: Doubleday.

Greenberg, Clement. [1944] 1986. "A Symposium on American Literature and the Younger Generation of American Jews." *Contemporary Jewish Record* 7 (Feb. 1944): 3–36. Reprinted in *Clement Greenberg: The Collected Essays and Criticism*, vol. 1, edited by John O'Brian, 176–79. Chicago: Univ. of Chicago Press.

Greenberg, Melinda. 1998. "Primary Colors." *Jewish Week*, Mar. Copy in Archie Rand's files.

Gross, Rita M. 1979. "Female God Language in a Jewish Context." In *Womanspirit Rising: A Feminist Reader in Religion*, edited by Carol P. Christ and Judith Plaskow, 167–73. San Francisco: Harper and Row.

Grossman, Emory. 1967. *Art and Tradition*. New York: Yoseloff.

Gutmann, Joseph. 1963. "Jewish Participation in the Visual Arts of Eighteenth- and Nineteenth-Century America." *American Jewish Archives* 15 (Apr.): 21–57.

Gutmann, Joseph, and Stanley F. Chyet. 1975. Introduction to Moses Jacob Ezekiel, *Memories of the Baths of Diocletian*, edited by Joseph Gutmann and Stanley F. Chyet, 15–73. Detroit: Wayne State Univ. Press.

Haas, Peter J. 1992. "Women in Judaism: Reexamining an Historical Paradigm." *Shofar*, Winter, 35–52.

*The Haggadah for Passover*. 1965. Illustrated by Ben Shahn. Boston: Little, Brown.

Hammer, Jill. 2001. *Sisters at Sinai: New Tales of Biblical Women*. Philadelphia: Jewish Publications Society.

Hamoy, Carol. 1992. "Artist's Statement." In *Carol Hamoy/Voices*, 9. New York: Ceres Gallery.

———. 1996. "Patterns." *Piecework* 4 (Sept.–Oct.): 83.

Hapgood, Hutchins. [1902] 1965. *The Spirit of the Ghetto: Studies of the Jewish Quarter of New York*. New York: Funk and Wagnalls.

Hegman, Susan. 1999. *Patterns for America: Modernism and the Concept of Culture*. Princeton, NJ: Princeton Univ. Press.

Herberg, Will. [1955] 1960. *Protestant, Catholic, Jew: An Essay in American Religious Sociology*. Garden City, NY: Doubleday.

Hertzberg, Arthur, and Aron Hirt-Manheimer. 1998. *Jews: The Essence and Character of a People*. San Francisco: Harper San Francisco.

Heschel, Abraham Joshua. 1955. *God in Search of Man: A Philosophy of Judaism*. New York: Farrar, Straus and Giroux.

———. 1996. *Moral Grandeur and Spiritual Audacity*. Edited by Susannah Heschel. New York: Farrar, Straus and Giroux.

———. [1951] 2005. *The Sabbath: Its Meaning for Modern Man*. New York: Farrar, Straus and Giroux.

Heschel, Susannah, ed. 1983a. *On Being a Jewish Feminist: A Reader*. New York: Schocken Books.

———. 1983b. Introduction to *On Being a Jewish Feminist: A Reader*, edited by Susannah Heschel, xxiii–xxxvi. New York: Schocken Books.

Higham, John. 1984. *Send These to Me: Immigrants in Urban America*. Rev. ed. Baltimore: Johns Hopkins Univ. Press.

Hirsch, Gilah Yelin. 1985–86. "Ruth Weisberg: Transcendence of Time through Perspective of Imagery." *Woman's Art Journal* 6:41–45.

Hirsch, Samson Raphael. 1969. *The Nineteen Letters of Judaism*. Translated by Bernard Drachman. Jerusalem: Feldheim.

Hoffman, Lawrence A. 1997. *My Peoples' Prayer Book*. Vol. 2 of *Traditional Prayers, Modern Commentaries: The Amidah*. Woodstock, NY: Jewish Lights.

Holo, Sarah. 1986. "*A Circle of Life*." In *Ruth Weisberg: A Circle of Life*, 9–18. Los Angeles: Fisher Gallery, Univ. of Southern California.

Hook, Sidney. 1949. "Reflections on the Jewish Question." *Partisan Review* 16 (May): 463–82.

Hurwitz, Rabba Sara. 2018. "What Is the Meaning of God Today? A *Moment* Symposium." *Moment* 43 (Mar.–Apr.): 46–57.

Hyman, Naomi Mara. 1998. *Biblical Women in the Midrash: A Sourcebook*. Northvale, NJ: Jason Aronson.

Idel, Moishe. 1988. *Kabbalah: New Perspectives*. New Haven, CT: Yale Univ. Press.

Isaacs, Ronald H. 1996. *Mitzvot: A Source/Book for the 613 Commandments.* Northvale, NJ: Jason Aronson.

Jablons, Pamela. 1978. "Archie Rand." *Arts Magazine* 53 (Sept.): 15.

Jackson, Marion E. 1988. "Accompanied Journey." In *Ruth Weisberg: Paintings, Drawings, Prints, 1968–1988*, 8–16. Ann Arbor: Univ. of Michigan School of Art.

Jaffe, Irma B. 1980. *The Sculpture of Leonard Baskin.* New York: Viking.

Jaynes, Julian. 1976. *The Origin of Consciousness: The Breakdown of the Bicameral Mind.* New York: Houghton Mifflin Harcourt.

*The Jewish Study Bible.* [1985] 2004. Edited by Adele Berlin and Marc Zvi Brettler. New York: Oxford Univ. Press.

*Jewish Themes/Contemporary American Artists.* Vol. 2. 1986. New York: Jewish Museum.

*Jo-El/Jore-El: Superheroes, Autobiography, and Religion: The Art of Joel Silverstein.* 2014. New York: Hadas Gallery, Rohr Center, Pratt Institute.

Josephs, Susan. 1995. "Manhattan Cultural Threads." *Jewish Week*, Jan. 15.

Josephus. 1984. *The Jewish War.* Translated by G. A. Williamson. New York. Penguin Books.

Kahn, Tobi. C. 1985. "Creation and Re-creation." Typed sheet in Tobi Kahn's files.

———. 2004. "Chronology." In *Objects of the Spirit: Ritual and the Art of Tobi Kahn*, edited by Emily Bilski, 141–43. New York: Hudson Hills.

———. 2009. "The Meaning of Beauty." In *Tobi Kahn: Sacred Spaces for the 21st Century*, edited by Ena Giurescu Heller, 11–13. New York: Museum of Biblical Art.

———. 2011. "An Installation." In *Embodied Light: 9-11 in 2011: An Installation by Tobi Kahn*, 11. New York: Educational Alliance.

Kainen, Jacob. 1938. "Friends of Jewish Culture Hold Fine Arts Exhibition." *Daily Worker*, Mar. 4.

Kallen, Horace. 1915. "Nationality and the Hyphenated American." *Menorah Journal* 1 (Apr.): 79–86.

Kampf, Avram. 1990. *Chagall to Kitai: Jewish Experience in 20th Century Art.* London: Barbican Art Gallery.

Kaplan, Arie. 2008. *From Krakow to Krypton: Jews and Comic Books.* Philadelphia: Jewish Publication Society.

Kaplan, Aryeh. 1985. *Jewish Meditation: A Practical Guide.* New York: Schocken Books.

———. 1990. *Innerspace: Introduction to Kabbalah, Meditation, and Prophecy.* New York: Moznaim.

Kaplan, Dana Evan. 2009. *Contemporary American Judaism: Transformation and Renewal.* New York: Columbia Univ. Press.

Kaufman, David. 2003. "Archie Rand's *The Eighteen* and Postmodern (Mis)Recognition." *Shofar* 21 (Winter): 120–33.

Kedar, Rabbi Karyn D. 2004. "The Prophetess Huldah." In *The Women's Haftarah Commentary*, edited by Rabbi Elyse Goldstein, 390. Woodstock, VT: Jewish Lights.

Keder, Benjamin Z., and R. J. Zwi Werblowsky, eds. 1998. *Sacred Space: Shrine, City, Land.* New York: New York Univ. Press.

Kessler, Barry, curator. 1998. *The Eighteen* (exhibit catalog). Baltimore: Jewish Museum of Baltimore.

Kierkegaard, Soren. [1843] 1985. *Fear and Trembling.* Translated by Alastair Hannay. London: Penguin.

Kirschbaum, Robert. 1990. "Jerusalem Gates Studies I–IV." *Avant Garde* 3 (Winter): 45–53.

———. c. 1998. "Artist's Statement." In *Robert Kirschbaum Prints*, not paginated. Jerusalem: Artists House.

———. n.d. *Squaring the Mount.* Brochure, Trinity College Hillel House, Hartford, CN.

Kitaj, Ronald. 1989. *First Diasporist Manifesto.* New York: Thames and Hudson.

———. 2017. *Confessions of an Old Jewish Painter.* Munich: Schirmer/Mosel.

Kleeblatt, Norman. 1996a. "'Passing' into Multiculturalism. In *Too Jewish? Challenging Traditional Identities*, edited by Norman Kleeblatt, 3–38. New York: Jewish Museum.

———, ed. 1996b. *Too Jewish? Challenging Traditional Identities.* New York: Jewish Museum.

Klein, Lillian R. 2003. *From Deborah to Esther: Sexual Politics in the Hebrew Bible.* Minneapolis: Fortress Press.

Kopman, B[enjamin]. 1928. "Max Weber: The Modern Jewish Painter Who Is Very Famous in the World and Is so Little Known among Jews." *Di Zukunft* 33 (June): 354–56.

Kraft, Dina. 2008. "The End of Mass Aliyah." *Jewish Week*, Apr. 4.

Kramer, Hilton. 1955. "Bloom & Levine: The Hazards of Modern Painting." *Commentary*, June, 583–87.

Krausz, Michael. 1993. "On Being Jewish." In *Jewish Identity*, edited by David Theo Goldberg and Michael Krausz, 264–78. Philadelphia: Temple Univ. Press.

Kresh, Paul. 1992. "Art Exhibit Combines Judaism, Feminism." *Jewish Week*, Mar. 6–12.

Kushner, Sherrill. 1998. "Making Book on Women's Lives." *Lilith* 23 (Spring): 4. At https://search-proquest-com.proxy.libraries.rutgers.edu/docview/19.

Kuspit, Donald. 2003. "Tobi Kahn's *Sky and Water Series.*" In *Tobi Kahn: Sky and Water*, 5–6. Purchase: Neuberger Museum of Art, Purchase College, State Univ. of New York.

Lacocque, André, and Pierre-Emmanuel Lacocque. 1990. *Jonah: A Psycho-religious Approach to the Prophet.* Columbia: Univ. of South Carolina Press.

Lane, John R. 1979. "Archie Rand: The Consistence of Choice." *Arts Magazine* 9 (Nov.): 133–35.

Laniak, Timothy S. 1998. *Shame and Honor in the Book of Esther.* Atlanta, GA: Scholars Press.

Lavin, Marilyn Aronberg. 1990. *The Place of Narrative: Mural Decoration in Italian Churches, 431–1600.* Chicago: Univ. of Chicago Press.

Lerner, Michael. 1994. *Jewish Renewal: Path to Healing and Transformation.* New York: HarperCollins.

Lester, Elenore. 1988. "Brooklyn Artist: Paintings Were His Path to Judaism." *Jewish Week*, May 13. Copy in Archie Rand's files.

*Let My People Go: A Haggadah.* 1972. Illustrated by Mark Podwal. New York: MacMillan.

Levenson, Alan T. 2000. *Modern Jewish Thinkers: An Introduction.* Northvale, NJ: Jason Aronson.

Levine, Jack. 1962. "Dialogues III: Jews in the Creative Arts." *Congress Bi-weekly* 29 (Sept. 24): 35.

Levinson, Julian. 2008. *Exiles on Main Street: Jewish American Writers and American Literary Culture.* Bloomington: Indiana Univ. Press.

Liebman, Charles. 1973. *The Ambivalence of American Jews: Politics, Religion, and Family in American Jewish Life.* Philadelphia: Jewish Publication Society of America.

Lifshitz, Ze'ev Haim. 1994. *The Paradox of Human Existence: A Commentary on the Book of Jonah.* Translated by Julie Goldwasser and Sarah Nathan. Northvale, NJ: Jason Aronson.

Linn, Denise. 1999. *Altars: Bringing Sacred Shrines into Your Everyday Life.* New York: Ballantine Wellspring.

Lippard, Lucy. 1981. "Breaking Circles: The Politics of Prehistory." In *Robert Smithson: Sculpture*, edited by Robert Carleton Hobbs, 31–40. Ithaca, NY: Cornell Univ. Press.

Livingstone, Marco. 1992. *Kitaj.* London: Phaidon Press.

Lombardi, D. Dominick. 2000. "Portraying the Past and the Present." *New York Times*, Westchester ed., June 4. Copy in Carol Hamoy's files.

Lozowick, Louis. 1924. "A Jewish Art School." *Menorah Journal* 10 (Nov.–Dec.): 465–66.

Lukacs, Georg. 1971. *The Theory of the Novel.* Translated by Anna Bostock. Cambridge, MA: MIT Press.

Margolis, Judith. 2011a. "Interview with Richard McBee." *Nashim* 22 (Fall): 202–5.

———. 2011b. "A Woman's Voice in a Man's Mouth: The Sarah Paintings by Richard McBee." *Nashim* 22 (Fall): 192–201.

———. 2013. "Resident Artist: Anonymous No More: Carol Hamoy's Visible Women." *Nashim* 24 (Spring): 139–45.

Mark, Jonathan. 2010. "What Were the First Words in the Bible Spoken by a Jew?" *Jewish Week*, Oct. 17. Copy in Richard McBee's files.

*Mark Rothko 1903–1970*. 1987. London: Tate Gallery.

Matt, Daniel C. 1995. *The Essential Kabbalah: The Heart of Jewish Mysticism*. San Francisco: Harper San Francisco.

*Mayamata: An Indian Treatise on Housing, Architecture, and Iconography*. 1985. New Delhi: Sitaram Bhartia Institute of Scientific Research.

Mayer, Egon. 2008. "A Demographic Revolution in American Jewry." In *American Jewish Identity Politics*, edited by Deborah Dash Moore, 267–99. Ann Arbor: Univ. of Michigan Press.

Mazar, Benjamin. 1975. *The Mountain of the Lord*. Garden City, NY: Doubleday.

McBain, Roger. 2010. "Artwork a Fitting Class Backdrop." *Evansville Courier and Press*, May 16. Copy in Toby Kahn's files.

McBee, Richard. 2003. "Biblical Contentions: Paintings by Janet Shafner." *Jewish Press*, Feb. 19.

———. 2004. "Archie Rand: 'Jewish Enough?'" *Jewish Week*, May 7. Copy in Archie Rand's files.

———. 2010. "The Enigma of the Name: *The 42 Letter Name* of Robert Kirschbaum." *Jewish Press*, Mar. 25.

———. 2011. Review of *Robert Kirschbaum: Small Paintings from the Akedah Series*. *Jewish Press*, Oct. 16.

———. 2013–14. "Contemporary Jewish Art: The Challenge." *Beloved Words: Milin Havivin* 7:41–57.

McCloud, Mac. 1990. "History as Renewal." In *Ruth Weisberg Prints: Mid-life Catalogue Raisonné, 1891–1990*, 21–25. Fresno, CA: Fresno Art Museum.

McMann, Jean. 1998. *Altars and Icons: Sacred Spaces in Everyday Lives*. San Francisco: Chronicle Books.

*Midrash Rabbah: Exodus*. 1983. Translated by Dr. S. M. Lehrman. London: Soncino Press.

*Midrash Rabbah: Genesis II*. 1983. 3rd ed. Translated by Dr. H. Freedman. London: Soncino Press.

*Midrash Rabbah: Leviticus*. 1983. Translated by Judah J. Slotki. London: Soncino Press.

*Midrash Tanchuma*. 1996. In Hebrew and English, translated by Samuel A. Berman. Hoboken, NJ: KTAV. At https://www.sefaria.org/Midrash_Tanchuma?lang=bi.

*Midrash Tanhuma: S. Buber Recession*. 1989. Translated by John T. Townsend. Hoboken, NJ: KTAV.

Milgrom, Jo. 1988. *The Binding of Isaac: The Akedah—a Primary Symbol of Jewish Thought and Art*. Berkeley: BIBAL Press.

Moorman, Margaret. 2001. "Spaces of the Spirit." *Art News*, Summer, 116.

Munich, Adrienne. [1985] 2005. "Notorious Signs, Feminist Criticism, and Literary Tradition." In *Making a Difference: Feminist Literary Criticism*, edited by Gayle Greene and Coppelia Kahn, 238–59. Boca Raton, FL: Taylor & Francis.

Myers, D. L. 2009. "The Judaism Rebooters." *Commentary* 127 (July–Aug.): 36–39.

Myers, Julia R. 2007. *Completing the Circle: The Art of Ruth Weisberg*. Ypsilanti: Eastern Michigan Univ. Art Gallery.

Nahas, Dominique. 1987. *Sacred Spaces*. Syracuse, NY: Everson Museum of Art.

Nelson, Mary Carroll. 1984. *Connecting: The Art of Beth Ames Swartz*. Flagstaff, AZ: Northland Press.

Newman, Barnett. 1990. "Art of the South Seas" (1946). In *Barnett Newman: Selected Writings and Interviews*, edited by John P. O'Neill, 98–102. Berkeley: Univ. of California Press.

Nilson, Lisbet. 1991. "Loyola Gallery Puts Its Faith in Religious Art Exhibit." *Los Angeles Times*, Mar. 17.

Oirich, Aklan. 2003. "Thwack! To Our Enemies." *Hadassah Magazine*, June–July. Copy in Archie Rand's files.

Olgin, Moissaye J. 1938. "First Exhibition." *World Alliance for Yiddish Culture (YUKF):*

*Art Section, USA*, no issue number or specific date. YKUF folder, Jewish Museum, New York.

*The Open Door: A Passover Haggadah*. 2002. Edited by Sue Levi Elwell. With drawings by Ruth Weisberg. New York: Central Conference of American Rabbis.

Orenstein, Gloria. 1988. "The Reemergence the Archetype of the Great Goddess by Contemporary Women." In *Feminist Art Criticism: An Anthology*, edited by Cassandra L. Langer and Joanna Frueh, 75–82. Ann Arbor, MI: UMI Research Press.

———. 1994. "Recovering Her Story: Feminist Artists Reclaim the Great Goddess." In *The Power of Feminist Art: The American Movement of the 1970s, History and Impact*, edited by Norma Broude and Mary D. Garrard, 158–87. New York: Harry Abrams.

———. 2000. "And Woman Creates God." *The Little Magazine* (Delhi, India) 1 (Sept.–Oct): 36–43.

———. 2007. "Torah Study, Feminism, and Spiritual Quest in the Work of Five American Jewish Women Artists." *Nashim* 14 (Fall): 97–130.

Ostriker, Alicia Suskin. 1993. *Feminist Revision and the Bible*. Cambridge, MA: Blackwell.

Ozick, Cynthia. 1983. "Notes toward Finding the Right Question." In *On Being a Jewish Feminist: A Reader*, edited by Susannah Heschel, 120–51. New York: Schocken Books.

———. [1980] 1990. "The Shawl." In *The Shawl*, 3–10. New York: Vintage.

*A Passover Haggadah*. 1974. Illustrated by Leonard Baskin. New York: Central Conference of American Rabbis.

*A Passover Haggadah*. 1993. Illustrated by Mark Podwal. Edited by Elie Wiesel. New York: Simon and Schuster.

Patai, Raphael. 1947. *Man and Temple in Ancient Jewish Myth and Ritual*. London: Thomas Nelson.

———. [1967] 1990. *The Hebrew Goddess*. 3rd ed. Detroit: Wayne State Univ. Press.

Paulson Michael. 2001. Untitled. *Boston Globe*, undated, not paginated. Copy in Helène Aylon's files.

Philipson, Rabbi David. 1922. "Moses Jacob Ezekiel." *Publication of the American Jewish Historical Society* 28:1–62.

Pianko, Noam. 2015. *Jewish Peoplehood: An American Innovation*. New Brunswick, NJ: Rutgers Univ. Press.

*Pirke de Rabbi Eliezer*. 2004. Translated by Gerold Friedlander. North Stratford, NH: Ayer.

Plaskow, Judith. 1979. "Bringing a Daughter to Covenant." In *Womanspirit Rising: A Feminist Reader in Religion*, edited by Carol P. Christ and Judith Plaskow, 179–84. San Francisco: Harper and Row.

———. 1989. "Jewish Memory from a Feminist Perspective." In *Weaving the Visions: New Patterns in Feminist Spirituality*, Edited by Judith Plaskow and Carol P. Christ, 39–50. San Francisco: Harper and Row.

———. 1990. *Standing Again at Sinai: Judaism from a Feminist Perspective*. San Francisco: Harper San Francisco.

———. 2005. *The Coming of Lilith: Essays on Feminism, Judaism, and Sexual Ethics, 1972–2001*. Boston: Beacon Press

Podwal, Mark. 1972. *Let My People Go: A Haggadah*. New York. Macmillan.

———. 1993. *A Passover Haggadah*. Edited by Elie Wiesel. New York: Simon and Schuster.

———. 1995. *Golem: A Giant Made of Mud*. New York: Greenwillow Books.

———. 2012. *Sharing the Journey: The Haggadah for the Contemporary Family*. New York: Central Conference of American Rabbis.

———. 2016. *Reimagined: 45 Years of Jewish Art*. New York: Glitterati.

———. 2018. *Kaddish for Dąbrowa Białostoka*. Amherst, MA: Yiddish Book Center.

Prescott, Theodore. 2001. "Tobi Kahn: A Profile." *Image* 33 (Winter): not paginated. Copy in Tobi Kahn's files.

Putnam, Hilary. 1993. "Judaism and Identity." In *Jewish Identity*, edited by David Theo Goldberg and Michael Krausz, 108–15. Philadelphia: Temple Univ. Press.

Rand, Archie. 1984. "Artist's Statement." In *Archie Rand: Paintings*, not paginated. Cincinnati: Contemporary Art Center.

———. 1999a. “On God (en Garde).” *New Art Examiner* 26, no. 6: not paginated. Copy in Archie Rand’s files.

———. 1999b. “Some Thoughts on Midrash and Art: Midrash as Parable.” *Living Text* 6 (Winter): 3–4.

———. 2003. “Archie Rand: The 19 Diaspora Paintings, 2002.” *Bomb* 84 (Summer). At https://bombmagazine.org/articles/the-19-diaspora-paintings/. Copy in Archie Rand’s files.

———. 2006. “Artist Statement: About the Creation of *The 39 Forbidden Labors of the Sabbath*.” In *Archie Rand: The 39 Forbidden Labors of the Sabbath*, not paginated. New York: UJA-Federation of New York.

———. 2014. “*Psalm 68*.” In *Archie Rand: Psalm 68*, 19–24. Riverdale, NY: Hebrew Home at Riverdale, Derfner Museum.

Raskin, Saul. 1911. “The Future of Jewish Art” (in Yiddish). *Dos Naya Land* 1 (Sept. 15): cols. 17–22.

———. [1940] 1969. *Pirke Aboth in Etchings*. New York: Bloch.

Raven, Arlene. 1973. “Women’s Art: The Development of a Theoretical Perspective.” *Womanspace Journal* 1 (Feb.–Mar.): 14–20.

———. 1988. *Crossing Over: Feminism and Art of Social Concern*. Ann Arbor, MI: UMI Research Press.

———. 1994. “Womanhouse.” In *The Power of Feminist Art: The American Movement of the 1970s, History and Impact*, edited by Norma Broude and Mary D. Garrard, 48–61. New York: Harry Abrams.

Reed, Mary Lou. 1981. “A Vital Connection: Artist and Topography.” *Woman’s Art Journal* 2 (Fall–Winter): 43.

Ribuffo, Leo. 1983. *The Old Christian Right: The Protestant Far Right from the Great Depression to the Cold War*. Philadelphia: Temple Univ. Press.

*Richard McBee: Relative Narratives*. 2016. Riverdale, NY: Hebrew Home at Riverdale, Derfner Judaica Museum.

Rifkin, Ned, and Lynn Gumpert. 1984. “On Power and Vulnerability: The Art of Leon Golub.” In *Golub*, edited by Ned Rifkin and Lynn Gumpert, 11–66. New York: New Museum of Contemporary Art.

Rodman, Selden. [1957] 1961. *Conversations with Artists*. New York: Capricorn.

Ronson, Barbara L. Thaw. 1999. *The Women of the Torah*. Northvale, NJ: Jason Aronson.

Rosen, Lia Lynn. 2001. “Wisdom of the Heart: Portraits of Five Contemporary Jewish Visual Artists.” Master’s thesis, Teachers College, Columbia Univ.

Rosenberg, Harold. 1950. “Jewish Identity in a Free Society: On Current Efforts to Enforce Total Commitment.” *Commentary* 10 (June): 508–14.

Rosenblatt, Gary. 2007. “A Welcome Ceremony for Baby Girls.” *Jewish Week*, Sept. 14.

Rosenblatt, Naomi Harris. 2005. *After the Apple: Women in the Bible*. New York: Miramax.

Rosensaft, Jean Bloch, ed. 2004. *Archie Rand: The Nineteen Diaspora Paintings*. New York: Hebrew Union College–Jewish Institute of Religion Museum.

———. 2005. *Carol Hamoy: PsalmSong*. New York: Hebrew Union College–Jewish Institute of Religion Museum.

Roskies, David G. 1984. *Against the Apocalypse: Responses to Catastrophe in Modern Jewish Culture*. Cambridge, MA: Harvard Univ. Press.

Rotberg, Rabbi Tzvi. 1983. *Sefiras HaOmer*. New York: Moznaim.

Rubin, Barry. 1995. *Assimilation and Its Discontents*. New York: Times Books.

Rubin, David S. 2002. “Ritual and Transformation: An Introduction to the Art of Beth Ames Swartz.” In *Reminders of Invisible Light*, 9–24. New York: Hudson Hills Press.

*Ruth Weisberg: The Scroll*. 1987. New York: Hebrew Union College–Jewish Institute of Religion.

Sandler, Irving. 1970. *The Triumph of American Painting: A History of Abstract Expressionism*. New York: Harper and Row.

*Sarah’s Trials*. 2010. New York: Jewish Community Center in Manhattan.

Sarna, Jonathan D. [1986] 1997. Introduction to *The American Jewish Experience*, edited

by Jonathan D. Sarna, xiii–xix. New York: Holmes and Meier.
———. 2004. *American Judaism: A History*. New Haven, CN: Yale Univ. Press.
Sartre, Jean-Paul. 1947. *Existentialism*. New York: Philosophical Library.
Sasson, Jack M. 1990. *Jonah*. New York: Doubleday.
Schachter-Shalomi, Zalman. 2001. "On Renewing God." In *Best Contemporary Jewish Writing*, edited by Michael Lerner, 103–12. San Francisco: Jossey-Bass.
Schneider, Tammi J. 2004. *Sarah: Mother of Nations*. New York: Continuum.
Scholem, Gershom. [1941] 1961. *Major Trends in Jewish Mysticism*. New York: Schocken.
———. 1965. *On the Kabbalah and Its Symbolism*. Translated by Joachim Neugroschel. New York: Schocken Books.
———. 1971a. "The Messianic Idea in Kabbalism." In *The Messianic Idea in Judaism and Other Essays in Jewish Spirituality*, 37–48. New York: Schocken Books.
———. 1971b. "Revelation and Tradition as Religious Categories in Judaism." In *The Messianic Idea in Judaism and Other Essays in Jewish Spirituality*, 282–303. New York: Schocken Books.
———. 1971c. "Toward an Understanding of the Messianic Idea in Judaism." In *The Messianic Idea in Judaism and Other Essays on Jewish Spirituality*, 1–36. New York: Schocken Books.
———. [1974] 1978. *Kabbalah*. New York: Meridian.
———. 1991. *On the Mystical Shape of the Godhead*. Edited by Jonathan Chipman. Translated by Joachim Neugroschel. New York: Schocken.
Schwabsky, Barry. 1986. "The Invisible Scene: Some Artists in Brooklyn." *New York/Berlin* 2:not paginated.
———. 1987. "What Is Painting All About? A Conversation with Archie Rand." *Arts Magazine* 61 (Apr.): 23–24.
Schwartz, Anita. 1984. "Ethnic Identity among Leftwing American Jews." *Ethnic Groups* 6, no. 1: 65–84.
Scott, Jamie, and Paul Simpson Housley, eds. 1991. *Sacred Spaces and Profane Places: Essays in the Geographics of Judaism, Christianity, and Islam*. Westport, CN: Greenwood Press.
*Sefer Yetzirah: The Book of Creation*. 1997. Rev. ed. Edited by Aryeh Kaplan. York Beach, ME: Samuel Weiser.
Seidman, Hillel. 1969. *Glories of the Jewish Holidays*. Edited by Moses Zalesky. New York: Shengold.
Selz, Peter. 1997. Introduction to *Tobi Kahn: Metamorphoses*, edited by Peter Selz, 11–28. Seattle: Univ. of Washington Press.
Shafner, Janet. 2003. *Women of Mystery, Men of Prophecy: Biblical Visions*. New York: Jewish Heritage Project for the Lyman Allyn Art Museum.
Shahn, Ben. 1963. *Love and Joy about Letters*. New York: Grossman.
———. 1965. *The Haggadah for Passover*. Boston: Little, Brown.
*Sharing the Journey: The Haggadah for the Contemporary Family*. 2012. Illustrated by Mark Podwal. New York: Central Conference of American Rabbis.
Sheeler, Charles. 1916. "Statement." In *Forum Exhibition of Modern American Art*, not paginated. New York: Anderson Galleries.
Shluker, Zelda. 1996. "Too Jewish to Be Hip?" *Hadassah Magazine*, Nov. Copy in Archie Rand's files.
Silberman, Charles E. 1985. *A Certain People: American Jews and Their Lives Today*. New York: Summit.
Snell, Bruno. 1982. *The Discovery of Mind in Greek Philosophy and Literature*. New York: Dover.
Soloveitchik, Rabbi Joseph B. 2000. *Family Redeemed: Essays on Family Relationships*. Edited by David Shatz and Joel B. Wolowelsky. Jersey City, NJ: KTAV.
Soltes, Ori Z. 2008. *Judaism, Christianity, and Islam: Searching for Oneness*. Lanham, MD: Rowman and Littlefield.
———. 2016. "Home Is Where I Pitch My Tent: The Art of Siona Benjamin." In *Siona*

*Benjamin: Beyond Borders*, edited by Elizabeth Greenberg, 6–14. Albany, NY: Opalka Gallery, Sage Colleges.

Somerstein, Rachel. 2006. "Art Talk." *Art News*, June. Copy in Archie Rand's files.

*Song of the Land*. 2012. Los Angeles: Hebrew Union College–Jewish Institute of Religion.

Spiegel, Shalom. 1993. *The Last Trial: On the Legends and Lore of Covenant to Abraham to Offer Isaac as a Sacrifice: The Akedah*. Translated by Judah Goldin. Woodstock, VT: Jewish Lights.

Stanger, Ilana. 1996. "Liberating God." *Lilith* 21 (Fall): 40.

Steiner, George. 1996. "Our Homeland the Text." In *No Passion Spent: Essays 1978–1995*, 304–27. New Haven, CN: Yale Univ. Press.

Steinfels, Peter. 2008. "Artist Brings Religion into His Work, in Bold Style." *New York Times*, June 7. Copy in Archie Rand's files.

Steinmetz, Devora. 1988. "A Portrait of Miriam in Rabbinic Midrash." *Prooftexts* 8 (Jan.): 35–65.

Steinsaltz, Adin. 1980. *The Thirteen Petalled Rose*. Translated by Yehuda Hanegbi. New York: Basic Books.

——— 1984. *Biblical Images*. Translated by Yehuda Hanegbi and Yehudit Keshet Benjamin. Northvale, NJ: Jason Arson.

Stern, David. 2004. "Midrash and Midrashic Interpretation." In *The Jewish Study Bible*, edited by Adele Berlin and Marc Zvi Brettler, 1863–75. New York: Oxford Univ. Press.

*Talmud Bavli: Tractate Kiddushin*. 1993. New York: Mesorah.

Tanning, Dorothea. 1998. *Another Language of Flowers*. New York: George Braziller.

*Temple*. 1997. New Delhi: Fulbright House.

Teubal, Savina J. 1997. *Ancient Sisterhood: The Lost Traditions of Hagar and Sarah*. Athens: Swallow Press of Ohio Univ. Press.

Tigerman, Stanley. 1988. *The Architecture of Exile*. New York: Rizzoli.

Tishby, Isaiah, ed. 1989. *The Wisdom of the Zohar: An Anthology of Texts*. Vol. 2. Translated by David Goldstein. London: Littman Library of Civilization.

Tofel, Jennings. 1927. "Jewish Art Center" (in Yiddish). *Der Hamer* 11 (Mar.): 53–56.

*The Torah: A Modern Commentary*. 1981. Edited by W. Gunther Plaut. New York: Union of American Hebrew Congregations.

Trible, Phyllis. 1999. "Genesis 22: The Sacrifice of Sarah." In *Women in the Hebrew Bible*, edited by Alice Bach, 271–90. New York: Routledge.

Tuchman, Shera Aranoff, and Sandra E. Rapoport. 2004. *The Passions of the Matriarchs*. Jersey City, NJ: KTAV.

Tye, Larry. 2012. *Superman: The High-Flying History of America's Most Enduring Hero*. New York: Random House.

Umansky, Ellen M. 1988. "Females, Feminists, and Feminism: A Review of Recent Literature on Jewish Feminism and the Creation of a Feminist Judaism." *Feminist Studies* 14 (Summer): 349–65.

Valdes, Marcela. 2018. "The Revisionary." *New York Times Magazine*, Dec. 16.

Van Biema, David. 2016. "Tobi Kahn's Soulful Art Is for Jews—and Non-Jews Too." Religion News Service, Apr. 25. At http://religionnews.com/2016/04/25/tobi-kahns-soulful-art-is-for-jews-and-non-jews-too.

*Vastusutra Upanishad: The Essence of Form in Sacred Art*. 1982. Delhi: Banarsidass.

Vatsky, Sharon. 1994. *Wonder Women*. New York: Ceres Gallery.

Verschaffel, Bert. 2012. "(Sacred) Places Are Made of Time: Observations on the Persistence of the Sacred in Categorizing Space in Modernity." In *Loci Sacri: Understanding Sacred Places*, edited by Thomas Coomans, Herman de Dijn, Jan de Maeyer, Rajesh Heynickx, and Bert Verschaffel, 49–56. Leuven, Belgium: Leuven Univ. Press.

Vorspan, Albert, and Eugene J. Lipman. 1956. *Justice and Judaism: The Work of Social Action*. New York: Union of American Hebrew Congregations.

"*Voyage of the* St. Louis." n.d. United States Holocaust Museum, exhibition description. At https://www.ushmm.org/exhibition/st-louis/.

Waldman, J. T. 2005. *Megillat Esther*. Philadelphia: Jewish Publication Society.

———. 2008. “Comix, Judaism, and Me.” In *The Jewish Graphic Novel: Critical Approaches*, edited by Samantha Baskind and Ranen Omer-Sherman, ix–xiii. New Brunswick, NJ: Rutgers Univ. Press.

Wander, David. 1985. *Wolloch Haggadah in Memory of the Holocaust*. Haifa: Goldman’s Art Gallery.

Waxman, Chaim. 1983. *American Jews in Transition*. Philadelphia: Temple Univ. Press.

Wecker, Menachem. 2004. “Painting Midrash in Tarot Cards and Cartoons: How to Pray in Color.” *The Commentator* 68 (May 11): pages unavailable. Copy in Archie Rand’s files.

———. 2009. “The Amulet, the Temple, the Disfigured Book, and the Butterflies: The Art of Yona Verwer, Robert Kirschbaum, David Friedman, and Joel Silverstein.” *Jewish Press*, May 27.

———. 2010. “Tobi Kahn’s Sky and Water Meditation Paintings.” *Houston Belief*, July 9.

Weisberg, Ruth. 1999. “Artist’s Statement.” *Living Text* 5 (Summer): 2–4.

———. 2002. *The Open Door: A Passover Haggadah*. Edited by Sue Levi Elwell. New York: Central Conference of American Rabbis.

———. 2004a. “Creating Midrash: An Artist’s Perspective.” In *Objects of the Spirit: Ritual and the Art of Tobi Kahn*, edited by Emily Bilski, 138–39. New York: Hudson Hills.

———. 2004b. “A Life in Art.” *Nashim* 7 (Spring): 231–32.

Weisman, Jonathan. 2018. *(((Semitism))): Being Jewish in America in the Age of Trump*. New York: St. Martin’s Press.

Weissler, Chava. 2005. “Meanings of the Shekinah in the ‘Jewish Renewal’ Movement.” *Nashim* 10 (Fall): 53–83.

Wellisch, Erich. 1954. *Isaac and Oedipus: A Study in Biblical Psychology of the Sacrifice of Isaac: The Akeida*. London: Routledge.

Werner, Alfred. 1976. Introduction to J. Arthur Granick, *Jennings Tofel*, 9–13. New York: Harry Abrams.

Wertheimer, Jack. 2018. *The New American Judaism: How Jews Practice Their Religion Today*. Princeton, NJ: Princeton Univ. Press.

Wertlowsky, R. J. Zwi, and Geoffrey Wigdor. 1999. *The Oxford Dictionary of the Jewish Religion*. New York: Oxford Univ. Press.

White, Mark. 2003. *Paradisus: Paintings by Tobi Kahn*. Stillwater: Gardner Art Gallery, Oklahoma State Univ.

Whitfield, Stephen J. 1985. “Jews by Choice: A Review Article.” *Shofar* 4 (Fall): 46–52.

———. 1999. *In Search of American Jewish Culture*. Hanover, NH: Brandeis Univ. Press.

Wiesel, Elie. 1983. *The Golem: The Story of a Legend*. With drawings by Mark Podwal. New York: Summit.

Wight, Frederick S. 1954. *Charles Sheeler: A Retrospective Exhibition*. Los Angeles: Art Gallery of the Univ. of California.

Williams, Dolores S. 2006. “Hagar in African American Biblical Appropriation.” In *Hagar, Sarah, and Their Children: Jewish, Christian, and Muslim Perspectives*, edited by Phyllis Trible and Letty M. Russell, 171–84. Louisville, KY: Westminster John Knox Press.

Wise, Michel Z. 2009. “Sacred Spaces: Tobi Kahn and the Art of Creative Reverence.” *Tablet*, Nov. 5. Copy in Tobi Kahn’s files.

*Wolloch Haggadah in Memory of the Holocaust*. 1985. Illustrated by David Wander. Haifa: Goldman’s Art Gallery.

Wortz, Melinda. 1982. *Tradition in Transition: Bruria, Gilah Yelin Hirsch, Beth Ames Swartz, Michel Zackheim*. Irvine: University Fine Arts Gallery, Univ. of California.

Wulkin, Reba. 2002. Preface to *Microcosmos*, 7. New York: Yeshiva Univ. Museum.

Yau, John. 1989. *Four Painters*. Flint, MI: Flint Institute of Arts.

Yerushalmi, Yosef Hayem. 1982. *Zakhor: Jewish History and Jewish Memory*. Seattle: Univ. of Washington Press.

*Yonah/Jonah: A New Translation with a Commentary Anthologized from Talmudic, Midrashic, and Rabbinic Sources*. 1978. Translated by Rabbi Meir Zlotowitz. New York: Mesorah.

Young, Dede. 2003. “Tobi Kahn: *Sky & Water*.” In *Tobi Kahn: Sky and Water*, 5–11. Purchase:

Neuberger Museum of Art, Purchase College, State Univ. of New York.

*Zohar: The Book of Enlightenment*. 1988. Translated by Daniel C. Matt. New York: Paulist Press.

*Zohar: The Book of Splendor, Basic Readings from the Kabbalah*. 1977. Edited by Gershon Scholem. New York: Schocken.

*The Zohar: Pritzker Edition*. 2009. Vol. 5. Translated by Daniel C. Matt. Stanford, CA: Stanford Univ. Press.

Zornberg, Avivah Gottlieb. 1995. *Genesis: The Beginning of Desire*. Philadelphia: Jewish Publication Society.

———. 2009. *The Murmuring Deep Reflections on the Biblical Unconscious*. New York: Schocken.

———. 2018. "What Is the Meaning of God Today? A *Moment* Symposium." *Moment*, Mar.–Apr., 46–57.

# Index

*Page numbers in italics refer to illustrative material. Titles of artworks are indexed under the artist.*

**Matthew Baigell** holds the rank of professor II emeritus in art history at Rutgers University. He has written, cowritten, edited, and coedited more than twenty books and has authored dozens of articles on aspects of American art. He has also published material on recent Russian art. This is his sixth book on Jewish American art.

**Select Titles in Judaic Traditions in Literature, Music, and Art**

*After Weegee: Essays on Contemporary Jewish American Photographers*
Daniel Morris

*Diary of a Lonely Girl, or The Battle against Free Love*
Miriam Karpilove; Jessica Kirzane, trans.

*The Implacable Urge to Defame: Cartoon Jews in the American Press, 1877–1935*
Matthew Baigell

*The Odyssey of an Apple Thief*
Moishe Rozenbaumas; Isabelle Rozenbaumas, ed.; Jonathan Layton, trans.

*Paul Celan: The Romanian Dimension*
Petre Solomon; Emanuela Tegla, trans.

*Petty Business*
Yirmi Pinkus; Evan Fallenberg and Yardenne Greenspan, trans.

*Red Shoes for Rachel: Three Novellas*
Boris Sandler; Barnett Zumoff, trans.

*Social Concern and Left Politics in Jewish American Art: 1880–1940*
Matthew Baigell

---

For a full list of titles in this series, visit https://press.syr.edu/supressbook-series/judaic-traditions-in-literature-music-and-art/.